Studies in Global Justice

STUDIES IN GLOBAL JUSTICE

VOLUME 15

Aims and Scope

In today's world, national borders seem irrelevant when it comes to international crime and terrorism. Likewise, human rights, poverty, inequality, democracy, development, trade, bioethics, hunger, war and peace are all issues of global rather than national justice. The fact that mass demonstrations are organized whenever the world's governments and politicians gather to discuss such major international issues is testimony to a widespread appeal for justice around the world.

Discussions of global justice are not limited to the fields of political philosophy and political theory. In fact, research concerning global justice quite often requires an interdisciplinary approach. It involves aspects of ethics, law, human rights, international relations, sociology, economics, public health, and ecology. Springer's new series *Studies in Global Justice* up that interdisciplinary perspective. The series brings together outstanding monographs and anthologies that deal with both basic normative theorizing and its institutional applications. The volumes in the series discuss such aspects of global justice as the scope of social justice, the moral significance of borders, global inequality and poverty, the justification and content of human rights, the aims and methods of development, global environmental justice, global bioethics, the global institutional order and the justice of intervention and war.

Volumes in this series will prove of great relevance to researchers, educators and students, as well as politicians, policy-makers and government officials.

For further volumes:
http://www.springer.com/series/6958

Jonathan Bowman

Cosmoipolitan Justice

The Axial Age, Multiple Modernities, and the Postsecular Turn

Springer

Jonathan Bowman
St. Charles College
St. Peters
MO USA

ISSN 1871-0409
Studies in Global Justice
ISBN 978-3-319-12708-8 ISBN 978-3-319-12709-5 (eBook)
DOI 10.1007/978-3-319-12709-5

Library of Congress Control Number: 2014956763

Springer Cham Heidelberg New York Dordrecht London

Printed on acid-free paper

Springer is part of Springer Science+Business Media (www.springer.com)

Acknowledgements

I would like to dedicate this book to my wife Meagan, and sons Jonny and Robbie. My boys served as constant inspiration for helping project what justice might look like for future generations. My wife provided an unending source of encouragement.

The Council for Research and Values in Philosophy (www.crvp.org) under the guidance of Prof. George Mclean and Prof. Edward Alam first provided the international forum in the fall of 2010 for me to realize that cosmoipolitan justice needed a theoretical formulation. In addition, Hu Yeping facilitated the indispensible contacts for presenting the early drafts of Chaps. 1, 2, and 6 in October of 2012 in at the China School of Law and Political Science of Beijing, Shanghai Academy of Social Sciences, and Renmin University of Beijing respectively. I am deeply grateful for the tireless work of the translators and the audience feedback that helped give the work a truly transcivilizational dimension.

I am indebted to the major centers of critical theory at Saint Louis University, Boston College, and Frankfurt University for the opportunities to present and garner feedback on Chaps. 1, 4, and 6. I am especially grateful to William Rehg, David Rasmussen, Matthius Lutz-Bachmann, and Thomas Schmitt for their work in this regard. I would also like to thank a long list of persons who provided direct feedback to one or more of the chapters over stages of development or graciously offered their time to entertain my questions that stirred on the research behind this work. These include, but are not limited to Amy Allen, Michael Allen, Michael Barber, Jose Casanova, Andreas Follesdal, Jurgen Habermas, Eduardo Mendieta, John Milbank, Eleonore Stump, Charles Taylor, and Theodore Vitali. I should also not forget the anonymous reviewers provided by Springer, the editorial direction for the series provided by Prof. Chatterjee, and the ever-helpful support team at Springer.

The research would not have been possible without my Fall 2012 sabbatical generously provided by St. Charles College. SCC also helped fund my travel for presentations in China that semester. In addition, they supported my travel to present the initial draft of Chap. 4 at the international conference on Taylor's *A Secular Age* at Mater Dei Institute in Ireland in June 2009. Likewise, they supported my travel and even helped rearrange my teaching schedule in order to ensure attendance at the Fall 2010 CRVP Washington DC conference that allowed for further presentation and development of my Chaps. 1, 3, and 4 research. For these arrangements, I especially thank my enthusiastically supportive colleagues Isaac Ruedin (chair), Stephen Snyder, and Jim McCollum. I also thank Tana Burton, Vicky Tesson, and Karen Jones for their administrative support. A special gratitude goes to my mom, Lynda, for teaching and modeling the joy of prolific reading.

Lastly, I express a special debt of gratitude to Prof. James Bohman of Saint Louis University. His leadership of the annual Critical Theory Roundtable, direction of numerous reading groups at SLU, and continual forging of new innovative institutional ties with Frankfurt bring to light the critical theorist task positively to change and not merely critique the world. His ongoing critical feedback has shaped every chapter of the book, to which I cannot ever repay in similar act or deed.

Contents

1 **Introduction: Why Cosmoipolitan Justice? Species-Ethics and the Competing Ecumene of the Axial Age** ... 1
1.1 Introduction: Justice as Universal Species-Ethic ... 1
1.2 Karl Jaspers: Conditions for the Renaissance of Axial Age Scholarship ... 6
1.3 Jaspers and Contemporary Critics: The Axial Age as Contested Concept ... 11
1.3.1 Axiality, Transcensus, and the Core to Periphery Tensions of Voegelin's Ecumene ... 12
1.3.2 Nothing Is Ever Lost? Evolutionary Accounts of Stages of Axial Breakthroughs ... 16
1.3.3 Habermas on the Axial Age as Rite of Initiation Into Modernity: The Bio-Social Genealogy of the Second Person... 21
1.4 The Axial Age(s) in Stepwise Historical Iterations: Axial Age 1.0, Axial Age 2.0, and Axial Age 3.0 ... 23
1.4.1 Axial Age 1.0: The Onset of Philosophical Reflexivity ... 23
1.4.2 Axial Age 2.0: Modernity as Multiple Modernities... 27
1.4.3 Axial Age 3.0? Taylor's Nova Effect, Supernova Effect, and the Postsecular Age ... 29
1.5 Brief Excursus for Clarification by Rough Analogue: Cosmoipolitan Justice as Original Position 3 ... 31
1.6 Completing the Turn from Modernization Theory to Multiple Modernities: Why the Social Scientific Shift from Weber to Jaspers? ... 39
1.6.1 The Rebirth of Ethnic and Religious Nationalism (Chaps. 2 and 3) ... 40
1.6.2 Industrialization and Religion (Chap. 4) ... 41
1.6.3 European Modernization as Always Already Inherently Cultural (Chap. 5) ... 42
1.6.4 Neo-Colonial Patterns of Developmental Economics (Chap. 6) ... 43
References ... 43

Part I Axial Period One—The Great World Religions

2 Extending the Dialectics of Secularization Eastward: Scriptural Hermeneutics and Discursive Insights from Hindu, Buddhist, Confucian, and Taoist Philosophy of Language 49
2.1 Introduction 49
2.2 Habermas on Recasting the Second-Person Grammar of Communication 54
2.2.1 Pragmatic Presuppositions of Mutual Understanding 55
2.2.2 Three Media of Social Integration: Macro-level Discourse 56
2.2.3 Evolutionary Origins: Axial Ritual, Civilizational Critique, and the Second Person 57
2.3 Reciprocal Role-Taking, Right Speech, Name Rectification, and Truth Disclosure: Revolutionary Axial Breakthroughs from Four Eastern Philosophies 61
2.3.1 Hinduism: Epistemic Authority, Social Roles, and Vedanta as Axial Breakthrough 61
2.4 Kinship, Hierarchy, and the Legitimation of Social Roles 62
2.5 Axial Breakthrough? Rationalization of Ritual Praxis 65
2.6 The Out-worldly Role of the Ascetic Renouncer 66
2.7 Intra-Axial Center to Periphery Tension: The De-territorialized Polity 69
2.8 Conclusion: A Non-Subjective Genealogy of Hindu (and Modern) Individuality? 71
2.8.1 Buddhism: The Species-Ethical Soteriology of Right Speech 73
2.9 Biographical Remarks: Caste Hierarchy to Radical Egalitarianism 73
2.10 Right Speech: Language as Moral-Practical Ontology 74
2.11 Buddhist Inter- and Intra-Axial Competition: Common Vernacular, Parallel Social Orders, and the Proliferation of Sects 79
2.12 Conclusion: Towards the Buddhist Galactic Polity 83
2.12.1 Confucianism and the Rectification of Names: A Normative Semantics 86
2.13 The Historical and Materialist Dynamics to Confucian Axiality: The Period of Warring States (800 BCE to 300 BCE) 86
2.14 The Species-Ethics of Jen Rendered Communicative: The Universal Pragmatics of Name Rectification 89
2.15 The Five Constant Relations: Ecumenic Social-Political Order or an Ethics of Kinship? 92
2.16 The Internal Heterodoxy of Deliberate Tradition: Mohists, Realists, and the Classics 95
2.17 Towards Some Contemporary Concluding Themes: The Mandate of Heaven and the Dialectics of Secularization 97
2.17.1 The Disclosive Power of the Tao: Liminal Anonymity in Taoist Language and Ritual 99

2.18 Enigmas of the *Tao Te Ching:* An Elite Hermeneutics for Humble Teachings ... 100
2.19 The Taoist Sage: Namelessness, Silence, and Truth Disclosure ... 102
2.20 Micro-Level Discourse Politicized: Towards a Macro-Level Reconstruction of the Taoist Polity ... 106
2.21 Why Jaspers? Why Reset Political Theory to the Onset of the Axial Age? Revisiting Habermas's Critique of Heidegger's History of Being ... 108
2.22 Brief Speculative Conclusion for Inter-Axial Discourse: Breadth Versus Toleration? ... 113
References ... 116

3 Jasper's Axial Prophesy Fulfilled? The Origin and Return of Biblical Religion, Abrahamic Hermeneutics, and the Second Person ... 119
3.1 Introduction ... 119
3.2 Jaspers on Biblical Religion ... 120
3.2.1 Judaism as the Onset of Biblical Religion:Yahweh, Theopolity, and Second Personal Discourse ... 122
3.2.2 The Promissory Narrative as a Composite Christian Hermeneutic? Reconciling John's Logos with the Synoptic Gospels' Sermon on the Mount ... 150
3.2.3 Islam: The Axial Dynamics of Culture, Internal Transformation, and Universality ... 177
3.2.4 Concluding Speculations: The Pragmatics of Biblical Religion in a Multi-polar World ... 204
References ... 206

Part II Axial Period Two—Multiple Modernities

4 Whose Justice? Which Modernity? Taylor and Habermas on European versus American Exceptionalism ... 211
4.1 Introduction ... 212
4.2 Taylor's Evocative Classification of the Three Varieties of Secular ... 214
4.3 Taylor's Critique of Habermas's Constitutional Patriotism: Two False Exceptionalisms ... 215
4.3.1 Constitutional Patriotism—Ideologically Construed as American Exceptionalism? ... 218
4.3.2 European Exceptionalism: Ideologically Contrived as Euro-Secularity? ... 219
4.4 Secularization and Integration of Religious Minorities: Islam as Litmus Test? ... 223
4.4.1 United States: Stretching the Limits of a Civic Religion? ... 224
4.4.2 European Union: Immigrants as the 'Missing Nation' in an Ongoing Constitutionalization? ... 225
4.5 Concluding Recommendations: Towards Cosmoipolitan Justice ... 228
References ... 233

5 The Fiction of a European Secular Modernity: Rationalists, Romantics, and Multiple Modernists ... 235
5.1 Introduction ... 236
5.1.1 Three Narratives to Modernity, Three Social Imaginaries: Locked Iron Cage, Clash of Fanatic Affectations, or Multiple Modernities? ... 240
5.1.2 Democratizing European Subsidiarity Under the Aegis of Multiple Modernities ... 248
5.1.3 Recasting Follesdal's Analysis of Subsidiarity for Multiple Modernities: Nordic/Scandinavian Subsidiarity as a Template for a More Liminal Europe? ... 254
5.2 Conclusion: The Multiperspectival Principle and the Political Ethics of Global Subsidiarity ... 270
References ... 274

Part III Axial Period Three—The Postsecular Turn

6 Conclusion—Western vs. Eastern Replies to the Inverse Economic Pyramid: Innovation, Development, and the Material Future of Cosmoipolitan Justice ... 283
6.1 Introduction ... 284
6.1.1 Landes on the Historical Conditions for the European/British 'Invention of Invention' ... 287
6.1.2 Onuma on the Transcivilizational Alternative to Eurocentric Imperialism ... 289
6.1.3 Sen on Capabilities: A Revisionist Understanding of Non-Western Contributions to Global Innovation ... 292
6.1.4 Reverse Innovation, Human Nature, and a Renewal of Humanity: Four Non-Western Epistemic Contributions to Enhanced Global Material Justice ... 295
6.1.5 Concluding Lessons for Realizing Cosmoipolitan Justice as a Political Program: Towards a More Egalitarian Economic, Social, and Moral Interdependence ... 305
References ... 311

Index ... 313

Chapter 1
Introduction: Why Cosmoipolitan Justice? Species-Ethics and the Competing Ecumene of the Axial Age

Abstract While I want to retain a commitment to justice as inherently universal, the Axial Age proposes a plurality of historical forms for achieving such universality as a species-ethic. Karl Jaspers elaborated the concept of the Axial Age as an attempt to reset the initiation of modernity at the seminal 800–200 BCE dates. He also sought to integrate these distinct cultural heritages more deeply into the post-WWII, decentered, multi-polar, and non-Eurocentric onset of what he terms global philosophy. While the Axial Age remains a contested concept, Jaspers' confidence in the prospect of boundless communication provides us with a linguistic medium for reorienting the roots of political theory. My focus on the universal role of the second person in each tradition offers an abiding constant even in light of my endorsement of multiple modernities as a necessary consequence of the Axial Age—stemming simultaneously from cultural elites in India, China, the Hebrew prophetic heritage, and Greek philosophy. As a philosophical complement to Jaspers and the growing social scientific literature on multiple modernities, I amend his views by highlighting three contemporary appropriations of his Axial thesis. These include Taylor's probing genealogical analysis of secularity, Habermas's proclamation of the onset of a postsecular age, and my own transcivilizational recasting of Rawls' overlapping consensus. My defense of cosmoipolitan justice seeks agreement upon shared sets of species-ethical norms that nonetheless take distinct legal forms and divergent background justifications.

Keywords Axial age · Cosmoipolitan · Ecumene · Jurgen Habermas · Karl Jaspers · Multiple modernities · Original position · John Rawls · Second person · Stadial consciousness · Charles Taylor · Transcensus · Eric Voegelin

1.1 Introduction: Justice as Universal Species-Ethic

When approaching concerns of global justice, philosophical methods couched in the communicative medium of rational justification should realize universal capacities for species-wide participation. Insofar as problems like immigration, the environment, international crime, regional warfare, human rights abuses, and vast material

J. Bowman, *Cosmoipolitan Justice*, Studies in Global Justice 15,
DOI 10.1007/978-3-319-12709-5_1

inequalities require international solutions, the requirements of justice are truly concerns affecting all humanity. The intuitive appeal of cosmopolitanism builds upon the presumption of global institutions as the crucial player in serving to protect the particular individual as global citizen. Cosmopolitan institutions as multi-polar in functionality and decentralized in loci of power—like the United Nations, International Criminal Court, the World Trade Organization, the International Monetary Fund, and UNESCO—thereby protect individuals from domination from multiple possible sites. These include but are not limited to other individuals, family, city, kingdom, nation-state, peoples, empire, and even emergent regional/continent-wide networks.

However, as much as cosmopolitanism meets maximal thresholds of scope and scale for the growing sets of problems affecting all humanity, in the parlance of Jurgen Habermas (but antithetical to his lexical priority of the moral over the ethical), my focus on justice will privilege the universality of a species-ethic (Hegel/Marx/Kierkegaard) over moral universality (Kant). Even within Habermas' own work, his political cosmopolitanism all too hastily presumes deontological moral universality as the primary concern of his works on global political justice, especially when doing so produces the unintended consequence of legal-juridical domination. In addition to the endemic sources of conflicting levels of political authority, as the famous debates between Habermas and Rawls have demonstrated, there are myriad equally plausible contexts in which more specific ethical concerns tied to race, gender, age, generation, religion, or ethnicity might seem more fitting for the particularity of the ethical over the universality of the moral. We could thus heed the forewarnings of Kant—as affirmed in Rawls' *Law of Peoples*—of not lapsing into a legal-juridical soulless despotism. Particularly, we must grant proper consideration to the historical injustices of European colonialism and disaggregated neo-colonialisms as reasons for due skepticism over the purported impartial universality of cosmopolitan institutions. Demographically, it would be no stretch to assume testimonial accounts from the majority of those affected by purportedly universal claims to justice—if given the requisite communicative capabilities—might instead produce another chapter to the long grand-historical narrative of neo-colonial imperialism. Replete references to material motives of cyclical domination rendered legal-juridical would predominate: first-world over second-world and third-world, Western over East/Non-Western, North over South, wealthy elites exponentially increasing profits at the cost of spreading global poverty among masses—even internal to civilized states.

In light of the latest waves of neo-colonialism stirred on by the globalization of inequitable flows of capital, another contributing source of further material injustice would be the species-ethical dimensions of a global epistemic gap. Insofar as the benefits of globalizing trends are asymmetrically distributed, the innovations unleashed by the technological age create rather than eviscerate new classes of haves and have-nots (see Chap. 6). The deepest structural dynamics made most visible through the new social science of capability sets in development literature propose we frame our considerations of potentially tyrannical cosmopolitanism as a reciprocal reinforcement of material *and epistemic* causes. Such a functionalist approach successfully weds the teleological with the deontological, particularly when employing counter-factual reflection to assess functional asymmetries. Casting the technologically fast within a distinctly privileged capability set would fail tests of universal justice when dividing humanity into two species, placing the cognitively, materially, and politically advantaged over the lagging, primitive, and non-technologically endowed.

In light of two-track teleological and deontological rubrics for comparative analysis of forms of injustice, I want to retain the species-wide scope of ethical (and, thus, romantic) cosmopolitanism (Kleingeld 1999), while being mindful of the critical theorist commitment to stave off all forces of domination. Taking the full human emancipation of both species and individuals as the highest goal, I will opt for a comparative civilizational framework that I have elsewhere called *cosmoipolitan justice* (Bowman 2012).

In line with the critical theorists of yesterday, today, and tomorrow, we must relearn the initial lessons of a critique of modernity by reassessing the pre- and post-WWII philosophical landscape. Reason emerging in that period from a tradition of negative dialectics can resonate from multiple voices in a multi-polar world. While in post-World War II Europe, Jaspers' philosophical-faith was the heavy object of critique in Adorno's *Negative Dialectics* for its purportedly subjectivist existentialist overtones (Adorno 1966, p. 113, 122–123, 127–128), Jaspers did share with Adorno (and thereby Horkheimer too) the Nietzschean insight that a critical conception of reason derived by multiple empirical and normative sources need not lapse into relativism or nihilistic defeatism. The renaissance of philosophical interest in Jaspers by the likes of Habermas, Taylor, and Bellah after decades of philosophical obscurity places his work in a dubious position. While, until only very recently, Jaspers had all but been ignored by philosophers, social scientists like S.N. Eisenstadt had continued surreptitiously to do the difficult empirical, historical, archeological, and anthropological work to both affirm and redact many of the empirical components of his original Axial thesis.

This long philosophical caesura with its timely renaissance has served my present purposes well in a doubly fortuitous sense. On the one hand, we can reassess Jaspers' status among critical theorists by placing his insights closer to the communicative optimism of second-generation critical theory as most comprehensively developed by Habermas. On the other hand, we can make an epistemic virtue of the burgeoning social science literature advancing, redacting, and critiquing Jasper's original axial thesis. Deriving a philosophical program adequately informed by the social sciences offers a richer and increasingly more complex narrative of the emergent cross civilizational Axial backdrop, closest to the political and moral innovations associated with alternate and multiple modernities (Taylor 2001; Rasmussen 2010, 2012). The plurality implied by multiple modernities, nonetheless, need not cloud our irrevocable normative threshold of universal species-wide justice. Cosmoipolitan justice as a viable philosophical theory discloses yet unexplored realms of overlapping consensus on common goods as diverse as peace, security, material well-being, and a sentiment for humanity without necessarily presupposing shared background justifications for why we hold those norms nor presuming agreement over the best legal forms for institutionalizing these ideals.

Also of a critical theorist bent, but more along the lines of attentiveness to social-scientific detail, Jaspers' Axial thesis has likewise been re-appropriated by those challenging—on an empirical basis—neo-Weberian and neo-Durkheimian proclivities to collapse the classically formulated secularization thesis with an objective value-free social science. In this second camp, the sociology of religion also deeply informed by the lifework of S. N. Eisenstadt currently offers the best available social science literature required to construct an empirically informed radical critique of global modernities. Pairing together the great axial traditions with the great revolutions that led to the civilizations of modernity (EIsenstadt 2006), we can develop a political theory with a deeper basis for its legitimation. Cosmoipolitan justice moves us beyond the hegemony and neo-colonial excess of conflating moral progress, impartial reason, and the secular constitutional state. We must wholeheartedly avoid making an administrative fetish of the species-ethical universality of the Axial traditions that are nonetheless certainly among leading institutional candidates as alternatives to the perpetual misuses of state and cosmopolitan coercive power. Highlighting the revolutionary impulses inherent to each Axial tradition as an alternative source for checking administrative drives toward empire and colonial expansion, we avoid imposing a narrative of Western secular progress as the sole guarantor of ongoing rationalization.

Lastly, in the third camp of those most interested in deriving normative correctives to tyrannical forms of legal-juridical domination, theorists of transnational governance offer some much needed practical direction as pertains to the best routes to institutionalizing cosmoipolitan justice as a political program, primarily and most developed via the critique and analysis of the EU (Bohman 2007; Follesdal 2013; MacCormick 2002). Loosely included among these figures include critical theorists skeptical of cosmopolitan imperialism (McCarthy 2009, 2013; Bellah 2011, pp. 567–608), and non-Western critiques of the European biases that purportedly pervade the prevailing international legal framework (Koskeneimi 2011; Onuma 2010; Mendieta 2009; Asad 2003). The growing suspicion towards a characteristically European reading of a secular modernity also serves as consistent with the critical theorist slant of this text that believes our normative conclusions must be continually informed and redacted appropriately. The pursuit of a reflective equilibrium must both adequately describe the increasingly plural social world as it is and prescribe empirically informed ethical, moral, and political norms for how we would like the world to be.

Since the social scientific terrain as yet to be charted has heretofore traveled down these three distinct roads, I will make the preliminary move toward disclosing a philosophical method to direct the path where they might, at least under an ideal theoretical construct, coalesce. My general notion behind the term *cosmoipolitan justice* would be to make the post-secular turn of rehabilitating the cosmic and/or transcendent dimensions of civilizational analysis that have so far been overlooked in modernization theory. Eliding the conceptually myopic straight-jackets of grand-theory, we refrain from a making a comprehensive endorsement of the administrative commitments of Weber, economic industrialization of Marx, and democratic politicization of Habermasian neo-Kantian cosmopolitanism (Chap. 4).

I will instead employ the multiple modernities thesis as the justification for my privileging of cosmoi over cosmos, including the related assumption that modernity, while usually cast in the singular, has actually derived its reflective character from a rich hybrid of multiple sources of inter-axial borrowing. Even the most uncontested genealogies of Western modernity have treated as canonical an inherently dyadic universe strained by the agonistic tension between the mundane and transcendent, the secular and sacred, or more generally, the inter-Axial co-originally of Athens and Jerusalem (Chap. 3). In another iteration of the pluralized cosmoi, my aim via appeal to recasting a de-territorialized principle of subsidiarity (Chap. 5) will also be to reconstruct a more accurate genealogy of these interlocking tensions, as I intentionally avoid legal-juridical sources of structural domination by turning to civil society and the local rather than human rights and the global. This will offer a means to tap into the moral ethical norms that traverse, sometimes encumber, and occasionally overlap as the inter-axial social currents that continue to this day to feed into transnational governance mechanisms.

My use of the term cosmoipolitanism carries many additional intended connotations. On the one hand, I want to concede to cosmopolitans that, under conditions of globality (namely, that shared transnational problems do not necessarily entail any uniform movement toward greater politico-institutional progress collectively among humanity—or greater regress—but rather under pervasive conditions of worldwide interdependence suggest hints of both), the moral demands of justice extend universally as competing ethical claims to envelop the entire species. The plurality of cosmoi plays off of (a) the incorporation of non-Western forms of modernity including the prospect of multiple world histories (Chaps. 2 and 3), (b) the recent theoretical insight that Western modernity has also historically taken on multiple forms (Chap. 5), (c) the concession that shared normative ideals, even when derived from equally 'Western' contexts—the EU and US—need not presuppose consensus over their background justifications nor agreement on an ultimate convergence toward ever-more encompassing transnational (or global) federations (Chap. 4), (d) the ongoing development of the major Axial traditions that have informed conceptions of modernity when characterized by species capacities for second-personal reflexivity (see Chaps. 2 and 3), and (e) the cosmic dimensions shaped by the major world religions that have modified the social science rubrics for inter-civilizational comparisons away from a temporal casting of stadial consciousness guiding history toward rational progress to a spatial emphasis upon opening new public realms for inter-Axial debate.

Therefore, in this opening chapter, following the philosophical methodology of Habermas and historical spirit of Jaspers (Habermas 2002a, b; Habermas 2013, pp. 364–365), I will be most interested in providing a deeper theoretical basis to the work of S. N. Eisenstadt in light of his pioneering sociological comparative set of civilizations initiated by the Axial Age (approximately 800–200 BCE). In the parlance set forth by S.N. Eisenstadt, I will be focused on the sociological context that he—and now more fully articulated by Taylor, Rasmussen, McCarthy, and Casanova—respectively call alternate or multiple modernities (Casanova 2006, pp. 13–14). The ultimate goal of this text would be a critical appraisal of the Western biases of political theory as rooted in significant shifts in secularization theory. Such a revisionist approach both to critical theory and the emergent tradition of global philosophy (a) replaces the post-modern with multiple modernities as a rehabilitation of reason and (b) explores creatively the fruitful transnational gaps between global and local as best mediated by the great traditions of the Axial Age. While seeking both to preserve and reform new transnational types of political governance, this project also seeks to explore the increasingly de-territorialized but nonetheless transnational entities comprised by the epistemic, moral, and truth-disclosive qualities of the great Axial traditions. Each carries the unique tension that will define the future shape and ideals of the modern polity. In doing so, we must reconcile internal claims to ethical-moral species universality while conceding to axial traditions the status of perpetual minorities/outsiders when compared to the sheer demographics of the rest of the species. Lastly, in offering cosmoipolitanism as a viable alternative to cosmopolitanism, I will be employing the legal-juridical critical realism proposed by Onuma (2010) and Asad (2003) as a corrective to the neo-colonial tendencies that come invariably with the presumption of tying rational reflection to secular normative justification.

1.2 Karl Jaspers: Conditions for the Renaissance of Axial Age Scholarship

For Jaspers, what makes the Axial Age so axial (Casanova 2012, p. 191)? For Karl Jaspers, the Axial Age refers to the time period spanning 800–200BCE that witnessed the astonishing simultaneity of incredible cultural elites such as Confucius, Mencius, Lao Tzu, Buddha, the Hebrew prophets, and the Greeks Socrates, Plato, and Aristotle. Jaspers most succinctly defined the 'axial age' to initiate the birth of modern humanity as we know it to be comprised of existentially responsible historical beings. Although European scholarly reflection on the intellectual flourishing of this era among Egyptologist and Persian scholars had already begun as early as the 1770s, Jaspers' seminal *Origin and Goal of History* (1949) suggests a unique blend of autobiographical and scholarly aims in the immediate post-WWII context.[1] These include but are not limited to: decentering the axis of world his-

[1] According to Thomassen's analysis of the role of reflectivity in Jaspers' philosophical methodology, 'Karl Jaspers' idea of the axial age and his search for 'the origin and goal of history' was directly related to his generation's experience of a total collapse of order, and the subsequent search for order in the midst of the possibly most extreme hopelessness humanity has ever faced: Germany at the end of the Second World War….The reflexive exercise goes much beyond the experiences of the single person, although those experiences are indeed both real and vital, and absolutely necessary to understand. Jaspers himself repeatedly emphasized the centrality of reflexivitiy: he found it constitutive of the very spirit of the axial age period, but despite the enormous difficulties of his own historical moment he also believed in a 'new historical consciousness' of the present period….This all indicated that the search for a new historical-global perspective was intimately linked to an experience of a collapse of order; it implied a search for a perspective of the present as rooted in an understanding of human history taken in its widest depth and globality' (Thomassen 2010, p. 331).

tory away from a Eurocentric and/or Christocentric axis, stimulating future scholarship on comparative civilizational philosophies, and unleashing the full potential of limitless communication between cultural contexts bound in irrevocable ties of economic, historical, and global interdependence.

In the contemporary language of Charles Taylor, Jaspers foresaw the pressing need to shift our entire social imaginary toward what I will redact to the conditions of the present as the normative and descriptive features to inhabiting the epistemic perspective offered by cosmoipolitan justice. While conceding the epistemic humility that such a project perhaps surpasses the expertise any single individual alone could master, along with Jaspers (1953), and then Eisenstadt (2003a, b), Bellah (2011), and soon, Habermas (2015)—I have likewise undertook 'the necessity to attempt the impossible':

> Because the conception of its entire history is indispensable for philosophizing itself and can be performed only by a single mind, the impossible will have to be attempted...[W]e are on the road of the evening-glow of European philosophy to the dawn of world philosophy. On this road all of us individuals will be left. But it will go on into a future which, in addition to the most terrible, also shows the brightest possibilities. (Jaspers 1981, pp. 83–84)

Therefore, I concede with the work of Habermas in progress (Mendieta 2013), that in its nascent fragmentary and amorphous shape nonetheless clearly argues that to make the postsecular turn requires making an epistemic virtue of pluralism that in turn demands an in-depth understanding of *all* of the great axial traditions.

While devoting the greater weight of his attention to the cognitive, historical, and philosophical dynamics of the Axial Age, Jaspers regards its aggregate affect upon the species in spiritual terms as analogical to a global rite of initiation.

> Once the break-through of the Axial Period had taken place, once the spirit that grew up in it had been communicated, through ideas, works and constructs, to all who were capable of hearing and understanding, once its infinite possibilities had become perceptible, all the peoples that come after were historical by virtue of the intensity with which they laid hold of that breakthrough and the depth at which they felt themselves spoken to by it.
>
> The great break-through was like an initiation of humanity. Every later contact with it is like a fresh initiation. Subsequent to it, only initiated individuals and peoples are within the course of history proper. But this initiation is no hidden, anxiously guarded Arcanum. Rather has it stepped out in brightness of day, filled with a boundless desire for communication, laying itself open to every test and verification, showing itself to all, and yet an 'open secret' in so far as he alone who is ready for it, he who, transformed by it, comes to himself.
>
> The fresh initiation takes place in interpretation and assimilation. Conscious transmission, authoritative writings and study become an indispensable element of life. (Jaspers 1953, p. 55)

For Jaspers, the term Axial itself elicits a sense of turning about or entering into a historical stage uniquely differentiated from that which came prior (Eisenstadt 2003, p. 198; Schwartz 1975; Bellah 2011, p. 272; Bellah 2012; Joas 2012, p. 9; Roetz 2012, pp. 250–253). Perhaps better captured in the German term *Achtenzeit*, independent albeit simultaneous social transformation occurred via elites including Confucius, Buddha, Socrates, and the Hebrew prophets (Jaspers 1957, p. 90; Taylor 2007, p. 151).

Jaspers claims a transition more radical than historical differentiation by pronouncing history as we know and experience it in the present had originally initiated at the turn of the Axial Age.

> This axis would be situated at the point in history which gave birth to everything which, since then, man has been able to be, the point most overwhelmingly fruitful in fashioning humanity; its character would have to be, if not empirically cogent and evident, yet so convincing to empirical insight as to give rise to a common frame of historical self-comprehension for all peoples—for the West, for Asia, and for all men on earth, without regard to particular articles of faith. It would seem that this axis of history is to be found in the period around 500 BC, in the spiritual process that occurred between 800 and 200 BC. It is there that we meet with the most deep cut dividing line in history. Man, as we know him today, came into being. For short we may style this the 'Axial Period'. (Jaspers 1953, p. 1)

While there seem to be others that had entertained the notion of the distinctiveness of the Axial Age, such as Max Weber's reference to the 'prophetic age' (1920), Lasaulx (1856), Victor von Strauss (1870), Eric Voegelin (1974) and to a limited extent Alfred Weber (1935), it was Jaspers that provided the first fully developed historical characterization of the age from the decentered perspective of humanity as a species despite distinct simultaneous centers from the West (Athens and Jerusalem), Asia, and India (Jaspers 1953, pp. 8, 15–16; Eisenstadt 2003, p. 198).

Demonstrating uncanny insight into the contours of where future queries to address the enigmatic character of the tripartite *and* simultaneous emergence of the Axial Period, he evades neo-Hegelian proclivities toward offering a grand-historical narrative of Spirit. In agreement with the onslaught of criticisms of Hegel for engaging in gnostic speculations and for regarding humanity from the third-person perspective of a stadial consciousness, Jaspers rejects reconstructing it's step-wise development from the myopic biases of a European world-view. Akin to Taylor's own criticisms of the secular tendency to employ the past perfect tense of 'having overcome' the inherent irrationality of belief, Jose Casanova offers a succinct description of this 'stadial consciousness' he ascribes to the neo-Hegelian proclivity behind the false assumption of falling into a global narrative of Western secular progress.

> Intrinsic to this phenomenological experience is a modern "stadial consciousness," inherited from the Enlightenment, which understands this anthropocentric change in the conditions of belief as a process of maturation and growth, as a "coming of age" and as progressive emancipation. (Casanova 2013, p. 32)

My own view agrees with Jose Casanova's cosmic shift in perspective from a univocal historical frame of reference to the simultaneity allowed by dispersed spatial references:

> [O]ne could say that the social scientific study of religion had been permeated by a modern, secularist, stadial consciousness that placed the social scientists 'here and now' in secular modernity while placing their object of study, religion, 'there and then', as the 'other' that somehow persisted as a pre-modern anachronistic survivor in a time not contemporary with our secular age (Fabian 1983). This was the fundamental premise on which every theory of modernization and every theory of secularization were built. Our age of globalization, however, is changing this perspective. Globalization is the new philosophy of space that has come to replace the modern philosophy of history. In a sense, with globalization the spatial metaphor has begun to replace the dominant temporal-historical metaphor of Western secular modernity. (Casanova 2013, p. 32)

In light of the spatial reframing introduced by globalization, Jaspers had already foreseen the entailed communicative presuppositions that came with engaging in the perspective of cosmoipolitan justice as an alternative to viewing history from a stadial consciousness. By rendering the pervasive interdependence posed by globalization from the social-scientific participant perspective of an ongoing engagement of the species in potentially boundless communication, we must follow by Jaspers, and now Casanova, in adopting spatial rather than temporal metaphors. The spatial turn better captures the decentered, simultaneous, and agonistic formation of public spaces contesting both the hegemony of the secular narrative and permitting inter-axial debate over shared problematic circumstances (Knott 2014, p. 40). Jaspers posits this as a necessary pragmatic presupposition of human understanding that we cannot expect empirically to prove or deny: 'we cannot deduce the unity of mankind and the existence of human solidarity from empirical investigations, even though these give us some pointers; nor can we refute this unity and solidarity by empirical investigations' (1953, p. 42).

In addition, anticipating very likely advances in biological and anthropological research into the evolution of the species, he nonetheless remains skeptical of evolutionary premises giving a satisfactory account for the historically-unparalleled emergence of the Axial Age. By leaving the question of precise empirical explanation of the 'why?' of such a unique emergence, he nonetheless does find the prospect of universal human communication as *both* a necessary capacity to be assumed for the Axial turn and the point of departure from which the history of the species as such can, in a sense, be said to have begun:

> We—all men—can share the knowledge of the reality of this universal transformation of mankind during the Axial Period. Although confined to China, India, and the West, and though there was to begin with no contact between these three worlds, the Axial Period nonetheless founded universal history and, spiritually, drew all men into itself. The fact of the threefold historical modification effected by the step we call the Axial Period acts as a *challenge to boundless communication*. To see and understand others helps in the achievement of clarity about oneself, in overcoming the potential narrowness of all self-enclosed historicity, and in taking the leap into expanding reality. This venture into boundless communication is once again the secret of becoming-human, not as it occurred in the inaccessible prehistoric past, but as it takes place within ourselves. (Jaspers 1953, p. 19)

With respect to the risk of historical reductionism, and as confirmed in Voegelin's own reflections on the insurmountable historical gaps encountered in reconstructing what Voegelin termed the *Ecumenical Age* (1974), Jaspers argued that one grand historical metanarrative will not do justice to the threefold parallel emergence of the Axial Period. As for the latter risk of biological reductionism, Habermas (2008a), Bellah (2011), and others have reaffirmed the dilemmas Jaspers had already anticipated in applying the empirical assumptions of natural biological evolution to the distinct realm of social evolution.

By rejecting the likely prospect of an ultimate evolutionary or historical narrative fully to explain the coming of the Axial Period, if the event itself were so anomalous as to evade natural explanation, we might expect his final appeal would be to point to God. However, he seems to anticipate precisely such an objection and find in it the pragmatic motive for continuing empirical investigation rather than bringing research to a close:

> It might seem as though I were ought to prove direct intervention on the part of the deity, without saying to openly. By no means. For that would not only be a *salto mortale* of cognition into pseudo-knowledge, but also an importunity against the deity. I want rather to prevent the comfortable and empty conception of history as a comprehensible and necessary movements of humanity; I should like to maintain awareness of the dependence of our cognition upon current standpoints, methods and facts and, thereby, of the particularity of all cognition; I should like to hold the question open and leave room for possible new starting points in the search for knowledge, which we cannot imagine in advance at all. Wonder at the mystery is itself a fruitful act of understanding, in that it affords a point of departure for future research. It may even be the goal of all understanding, since it means penetrating through the greatest possible amount of knowledge to authentic nescience, instead of allowing Being to disappear by absolutizing it away into a self-enclosed object of cognition. (Jaspers 1953, p. 18)

His remarks earlier in the text would affirm solid ground for the above critique directed toward the Hegelian Absolute. In addition, the reemergence of Jaspers in circles associated with critical theory find a more amenable target of the above remarks in Heidegger's renunciation of the achievements of modernity for a non-normative history of Being.

However, Jaspers' suspicions toward theological and ontological metaphysics do not alone render all his reflections reducible to pragmatically historical analysis. For instance, despite the historical data of Indo-European horsemen as perhaps the empirical condition to bring about the transfer of seemingly overlapping phenomena in distinct regions of the globe and sociological data to provide the political conditions to make the historical age ripe for transformation on a grand scale, the description of preconditions does not translate to a causal explanation:

> [T]he simplest explanation of the phenomena of the Axial Period seems to lie in common sociological preconditions favourable to spiritual creativeness: many small States and small towns: a politically divided age engaged in incessant conflicts; the misery caused by wars and revolutions accompanied by simultaneous prosperity elsewhere, since destruction was neither universal nor radical; questioning of previously existing conditions....They are preconditions of which the creative result is not a necessary sequel; as part of the overall pattern of their own origin remains in question. (Jaspers 1953, pp. 17–18)

Nor do updated empirical assessments of contemporary authors put to final rest the questions of ultimate origin. These include a widening gap between the transcendent and mundane, the radical revision of prior held conceptions of the human good, the purging of society of paganism and idolatry (Taylor 2007, p. 770), and a growing conception that violence can legitimately be brought about when done in service of the divine (Taylor 687).

Also akin to the general spirit of Taylor's affinity for Jaspers in his select remarks of his *A Secular Age*—and likewise, Habermas's new attention paid to the existential authenticity espoused by Kierkegaard—Jaspers' account of the reflection and critique characteristic of the Axial Age is given an existential twist as a crisis for melding authentic selfhood (Jaspers 1953, p. 2; Taylor 2012). Jaspers seeks to embrace the internal plurality of the tripartite split between the West, India, and China rather than overcome it at a higher level of conceptual abstraction. The crisis-induced new realization of human limitations and growing skepticism towards the dual promises of deliverance via scientific progress or technological industrialization also introduced new prospects for liberation akin to Weber's salvational impulse ascribed to the great Axial traditions.

For even Habermas, the appeal to the content of the Axial traditions as associated with an aggregate increase in human freedom does illicit justifiable concerns of religious dogmatism and epistemic imperialism (Cooke 2013). Nonetheless, Jaspers' conception of the Axial traditions includes as an essential component of each axial breakthrough an increase in our attendant powers and capacities for second-order rational reflection (Jaspers 1953, p. 2). In contrast with the dogmatic kernels often associated with appeals to the great axial traditions as philosophical faith, Jaspers views them as arising in the contexts of inherent inter- and intra-Axial tension and conflict (Jaspers 1967). This agonistic model of rational argument, while not necessarily guaranteeing consensus, was the entry into essaying every possible prospect for reflective universality (Jaspers 2). On the one hand, the subjection of all contents of life to rational scrutiny left nothing immune from critique. On the other hand, Jaspers does not buy into the secularization thesis that this critique of custom, tradition, and even authority of accepted canons of scripture will lead to the impending demise of the Axial traditions. Instead, that which passes these ongoing tests of critical rational scrutiny may contribute increased vitality to the scarce sources of social solidarity that also feed into the appeal of these revitalized traditions from figures as diverse as Habermas, Bellah, and Taylor.

1.3 Jaspers and Contemporary Critics: The Axial Age as Contested Concept

So, in yet further clarification of Jaspers' vocabulary for this wider social imaginary: what makes the Axial Age so axial? The conceptualizations regarded as characteristic of the age vary by virtue of professional persuasion of the assessor. Weber highlights the salvation impulse and differing degrees of rationalization potential of each tradition. Voegelin reconstructs these 'parallel spiritual outbursts' of the ecumenical age to replace grand-historical narratives with multiple world histories (1974, p. 4; McKnight 1975, p. 364). Eisenstadt regards each as evincing variant grades of tension between the transcendent and mundane (2003). Charles Taylor accentuates the unprecedented moral-ethical guarantee of the ultimate triumph of good over evil for diverse teleological understandings in each that reach beyond mere human flourishing (Taylor 2012). Habermas champions the great axial religions as each providing the minimal species-ethical self-understanding required to sustain an autonomous morality (2001, pp. 30–45, 2003, p. 40). Lastly, Robert Bellah's account of religion and human evolution celebrates the axial traditions' triumphant theoretical supersession over prior episodic, mimetic, and mythical phases (2011).

While each of these key contributions to the axial debate yield their respective merits, they fare worse when over-generalizing a divergent array of particular phenomena in the hope of capturing some crucial conceptual quality that will redeem axiality in preserving, ironically, it's growing quasi-mythic status. In the immediate wake of Bellah's *Religion and Human Evolution* (2011), my contribution to the current state of the debate will focus most specifically on the work of Jaspers and Habermas as skeptical critiques to Bellah's (and Merlin Donald's) construal of capturing the axial quality of this epoch in (third-person) social-evolutionary terms (Donald 2012).

1.3.1 Axiality, Transcensus, and the Core to Periphery Tensions of Voegelin's Ecumene

I am most in agreement with the more historically acute work of Johann Arnason's "Rehistoricizing the Axial Age" (2012), and his overt appeal to Jan Patocka's notion of existential *transcensus* that I would like to develop as a response to our original question: what makes the axial age so axial? Dual trends of over-evolutionizing the axial break and over-essentializing the axial traditions converge when treating these traditions as devoid of deep internal conflict, as if we could suspend the horizon of the present and surreptitiously project it onto the past. In this manner, akin to the existential overtones of Jaspers' (and Voegelin's) lifework, the historicity of believers engaged in critical exegesis of canonical texts, and perhaps even redacting interpretive precedent in light of their embodied existential concerns acknowledges Taylor's distantiated and buffered self (Taylor 2007). The disembedding of individual, cosmos, and collectivity continually gets negotiated over time, particularly in light of a meta-level, second-personal cultural memory that already presupposes and addresses a community of fellow readers. The Jaspers'-inspired historicist appeal of transcensus calls attention to what may be perceived as the most intensely transcendent qualities of a particular tradition finding their genesis out a particular problematic lifeworld context that eventually bifurcates into the classics of antiquity versus the historical context of modernity. Thus each is always already immersed with the profane context to which it is indelibly forced to respond—even in world-renouncing acts of withdrawal, rebellion, or extremist political mobilization. Such willful and conscious critical opposition runs directly counter to macro-social evolutionary trends that devalue the internal cognitive variability of axial traditions that have in most cases contributed as much to their ongoing survival as also to their darkest moments. Jaspers' original notion of particular traditions constantly foundering in their striving to attain pure transcendence resonates with Arnason's pragmatic applications of the variegated pasts of each axial faith to contemporary dynamics set in motion by the initial inter-axial polemics between Judaism, Christianity, and Islam; Hinduism and Buddhism; Confucianism and Taoism.

These tensions characteristic of transcensus accentuate center to periphery strife within both the concrete and idealistic constructs of the polities I will associate with the *politan* of cosmoi-*politan* justice.[2] Transcensus applies to the polities of each axial context while rendering futile insular attempts at internal purification

[2] Thomassen—in a move not surprising for a theorist of liminality—notes the general uniformity of axial 'free-standing' intellectuals emerging at the fringes of civilizations: '[R]eferring to the spatial co-ordinates, the axial 'leaps' all happened in in-between areas between larger civilizations, in liminal places: *not* at the centres, nor outside the reach of main civilizational centres but exactly

from outside corruption and also assuaging Voegelin's concern of axial transcendence lapsing into ideological dogmatism and gnostic disengagement.[3] The tensions inherent to the concept transcensus perhaps receive their clearest elucidation under the historical pragmatics Voegelin associates with the initial emergence of the Greek term ecumene (literally: the known inhabited universe, world, and/or cosmos) informing the title of his perennial work, *The Ecumenic Age*, as a philosophical reconstruction of the concrete social, political, and historical conditions leading up to the emergence of the Axial Age:

> The carriers of spiritual order tend to separate from the societies of their origin because they sense the unsuitability of the concrete society as a vessel for the universality of the spirit. And the new empires apparently are not organized societies at all, but organizational shells that will expand indefinitely to engulf the former concrete societies. The universality of spiritual order, at this historical epoch, meets with the indefinite expansion of a power shell devoid of substance. From the one side, the universality of spiritual order seems to reach out for the human *ecumene* rather than a concrete society as the field of realization. From the other side, the new empires tend to expand over the whole *ecumene* and to provide an institutional order ready to receive the spiritual substance. (Voegelin 1974, p. 117)

Voegelin's philosophical query judges that these new ecumene do not belong to the same type of order as older Near Eastern societies insofar as their potential scope remains universal in a double sense that mutually undermine ultimate success as concrete orders. On the one hand, Voegelin refers to the original sources of these insights found in *The Histories* of Greek historian Polybius (200–118 BC) that detailed the historical conditions accounting for the rise of the Roman Empire from approximately 264–146 BC to the status of 'ecumene,' or truly species-universal world power. According to Voegelin, Polybius found that this new typology introduced by the Roman Empire was truly global in scope in knowing no fixed or settled territorial limits that thus differentiated it from prior imperial forms (McKnight 1975, p. 362). However, on the other hand, the spiritual content as substance of the ecumene remained unrealized by reaching for universal species extension in a world that to that point had only evinced the political establishment of societies claiming uniqueness of particular histories as opposed to universal species applicability. The enduring sustainability of potential societies ordered in accord with proclaimed truths concerning the reality of existence, for Voegelin, also seemed to belie the practical observations for Polybius that the Greeks were unable to organize

at the margins, and that quite systematically so in the eastern Mediterranean, China and India' (2010, p. 333–334).

[3] This reinforces the autobiographical imprint of Eric Voegelin's early academic forays with the appeal of American pragmatism he perceived as a necessary alternative to the third-person objectivigating stance of dead-end positivism to which he was so deeply indoctrinated in his Austrian academic ties to Kelsen, Hayek, and others. However, McKnight also notes that Voegelin concedes too that pragmatism alone cannot exhaust the richer ontology needed to expand the scope of the domain of the political: 'The *ecumene* becomes a field of human action, primarily the *libido dominandi*. Political action becomes conquest and expansion and sound political action is measured not as attunement to the *arche* but in utilitarian or pragmatic terms. So the ecumenic expansion which is potentially a great breakthrough in human consciousness, results in a contracted, deformed view of reality' (McKnight 1975, p. 362).

an enduring order around the love of wisdom while the Israelites were likely unsuccessful in creating a sustainable order around the revealed word (Voegelin 1974, p. 115). Lastly, as for the newness of the Roman case, while its imperial expansion seemed limitless—from the historical perspective of Polybius—at that point, it was still devoid of spiritual content.

In another point of affinity between my approach to political justice and the methodological commitment of Voegelin would be to approach the perspective of the political from a much wider rubric of analysis that not only includes human to human relationships but also the relation between human to cosmos and human to the gods (Voegelin 1974, p. 93). In this respect, McKnight's "Review Essay" of Voegelin's *Order and History* (1974) employs the term 'cosmion' to highlight the cosmic overtones of Voegelin's understanding of political societies in correspondence with my own employment behind the term in cosmoipolitan justice and again remains consistent with characterizing the axial age as an age of transcensus:

> Under cosmological, mythic experience, society is not conceived as a "secular" power organization whose function is pragmatic or utilitarian. A society is a "cosmion," a vital part of the cosmos and the consubstantial community of God and man, world and society. The rule of the king over his subjects is understood to be both *analogous* and complementary to the role of the intracosmic gods over the rest of creation. The society, then, functions as the locus of meaning and the source of human understanding. (McKnight 1975, p. 357)

Although I will use the qualifier cosmoi for the account of cosmoipolitan justice, I do not intend to suggest that each Axial tradition projects its own independent universe comprised of its various internal tensions, struggles, and anxieties of its attendant participants whereby we must assume an incommensurability of translated contents. Nor will I go to the extreme of professing a commitment to a univocal cosmic realism that serves as the undisclosed backdrop uniting each distinct Axial attempt to communicate the ineffable nor to the radical extreme of incommensurate subjective monads each with their distinct syncretic mixes of articulate and inarticulate inter- and intra-Axial commitments. Rather, my own approach would be closest to a cosmic and political appropriation of Gadamer's hopeful confidence in a fusion of horizons given its appropriate pragmatic twist, as also initially intended by Voegelin as an open-ended and inherently historical convergence of participatory discourse initiated between otherwise disparate symbolic narratives with the Axial Age connoting a non-linear history of histories.

> Since we are human beings and not disembodied consciousness, the field of history has no other meaning for us except the one recognizable through the *ratio* and *noesis* and the development of type-concepts relating to the phenomena of participation. Should we attempt to transcend our own transcending toward the ground and to outstrip our perspectival knowledge of reality in a kind of absolute knowledge, we derail into gnosticism. (Voegelin 1978, p. 180)

In Voegelin's language, I would be comfortable accepting the Axial construct as a common type token of species historiogenesis,[4] which he most simply describes as

[4] McKnight defines historiogenesis as follows: 'its function is to move from the author's present, back through mythic history to the beginning of the cosmos in order to align the social creation with the cosmic. The principle motive in historiogenesis is the same as in the order of mythospecu-

'speculation on the origin and cause of social order' (1974, p. 109).[5] In addition, like Voegelin, I also reject any and all attempts at gnostic claims to privy access to—or closure of—an otherwise second-personal participation between a symbolic beginning and an eschatologically open historical horizon.

However, as an analogue to the tensional instability of the initial ecumenic orders, nonetheless, moving to the present tensional strife of the transcensus that permeates each Axial cosmic order, even if no Axial tradition, ritual, or claim can profess permanent immunity from critique, neither Jaspers nor Arnason would ever imply going to the extreme of rendering each axial tradition as though it had no doctrinal core, internal integrity, or authoritative hierarchy. As for the latter, Voegelin gives a pragmatic construal for what otherwise may seem to violate post-metaphysical assumptions. As evidence for a hierarchical ordering of the cosmos, he reads the symbolic role of the king or ruler played in each of the axial traditions to be discussed in the ensuing two chapters as reflective of the deeper cosmic hierarchy of the gods/god over man. As for the associated risks that might hint at epistemic authoritarianism via the introduction of a cosmic hierarchical order, existential transcensus has both horns of the fundamentalist versus relativist dilemma covered. On the one hand, the 'trans,' for axial historicist Jan Assman (2012) appeals **not** to the seminal breakthrough personalities and their dates of birth and death but instead to the historicized, ongoing redaction, and eventual canonization of sacred scriptures that had become the core locus of doctrinal integrity for each axial tradition roughly around 200 BCE to 200CE. On the other hand, the 'census' appeals to the ongoing center to periphery strife between orthodox and heterodox traditions of scriptural precedent that often owe secondary and tertiary axial breakthroughs to novel interpretations of canonical works that speak to problematic circumstances in a pragmatic encounter. That allows the canon of what Jaspers calls in its Western variant 'biblical religion' to extend to the later dates of Islam (Chap. 3) and in the Indian and Chinese contexts (Chap. 2), their respective scriptural canons retain their ongoing contact and vitality with profane realms that thereby initiate historical archives of interpretation. However, openness to ongoing redaction simultaneously must allow for the doctrinal conferral of authority over arbitrary interpretations that bear no scholarly precedent or no internal consistency with the larger canonical doctrine. Each set of canonical scripture partially retains immunity from arbitrary overhaul by virtue of ossification

lative constructions. It is an attempt to supply a lasting, eternal ground for social order which will be able to resist the corrosive, destructive flow of time' (1975, p. 359).

[5] In his own more lengthy explanation, Voegelin characterizes historiogenesis in light of the participant perspective of concrete membership in a particular community of being that nonetheless attempts a mix of both mythic and social scientific speculation as to a society's origins: 'There is more to this classification than the possibility of defining historiogenesis by the rule of genus and specific difference. The recognition of the class discloses its full importance, if one remembers that gods and men, society and the cosmos exhaust the principle complexes of reality distinguished by cosmological societies as the partners in community of being. The complexes in their aggregate comprehend the whole field of being, and the four symbolisms enumerated form a corresponding aggregate covering this field. Through the addition of historiogenesis to the other three varieties [(1) gods and men, (2) society, and (3) the cosmos], the aggregate becomes the symbolism that is, in the language of cosmological myth, equivalent to a speculation on the ground of being in the language of noetic [rational/mental] consciousness' (1974, p. 109).

in sacred languages that still foster continuity of elite-educated access to core meanings, balanced also by the ongoing education of the masses as a worthy material ideal, yielding negotiated translations into the common vernacular that run in both directions. They speak to the present and call for ongoing interpretive acts eventually archived as cultural memory. Once archived in competing historical schools, subjection to the historical-critical method of hermeneutic exegesis need not force elites or lay believers to forfeit the allegorical, symbolic, or revelatory qualities required to maintain canonical integrity.

In summation, and in partial response to Voegelin's critique of Jaspers' biblical religion and core dates as excluding Moses and Jesus, by shifting out focus to canonical schools established loosely from about 200BCE to 200 CE, we (a) allow for a vicarious inclusion of the Greeks, including seminal figures like Philo of Alexandria without the contentious invention of a purported canon of Greek philosophy or dubiously exalting it to the status of a major world religion, and (b) de-mystify the axial achievements of historically contested charismatic personalities in shifting our focus upon hermeneutic redaction, exegesis, and ongoing reinterpretation of the traditions as tied to canonical texts. In modifying our axial dates and focus of philosophical reflection we also respond to Voegelin (and others') critique of the purported species universality of the 800–200 BCE breakthrough insofar as the variant traditions may not be classified as truly universal until bearing at least the real capacity of cultural dissemination and interaction with humanity on a more truly universal scope and scale.

1.3.2 Nothing Is Ever Lost? Evolutionary Accounts of Stages of Axial Breakthroughs

In this section, I explore the contributions of the great axial traditions to moving beyond myth to the more reflective and inherently discursive employment of logos, particularly via Habermas's growing interest in providing a discourse-theoretic account of the emergence of ritual at the onset of the axial period. For Habermas, the second-person sense of communicative action oriented toward mutual understanding presupposes a motivational source of affective trust as the socially learned empathetic capacity for role-reversal characteristic of rational reflexivity.[6] The

[6] According to James Bohman's neo-pragmatic and distinctly Habermasian social-scientific approach, 'second-person approaches see interpretation as dependent on the right sort of performative attitude typical of ordinary conversation and upon complex practical abilities to triangulate behavior, intentions, and reference to the common world in which agents interact' ('The Importance of the Second Person,' Boulder: Bohman, 2000, p. 224). In contrast to the continental overtones of Bohman's explanation, throughout the remainder of the book I will also draw upon more recent analytic philosophies of the second person, particularly those of a neo-Thomistic and narrative bent. While those referenced tend to employ these rubrics of analysis upon Hebrew and Christian scriptural narratives, my project will attempt to employ the same sort of hermeneutic to the canonical scriptures of all of the great Axial traditions, particularly in my ensuing Chaps. 2 and 3. For example, Eleonore Stump describes the second person philosophical analysis of biblical texts from

un-coerced extension of empathetic trust will thus be required and presumed in order to act on behalf of the common good of one's fellow citizen or fellow member of the literate global public. In carrying out his intriguing proclamation that: 'post-secular society continues the work, for religion itself, that religion did for myth' (2003, p. 114), we will shift our axial focus upon the respective canons. This allows us also to construe the elite emergence of the onset of a nascent corpus of inter-axial comparative literature as the birth of a 'republic of republics of letters' continuing Japers' original hope for universal second-personal communication initiated across civilizational divides. We can now survey the Western ranks to include the likes of Eisenstadt (2003), Voegelin (1974), Taylor (2007), Casanova (1994), and Bellah (2011) and non-Western elites such as Talal Asad (2003), Abdullah An-Naim (2008), Raimon Pannikar (1993), Amartya Sen (1999), and Onuma Yasuaki (2010).

My appeal to the second person perspective as a modicum of inter-axial communication thus treats embodiment, moral-cognitive maturation, and social evolution as inseparable given a multi-perspectival approach drawing on innovative research of child development (Stump 2010), sociology of religion, moral psychology, social anthropology, and evolutionary theory. On the one hand, by appeal to historical, archeological, and empirical data concerning the evolutionary process as its bears on the initial formation of ritual, Eisenstadt (2003), Voegelin (1974), Jaspers (1953), Habermas (2008), Charles Taylor (2007), and Talal Asad (2003), are in general agreement in not thinking a third person social-evolutionary description of facts will capture the unique linguistic, moral, and social achievements of the species-wide practices of individuation via process of socialization that have come about through ritual. Consider the initial claims from Eisenstadt on this issue that eventually led him to reject functionalist sociology in pursuit of civilizational analysis and the postulation of multiple modernities:

> [I]t is these problems—of the regulation of power, the construction of trust and solidarity and legitimation and meaning that designate the conditions, which have as it were, to be "taken care of"—in order to ensure the continuity of any pattern of social interaction, i.e., of relatively continuous boundaries of such interaction. It is these problems which define the systemic tendencies and sensitivities, the "needs" or prerequisites of such continuous

---

this narrative angle: 'A story takes a real or imagined set of second-person experiences of one sort or another and makes its available to a wider audience to share. It does so by making it possible, to one degree or another, for a person to experience some of what she would have experienced if she had been an onlooker in the second-person experience represented in the story. That is, a story gives a person some of what she would have had if she had had unmediated personal interaction with the characters in the story while they were conscious and interacting with each other, without actually making her part of the story itself. The re-presenting of a second-person experience in a story thus constitutes a second-person account. It is a report of a set of second-person experiences that does not lose (at least not lose extremely) the distinctively second-person character of the experiences'(78). For a more comprehensive analysis of what she terms 'second-person experiences,' see her 'Narrative and the Analysis of Persons,' Chap. 4 in her *Wandering in Darkness*, Oxford, 2010, pp. 64–81; see especially pp. 77–80). For a more direct tie of the requisite socialization processes of the second person perspective to the philosophy of Aquinas, see Andrew Pinsent's *The Second Person Perspective in Aquinas's Ethics: Virtues and Gifts* (New York, Routledge, 2012). Pinsent's work represents the book version of his original doctoral thesis written under the direction of Prof. Stump under the same title.

> interaction, and which have been strongly emphasized by the "structural functional" school of sociology. However, contrary to the usual interpretation of the structural-functional approach, the concrete specification of such needs and prerequisites is not given by some "internal" features of these systems, i.e., by the level of technological development or of structural differentiation, but is effected by specific social processes, in which the construction of meaning plays a central role. The social activities oriented to these problems can be defined as elite functions and are indeed distinct from those engendered by the social division of labor. This distinction has, however, not been fully recognized in the relevant literature and it is the examination of this distinction and its implications for sociological analysis that constitute the starting point, or the reappraisal, of structural-evolutionary perspective which will be presented here. (Eisenstadt 2003a, pp. 59–60)

In other words, while Eisenstadt would certainly agree with the critical theory tradition in finding the empirical work of objective scientific research indispensable to technological progress and necessary for any data-driven theoretical enterprise, the socio-evolutionary reduction of communicative action to the third-person structural functional perspective fails. The long litany of multi-disciplinary examples subject to such critique include rejections of neuronal-scientific observations of brain functioning, the grand historical evolutionary narrative of a purely biological rendition of the species, dubious appeals to the social-scientific expert authority of the objective social engineer, and even emergent critiques of the methodological paucity of the third-person historical critical hermeneutic deflation of the narrative second-personal dimensions of axial scriptures (Stump 2010).[7]

On the other hand, bringing critical theorist/materialist modes of assessment to bare upon the social and species dimensions of evolutionary theory will provide an initial benchmark by which we might assess what would constitute elite-driven epistemic and moral progress in conferring axial literature as canonical breakthroughs over episodic, mimetic, and ritual stages of religion (Habermas 1979; Bellah 2011).[8] Although bearing the somewhat misleading title "*Theory*" *of Communicative Action*, by shifting our axial focus to the cultural memory induced by canonical traditions, we ought experimentally to attempt to apply Habermas's linguistification of the sacred as pragmatically applicable to *all* the world religions, specifically not to just Western culture nor by beginning a biased reconstruction with the Greeks, into European enlightenment, as evidenced in greater critical theorist comfort in renouncing the default rational stance as strict methodological atheism.

---

[7] Communicative action presupposes among each actor the cognitive, social, and moral capacity simultaneously to switch between observer and participant roles in the same communicative interaction. What the objective-theoretical perspective overlooks is our capacity to play participant role, and thus take 'yes' and 'no' stances upon the observed claims that social and empirical sciences make concerning the intentional states of the observed. Therefore, the observer-theoretic perspective belies a basic pragmatic assumption of free consent that we must presuppose in attributing responsible moral action to the observed behaviors of others.

[8] In providing a micro-analysis of the discursive interaction of subjects for a postsecular pragmatic of discourse, as an axial constant across traditions—even when initially unsuccessful—each had historically overcome various material manifestations of civilizational crisis by encouraging diverse forms of reflexive contestation, protest, and periphery to center critiques over the social distribution of power and wealth (Eisenstadt 2003a, pp. 249–277).

In his essay 1976 "Toward a Reconstruction of Historical Materialism" (English 1979) in *Communication and the Evolution of Society*, Habermas argues that the social leap forward to legal institutions as a means of state coercion comes to a crisis in socially-conferred legitimacy when retroactively assessed against the family and tribal kinship network as the historically super-ceded mode of social organization. On the one hand, as a socio-biological explanation, he finds that the ritual proprieties tied to birth, marriage, death, and rites of passages in institutionalized modes of social organization are unique to humans among primate species. As perhaps the nascent origins of the co-originality of private and public autonomy, these rites eventually required quasi-legal juridical protections for the extension of their legitimacy via procedures that socialize members of a given social network into the proprieties tied to family units. On the other hand, as the direct tie between the seemingly disparate themes of ritual socialization and a critical theorist adaptation of the premises of historical materialism, Habermas ultimately concludes that the legitimacy of the transfer of authority out of the family/kinship unit to the state can *only* be achieved through the co-originality of the emergence of the materially *and* morally conferred individual and social statuses by institutions beyond kinship solidarity. Here the analogous shift in the great axial traditions away from kinship to other ties of solidarity constitutes the salvation promise of an alternate yet to be realized social order, initially elite-driven, as a competing organizational form distinct from the mundane order.

As a materialist test for the legitimacy of alternate orders of bonds of solidarity beyond kinship, for Habermas, the moral equality conferred to individuals via social rites must tie directly to the resource equality of institutionalized modes of production and the increasingly differentiation forms of labor.[9] In other words, if we are going to deem axiological salvation visions moral and social progress—to justify the move from kinship networks of social organization to normative orders constituted by rational justification—then we must be able to take a 'yes'/'no' position that gives its assent for reasons beyond mere naturalistic enhanced group/species survival and beyond meta-narrative ideological projections of a fateful eschatological breakthrough impending for the history of collective spirit.

We must therefore avoid being initially misled down the path of naturalistic reductionism by Bellah and Donald's revisionist appeals to an evolutionary account of ritual as an historical, empirical, and anthropological attempt to trace out the socio-biological origins of axiality. While Habermas concedes that the evolutionary

[9] In *Communication and the Evolution of* Society, Habermas argues that a strict adherence to the objectivigating third-person perspective of the expert social scientist undermines both our cognitive learning potential and our moral-practical sensibilities: 'If we are not free then to reject or to accept the validity claims bound up with the cognitive potential of the human species, it is senseless to want to "decide" for or against reason, for or against the expansion of the potential of reasoned action. For these reasons I do not regard the choice of the historical-materialist criterion of progress as arbitrary. The development of productive forces, in conjunction with the maturity of the forms of social integration, means progress in learning ability in both dimensions: progress in objectivating knowledge and in moral-practical insight' (Habermas 1979, p. 177; see also Bellah 2011, pp. 573–574).

capacities for labor and linguistic communication have complex empirically-supported manifestations outside of and/or earlier than the human species, the unique collective practice of reproducing cultural memory through learning, institutionalizing, redacting, and codifying rituals and texts offers a significant differentiation of our species from even the most advanced primates. Habermas has three main routes for his multi-disciplinary support of these findings. First, he points to cases of aberrant moral and cognitive development in human children, specifically in cases of autism, that show what the child lacks would be akin to the uncanny ability of morally responsible agents to regard their own behavior, gestures, and veridical claims from dual participant-observer perspectives (see also Stump 2010; Pinsent 2012).

Secondly, he appeals to research among primatologists in Leipzig that have studied the linguistic capacities of chimpanzees. While, indeed, these primates can communicate shared words and concepts to one another, the findings indicate that they can only successfully express themselves in ways that are characteristic of strategic and objective reason most typified by the human equivalent of the above-mentioned aberrant realization of socialization processes.

Thirdly, although Bellah likewise agrees that the rudimentary origins of ritual can be found in pre-axial civilizational forms, the axial breakthrough first articulated by Jaspers as the global rite of initiation into the uniquely historical species we have grown to understand ourselves as could be recast in an axial sense. If viewing the Axial Age as the multi-polar onset of species natality, we displace the dubiously myopic Western claim of modernity beginning in the historical context of the early modern period. In addition, while the purported objectivity of Enlightenment reason celebrates its revolutionary break with the fetters of tradition, the Axial Age resets our species self-understanding to encompass both revolutionary social transformations and the crucial salience of tradition to the healthy socialization of individuals:

> While the axial age certainly produced many of the foundational 'isms' that have since shaped the world, and in many ways must be seen as 'revolutionary', what characterizes axial thought is at the same time something very different: a respect for and indeed a return to 'tradition.' What unites such diverse figures as Lao-Tse, Confucius, Buddha, Socrates and Plato—besides the fact that they more or less lived in the same period—is there search for the unchanging, and their insistence that human beings cannot, and should not, create everything anew….For axial philosophers, this meant a self-restraint or 'civilized directing' of the most basic human instincts, searching for a path of moderation, taming greed, hate, uncontrolled lust and violence. They all turned away from what they saw as the excessive reliance on material welfare and the pursuit of the pleasure principle….I state all this as an empirical fact, though not disregarding its possible normative implications. To the extent that we have anything to learn from the axial philosophies, it must be recognized that the spirit of axial thought was deeply anti-revolutionary, and involved a personal conversion away from the excess and spiral logics of the ecumenic age. (Thomassen 2010, p. 337)

In creatively selective second-personal appropriation of ritual behavior we find the normalized practice of what Habermas admittedly borrows from the American pragmatist tradition of Pierce, James, and especially Mead that: 'successful individuation proceeds through processes of socialization.' If all axial traditions indeed engage in second-personal reproductions of cultural memory that fail the test of legitimate conferral when bypassing the criterion of fit for the uniqueness of each individual that comprises the inalienable locus of legitimate appropriation, we can say that Habermas has offered us with communicative norms that we can take as foundational to not just Westernized forms of modernity, but to the growing social scientific interest in exploring the deeper axial roots behind the rich genealogies of multiple modernities. Such an array of paths of potentially open forms of narratively constituted socialization offers a better description of a multi-polar globalized world that eviscerates the efficacy of Western versus Eastern dualisms.

1.3.3 Habermas on the Axial Age as Rite of Initiation Into Modernity: The Bio-Social Genealogy of the Second Person

Casting cosmoipolitan justice in the direction of a normative project, second-person perspective taking can be applied to a more democratic, culturally rooted, and existentially rich praxis of communicative action that can open civic avenues for open contestation between these plural—albeit, each immanently universal—species ethics. One latent feature of a postsecular age extended globally would be the social fact that all the axial traditions are minorities among minorities when comparing demographic indices, public spaces, and private domains protected by each, including European secularists as minorities when assessed relative to the entire human species. Jose Casanova articulates this dubious quality of the postsecular as not so much standing in opposition to the historical achievements of secular modernization, but instead viewing the secular de-confessionalization of nation-states as enabling conditions to open up real, imagined, virtual, and noetic spaces for inter-axial discourse under pervasive globalization:

> Globalization is the new philosophy of space that has come to replace the modern philosophy of history. In a sense, with globalization the spatial metaphor has begun to replace the dominant temporal-historical metaphor of Western secular modernity. Paradoxically, with its institutionalization first in the West and then globally, ensuing globalization, the secular immanent frame becomes the very guarantor of the post-axial secular/religious system which guarantees equal, non-hierarchical free exercise of religion to all forms of religion, pre-axial, axial and post-axial. (Casanova 2014, p. 32)

On the one hand, the democratic dimension to the postsecular requires granting religious individuals and groups the institutional capabilities necessary to allow their voices to be heard in public spaces in the language most comfortable to their self-understanding.[10] Moreover, in the more metaphorical sense of space, in applying identity formation to texts and not territories, we can apply these second-personal

[10] Nussbaum has even granted religious and ritual praxis as among her basic list of capabilities (2011).

insights not just at the micro-level of debates within particular bounded polities but also at the macro-level of an increasingly decentered and multi-polar global politics whereby European secularity has thus proven the exception to the global norm (Bowman 2012). On the other hand, taking account of Voegelin's famous 'mortgage' insight, significant secular carryover remains in our re-articulation of political spaces from the dialectics of prior stages of the ongoing rationalization of society (Casanova 2013, p. 48; Bellah 2011). These include the expectation on the part of believers that their transcendent claims will be subjected publically to the rational scrutiny of the historical-critical method, the assessment of the efficacy of religious claims more in terms of instrumental capacity for pragmatic problem-solving than on the intrinsic worth of spiritual sanctification, and the concomitant evaluation of religious truth content less on metaphysical grounds and more in light of enhancing depleted ties of social solidarity (Habermas and Ratzinger, 2006).

Therefore, the postsecular turn does not connote turning back the achievements of state neutrality toward endorsing any particular religious worldview, nor does it prognosticate the unlikely wide-scale demographic spiritual renewal in populations already comprised of vast majorities of unbelievers. Instead, in Taylor's parlance (2007), since a postsecular age endorses the common sense view that both non-believing and believing citizens can mutually pursue morally righteous lives of authentic fullness, religious forms of authenticity must not be regarded as inherently irrational nor as mere matters of privately personal reflection from the outset (predominately with direct focus on Europe; see also Talal Asad 2003).[11]

Moreover, as a potential explanation of why the axial transformation initially occurred among the vast minority of civilizational forms, it initiated human potentials for moral, affective, mimetic, and cognitive development merely latent in the species that now, we can argue from a capabilities-based material justification thereby require appropriate institutional, epistemic, and cultural conditions of socialization for them to come to full fruition (Nussbaum 2011; Onuma 2010). Not only are these capacities for transcendence always in tension with our immediate lifeworld context, Habermas finds that they today are uniquely threatened by the over-incursion of market and power imperatives undermining the moral learning needed to generate new sources of social solidarity. Second-person means of healthy moral and cognitive development are thus required for the maintenance of the social-psychological conferral of moral responsibility characteristic of variant institutional forms that began in the great axial civilizations. Via ongoing cultural

[11] Some of the confusion in terms has, to no fault of his own, stemmed from lax scholarly misunderstandings of Taylor's *A Secular Age* that mistake his evocative title for the nuanced themes in the book. My view on Taylor's 'secular 3' would be to place it already fully within the basis requirements needed for qualifying his seminal work as a discourse on the postsecular as much as or even more so than in line with classical secularization theory. Given the acknowledged reflexive dialect between the secular and reason in a postsecular context, Taylor's focus on moral-ethical authenticity (secular 3) over church-state separation (secular 1) or demographic declines in belief indices (secular 2), and his account of fullness ascribed to the buffered self of the believer under conditions of secular 3, he could just as fittingly (but less provocatively) titled his book *A Genealogical Account for How We Have Arrived at Our Current Postsecular Age*.

transformation, these still bear testament to Eisenstadt's repeated observation of the center-periphery axial tensions that have since been intensified by both the emergence of a multi-polar world and the global demographic shift whereby the majority of the human population has migrated to urban settings. In reflection, is the last best hope then for critical theorists the active engagement in collaborative projects of institutionalized means to disclose the full species potential in all its material *and* spiritual forms? Would the eradication of domination in all of its pernicious forms, entail the startling (albeit necessarily post-metaphysical) guarantee of the cognitive, material, communicative, and ritual capacities for full participation in an inter-axial apologetic contest between the species-ethical cosmopolitan*isms* begun at the onset of the axial age?

1.4 The Axial Age(s) in Stepwise Historical Iterations: Axial Age 1.0, Axial Age 2.0, and Axial Age 3.0

I provide an emendation to the historical materialist systems theory insofar as I want to concede to Voegelin that perhaps it serves, like positivism, as another veiled form of Gnosticism. While I will endorse the Marxist and Habermasian notion that increases in cognitive capacities for moral learning are the best forms of legitimation for any type of political coercion, what I will resist would be to treat the utopian closure of the end to moral and material forms of political domination as if it were adequate to satiate the deepest symbolic longings for individual, group, and species salvation.

1.4.1 Axial Age 1.0: The Onset of Philosophical Reflexivity

The argument of this section will be to extend the advent of multiple modernities back to their inter-Axial origins—precluding the assumption that modern political theory should begin with Machiavellian, Hobbesian, and Cartesian assumptions. In addition, in evading the standard narrative of political theory expounded by Western philosophy, merely the inclusion of Medieval and Ancient influences will not suffice as a comprehensive political theory under the auspices of what Jaspers had termed truly global philosophy.

As for an abiding constant to Axial Age 1.0, we find a conception of reflectivity that builds upon the notion of transcensus introduced in the opening remarks of the chapter. Insofar as reflexivity allows one to bridle the constant tension between transcendent and mundane views of social order, it best captures the assumption of individuality. In addition, as reflexivity emerges in forms particular to each Axial tradition, it demonstrates the extension of variegated species ethics that are subject to the unique cosmic perspectives of those affected—without any direct ties to territorial jurisdiction as the arbiter of competing norms. Perhaps the greatest risk associated with a non-territorial, idealized frame of reference as a civilization, Axial tradition, and/or form of modernity will be the ambiguity that the lack of fixed borders will pose for considerations of political justice. In that light, throughout the remainder of the text, I will attempt to theorize an adequate principle of functional differentiation (as opposed to legal-juridical) of the desserts of justice via presenting four respective conceptions of reflexivity and their attendant scope. In order of philosophical and historical development, I will begin with Jaspers on Axial reflexivity, and then proceed forward to Eisenstadt, Bellah, and Habermas respectively. In the end, the goal will be most closely to follow Habermas and the critical theory tradition in hypostasizing a fully discursive account of reflexivity along with its nascent genealogical kernels of communicative development found among the other three previous views.

Jaspers on Reflection, Historicity, and Universality

What Jaspers highlights as unique with the onset of the Axial Age carries undeniably existential components. He refers to the anguish brought about the new awareness of self-limitation paired with the responsible recognition of requisite necessity to press for answers and meaning against insurmountable odds:

> What is new about this age, in all three areas of the world [China, India, and the West], is that man becomes conscious of being as a whole, of himself and his limitations. He experiences the terror of the world and his own powerlessness. He asks radical questions. Face to face with the void he strives for liberation and redemption. By consciously recognizing his limits he sets himself the highest goals. He experiences absoluteness in the depths of selfhood and the lucidity of transcendence. All this took place in reflection. (Jaspers 1953, p. 2)

His appeal to reflection reciprocally ties to a conception of selfhood and the crises of the individual subject (Thomassen 2010, p. 331).

> Consciousness became once more conscious of itself, thinking became its own object. Spiritual conflicts arose, accompanied by attempts to convince others through the communication of thoughts, reasons and experiences. The most contradictory possibilities were essayed. Discussion, the formation of parties and the division of the spiritual realm into opposites which nonetheless remained related to one another, created unrest and movement to the very brink of spiritual chaos. In this age were born the fundamental categories within which we still think today, and the beginnings of the world religions, by which human beings still live, were created. The step into universality was taken in every sense. As a result of this process, hitherto unconsciously accepted ideas, customs and conditions were subjected to examination, questioned and liquidated. Everything was swept into the vortex. In so far as the traditional substance possessed vitality and reality, its manifestations were clarified and thereby transmuted. (Jaspers 1953, p. 2)

While the existential overtones of conscious subjectivity resonate, Jaspers also turns reflexivity in the communicative direction. Groups frame problematic circumstances to place under scrutiny, form competitive collectives around sources of shared agreement and disagreement, and realize that even the passing on of the traditional must first pass the tests of critical collective scrutiny.

Eisenstadt: Inter-Civilizational Dimensions of Reflexivity

Eisenstadt develops a position on reflexivity that proves doubly reflexive through, firstly, the transcendent and mundane split, and secondly, via the ensuing protest movements initiated by the great cultural elites.

> One of the most important manifestations of such attempts [of elites to propose transforming the mundane order to reflect a higher transcendental vision] was a strong tendency—manifest in all of these civilizations—to construct a societal center of centers to serve as the major autonomous and symbolically distinct embodiments of respective ontological visions, and therefore as the major loci of the charismatic dimension of human existence. But at the same time the "givenness" of the center (or centers) could not necessarily be taken for granted. The construction and characteristics of the center tended to become central issues under the gaze of the increasing *reflexivity* that was developing in these civilizations and which focused above all on the relations between the transcendental and mundane orders. The political dimensions of such *reflexivity* was rooted in the transformed conceptions of the political arena and the accountability of rulers. The political order as one of the central loci of the "lower" mundane order has to be restructured according to the precepts of the transcendental visions. (Eisenstadt 2003a, p. 37)

As one of the endemic features that Eisenstadt ascribes to axial reflexivity would be continual core-to-fringe and center-to-periphery tensions concerning what objects of investigation will be the locus around which a particular tradition confers legitimacy upon even the themes and topics for critical scrutiny. Insofar as Eisenstadt characterized the spiritual core, or Weberian salvation-impulse, as the central emphasis upon which Axial discourse proceeded, while certain political conditions seemed necessary for such open debate to occur, the structure, style, stability, and center-to-periphery axis upon which the profanely political would be situated became secondary to the transcendent thrust of the community.

Bellah: Axial Age Reflexivity as Initiating an Age of Criticism

Bellah, on a number of occasions, quite explicitly notes that the evolutionary supersession of prior stages does not mean that they entirely disappear from playing any meaningful functions for human language and behavior. His main point though, in the large citation to follow, clarifies that theoretical culture would constitute a necessary condition for what we cherish as the best characteristics of the traditions brought about at the onset of the Axial Age.

> In discussing the axial age it is all too easy to read in our own presuppositions or take one of the four cases (usually Israel or Greece) as paradigmatic for all the others. Is there a theoretical framework in which to place the axial age that will help us avoid these pitfalls as much as possible? I believe there is: the framework of the evolution of human culture and cognition that I outlined in Chapter 3…Earliest is episodic culture, in which humans, along with all higher mammals, learn to understand and to respond to the immediate situation they are in. Then, perhaps beginning as early as 2 million years ago, came mimetic culture, the prelinguistic, but not necessarily prevocal, use of the body both to imaginately enact events and to communicate with others through expressive gesture. Then, some 100,000 or more years ago, with the development of language as we know it, came mythic culture,

> which Donald describes as "a unified, collectively held system of explanatory and regulatory metaphors".....It will be my argument that the axial breakthrough involved the emergence of theoretical culture in dialogue with mythic culture...The key elements of theoretic culture developed gradually; they consisted in graphic invention, external memory, and theory construction. (Bellah 2011, pp. 272–273)

In Bellah's words later in the same section: [I]t is precisely the emergence of second-order thinking, the idea that there are alternatives that have to be argued for, that marks the axial age (275). The condition of rational justification as a prerequisite for legitimacy marks for Bellah a paramount feature of the Axial breakthrough.

However, as remarked earlier in my exposition of Axial transcensus as perhaps the defining common denominator of each of the great Axial traditions, the account that I present construes transcensus not only as fundamentally communicative and dialogical, I also regard it as ensconced within a particular narrative to account for the differentiation in views on what constitutes the universality of each competing Axial species-ethic. On the one hand, Bellah describes the theoretical mode of thought as involving "a break with the dominance of spoken language and narrative styles of thought" (273). Since my emphasis on transcensus applied to each Axial tradition of canonical scripture, I cannot fully accept his criteria of breaking with spoken language and the attendant collective sharing of giant cataloguing of 'external memory' in distinct canonical traditions that run internal to a particular Axial tradition and include subtle nuances that escape the capacity of any single individual alone to master. Therefore, I am wary of accepting the third-person overtones of theoretical culture as an evolutionary advance upon the more second-personal overtones of a narrative self-understanding.

Habermas: Reflexivity Rendered Inherently Social

Returning to his essay "Toward a Reconstruction of Historical Materialism," in *Communication and the Evolution of Society,* Habermas argues that in cases such as evolutionary theory or even historical-materialist modes of analysis, the very capacity of a theory to serve as a justified explanatory mechanism would be the conferral to a particular subject of enhanced learning potential that changes their ethical-moral self-understanding:

> I have proposed a spectrum of problems connected with the self-constitution of society, ranging from demarcation in relation to the environment, through self-regulation and self-regulated exchange with external nature, to self-regulated exchange with internal nature. With each evolutionarily new problem situation there arise new scarcities, scarcities of technically feasible power, politically established security, economically produced value, and culturally supplied meaning; and thus new historical needs come to the fore. If this bold schema is plausible, it follows that the logical space for evolutionarily new problem domains is exhausted with the *reflexive turn* of motive formation and the structural scarcity of meaning; the end of the *first* run-through could mean a return, at a new level, to problems of demarcation—namely, to the discovery of internal limits which the socialization process runs up against—and to *the outbreak of new contingencies at these limits of social individuation.* (Habermas 1979, pp. 166–167)

In other words, at the macro-level, for an evolutionary theory to gain in explanatory potential always already presupposed a new problem-domain to resolve brought about not merely by a third-personal lack of objective facts, but a first-personal motivational factor of scarcity of meaning. As a practical corollary in his overall theory of communicative action, at the micro-discourse level, Habermas gives reflexivity its inherently social characterization via the yes versus no conferral of mutual understanding required for the legitimacy of a validity claim. We could also put this in moral egalitarian terms for why Habermas opts for the historical-materialist criteria of moral progress in self-understanding as preferable to a social-evolutionary understanding of human history. Since he finds that the historical-materialist mode better accounts for rational justification as an achievement in conferral of moral status, the risk of naturalistic reduction requires that even the subject of a grand-evolutionary meta-narrative cannot escape the pragmatic assumption that their behavior—including opting for, against, or suspending judgment upon the adoption of a particular Axial tradition or some combination thereof—still stands as the hypothetical conferral of free consent granted to an equal partner engaged in a common praxis of rational justification.

1.4.2 Axial Age 2.0: Modernity as Multiple Modernities

My use of the multiple modernities thesis agrees with the notion Taylor employs to describe what he calls an alternative modernity to a predominately secular one often presumed by Western intellectuals (Taylor 2000). Insofar as the Axial Age brought about a new current of reflexivity whereby the Axial traditions offer an alternative picture of the cosmos than the prevalent mundane state of affairs, the notion of alternative modernity concedes and reinforces this split reality. According to Smith and Vaidyanathan, numerous developments in the social sciences in the recent decades 'have opened up an important theoretical space for the reconsideration of modernity in more empirically realistic and metaphysically open terms' (2010, p. 351).

> [T]he most promising of these is the multiple modernities thesis, which proposes that modernity and its features and forces can actually be received, developed, and expressed in significantly different ways in different parts of the world and—by extension, I suggest—by different communities living in different societies. Thus, while the long-observed forces of modernization still operate through powerful historical changes around the globe, the original thesis of uniformity and standardization, including the related inevitable-secularization thesis, are suspended, if not rejected. This simple yet fundamental, even radical, change in the old assumptions, images, and expectations about modernity and modernization opens up at this moment an opportunity for rethinking, retheorizing, and reframing our empirical analyses in the social sciences, particularly with regard to religion. (Smith and Vaidyanathan 2010, pp. 351–352)

This variation upon our prior theme of Axial transcensus opens room for reflection upon the prospect that a sufficient account of modernity must carry all of Jaspers' attendant criteria. These include individual subjectivity, responsible moral action, authentic ethical self-understanding, and justificatory recourse to rational legitimation of claims. One or more variations upon modernity nonetheless could reside fully within the domain of an inter-Axial or intra-Axial self-understanding exhausted by one or more reflexive transformations of the great Axial traditions.[12]

According to Eisenstadt, the distinguishing feature of the Second Axial Age of multiple modernities from Axial Age 1.0 is the enhanced politicization of the reflective process.

> It was the combination of the awareness of the existence of different ideological and institutional possibilities with the tensions and contradictions inherent in the cultural and political program of modernity that constituted the core of modernity as the Second Global Axial Age. This combination gave rise—through the activities of multiple cultural and political activists who promulgated and attempted to implement different visions of modernity in their interactions with broader strata of society, and through the continual contestations between them—to the crystallization of different patterns of modernity, of multiple modernities. (Eisenstadt 2006, p. 501)

Eisenstadt (and Jaspers and Voegelin) notes that while the initial axial breakthroughs offered distinct modes of self-understanding together with alternative utopian visions for organizing societies, particularly with respect to the latter prospect of wide-scale social mobilization, for all practical purposes the Axial 1.0 initial attempts at radical social reorganization all ended in failure.

While the great Axial traditions survived beyond their various iterated attempts at social mobilization, in many cases, as noted in Voegelin's *The Ecumenic Age*, when eventually wedded to imperial ecumene devoid of any particular cultural content, these great Axial traditions were often much needed sources of solidarity to provide the species-ethical cultural content required to attempt the stretching of kingdoms to all corners of the earth. Eisenstadt expounds:

> The prevalence of these components [the transcendental-mundane chasm and groups of autonomous intellectuals at the institutional level] explains at least to some extent the relative responsiveness of many civilizations beyond Europe to some of the themes promulgated by Western modernity, above all indeed of revolutionary visions, themes, and activities, even if such responsiveness developed under the impact of colonial imperial expansion and domination.
>
> At the same time, the fact that within these civilizations there developed different conceptions of the Axial cosmology, which became combined with different constellations and historical contingencies and with the composition of autonomous intellectuals, gave rise within these civilizations to different patterns of modernity. Whatever the common core of these Great Revolutions—first, the European and American, later the Chinese and Vietnamese, and indeed also the Iranian revolution—and of their relation to modernity, the

[12] Yves Lambert points out that Jaspers even considered the prospect of hypothesizing a 'second axial period' that one might situate somewhere between my formulation of Axial 2.0 (multiple modernities) and Axial 3.0 (the postsecular age). She remarks that 'Jaspers, while in fact considering modernity as being a new axial period, regarded the turn taken by modernity in the nineteenth century as the harbinger of a probable "second axial period" (Jaspers 1954, p. 38). He hesitated because globalization was not yet a widespread phenomenon when he first wrote this in 1949, although we can assume that this is the case today. Jaspers identified modernity with four fundamental distinguishing features: modern science and technology, a craving for freedom, the emergence of the masses on the historical stage (nationalism, democracy, socialism, social movements), and globalization' (Lambert 1999, p. 305).

differences between these revolutions are also of importance in shaping the crystallization of different programs of modernities, or of multiple modernities. (Eisenstadt 2006, pp. 6–7)

In terms of an historical outline, Eisenstadt gives a genealogy to multiple modernities that ultimately finds their expression outside of the conventional anthropological association of Europe with the onset of modernity. For instance, he wonders whether historically there has been a successful case of a univocal institutionalization of a particular form of modernity, insofar as he agrees with Voegelin that given the social-scientific assumptions that come with transcensus, the real historical attempt to concretize utopian Axial (or even counter-Axial—as in communism or fascism) visions into a specific profane world-historical mold will *always* invariably end in failure.

In accord with the thesis of multiple modernities to reject the conventional association between Europe and modernity (Smith and Vaidyanathan 2011, p. 251; see also my Chap. 5), Eisenstadt actually considers the case of the North and Central Americas as perhaps the first historical instance of the multiple modernities trend that has now extended globally to every continent. Among the groups party to this initial example include Protestant Puritans in the Northeast, Spanish Catholics in the Southeast, various Native American groups dispersed across the continent, the Catholic Portugese in the South, Africans spread across the continent due to the colonial slave trade, in addition to small contingencies of British Anglicans continent-wide (Eisenstadt 2003b, pp. 701–722). What Eisenstadt finds in this creative mix comprises as many cases of outright conflict as complex cross-hybridization that yield competing, albeit equally plausible accounts, of authentic American histories (or world histories) to the present day.

1.4.3 Axial Age 3.0? Taylor's Nova Effect, Supernova Effect, and the Postsecular Age

In the domain of the life project of the particular individual, Eisenstadt and Taylor regard the Axial Age as leading to the hybridization of potential views of the good life across three overlapping planes. With respect to this first plane, the Axial traditions initially introduce alternative visions of the good life that challenge the mundane order of things. On the one hand, Taylor refers to this as competing visions of fullness and/or authenticity comprising his preferred characterization of secularity 3. On the other hand, by virtue of his indebtedness to Max Weber, Eisenstadt describes the similar phenomena of a differentiation of salvation impulses that extend beyond the mundane-ordinary and in the direction of transcendence.

In light of the second plane of hybridization of conceptions of the good that become potential sites of socialization, alternative views of the sacred and profane eventually vie to compete for adherents. Therefore, as a particular Axial tradition develops, internal heterodoxy follows as elites internal to a tradition develop competing accounts of fullness or salvation that simultaneously buttress against the mundane order. The profane or ordinary realm may also borrow and draw from the initial transcendental orientation of Axial views of the good as new problems arise in a particular civilizational complex. In addition, since any given Axial tradition need not wed its claims to species-ethical universality to any particular polity, Axial traditions historically tend to migrate and adapt well into entirely unique geographic locations. In describing the empirical conditions for what we will term Axial 3.0—or better, the onset of the postsecular age—large, culturally diverse, and materially rich, urban centers make realizable the inherent Axial promise of universal species-ethical viability across identical territorial domains. The metropolitan centers thereby render potential adherence to any one or syncretic mix of the great Axial traditions as Jamesian 'live options.' As warrant for postsecular modernization, access to each of the major Axial traditions with their attendant very public and universally accessible places of worship is taken as a political necessity. Such open access serves as a necessary precondition for sustaining the mass migratory movements and heterogeneous cultural mixes required to balance perpetual transience with richly endowed cultural sources of solidarity that contemporary mega-metropolitan centers can tap into from the great Axial traditions (Taylor 2007 pp. 549–551; 592–593).

Lastly, as for the third plane of hybridization, Eisenstadt in particular highlights the inter-Axial competition that often occurred close to founding periods as a means to buttress the claim that inter-axial competition should be curtailed for the sake of enhanced political stability. For instance, Eisenstadt points to the original axial breaks between Judaism and Christianity at the origins of the latter; Taoism and Confucianism as competing early visions for how best to bring about an end to the Period of Warring States; or Hinduism and Buddhism respectively again at the context of the origin of the latter and also as characterized by de-territorial mobilizations in the distant past (for instance, with the gradual migration of Buddhism from its origins in India northward into China). Lastly, Eisenstadt emphasizes that inter-Axial and intra-Axial competition may contribute to the ongoing health of a society as much as detract (for instance, with Hinduism and Islam in India; Hinduism, Buddhism, Islam, and Christianity in Malaysia; or the intense spiritual pluralism in the United States including traces of and completion among all the major Axial traditions).

Taylor, in the predominately American and European backdrop to *A Secular Age*, describes this new global context as follows, perhaps even pointing to the contemporary conditions for the initiation of what I have already denoted as Axial Age 3.0:

> The connection between pursuing a moral or spiritual path and belonging to larger ensembles—state, church, even denomination—has been further loosened; and as a result the nova effect has been intensified. We are now living in a spiritual super-nova, a kind of galloping pluralism on the spiritual plane. (Taylor 2007, pp. 299–300)

Despite the similarities between Axial Age and the Second Global Axial Age—Axial Age 3.0 offers some key differences that might indicate something akin to a globalized new historical consciousness as a species (Habermas, five chapter book on Ritual, Socialization, and the Axial Age, forthcoming 2015).

For instance, while Jaspers offered *The Origin and Goal of History* as an introduction of history as such in the singular, Eisenstadt (and perhaps more radically, Voegelin) have experimented with the notion of competing histor*ies* in the plural as shaping not just one's conception of the good, but offering different cosmic understandings for what indeed serve as the central axes (again, plural) upon which history turns—even if the diverging axes roughly fell within the same overlapping temporal plane of the Axial Age (800–200 BCE). While Taylor characterizes the iterated stages of Axial 1.0 going through an initial introduction of civilizational crisis, proceeding into the initiation of alternative cosmic understandings of cultural elites, and finally, disseminating into the wider appropriation by a general public, Axial 3.0 elicits some stark contrasts.

Instead of dispersed but relatively simultaneous civilizational crises that led to Axial founding moments in India, China, Greece, and the Near East, respectively, we could proffer that Axial 3.0 shares a common set of converging civilizational crises for humanity as such with the shared geographic plane as the globe, common communicative media, and temporal simultaneity that extends across decades rather than centuries. In addition, while Axial 1.0 was initiated by the rare cultural elites following in the distinct schools of Socrates in Athens, Buddha in North India, Confucius in China, and the Hebrew prophets, Axial 3.0 again proposes a distinct type of radical historical turn. While the initial triumph of the Axial traditions was to carry the cultural current of their respective centers from elite minorities to a gradual lay popularization, we might witness a reversal of trends in the Axial 3.0. Even though the Axial traditions have endured over millennia, we can now say that the likely trends of dissemination—even in the most successful cases (Christianity, Islam, and even atheistic/agnostic non-confessional secularism?)—will in the context of a global/species civilizational complex be guaranteed permanent minority status with regard to the remainder of the human population. Lastly, while the initial advent of the Axial Age 1.0 produced a social dissemination that eventually would give variant strands of multiple modernities their distinct cultural forms in Axial 2.0, Axial 3.0 may be leading toward a common vernacularization of each Axial tradition (particularly given the growing scope of English), spread by a thin global culture of shared technological media as the necessary empirical condition for the true global dissemination of each as a potential live option for every and any member of the species.

1.5 Brief Excursus for Clarification by Rough Analogue: Cosmoipolitan Justice as Original Position 3

As a means to elucidate what precisely I mean by *cosmoipolitan justice*, I will borrow from John Rawls' well-known original position he uses to establish the characteristic impartiality he attaches to justice as fairness. While in what follows, it will be clear that my philosophical commitments differ from Rawls in crucial ways that would make it misleading even to assume my approach as characteristically

Rawlsian, I will adopt the usage of the original position more so due to sheer expedience and familiarity among political theorists with the work of Rawls and less so by virtue of any special claim to a family resemblance of our views.[13]

Also for the sake of clarification of what I perceive to be a useful metric of comparison to help the reader understand my view, I will take license to call original position 1 that formulated by Rawls in *A Theory of Justice* (1971) and elaborated in *Political Liberalism* (1993). Akin to Rawls' own diction, original position 2 refers to his formulation of the concept as developed in his *Law of Peoples* (1999). Original position 3 will be the standpoint of cosmoipolitan justice yet to elucidate.

As a point of reference for the ensuing affinities and contrasts to underscore, the reference to Rawls' employment of original position 1 most typically calls attention to what we do *not* know behind the veil of ignorance. For instance, we do not know our race, gender, socio-economic standing, comprehensive doctrine, generation, psychological disposition toward risk, etc. However, relatively scant attention gets paid to the underlying assumptions concerning what we *do* know that actually amounts to a fairly robust view of human nature that cannot be explained without reference to the socialized capacity for second-personal reciprocal role-taking. These unique moral-pragmatic abilities include our status as a citizen, that we are rational in the sense of capable via enculturation of pursuing some (albeit unspecified) conception of the good life, that we are reasonable insofar as we have the capacity for reciprocity and at least loosely universalizable claims, that we have a basic sense of justice, that we are social, and that we are political self-authenticators of our claims, capable of responsible claim-making, and have the ongoing capacity to revise and amend our commitments (Rawls 1993, pp. 18–35).

As for Rawls' attempts to derive a hypothetical foreign policy acceptable to the Society of Peoples in his work *Law of Peoples*, this time the subject in original position 2 behind the veil of ignorance must take up the perspective of a representative of a particular liberal peoples, neither as a state actor nor as an individual citizen. While such a move takes Rawls many pages fully to explain, I will briefly cast again what we do and do not know in this perspective and then make theoretical reflections only insofar as they bear relevance for my impending introduction of original position 3. This time, behind the veil of ignorance, we *do not* know 'the size of the territory, or the population, or the relative strength of the people whose fundamental interests they represent' (1999, p. 32). In other words, while one does know they represent a liberal peoples that respects basic freedom and equality, they do not know which one, including in addition to the above constraints, their resources, their relative socio-economic conditions with respect to other liberal peoples, nor their military and/or geo-political clout. However, what we can assume they *do* know would be all the attendant second-personal assumptions behind what one knows of their cognitive, moral, social, political, and psychological capacities be-

[13] As far as I can tell, actually, the closest equivalent to my view comes from the non-Anglo-American, non-Western, anti-colonial outlook masterfully espoused in the 2010 Hague Lectures by the Japanese jurisprudence of Yusuaki Onuma which he fittingly terms his *transcivilizational perspective* in his *A Transcivilizational Perspective on International Law* (2010).

hind the veil of ignorance of original position 1. In addition, they *do* know that their particular people(s) have a distinct history of Mead's 'individuation via processes of socialization' that contributes to one's social basis of self-respect and social, political, and psychological identity (Habermas 1987, pp. 23–25). Rawls even goes as far as to say that this quasi-Humean sentiment of affinity to a particular people(s) may even border on a healthy sense of patriotic political identification matched by the capacity empathetically to extend these same sort of affinities to other representatives of peoples behind the veil of ignorance in original position 2. As a set of two final preliminary clarifications, representatives in original position 2 are proxies for peoples and not states insofar as peoples must formulate a law of peoples in light of the reasonable as opposed to the rational more strategically oriented interests often even expected by citizens to be pursued aggressively by states. Lastly, in comparison to original position 1, whose exemplar of public reason Rawls posits as akin the US equivalent of a Supreme Court Justice, the ideal representative in original position 2 would be the statesman with the capacity to make decisions of political leadership based on their contributions to posterity in furthering the spread of the ideals of the Society of Peoples beyond just their own national constituents and beyond the near-sighted perspective of the political expediency of the present.

As for the perspective of cosmoipolitan justice tentatively formulated under the loose analogy of an original position 3, the subject—or better, participant—I should clarify first in terms of negative formulations. In partial agreement with Rawls' original position 2, the subject behind the veil of ignorance I will *not* couch as an individual citizen of a liberal people or as a rights-bearing individual subject of the cosmopolitan global community as conferred by the institutions of the United Nations and the Charter on the Fundamental Rights of Man. However, in disagreement with Rawls, the party in original position 3 will not be a representative of a people(s) with the attendant loose analogies to the sympathetic identifications Rawls observes between subjects that share a common nationality.

While I am certainly drawn to the transcivilizational perspective of Onuma (briefly cited parenthetically above; and one might also find nascent transcivilizational comparative metrics in Toynbee's gigantic multi-volume analysis: *A Study of History*), I am in general agreement with the more specialized sets of debates that have occurred so far in Western academic discourse as critiques of Toynbee's employment of civilizational modes of analysis (Toynbee 1948). Conceding the risk of loosing the reader in hair-splitting distinctions that will take the remainder of this treatise fully to unpack, firstly, I am in partial agreement with S.N. Eisenstadt's adaptation of civilizational perspectives as the initial rubric from which multiple forms of modernity have since evolved. However, I am also agreement with Eric Voegelin's critique of Toynbee on civilizational matrices as the hypothetic construct from which a subject might be drawn as the fundamental unit of representation (Voegelin 1974, pp. 271–272). Perhaps surprisingly, Voegelin's critique of Toynbee has less to do with problems of scale and scope and more to do with the patchwork historical inconsistencies that viewing a linear developmental progress of mankind's entrance into modernity. Presuming multiple parallel world histor*ies* (in the plural) appeals to the concrete historical experience of any given subject that may abstractly get characterized under crossing and competing (inter-Axial) civilizational matrices and socialization processes (1974, pp. 49–50; Voegelin 1952).

Negations aside now, the participant-subject of my original position 3 on the tenets of cosmoipolitan justice would most directly serve as a participant-in (second-personal perspective) rather than mere representative of (third-person perspective) an Axial Age tradition. The closest corollaries to the communicative participant inhabiting original position 3 would include but not be limited to the idealized appeals for boundless inter-Axial communication as initially developed by Karl Jaspers, Eric Voegelin, and S.N. Eisenstadt and more recently by Charles Taylor, Robert Bellah, and Jurgen Habermas. Here, I would agree with Habermas and others that the idealized liberal-individualist abstractions of the social-contract tradition informing Rawls' original position(s) build into the principles presumed behind the veil(s) of ignorance epistemic and normative commitments that could only warrant their legitimation through a discourse-theoretic employment of communicative action that Rawls seems paradoxically both to presume and altogether to bypass.

For initial sake of clarification, although my concern with justice will seek universal constants as the ideal outcome of intra- and inter-Axial communicative action, cosmoipolitan will also *not* refer to the semantic fallacy forewarned by Jose Casanova of referring to the Axial Age traditions as the great world religions (2013). Insofar as religion derives from Latin Christendom, Casanova effectively demonstrates that it fails the Habermasian pragmatic test of universal translatability into alternative Axial frameworks that either only suggest very loose corollaries or evince the utter absence of an equivalently translatable term (see also Voegelin 1974, pp. 43–48). In a prudential move too, I thereby bypass the messy hermeneutics that come with imposing the present upon the past, in addition to the countless warranted claims of unjustifiably imposing Western claims upon non-Western traditions. I avoid not only the use of the term religion in this particular work but also dismiss as misguided contemporary attempts to define a sufficient category religion that can adequately capture the diversity of pragmatic lived history associated with the great Axial traditions.

Therefore, according to cosmoipolitan justice, what does one know and not know in original position 3? Behind the associated veil of ignorance, one must assume membership in at least one of an unspecified number of the multiple manifestations of modernity. Within this hypothetical construct, one must also assume that their arrival at modernity must indelibly have passed through at least one or more of the major axial traditions. In addition, as the historical, genealogical, archeological, and social scientific data may become more comprehensive over time, original position 3 also assumes along with Jaspers that we should not expect the full array of inter-Axial cross-overs, borrowing, and redacting ever be fully exhausted empirically. While presuming original position 3 would be a standpoint within modernity, however, in tandem with the previous commitment to ongoing empirical and epistemic openness, we must grant the impossibility of a third-person grand-historical narrative that encompasses the full complexity of the initiation of the Axial Age, the onset of modernity, in addition to an impending openness to ongoing critical scrutiny of claims to privy access to how the eschatological fullness of history will eventually unfold. The original position epistemic constraints I propose run in the alternate direction too as far as we must preclude the prospect of verdicts upon an exhaustive finality to evolutionary questions of origins as a third-person consciousness that falls prey to the fallacy of supplanting the purported objectivity of the natural sciences to the social scientific and cultural dimensions of investigations that can only be postulated about the species from the second-personal participant perspective. In more technical terms, we must avoid the empirical third-personal deflation of our ultimately second-personal narrative self-understanding. Voegelin calls this necessity of a symbolic postulation of historiogenesis that would be spoiled by 'proof' via an exhaustive empirical justification. To make matters even more technical, what I am postulating would be a proposed reconstruction of the distinct symbolic onsets of historiogenesis from *each* Axial tradition as, within the standpoint of original position 3, presupposing the symbolic construct of the Axial Age as a share species-ethical point of historiogenetic reference for humanity as such in all of its historical manifestations into the present.

Lastly, what we *do not* know in original position 3 of cosmopolitan justice differs substantially from the legal-juridical and constitutionally oriented great works of Rawls on political justice in original position 1 and 2. For the astute expert in Anglo-American political theory, while I ultimately agree with Rawls (and Rasmussen 2010) that an overlapping consensus would be our best hope in establishing a realistic utopia comprised of multiple modernities, I will come closer to Charles Taylor's path to achieving the same end since Taylor's focus hones in upon the content of the norms of consensus instead of their particular legal-juridical constitutional forms [contra-Rawls] or background justification [pro-Rawls].

As for the merits of the original position abstraction in all of its forms, Rawls states bluntly that the ultimate purpose of such impartiality would be so that we do not tailor the principles/norms of justice to the unique nuances of our particular case. In other words, as part of the long tradition of social contract theory, the original position situates us in the standpoint required for justice as fairness in a hypothetically ongoing constitutional assembly that will seek reflective equilibrium between our principled ideals and the social world in which we live. In a related manner, Rawls repeatedly associates original position 2 of the *Law of Peoples* with the Kantian project of establishing a *foedus pacificum* (Rawls 1999, p. 10, 21, 54). While Rawls emphasizes that he does not espouse a world-state or a cosmopolitan regime of political and redistributive justice to individuals, he nonetheless seeks a principled account of justice that he says can achieve legal-juridical institutionalization in a variety of political forms.

In contrast, while the original position 3 of cosmoipolitan justice agrees with Habermas and others that only universalizable claims that run species-wide can warrant the claim to justice, in accord with Taylor's more juridically-underdetermined overlapping consensus (thus, in contrast here with *both* Rawls' and Habermas's constitutional fetish) I am not seeking the legal-juridical institutionalization of these ideals as the ultimate consummation of the ethical-moral justice that I will seek as universal across axial traditions. Most closely aligned with the warnings of Eric Voegelin (and Taylor not tying overlapping consensus to a constitution) at the risk of lapsing into an ideological Gnosticism of a particular Western constitutional slant, I cast the distinct salvational impulse of each of the great axial traditions as sharing in common the uncanny tension of not taking eschatological closure as plausible within the domain of idealized visions of perfect justice. Nonetheless, while avoiding the repetition of the colonial errors of coercively-imposed territorial, demographic, and constitutional forms of gerrymandered political closure from the outside, cosmoipolitan justice devoid of Western bias must ceaselessly continue to motivate human practical action that can respond to the unique problems of the day.

Stated more positively, we *can* know within the original position 3 of cosmoipolitan justice that, albeit from the inescapable constraints of a participant perspective, that the norms and ideals sought must at least bear potential universality for the species as such. In other words, here I may be closest to seeking what Habermas elsewhere has called a species-ethic that nonetheless carries the universality he usually reserves for the moral, nor merely ethical, domain (2003).

In addition, perhaps closest here to the work of Charles Taylor on the Jamesian open-space he finds characteristic of secularists and/or agnostics that truly take seriously the claims made by their fellow members of the species that derive from one or more axial tradition, we must assume the potential capacity for transcendence as a species constant. As clarified in the earlier exposition of transcencus, such a potentiality for pragmatically ideal transcendence does not thereby foreclose the immanent here and now of the profane realm. To the contrary, and again, likely closest to Voegelin—but also in line with the more general commitment of critical theory in its avowed commitment to eradicate domination in every and all of its historical forms—an appeal to transcendence does not require a disavowal of the profane as the concrete domain of realizing the historical project of bringing about justice as a realizable ideal.

As the most accessible point of departure for my final clarifications concerning the project of cosmoipolitan justice, I must return to an analogy from Rawls one last time. Insofar as the supreme court justice was the ideal exemplar of original position 1 and the statesman offers us an ideal to be met by the representatives in original position 2, it would seem most natural to posit the great axial personalities as the exemplars for inhabiting original position 3. However, as already hinted earlier, I expressly avoid such a hasty analogical move and will now elaborate with three additional reasons that are significant to the methodological commitments of my overall project. Most plainly, firstly, I take as one of the key achievements of modernity the unassailable dignity of the individual subject and the fullest possible realization of each individual's capacities as crucial to the historical dimensions of projects committed to an ideal of justice. In this respect, I adapt one of the characteristics of what Taylor calls the nova effect that has contributed to the onset of modernity, specifically whereby a defining component of the ongoing pertinence and success of the great axial traditions has been their gradual dissemination from cultural elites to infiltrating the common public and stirring on popular movements that realize originally Axial ideals and then the ensuing redaction of these commitments to the greatest possible scope of moral-ethical universality. As one of many possible instances from his *A Secular Age* (2007), we could point to the Christian Axial fundaments of love as *agape* as subjected to ongoing redaction until their ensuing translation into the less theologically-charged humanistic ideal of universal benevolence we have come to associate with a normative ideal of modernity.

Secondly, for openly strategic reasons in advancing my arguments to follow in the chapters addressing the historical unfolding of each major Axial tradition, we must also assume with original position 3 that—particularly, in agreement with Habermas—no claim advanced from the perspective of cosmopolitan justice carries special immunity from ongoing critique and rational justification. Here, we agree with Habermas that one of the problems with building too much content into the pragmatic presuppositions informing our original position(s) would be to render purported communicatively-established ideals from a critical-participant origination as if they were third-person objective achievements insulated from critically discursive redaction (Habermas 1998, pp. 56–59). Therefore, in direct opposition to Jaspers that associates the Axial Age with the great personalities that initiated these breakthroughs, the risk in doing so when subjected to the historical critical method would be attaching the accomplishments of several millennia of tradition, ritual, and even intra-Axial competition to the charismatic personalities of one or more small group of individuals that could not possibly have foreseen how even truly original axial breakthroughs of these elites would gain new layers of interpretive meaning that only millennia of tradition could endow with such rich content. While I agree with Eisenstadt that a stadial and evolutionary-functional view of history has trouble coming to terms with the sudden breakthroughs of charismatic individuals, nonetheless, the overt attachment of the Axial Age to a limited group of persons runs a greater risk of historical deflation in cases where that individual or group of prophetic personalities left behind either dubious sets of teaching that may or may not have received exact transcription or may have been historically known not to have written at all. When committed to the rational scrutiny of the historical-critical method, one risk of placing too much content into a single person or small charismatic group would be that an entire tradition of insight might be shortsightedly perceived to stand or fall on historical and empirical support, or lack thereof, from a predominately deflationary third-person perspective.

Thirdly, in light of my attention on the non-elite individual and the subjection of axial personalities to the historical-critical method, my shift of emphasis for participants in original position 3 would be the enhanced potential for multiple layers of interpretive learning and self-understanding via standing in as a hypothetical participant-interpreter of the canonical precedent of the great axial traditions. On the one hand, this puts emphasis on not overlooking the institutional prerequisites as part of the content of cosmoipolitan justice, including basic material capacities like literacy, numeracy, social recognition, low mortality rates, political participation, and generally stable economic conditions that can more closely tie together conventional capability sets in development literature with higher-order intellectual, psychological, and spiritual capabilities. On the other hand, as perhaps most acutely shown by the works of Eric Voegelin (see especially my Chap. 3, sections on Judaism), reducing canonical scriptures purely to the critical-historical comfort with a third-person reconstruction of linear time belies the best hermeneutic reconstructions of sacred texts that are often more richly understood as ongoing layers of historical redaction. These typically generate new participant-driven axial breakthroughs and symbolic insights only by engaging in the arduous hermeneutic labor of comparing and integrating multiple participant perspectives. While a more universal accessibility of the great axial traditions does run the risk of their trivialization, it also offers the prospect of creative syncretism, ongoing substantive apologetic critique from competitor traditions, and a greater sensitivity to areas where seemingly secular achievements owe their unleashed cognitive potentials to initial translation from one or more axial heritage.

Despite the array of contrasts with Rawls, in one academically unrecognized concurrence, my transcendentally pragmatic casting of original position 3 as distinctly second-personal resonates with a subtle feature of his original position 2 that he only reserves to limited reference in his textual notations. When he clarifies the notion of the perspective of the representative of a people, he refers specifically to 'the I and you, in the here and now' (Rawls 1999, p. 32 *and* note 35). My attention to this seemingly trite point emphasizes the participant role that one must assume when engaged in social-scientific practice. In other words, what I also want to retain in my casting of original position 3 as the starting point of cosmoipolitan justice would be the historicized, socialized, and moral-pragmatic layers that accompany this second person perspective. On the one hand, this notion of justice refers to the irreplaceability of each individual person addressed as a 'you' which also carries with it the irrevocable command of justice that ideally demands the consent or dissent of each and every person affected by a decision or particular scheme of action. On the other hand, 'you' in its plural form would not only comprise the entirety of the living human species as the hypothetically substantive content of each axial tradition, it also elicits implied commands of justice to reparation and reconciliation for past misdeeds and also engenders moral obligations to the future, specifically in light of growing problems of inter-generational scope including but not limited to environmental degradation, fiscal irresponsibility, new genetic and reproductive capacities, and the long-term effects of war and violence. As yet one related extension of the you standpoint, insofar as human survival indelibly ties to ecological responsibility, one of my intended connotations of the language of 'cosmoi'-politan justice would be to highlight the Thou or you quality of other organic communities to which we owe reciprocal (and sometimes asymmetrical) obligations of moral responsibility.

As for two final emendations to what I intend to convey by cosmoipolitan justice, the species component of these moral-ethical commitments also requires adding to original position 3 the pragmatically real potential of reproductive and/or familial ties of moral obligation to every other member of humanity. This may seem to overstretch both our capacities and our common sense sympathies. However, extending backwards, the embodied and even ritual dimensions of sexual reproduction presume common membership in a species bearing the capacity for propagation of itself. Even taking account of the most cutting-edge revisionist accounts of our evolutionary heritage, in light of the emergent prospect of past inter-species origins to humanity as brought about by genetic analysis of *Denisovan Hominins*, nonetheless that could widen our moral responsibilities backward as much as re-emphasize our biological and genetic common heritage in the present. As for the future too, with the onset of new reproductive technologies—of particular interest to Habermas in his (2003) *Future of Human Nature*—latent prospects for human reproduction of even quasi-asexual scientific procedures also seems to engender a heightened scope to our moral obligations to others that, may even be able to bypass formerly biologically imposed constraints on the composition of a genetic family, like challenging the assumption of tying the onset of moral personhood to the formation of a zygote combining the genetic inheritance of two sexually distinct male and female gametes.

As the final epistemic condition that we could say we *do* know from the original position 3 as it bears on the present renaissance of interest in the Axial Age as perhaps the new threshold for revising our non-Eurocentric reassessments of modernity, we could make a last normative claim in light of an empirical demographic observation. Since no single Axial tradition, (including those that would prefer ascription into the demographics of agnostic, atheist, and/or secularist) currently holds a majority relative to the rest of the human population, the standpoint of cosmoipolitan justice presumes that all persons are on the equal plane of Axial minorities with respect to the remainder of the human demographic. In what follows, this observation would be one of the many tensions implied by axial transcensus occurring between vying justificatory claims of universal and particular salience that cosmoipolitan justice wants to concede as a social fact of our postsecular condition (Bohman 2013). Somewhat akin to national constitutions professing claims about obligations and even entitlements to all humanity, the axial traditions hold this paradoxical quality of voicing epistemic, moral-ethical, and social claims for humanity as such while nonetheless having claimed self-authenticating justification from only portions of a composite whole.

1.6 Completing the Turn from Modernization Theory to Multiple Modernities: Why the Social Scientific Shift from Weber to Jaspers?

As a preliminary outline for the remaining chapters of the book, I will frame the themes to follow in the context of offering further justification for the social scientific viability and philosophical merits of the multiple modernities thesis. In addition, I would like to conjecture a response to a likely critique to my overall project: Why should we expect a social scientific trend of the last few decades to overturn the modernization theory that owes such an impressive heritage to the great achievements of the European Enlightenment? Or stated in less grandiose terms, why expect the relative philosophical obscurity of Jaspers to supplant the social scientific and philosophical prowess of Weber? Clearly the turn to Jaspers requires the much more laborious enterprise of engaging in the comparative inter-Axial reflection he effectively termed world philosophy. Therefore, what I am engaged in may seem to critics a prolonged and unnecessarily complex defense of Voegelin's eccentric claim that 'nothing much has happened in the last 2500 years.' In more philosophical parlance, must we renounce the achievements of modernity if we shift the axis of historical analysis away from the rational impartiality of the European Enlightenment *backwards* to the philosophical-faith(s) introduced at the onset of the Axial Age (800–200 BCE)? The same critics would likely point out the requisite lack of analytic rigor in abstracting wide generalizations from species-wide universal trends in these arcane traditions.

As a preliminary response to such critiques, I will amend the social scientific work of Smith and Vaidyanathan (2011) that has provided the most complete characterization of the empirical conditions that have led to the philosophical reframing of the relations between the great axial traditions and modernization into our current proliferation of multiple modernities. While I will endorse their four main causal trends, I will cast the empirical data philosophically and reorder the four trends as tailored to the thematic sequence of my five remaining chapters.

1.6.1 The Rebirth of Ethnic and Religious Nationalism (Chaps. 2 and 3)

While prior trends in modernization theory seemed to presume secular convergence as the only conceivable normative threshold for rational legitimacy, the opposite extreme would be to presume the incommensurability of multiple modernities, as perhaps most sensationalized in Huntington's *Clash of Civilizations* (1996). My project of multiple modernities seeks here to strike a mean somewhere between the overt acknowledgment of multiple forms of secularism together with an acceptance that new cultural programs of modernity may also be reshaped to conform with unforeseen patterns of religious resurgence. With the exception of Taoism and Confucianism (which one could argue still play an essential role in any sinological hybridized scheme—for instance, along with Buddhism, in what constitutes Chinese neo-imperialistic nationalism), we could find democratically elected forms of religious resurgence informing nation-state political mobilization of majoritarian groups of Axial origins—to name just a few—in India (Hindu nationalism), Israel (Hebrew nationalism), Turkey, Serbia, and/or Malaysia (Muslim nationalism), Thailand, Tibet, and/or Nepal (Buddhist nationalism), and/or Poland (Catholic), Ireland (Catholic), Britain (Anglican), Russia (neo-Orthodox) and in the Nordic states (secularized Lutheranism). Although I agree with Casanova and others that a prerequisite of modern justice best errs toward the side of deconfessionalized nation-states, with any variation of an Axial tradition rendered nationalist, the convergence trend upon overt secularization seems not only empirically implausible but also—at the opposing extreme this time—normatively proves a violation of basic justice.

Even when conceding the resurgence of variants of the axial traditions in nationalist form, my proposal for cosmoipolitan justice seeks to grant due recognition to each axial tradition (and their nuanced hybrids) as viable sites of political mobilization. I thus strongly discourage viewing their legal-juridical institutionalization within the confines of a sovereign state as an achievement of universal justice. On the one hand, for reasons akin to those expressed by Voegelin, repeating the errors of the ecumenic age at both the smaller national and larger imperial scales misses out on the axial impetus of universality that intentionally must evade attempts at institutional closure. On the other hand, I will concede a great deal of comfort with casting the great axial traditions internally as de-territorialized polities—that now via the technological prowess of mass global media—do indeed carry as a requisite of justice the real prospect of carving out a Jamesian open space of potential communicability of their distinct salvational impulses to a species-wide community of addressees. As de-territorial polities, in order to retain rational legitimation for the addressees that take up axial claims for possible conferral of warrant, first-person contestation, redaction, or responsible uptake renders each hypothetical polity subject to ongoing reconstruction.

My Chap. 2 will begin with the four non-Abrahamic axial traditions as distinct deterritorial iterations of species-ethical claims to universality, positing in some cases—via the mandate of heaven in its diverse forms—purely idealized cosmically-charged 'galactic polities.' My Chap. 3 then will address the Abrahamic axial forms that each provide distinct renditions of species-ethical universality with explicit ties to what Jaspers abstractly terms Biblical religion in a spatially open sense that belies institutional closure. Despite some avowed ambivalence on his part, my casting opts to include the Muslim tradition with the wider rubric of Biblical religion (even conceding sheer demographics could also merit among those traditions normally ascribed the classification of 'Eastern.')

1.6.2 Industrialization and Religion (Chap. 4)

Also contrary to the initial convergence theories of secular modernization, tradition can flourish and adapt under conditions of rapid industrialization. In my Chap. 4 comparison of the United States and Europe, I introduce both sides of the exceptionalist thesis. On the one hand, modernization theory initially regarded the United States religiosity as the exception to European secularization as the global norm. Now, the shift from modernization theory to multiple modernities has turned Europe into the exception to the norm of global industrialization *not* entailing the death of religion. However, I show that neither exceptionalist thesis captures the full complexity involved in deriving global conclusions from these singular cases. In addition, the market-like competitive conditions for axial traditions to offer pragmatic results garner proof of their enduring salience to solve concrete social problems. Such pragmatically oriented surface solidarity, while indeed trading off deeper bonds of trust for instrumental efficacy, has been among the keys to the enduring success of the US model for relating religion to the free-for-all market conditions of civil society networks missing in European states yet to undergo full processes of deconfessionalization.

On the other hand, immigration (largely often likewise market-driven) on both sides of the Atlantic—while exhibiting multiple manifestations of modernity—nonetheless has been driven by industrialization that has as much enhanced the ongoing salience of distinct axial traditions to discount the prognostication of industrialization and the immanent demise of tradition. For instance, in the US case, religion has proven to be a vehicle for social inclusion, immersion, and adaptation to distinct civic-national and localized-particular acculturation of new immigrants into society. In contrast, in the European case, industrialization—particularly, reconstruction post-WWII—saw huge waves of immigration (predominately without the conferral of citizenship status) from Muslim immigrants that have now become the driving force behind Habermas's proclamation of the onset of a postsecular age in Europe.

As far as the global dynamic of ongoing industrialization goes, sheer global demographics suggest entry into the first period in human history whereby the majority of the human population now resides in large metropolitan and urban centers. These large pluralistic metropolises also bring the onset of the postsecular city whereby one of the indices for advanced industrialization *includes* rather than precludes the formation of public spaces that enable the free practice of faith from any and all of the major axial traditions.

1.6.3 European Modernization as Always Already Inherently Cultural (Chap. 5)

In Chap. 5, not only do I argue along with the likes of Taylor, that European modernity presumes its own particular cultural backdrop, but I also show that Europe itself is, will be, and always has been comprised of multiple modernities. By parsing European modernities into at least three distinct historical iterations, we can begin to understand why one of the obstacles and internal structural dynamics of the European project has been the variegated administrative and institutional cultures associated with religion in private and public domains. In addition to categorizing what I term Anglo-Saxon, Continental, and Scandinavian forms of modernity, I also trace the religious, moral, and political genealogy of the principle of subsidiarity as articulated both in EU international covenants and in the broader religious histories of its Catholic, Protestant, and Anglican iterations. In the end, I conclude that a fuller articulation of the European experience with multiple modernities helps to reinforce Jose Casanova's sociological (and normative) conclusions that modernity cannot but be assessed in paradoxical terms, as all of its forms tends to secularize axial commitments at the very moment these become politicized. As the demands of justice point to the de-confessionalization of nation-states (not just in Europe, but also globally), the general trend of relegating *all* axial traditions to the domain of an emergent global civil society also contributes to the dynamic of what he terms 'global denominationalism'—thereby feeding into mass social movements that re-politicize these commitments at local, national, international, and global scales.

1.6.4 Neo-Colonial Patterns of Developmental Economics (Chap. 6)

In my concluding Chap. 6, I turn to development economics as yet the final major contributing empirical factor and normative basis for accepting and seeking further to institutionalize the multiple modernities thesis. Smith and Vadiyanathan put the issue well in highlighting that normative demands of justice warrant rectification of the neo-colonial excesses of coerced modes of development, even (and perhaps especially) in cases producing unintended economic consequences:

> [E]nthusiastic attempts in development economics to replace traditional forms with structures imported from the West led in many cases to embarrassing, if not disastrous, failures. As a result, development economists have recently begun to take much more seriously the importance of traditional communities and institutions, as well as religious and ethnic factors….This presented the possibility of a variety of pathways of "development" and, hence, forms of modernity. (2011, p. 252)

While an exhaustive treatment of both the many historical injustices and a comprehensive cataloguing of case studies of historical redress exceed the scope of this work—and the capacities of even the most astute of social scientists—I provide a sampling of cases predominately from developing economies. Nowhere can the multi-polarity of the cosmoipolitan scheme be seen better than through the emergence of China and India, the global repositioning associated with the demise of the Soviet empire, and the cultural nuances of the most egregious colonial and neo-colonial damage done to the Middle East, Central and South America, and Africa.

References

Adorno, Theodor. 1966. *Negative dialectics*. Trans: E. B. Ashton. New York: Continuum.

An-Nai'm, Abdullah. 2008. *Islam and the secular state: Interpreting the future of Shari'a*. Cambridge: Harvard University Press.

Arnason, Johann P. 2012. Rehistoricizing the axial age. In *The axial age and its consequences,* eds. Robert H. Bellah and Hans Joas, 337–365. Cambridge: Belknap Press of Harvard University.

Asad, Talal. 2003. *Formations of the secular: Christianity, Islam, modernity*. Stanford: Stanford University Press.

Assmann, Jan. 2012. Cultural memory and the myth of the axial age. In *The axial age and its consequences,* eds. Robert H. Bellah and Hans Joas, 366–406. Cambridge: Belknap Press of Harvard University.

Bellah, Robert. 2011. *Religion in human evolution: From the paleolithic to the axial age*. Cambridge: Belknap Harvard Press.

Bellah, Robert. 2012. The heritage of the axial age: Resource or burden? In *The axial age and its consequences,* eds. Robert H. Bellah and Hans Joas, 447–466. Cambridge: Belknap Press of Harvard University.
Bohman, James. 2000. The importance of the second person: Interpretation, practical knowledge, and normative attitudes. In *Empathy and agency: The problem of understanding in the human sciences,* eds. Hans Kogler and Karsten Stueber, 222–242. Boulder: Westview Press.
Bohman, James. 2007. *Democracy across borders: From demos to demoi.* Cambridge: MIT Press.
Bohman, James. 2013. A postsecular global order? The pluralism of forms of life and communicative freedom. In *Habermas and religion,* eds. Craig Calhoun, Eduardo Mendieta, and Jonathan VanAntwerpen. Cambridge: Polity Press.
Bowman, Jonathan. 2012. Why cosmoipolitan justice in a postsecular age? Taylor and Habermas on European versus American exceptionalism. *Philosophy and Social Criticism* 38 (2): 127–147.
Casanova, J. 1994. *Public religions in the modern world.* Chicago: University of Chicago Press.
Casanova, J. 2006. Rethinking secularization: A global comparative perspective. *The Hedgehog Review* Spring and Summer: 7–22.
Casanova, J. 2012. Religion, the axial age, and secular modernity in Bellah's theory of religious evolution. In *The axial age and its consequences,* eds. Robert H. Bellah and Hans Joas, 191–221. Cambridge: Belknap Press of Harvard University.
Casanova, Jose. 2013. Exploring the postsecular: Three meanings of "the Secular" and their possible transcendence. In *Habermas and religion,* eds. C. Calhoun, E. Mendieta, and J. VanAntwerpen, 27–48. Cambridge: Polity Press.
Casanova, J. 2014. The two dimensions, temporal and spatial, of the secular: Comparative reflections on the Nordic Protestant and Southern Catholic patterns from a global perspective. In *Secular and sacred? The Scandinavian case of religion in human rights, law and public space,* eds. Rosemarie van den Breemer, Jose Casanova, and Trygve Wyller, 21–33. Bristol: Vandenhoeck and Ruprecht.
Cooke, Maeve. 2013. Violating neutrality: Religious claims and democratic legitimacy. In *Habermas and religion,* eds. Craig Calhoun, Eduardo Mendieta, and Jonathan VanAntwerpen, 249–274. Cambridge: Polity Press.
Donald, Merlin. 2012. An evolutionary approach to culture: Implications for the study of the axial age. In *The axial age and its consequences,* eds. Robert H. Bellah and Hans Joas, 47–76. Cambridge: Belknap Press of Harvard University.
Eisenstadt, S. N. 2003a. *Comparative civilizations and multiple modernities, Part I,* 1–488. Leiden: Brill Publishers.
Eisenstadt, S. N. 2003b. *Comparative civilizations and multiple modernities, Part II,* 489–1055. Leiden: Brill Publishers.
Eisenstadt, S. N. 2006. *The great revolutions and the civilizations of modernity.* Leiden: Brill Publishers.
Fabian, J. 1983. *Time and the other: How anthropology makes its object.* New York: Columbia University Press.
Follesdal, Andreas. 2013. The legitimacy deficits of the human rights judiciary: Elements and implications of a normative theory. *Theoretical Inquiries in Law* 14 (2): 339–360.
Habermas, J. 1979. *Communication and the evolution of society.* Trans: Thomas McCarthy, Boston: Beacon Press.
Habermas, J. 1987. *Theory of communicative action. Vol. II—Lifeworld and system: A critique of functionalist reason.* Trans: Thomas McCarthy. Boston: Beacon Press.
Habermas, J. 1998. Reconciliation through the public use of reason. In *Inclusion of the other,* eds. Ciarin Cronin and Pablo de Greiff, 49–73. Cambridge: MIT Press.
Habermas, J. 2001. The conflict of beliefs: Karl Jaspers on the clash of cultures. In *The liberating power of symbols: Philosophical essays,* 30–45, Trans: Peter Dews. Cambridge: MIT Press.
Habermas, J. 2002a. Conversations about god and the world. In *Reason and rationality: Essays on reason, God and modernity.* Cambridge: MIT Press.
Habermas, J. 2002b. Glauben und Wissen. *Forum Philosophicum,* VII: 7–16.

Habermas, J. 2003. *The future of human nature*. Cambridge: Polity Press.
Habermas, J. 2008a. *Between naturalism and religion: Philosophical essays*. Trans: Ciarin Cronin. Cambridge: Polity Press.
Habermas, J. 2008b. Notes on a post-secular society, *SignandSight*, June 18.
Habermas, J. 2013. Reply to my critics. In *Habermas and religion,* eds. Craig Calhoun, Eduardo Mendieta, and Jonathan VanAntwerpen, 347–390, Trans: Ciarin Cronin. Cambridge: Polity Press.
Habermas, J., and Ratzinger, J. 2006. *Dialectics of secularization: On reason and religion*. San Francisco: Ignatius Press.
Huntington, Samuel. 1996. *The clash of civilizations and the remaking of world order*. New York: Touchstone.
Jaspers, K. 1949. *The perennial scope of philosophy*. Trans: Ralph Manheim. New York: Philosophical Library.
Jaspers, K. 1953. *The origin and goal of history*. Trans: Michael Bullock. New Haven: Yale University Press.
Jaspers, K. 1957. *Socrates, Buddha, Confucius, Jesus: The paradigmatic individuals* (from The Great Philosophers, vol. I), ed. Hannah Arendt, Trans: Ralph Manheim. San Diego: Harcourt Brace Jovanovich Publishers.
Jaspers, K. 1967. *Philosophical faith and revelation*. Trans: E. B. Ashton. New York: Harper and Row.
Jaspers, K. 1981. Philosophical autobiography. In *The philosophy of Karl Jaspers; Library of living philosophers*, Vol. IX, 5–94. Chicago: Open Court Publishing.
Joas, Hans. 2012. The axial age debate as religious discourse. In *The axial age and its consequences,* eds. Robert H. Bellah and Hans Joas, 9–28. Cambridge: Belknap Press of Harvard University.
Kleingeld, Pauline. 1999. Six varieties of cosmopolitanism in late eighteenth century Germany. *Journal of the History of Ideas* 60 (3): 505–524.
Knott, Kim. 2014. Interrogating the secular: A spatial approach. In *Secular and sacred? The Scandinavian case of religion in human rights, law and public space,* eds. Rosemarie van den Breemer, Jose Casanova, and Trygve Wyller, 34–55. Bristol: Vandenhoeck and Ruprecht.
Koskeneimi, Martii. 2011. Histories of international law: Dealing with Eurocentrism, 19 *Rechtsgeschichte,* 152–176.
Lambert, Yves. 1999. Religion and modernity as a new axial age: Secularization or new religious forms? *Sociology of Religion* 60 (3): 303–333.
Lasaulx, Ernst von. 1856. *Neuer Versuch einer alten auf die Wahrheit der Thatsache gegrundeten Philosophie der Geschichte*. Munich: Literarisch-Artistische Anstalt der J.G. Cotta'schen Buchhandlung. (New ed.: *Neuer Versuch einer alten auf die Wahrheit der Thatsache gegrundeten Philosophie der Geschichte*, ed. Eugen Thurnher. Munich: Oldenbourg, 1952).
MacCormick, Neil. 2002. *Questioning sovereignty: Law, state, and nation in the European commonwealth*. Oxford: Oxford University Press.
McCarthy, Thomas. 2009. *Race, empire, and the idea of human development*. Cambridge: Cambridge University Press.
McCarthy, Thomas. 2013. The burdens of modernized faith and postmetaphysical reason in Habermas's 'unfinished project of modernity'. In *Habermas and religion,* eds. Craig Calhoun, Eduardo Mendieta, and Jonathan VanAntwerpen, 115–131, Trans: Ciarin Cronin. Cambridge: Polity Press
McKnight, Stephen A. 1975. Recent developments in Voegelin's philosophy of history. *Sociological Analysis* 36 (4): 357–65.
Mendieta, Eduardo. 2009. From imperial to dialogical cosmopolitanism. *Ethics & Global Politics* 2 (3): 241–258.
Mendieta, Eduardo. 2013. Appendix: Religion in Habermas's work." In *Habermas and religion,* eds. Craig Calhoun, Eduardo Mendieta, and Jonathan VanAntwerpen, 391–407. Trans: Ciarin Cronin. Cambridge: Polity Press.

Nussbaum, Martha. 2011. *Creating capabilities: The human development approach*. Cambridge: Harvard University Press.

Onuma, Yasuaki. 2010. *A transcivilizational approach to international law*. (Pocketbooks of the Hague Academy of International Law). Leiden: Martinus Nijhoff Publishers.

Pannikar, Raimon. 1993. *The cosmotheandric experience: Emerging religious consciousness*. Maryknoll: Orbis Books.

Pinsent, Andrew. 2012. *The second person perspective in Aquinas's ethics: Virtues and gifts*. New York: Routledge.

Rasmussen, David. 2010. Conflicted modernity: Toleration as a principle of justice. *Philosophy and Social Criticism* 36 (3–4): 339–352.

Rasmussen, David. 2012. The emerging domain of the political. *Philosophy and Social Criticism* 38 (4–5): 457–466.

Rawls, John. 1971. *A theory of justice*. Cambridge: Harvard University Press.

Rawls, John. 1993. *Political liberalism*. Cambridge: Harvard University Press.

Rawls, John. 1999. *The law of peoples*. Cambridge: Harvard University Press.

Roetz, Heiner. 2012. A challenge to historicism or an explanatory device of civilizational analysis? With a look at the normative discourse in axial age china. In *The axial age and its consequences,* eds. Robert H. Bellah and Hans Joas, 248–273. Cambridge: Belknap Press of Harvard University.

Schwartz, Benjamin. 1975. *The age of transcendence*. Special issue on Wisdom, Revelation, and Doubt: Perspectives on the First Millennium BC. *Daedelus*, Spring, 1–7.

Sen, Amartya. 1999. *Development as freedom*. New York: Alfred Knopf Press.

Smith, Christian, and Brandon Vaidyanathan. 2010. Multiple modernities and religion. In *The oxford handbook of religious diversity,* ed, Chad Meister, 250–265. Oxford: Oxford University Press.

Strauss, Victor von. 1870. *Lao-tse's Tao te king*. Leipzig: Fleisher.

Stump, Eleonore. 2010. *Wandering in darkness*. Oxford: Oxford University Press.

Taylor, Charles. 2000. Modernity and difference. In *Without guarantees: In honour of Stuart Hall,* eds. Paul Gilroy, Lawrence Grossberg, and Angela McRobbie, 364–374. London: Verso.

Taylor, Charles. 2001. Two theories of modernity. In *Alternative modernities,* ed. Dilip Gaonkar, 172–196 Duke: Duke University Press.

Taylor, Charles. 2007. *A secular age*. Cambridge: Belknap Press of Harvard University.

Taylor, Charles. 2012. What was the axial revolution? In *The axial age and its consequences,* eds. Robert H. Bellah and Hans Joas, 30–46. Cambridge: Belknap Press of Harvard University.

Thomassen, Bjorn. 2010. Anthropology, multiple modernities and the axial age debate. *Anthropological Theory* 10 (4): 321–344.

Toynbee, Arnold J. 1948. *A study of history*. New York: Oxford University Press.

Voegelin, Eric. 1952. *The new science of politics: An introduction*. Chicago: University of Chicago Press.

Voegelin, Eric. 1974. *Order and history: The Ecumenic age, vol. IV*. Baton Rouge: Louisiana State University Press.

Voegelin, Eric. 1978. *Anamnesis*. Trans: and ed. Gerhart Niemeyer. Notre Dame: Notre Dame Press.

Weber, Max. 1920. *The sociology of religion*. Boston: Beacon Press. Trans: Ephraim Fischoff 1963.

Weber, Alfred. 1935. *Kulturgeschichte als Kultursoziologie*. Leiden: Sijthoff.

Part I
Axial Period One—The Great World Religions

Chapter 2
Extending the Dialectics of Secularization Eastward: Scriptural Hermeneutics and Discursive Insights from Hindu, Buddhist, Confucian, and Taoist Philosophy of Language

Abstract In light of Habermas's recent development of a socio-evolutionary account of the emergence of ritual introduced by the Axial Period, I focus most directly on the communicative ethic of achieving mutual understanding with a second person. I explore potential Eastern Axial contributions to this process providing a microanalysis of the interaction of discursive subjects in four traditions: for Hinduism, epistemic authority; Buddhism, right speech; Confucianism, the rectification of names; Taoism, truth disclosure. For the Hindu dynamic, I will examine the stages in dialectics of the second-personal reversal of social roles found in its axial period scriptures as they detail differentiation of sites of authority. Firstly, the Vedanta scriptures introduce the axial shift from ritual to cognitive transcendence via the rationalization of sacrificial rites. Secondly, the role of the renouncer transcends the worldly orientation of the caste hierarchy. Next, the appeal to Buddhist linguistic proprieties argues that true linguistic claims reflexively point to the moral and ontological status of the speaker more so than merely make factual claims about the world. The Confucian section provides a comparative analysis of its use of normative semantics to that employed by Habermas. Lastly, the Taoist portion of the argument highlights the holistic incompleteness of attempts at final closure upon the procedures and institutional contexts in which communicative action takes place. I conclude with reflections concerning the breadth that the Eastern traditions contribute in their relative comfort with experimental cross-Axial hybrids as compared to Western exclusivist norms of toleration.

Keywords Axial age · Communicative action · Epistemic authority · Jurgen Habermas · Karl Jaspers · Mandate of Heaven · Pragmatic presuppositions · Reciprocal role-taking · Rectification of names · Right speech · Second person · Transcensus · Truth disclosure

2.1 Introduction

Jurgen Habermas's pronouncement that we have entered a postsecular age runs a grave risk of philosophical distortion of its basic motivations (Habermas 2008b). Habermas outright rejects the potential misunderstanding of a postsecular age as

J. Bowman, *Cosmoipolitan Justice*, Studies in Global Justice 15,
DOI 10.1007/978-3-319-12709-5_2

bringing about a miraculous resurgence of spiritual commitments in the most secularized of European and Western states. He maintains in his *Dialectics of Secularization* that neither the modern state in its original form nor the many emergent transnational political regimes require faith-induced sources of moral solidarity. However, his ultimate rejection of any thick pre-political moral basis as the grounds for legitimacy does not thereby preclude foreclosure of the rational legitimacy of opting for or against faith in making contributions to public debate.

On the one hand, the achievements of modernity have rapidly spread species-wide through globalization (Eisenstadt 2003b, pp. 937–52). The global spread of state neutrality to religion necessarily entails the steady de-confessionalization of the nation-state. On the other hand, this secular achievement of neutrality becomes the very condition for the possibility of spiritual contributions to public debate. The growing recognition of the potential moral contributions of the great axial traditions to social solidarity also opens innovative epistemic, moral, and ethical inputs to shared problematic circumstances. The enigma in understanding the full import of Habermas's position rests upon the simultaneous opening of ethical and epistemic options for or against faith as equally rationally justifiable positions.

The ensuing problem with deriving a truly polycentric, multi-vocal, and inter-Axial politics of communicative action that begins with his Western-oriented and—nonetheless avowedly transcendentally ideal—theory is twofold (Habermas and Ratzinger 2006). Primarily, when dealing with non-Western traditions, we may be at risk of building into the pragmatic presuppositions of the discourse theory the sorts of Western outcomes we want them to produce. In order to alleviate some of the inevitable parochial biases of readers trained in critical theory and contemporary Western political theory, I will begin in critical theorist fashion with reconstructing the pragmatic presupposition of communicative action internal to the non-Western Axial traditions. The hope would also be to prevent reading the Abrahamic traditions into what ideally would constitute an impartial mode of analysis.

Secondly, while the program of cosmoipolitan justice may disclose innovative species-ethical justifications that contribute to the legitimacy of non-Western social orders, when moving from genealogy to transcendental implementation, they may fail pragmatic tests for rational universality originally cherished as a primary epistemic virtue. If misconstruing the cognitive motivations of those described as taking up these practices, we are left with a series of gaps between our expert transcendental theorizing and the more locally inscribed social imaginaries. In its worse forms, this could constitute yet another continuation of a hegemonic Westernization of not really taking up these alternative civilizational discourses on their own terms. Imposed transcendental justifications from the outside would lend further credence to the warranted bias that objectively impartial theorizing becomes another mode of surreptitious neo-colonialization. The dubious portrayal of law and universal morality as neutral will ultimately fail tests of legitimacy if not subjecting expert discourses to the rational assent or rejection of those most immediately affected by both our descriptive facts and prescriptive norms (Asad 1993).

On behalf of Habermas's increasing openness to imbue the universal with more localized ethical and cultural content, practical indeterminacy in the face of novel global problems can itself be turned into an epistemic virtue as a wellspring of species creativity. For instance, normative learning and ongoing reflexive redaction can be reconciled with compelling contemporary research into neonate and infant capacities for second person participation. An enriched contemporary understanding of our unique capacities to participate in another person's stance toward problematic circumstances can thereby heighten our sensitivity to providing more accurate rational reconstructions of how these universal capacities have been and continue to manifest themselves in non-Western communicative practices. In particular, the neonate practical capacity for joint attention precedes the later emergence of capacities for linguistic and propositional understanding (Pinsent 2012, p. 56). We will search for non-Western iterations of these practical capacities behind healthy cognitive flourishing and moral maturation as a means to encourage prolonged second-personal experimentation with both disclosing and resolving newly emergent species-wide problematic circumstances. In most general terms, the micro-level discourse analysis feeding into the project of cosmoipolitan justice presupposes neonate counterfactual experimentation with multiple realities as the very precondition for healthy individual and species moral maturation (Gopnik 2009, pp. 19–46, 86–91; Buber 1970/1923, pp. 75–79; Bellah 2011, pp. 1–11, 91–97). The collective learning process of ascribing shared propositional understandings for problems itself must always already include a reflective component when facing novel problems that yet require vocabularies for fully capturing their common species ramifications. I argue that such a dispositional comportment necessary for successful joint attention requires constant re-socialization as cognitive, moral, and affective buffers to our increasingly intense pressures to engage only in instrumental comportments to a shared social world. Without second person reflexive testing, we risk lapsing into either instrumental or objectivigating orientations of civilizing persons into linguistic practices that may do more cosmic, psychological, moral, and cognitive harm than good (Donald 2012; Bellah 2011).

The associated linguistic and communicative remedies I propose would be to render as a normative project Eisenstadt's empirical descriptions of both the tradition-preserving and revolutionary components common to the salvation impulse of all the axial traditions (Eisenstadt 2006). The initially unsuccessful Axial Age social movements projected disparate hopes for alternate civilizational orders. As the concomitant traditions have still survived, I will recast them more optimistically as the major drivers in realizing cosmoipolitan justice as an ongoing species vision of communicative experimentation with multiple potential realities subject to constant redaction. While the revolutionary movements were originally localized and elite-driven, the pragmatic presuppositions behind all the axial social imaginaries presumed potential communicability to a universally encompassing audience. Any person could be taken as at least a potential participant in communication, not just in reference to common objects of joint attention, but also in presuming the shared capacity to reshape a world of common reference as always already socially constituted. These revisionist emendations will draw upon Habermas's theory of communicative action as the best available template for this experimental syncretism of comparative analysis.

Learning by redaction through social protest and through creative extensions of millennia of tradition will also be transposed upon the initial species-wide rite of passage that Jaspers associates with the advent of the Axial Age. Instead of Habermas's original *TCA*-informed Weberian abstraction to a linguistification of the sacred that slowly progresses toward the methodogical atheism of a more fully mature modernity, upon reconstructing the basic pragmatic presuppositions of the axial period, we will actually find the richer genealogy (to follow in the next two chapters) to comprise opposite trends away from convergence. Again, allowing for some degree of necessary abstraction, we will instead presume (along with Eisenstadt, Taylor, and Casanova) the pre- and post-Axial linguistic/theoretical social imaginary as always already mimetic, inherently ritualistic, and politically constituted, via institutionalized transmissions of tradition and social protest in their performative address as second-personal.

We must therefore concur with Voegelin (and Bellah 2011), that while from hindsight we may execute rational reconstructions that delineate stages of enhanced reflexivity, 'nothing is ever lost' as the ritual stages of tradition can just as easily become cognitively imbued with new rational content when transmitting their originally embodied *habitus*. As communicatively transmitted, they may also become reflectively redacted via protest to give voice to the novel problems of the present. Pre and post-axial remnants of ritual socialization are thereby indelibly bent toward enduring degrees of prolonged reflexivity upon transcendence-immanence tensions from the outset. In the final analysis, I will construe each axial breakthrough as proposing a particular species-ethic fully embedded within the historicity of its mimetic and mythic ciphers. On this side of the particular, the performative attitude of a second-personal social imaginary must allow the first-person articulation of either transmitting prior socialized content or initiating axial protest—pairing both together as shared movements that belie too subjective of a construal of historical change. Here, while trading off the Axial Age simultaneity of distinct cultural transformations for his conventional stance of methodological atheism, we need not reinvent all aspects of Habermas's communicative ethic. Since we must allow for an adequate contextualization for our first-person articulations of responsible subjectivity, we can still follow the general spirit of Habermas's twofold linguistic turn laid out in *TCA*. First, we can provide even more detailed and tradition-specific rational reconstructions of the Durkeimian organic genesis of solidarity from the residues of the religious imaginaries. Secondly, we can also commit ourselves to adopting Mead's pragmatic maxim that 'individuation proceeds through processes of socialization' by applying neonate and adult linguistic capacities to the learning mechanisms required to reach mutual understanding. However, under the wider axial rubric of cosmoipolitan justice and the entailed project of presuming multiple modernities, we need not presume a single monolithic or hegemonic narrative of species maturation and must at least proffer the notion of never achieving convergence of background justifications and/or legal juridification when faced with the prospect of multiple world histories.

In recasting the communicative impetus of Habermas, we also must readdress the most likely critical query to arise. In proposing such an experimental overhaul of the critical theorist affinity for a methodologically atheist theory of communicative action, why revisit the positions of Jaspers? Why resuscitate his existential leanings from philosophical and social scientific obscurity—indeed if not ever as an all out replacement—but as among the foremost to consider as a viable emendation to social science traditions stemming from Weber?[1]

In response, since our capacities for second personal comportment are potentially unlimited, Jaspers had the keen insight to argue that a truly universal project of species communication must be presumed to have always already been intra-axial and inter-axial. In ascribing the present perfect sense to its theoretical warrant in *On the Origin and Goal of History*, his multi-vocal and decentered social imaginary presumes having always already started as an experimentally pragmatic project owing ultimate origin to the simultaneous emergence of an elite-driven republic of republics of letters from multiple civilizational sites. However, now, via globalization, the initially elite-driven process of inter-axial borrowing has truly become a live option for the wider public in both William James' and Taylor's senses. The practical efficacy of an alternative vision of social order rests upon breaching the elite horizon. Reaching the common understanding of realizing innate capacities for unlimited communication can only come about through the critical theorist hope for an educated and properly socialized global public. In reply to the 'why Jaspers?' question, we can also trace a clear line of development of insights taken to be found in Jaspers originally—inspired by his own explicitly anti-imperial rejection of an institutionally imposed Eurocentric global order to correct the myopic excesses of the original Eurocentric world histories found in both Hegel and Weber. As contemporary confirmation of the nascent global philosophy originally prognosticated by Jaspers, we can now appeal to the non-Eurocentric works of Eisenstadt, Bellah, Talal Asad, Onuma Yasuaki, Sen, and others to continue the realization of his social imaginary as a project that he also correctly predicted would create healthy empirical and normative dissonance in its development rather than ideological uniformity.

As Taylor has shown in the meandering narrative that comprises *A Secular Age*, even the European movements of social transformation characteristic of Latin Christendom had roots in alternate modernities that were always already imbued with thickly divergent cultural contents (see also my Chaps. 3, 4, and 5 for a longer development of this theme). However, instead of the adapting a neo-Weberian (and lopsidedly Protestant) subtraction narrative of cultural content as already ideological—that is, if owing its genealogy to Latin Christendom—the second-personal orientation of both furthering tradition and stirring on protest instead presumes persuasive attempts at rational justification as legitimate grounds for communicative action. Taylor interprets these movements of protest as second person appeals to a species-wide capacity for the rational warrant behind inter-axial epistemic claims:

> The background understanding which makes this act possible for us is complex, but part of what makes sense of it is some picture of ourselves as speaking to others, to which we are related in a certain way—say, compatriots, or the human race. There is a speech act here, addresser and addressees, and some understanding of how they can stand in this relation

---

[1] I am grateful to Eduardo Mendieta for having initially raised this question to me to address.

> to each other. There are public spaces; we are already in some kind of conversation with each other. Like all speech acts, it is addressed to a previously spoken word, in the prospect of a to-be-spoken word. The mode of address says something about the footing we stand on with our addressees. The action is forceful; it is meant to impress, perhaps even threaten certain consequences if our message is not heard. But it is also meant to persuade; it remains this side of violence. It figures the addressee as one who can be, must be reasoned with. (2007, p. 174)

Regarded in light of continuing the initial calls for radical social transformation initiated by the collective rites of simultaneous protest that came with the Axial Age, cosmoipolitan justice as an institutional program for practical realization therefore need not draw its hope from capacities outside the scope of healthy species functioning. Insofar as they are always already latent to healthy individuation via processes of socialization, we instead need to reconstitute new public spaces that redefine the political in a manner that better conforms to our most enduring cognitive, affective, and moral capacities.

In light of a more comprehensive review of the micro-level philosophy of language that informs Habermas's discourse theory, I will first briefly reconstruct how his defense of communicative action depends upon his rejections of strategic-instrumental and objectively-theoretical reason. Then, following his call for a multifaceted purification in the West whereby secular and religious commitments are subjected to mutual critique, in the remainder of this chapter, I explore potential epistemic contributions of Eastern axial traditions to moving beyond myth to the more reflective employment of logos, particularly via Habermas's growing interest in providing a discourse-theoretic account of the emergence of ritual at the onset of Jaspers' Axial Age.

In initially focusing my attention upon the Eastern contributions to this process, I will provide a micro-analysis of the interaction of discursive subjects in four traditions: for Hinduism, epistemic authority (as presuming capacities for joint attention) when applied to social role differentiation; for Buddhism, right speech; for Confucianism, the rectification of names; Taoism, truth disclosure. At the more macro-level of entire civilizational orders, I will also show how each overcomes various cultural manifestations of political crises by encouraging diverse forms of contestation, protest, and periphery to center critiques of the social distribution of coercive administrative power and material wealth.

2.2 Habermas on Recasting the Second-Person Grammar of Communication

Although Habermas's theory of communicative action has undergone numerous amendments, revisions, and multi-disciplinary supplements over his prolific career, in these brief remarks I will restrict my focus in the first two sections to the enduring constant to his view: the paramount importance of achieving mutual understanding with a second person. Then, in the last part of this section will I take on his most recent engagement with evolutionary theory and the great Axial traditions in so far as these new developments bear the most direct significance to his critical theorist ongoing commitment to bringing historical materialist modes of assessment to bear upon the institutional challenges of the present.

2.2.1 Pragmatic Presuppositions of Mutual Understanding

While perhaps his most pioneering work bears the somewhat misleading title "*Theory*" *of Communicative Action*, he finds that by observing normal everyday communication, we can reconstruct a weakly transcendental argument for the pragmatic presuppositions behind the successful achievement of mutual understanding. As it will bear on my analysis of the great axial traditions, if second person achievements of mutual understanding are truly species universal, we ought to find them emerge in *all* the world religions, specifically not in just Western culture nor by beginning a biased reconstruction with the Greeks, with European enlightenment, or the preferred stance of methodological atheism, for that matter.

In his potentially cross-cultural, pragmatic, and idealized reconstructions, Habermas employs the grammatically-driven, linguistically universal orientation toward achieving mutual understanding that requires that persons address one another in the performative attitude of a 'you.' In turn, in order to serve as a legitimate norm of concerted action, the party/parties addressed as a second person in communication must hold the capacity for either (a) accepting or (b) rejecting the proposed norm-generating behavior. For Habermas, the very thin neo-Kantian assumption of never involving another in a scheme of action to which they could not in principle consent thereby serves as the self-reinforcing basis for the legitimacy of moral-practical norms of collective action. In other words, he resists the necessity of any thicker basis of shared solidarity that would necessitate a commitment to natural law, theological underpinnings, or richly shared cultural resources as the motive for acting on behalf of one another.

To contrast with communicative action, Habermas proposes strategic action as a strictly first-person attempt to achieve an instrumental aim. In simplest terms, this type of linguistic claims fails to prove communicative, since its means-end orientation focuses almost exclusively on strategic success of the end under pursuit regardless of the acceptance or rejection of those affected by the proposed action. In accord with his characteristically neo-Kantian commitments, even if it were descriptively true that we can daily take notice of multiple instances in which we or others have successfully involved ourselves or others in schemes of action that did not receive the rational consent of those affected, we nonetheless ought normatively to regard these as morally illegitimate practices of communicative intercourse.

As an additional contrast with communicative action, he presents objective-theoretical reason as the concerted effort to employ third-person observer descriptions of a state of affairs upon others, irrespective of explicit consultation whether they could endorse such descriptions about them. In other words, while he finds the empirical work of objective scientific research indispensable to technological progress and necessary for any data-driven theoretical enterprise, the reduction of communicative action to the third-person perspective fails. The long litany of multi-disciplinary examples he subjects to such critique include his rejections of neuronal-scientific observations of brain functioning, the grand historical evolutionary narrative of a purely biological rendition of the species, or even dubious appeals to the social-scientific expert authority of the objective social engineer. For Habermas, each of these examples will ultimately fail on two fronts. On the one hand, communicative action presupposes among each actor the cognitive, social, and moral capacity simultaneously to switch between observer and participant roles in the same communicative interaction. What the objective-theoretical perspective overlooks is our capacity to play participant role, and thus take 'yes' and 'no' stances upon the observed claims that social and empirical sciences make concerning the intentional states of the observed. On the other hand, he finds the observer-theoretic perspective to belie a basic pragmatic assumption of free consent that we must presuppose in attributing responsible moral action to the observed behaviors of others.

As a neo-Kantian supplement to his rejection of first-person and third-person accounts of communicative action, he presents the performative attitude as weakly transcendental. Although it can be extended to an unlimited potential communicative community, since the idealization represents a species-wide capacity for healthy psychological and moral socialization, (he claims) it does not surreptitiously impute Western biases upon non-Western cultural contexts. Habermas regards the second person performative attitude as a presupposition behind many common culturally-universal daily behaviors, including but not limited to, getting and clarifying directions to an uncertain destination, establishing the normative framework upon which a new relationship will be guided, as an analogy for the efficient learning mechanism of any collectively coordinated problem-solving scheme that requires the competence of more than one agent for its successful employment, and as a presumptive capacity held by both speakers and hearers in social movements of protest that seek to derive their basis for rational legitimacy from the force of the better argument.

2.2.2 Three Media of Social Integration: Macro-level Discourse

Corresponding to the micro first-person instrumental, second-person performative, and third-person objective grammar of reasoning are three media for the macro wide-scale coordination of social action: the economic market (first-person), social solidarity (second-person), and bureaucratic power (third-person), respectively. In the first-person instrumental sense of reason, (whether local, state, or global) market satisfaction presupposes strategic self-interest of a particular individual or corporate entity as the prime motivational factor. In contrast, the second-person sense of communicative action oriented toward mutual understanding, presupposes a motivational source of affective trust as the socially learned empathetic capacity for role-reversal characteristic of rational reflexivity. The un-coerced extension of empathetic trust will thus be required and presumed in order to act on behalf of the common good of one's fellow citizen or fellow member of the literate global public. Lastly, in the third-person mode of bureaucratic power, the impersonal logic of coercion via power-oriented social steering mechanisms function according to the motivating factor of efficient management of coordinated behavior across mass levels of complexity, scope, and scale of jurisdiction.

While he concedes that markets and bureaucracy are indispensable dimensions of any modern complex society, if social solidarity does not or could not confer consent upon the spheres of interaction in which market and bureaucratic functions are then steered by law-generating norms of communicative action, then the state and market incursion into the social realm has lost its legitimating normative force. In his consistently pragmatic approach, the only solution to such a crisis in legitimation would be to regain the communicative steering of the other realms either through (a) passing them through the filters of procedurally legitimate channels or (b) as a last resort, to initiate wide-scale movements of social protest until the procedures themselves have undergone the requisite degrees of legitimate transformation.

2.2.3 Evolutionary Origins: Axial Ritual, Civilizational Critique, and the Second Person

As cautioned briefly in the first chapter, we must avoid being initially misled down the path of third person naturalistic reductionism. Habermas's most recent appeal to an evolutionary account of ritual offers an historical, empirical, and anthropological attempt to trace out the biological origins of communicative action. However, Habermas has repeatedly resisted reductionist functional accounts as capable of delivering on their promise to give an exhaustive reconstruction of cognitive functioning.[2] In terms of the grammar of communicative action mentioned in the earlier section: we are caught in a performative contradiction if we believe we can give a fully adequate third-person account of the second-person attribution of moral responsibility to another agent in communicative discourse. The contradiction resides in claiming to those being described that this objective account applies to *you*, while foreclosing the prospect that they—particularly when dealing with behaviors of a moral motivation—can, from a first person stance, accept or reject the account as legitimate provided by the third person observations of the expert theoretician.

Likewise, by appeal to historical, archeological, and empirical data concerning the evolutionary process as its bears on the initial formation of ritual, Habermas does not think a third person description of facts will capture the unique linguistic, moral, and social achievements of the species-wide practices of individuation via process of socialization that constitute the correct performance of these behaviors. While offering a precise historical date of their evolutionary development goes far

[2] In Eisenstadt's own biographical reflections, he reveals his discontent with evolutionary functional approaches predominating early in his intellectual career. Eisenstadt's postulation of multiple modernities served for him as an explicit attempt to resist the generalization of diverse sociological and empirical observations into a single grand-historical narrative.

beyond his motives (and beyond what he believes can be inferred from the incomplete relevant archeological and historical data), he follows Jaspers in arguing that the species-wide rite of initiation into these historical modes of socialization has found their fullest expression in the Axial Period (800–200 BCE) that had birthed the great world religions (Habermas 2003, p. 40).[3]

What can we now make of these cursory programmatic themes for how they bear on his current interest in the non-Western traditions that had emerged in the Axial Period? For starters, one might find such a turn in his scholarly interests to the great Axial traditions surprising for a critical theorist of a Marxist heritage, deeply committed to eradicating material injustice as the means to widening the overall scope of human emancipation from ideology in every possible form. In addition, contributing to the counter-intuitive thrust of this new research program, from his growing collection of writings on processes of secularization in contemporary societies, we do know that although second-personal forms of socialization may have had their emergence in the rituals of the great axial traditions, the onset of a postsecular age *does not* mean he thinks the modern state requires any pre-political moral (and/or religious) foundation for its legitimacy. However, since his large book on these themes still remains under construction, for some further clarification of his other impending motives and themes for a large-scale book specifically addressing these themes, we might be better briefly to return again to one of his earlier writings in *Communication and the Evolution of Society* (1976) that can begin to pull together otherwise disparate trends within his wider corpus of writings.

Let us start with an opening necessary presupposition of a materialist motivation: for Habermas, the moral equality conferred to individuals via social rites must tie directly to the resource equality of institutionalized modes of production and the free rational endorsement of increasingly differentiation forms of labor. In other words, as a consistent Kantian, gains incurred via the new socialization statuses brought about by the unique Axial evolutionary stage, lose their transcendental legitimacy if bought at the price of a decrease in moral and resource equality. Perhaps best expressed in Habermas's own words, his earliest attempts to resuscitate historical materialist modes of critical social analysis must not be cast as the hapless and/or arbitrary processes guided by autopoetic structures immune from cognitive steering:

> If we are not free then to reject or to accept the validity claims bound up with the cognitive potential of the human species, it is senseless to want to "decide" for or against reason, for or against the expansion of the potential of reasoned action. For these reasons I do not regard the choice of the historical-materialist criterion of progress as arbitrary. The development of productive forces, in conjunction with the maturity of the forms of social integration, means progress in learning ability in both dimensions: progress in objectivating knowledge and in moral-practical insight. (Habermas 1979, p. 177; Bellah 2011, p. 573–574)

[3] While I follow Habermas in using the description of the Axial Age birthing the great world religions, I still retain the skepticism voiced in Chap. 1 on the use of religion in Latin Christendom that does not accurately translate across traditions. In this respect, I agree with Casanova that the term religion caused more problems in these contexts than it solves. Particularly, the term itself, on my reckoning, fails communicative tests for universal translatability across axial traditions.

In other words, if we are going to deem it moral and technological progress—that is, to call the move from kinship networks of social organization to state-mediated forms constituted by law—then must be able to take a 'yes'/'no' position that gives its free assent on a normative basis beyond mere naturalistic descriptions of enhanced group/species survival. We must also move beyond mere meta-narratives of the history of the moral progress of collective spirit that likewise risks silencing individual autonomy. In these respects, he retains the commitment to the revolutionary potential born in the materialist analysis. True moral egalitarianism would only be deemed normatively legitimate through the collective ownership and redistribution of goods in line with the cognitive steering of resource egalitarianism. In characteristic critical theorist form, he regards this too as a learned collective phenomenon. As a clarification of the critical thrust of Marx's species-ethic that lacked a concrete institutional program, moral learning must ideally transcend even the particularities of the state legal apparatus. Habermas's turn from morally universal cosmopolitanism to politically democratic cosmopolitanism confers legitimacy upon its transcendental aims via boundless networks of social communication that transcend national borders, cultures, and languages as an all-encompassing project of a democratized species ethic.

In assessment, I am in agreement with Hans Joas that more contemporary attempts to rejuvenate materialist theory in light of a reconstruction along the Axial thesis requires much further development, particularly in seeking out alternatives to the legal-juridical excesses of a political cosmopolitanism. I also agree with Joas that Habermas, until quite recently, had predominately seemed to endorse the historicized 'stadial consciousness' (as critiqued in Chap. 1 by Casanova) that the inherent rationality of the secularization process pointed to the eventual supersession of religion in the realization of cosmopolitan democracy (Joas 2012). However, more in line with Habermas's more recent attempts to depart from the secularization narrative of progress, we will find the species-ethical universalistic norms of each Axial tradition fit within the pragmatic experiential criteria of his increasing openness to developing an inter-Axial narrative while nonetheless retaining post-metaphysical commitments. Habermas has even gone as far as arguing that a democratic cosmopolitanism, with global constitutional procedures to regulate widening global disparities in capital, may offer the best available means to preserve rather than supersede multiple modernities (Habermas 2008a, pp. 351–352).

Habermas provides us with three generalizable principles to guide our assessment of the true universality of his species-ethic assumptions (2003, pp. 16–74). Although initially developed in *The Future of Human Nature*, I would like to apply them politically to his conclusions drawn in his later *Dialectics of Secularization* (2006). As a final step, I will subject them to a universalizability test as they potentially bear on four non-Western axial traditions.

1. The modern secularized state, while perhaps owing the genealogical origins of its socialization practices to one or more of the great Axial traditions, does not require any pre-political moral foundations for its legitimacy (Habermas 2006, pp. 21–23, 27–34).
2. The most promising philosophical justifications for the transfer of legitimacy from kinship to state-mediated, regional, and cosmopolitan networks of

solidarity would be through historical materialist criteria for moral and cognitive progress in forms of complementary learning processes (Habermas 2006, pp. 35–39, 43–47).

3. In assuming the social-evolutionary account of the achievements of the Axial period, we must draw upon the internal reflection required to insulate the nexus of social-solidarity mechanisms from the over-incursion of first-person market and third-person political power logics (Habermas 2006, pp. 35–37, 45–46).

In what follows in the rest of the chapter, if the ensuing four non-Western axial traditions indeed provide alternate renditions of s species-ethic that meets the guiding principles above, we can say that Habermas has offered us with three norms that we can take as foundational to not just Westernized forms of modernity, but to the growing social scientific interest in exploring the prospect of multiple modernities as a better description of a multi-polar globalized world. However, if there are failures on the three rubrics of assessment, we will (i) need to challenge Habermas's conclusions as overtly Western and/or historical materialist, (ii) look for ways to amend all Axial traditions in ways that count for legitimate innovation on Habermas's criteria of learned progress, or (iii) perhaps conclude that there are yet no species-universal moral and social criteria for legitimacy sufficient to encompass the global proliferation of multiple modernities.

As a foretaste of the direction my own assessments of the principles, much of the success or failure of both descriptive and prescriptive conclusions will rest on the state-centric features of (*2) as articulated above. Although we will find that each of the Axial traditions offer distinct normative bases for transferring conferred legitimacy outside the nuclear family nexus, we need not jump to the state-mediated, regional, and cosmopolitan juridical conferrals of justification too hastily. In this manner, I will seek to advance an admittedly non-conventional view of the polity as an institutional form that in its various axial forms may belie distinct features often ascribed to states, such as (but not limited to): territoriality, clear delineations of center to periphery distributions of coercive power, a shared language and/or culture, some primordial tie to a particular people or region, and legal-juridical institutions designed to confer clear lines of inclusion and/or exclusion within a particular polity. While it is not my motivation to undermine the achievements of democratic constitutionalism as an important site of the requisite state-neutrality that seems indispensible to modernity in its myriad forms, I would also like to challenge the hasty assumption of tying the political to an overtly Western (and thereby colonial) narrative, especially when dealing with these Eastern traditions. For the most part, while we do witness a shift in legitimacy from familial to Axial communities with their varied salvational impulses, insofar as they each contain the nascent kernels of species-universality, we will find these generally to resist territorial and institutional confines. Since they each evince novel means for translation of elite discourses ensconced in dead languages to more expansive translations into common vernacular, they overcome barriers that tie one axial narrative to a particular language and culture. As an additional means of transfer of axial universality to more dispersed renditions of modernity, each also suggest hints of periphery to core tensions when imperial powers at the center of a given axial movement seek to usurp exclusive juridical control over doctrine, ritual, and/or conferral of legitimate membership.

2.3 Reciprocal Role-Taking, Right Speech, Name Rectification, and Truth Disclosure: Revolutionary Axial Breakthroughs from Four Eastern Philosophies

The linguistic turn in Western philosophy has led to three major influences on the critical theory tradition that contribute to its overall materialist and moral goal of species-wide human emancipation. The first, macro-level trend, appeals to the explicitly democratic construction of regional, transnational, and cosmopolitan political institutions in light of the widening scope of the flows of communication of modern subjects that transcend the sovereign state, local markets, and nationally oriented popular media. The second—the analysis of the micro-level communicative interaction among discursive subjects—has typically fallen under the domain of discourse ethics, with much focus on pragmatically reconstructing and morally ensuring presuppositions of legitimate communicative action. The third, most recent effort has thus far received the least comprehensive development, initiated by Habermas's attempts to deploy both the macro and micro dimensions of discourse theory via his reconstruction of the linguistic dimensions of Axial ritual.

My provisional attempt at laying out the discourse theoretic program of cosmoipolitan justice, while true to varying degrees to all three movements internal to critical theory, admittedly bears no theoretical precedent. My effort to embed the micro-discursive components of the Eastern traditions (and then, in Chap. 3, the Abrahamic ones) within his more transcendental rubric of the second-person perspective will thus flesh out the context and implications of an Axial ritualization of practices of joint attention among discursive subjects oriented to mutual understanding. While, on his view, the third approach—Axial ritual—assumes an evolutionary narrative, we will also embed it within a historical materialist framework of socialization. This material line of development ultimately confers legitimacy upon traditions as moral progress only when introducing reflexively learned innovations beyond prior modes of decadent, imperialistic, and war-torn modes of civilizational organization. Although I treat each distinctly, the abiding constants for comparative focus include the significance of social protest oriented toward extensions of more universal species justice, the unique role of the renouncer-philosopher in each, and the communicative dynamics of recasting Axial insights within their respective scriptural canon. These comparative scriptural hermeneutics are typically imbibed in some variant of formalized or informal scriptural tradition among elites. Competing schools gradually gain mobility in professing salvation impulses more universally—eventually spilling over into the common vernacular for the critique, assessment, and redaction from multiple, often internally heterodox, general publics.

2.3.1 Hinduism: Epistemic Authority, Social Roles, and Vedanta as Axial Breakthrough

While no real consensus has yet emerged on whether to include Hinduism within the great traditions granted Axial status, in what follows, I will argue that on more than one substantive criteria the Hindu traditions suffice. Moreover, opening the pragmatic reconstructions of discursive praxis with Hinduism serves two purposes beyond just proceeding historically or merely deflecting hegemonic Western biases. It effectively introduces the role of the out-worldly renouncer that runs as a subtle constant to all the axial traditions. The renouncer introduces a new type of participant perspective to social roles that effectively bridles the tension between projecting an alternative social order while nonetheless operating efficaciously within the concrete limits of this one. Moreover, I hope to render at least plausible the admittedly peripheral intellectual conjecture—though with its due empirical support—that the Hindu renouncer may via cultural diffusion had contributed significantly to the Greek role of the philosopher. We thereby implicitly challenge the already dubious intellectual construct of an impervious East-West divide running as a constant fissure through the non-Abrahamic and Abrahamic axial traditions. I am therefore in general agreement with H. Kulke in conferring Axial status upon the Hindu traditions, in his "The Historical Background of India's Axial Age":

> It turns out that the development in India had several very general, though significant features in common with the development in Persia, Greece and Israel. Firstly, all these Axial Age civilizations originated from former nomadic or semi-nomadic peoples who has settled down in their new homelands only 500–1000 years before the Axial Age. Secondly, all these newcomers had chosen as their early habitation the neighbourhood or even frontier regions of early *Hochkulturen*. Thirdly, all these peoples had undergone in a relatively short period a social change from ranked tribal to emerging stratified agro-urban societies. Fourthly, out of this rapid social change in all these societies a group of influential intellectuals arose outside or even in opposition to the established priesthood. Fifthly, during the period of their Axial breakthrough all these civilizations from India in the East to Greece in the West stood in very direct contact with one or several of the imperial states of the Near East….[A]fter Persia took the lead under the Achaemenids, Israel, Greece and India experienced, though to a different extent, the neighbourhood of this largest empire of early history. (Kulke 1986, pp. 390–391)

Even for the reader still skeptical of Kulke's inclusion of Hindu developments within the axial period, this tradition affirms the claim that 'nothing ever is lost' as it includes necessary presumptions that will serve as the basis for detailing the attendant inter-Axial dynamics with Buddhism and the other great traditions ultimately granted axial status.

2.4 Kinship, Hierarchy, and the Legitimation of Social Roles

The initial separation of the social roles of the priest and king offers a unique perspective from which we can assess the legitimation of both spiritual and political authority within a Hindu context (Shulman 1986, pp. 424–25). The ability to inhabit distinct social roles and still to engage in joint attention across statuses presumes the capacity for reciprocal role taking. The pragmatist tradition has historically associated this capacity with developing the empathetic and rational skills for the practical employment of the second-person perspective. Once a society begins differentiation of social roles towards more complex divisions of material and epistemic labor beyond the simplistic norms ties to a kinship model of organization, they attempt to overcome the initial estrangement accompanying the loss of a prior mode of socialization. Kinship bonds initially loosen as they extend openness to new bonds of trust species-wide by constructing a social order grounded upon learned capacities to take up new perspectives and roles. To retain a more abstract moral legitimacy outside the family context, these hypothetical abstractions necessarily require the practical agent to confer political authority on the basis of rational justification and not merely upon a pre-ordained cosmic order:

> These theories reflect an increasing sense of alienation where it becomes necessary to enforce harmony, since the pristine natural harmony of society has disappeared. They also reflect the acceptance of the idea of authority based on power and not necessarily on kinship alone. The *janapadas* were coalescing into territorial states. By the fifth century B.C. competition for power had already developed among the stronger of the major *janapadas*, such as Kasi, Kosala and Magadha, where even close kinship ties were ignored to further political gains. (Thapar 1975, p. 122)

In accord with one of Kulke's earlier criteria for granting Hindu traditions that status of axiality, we see this occurring within the wider context of a large shift from ranked tribal kinship orders to the more complex differentiation into agro-urban social roles. Here we also find the nascent origins of the political hierarchy of the caste system that eventually will become one of the major non-territorial cultural features of the emergent Hindu practices that allows its precedent of hierarchy by social roles to spread eastward to other non-Hindu regional contexts. On this front, we satisfy yet another of Kulke's Axial conditions: the nomadic de-territorial drift of early Hindu patterns of socialization into a new homeland increasingly spreading eastward.

As these new Hindu practices eventually spread, the third-highest caste—that of the warrior administrative king—was eventually super-ceded by the priestly caste. On the one hand, originally, blood sacrifice in battles allowed for a prolonged period of perceived social legitimacy to imperial conquests eastward into less nomadic and more agricultural modes of social organization. However, we find that in the Hindu corpus of scriptures that carried quasi-historical narrative reconstructions of these conquests, the sacrificial nature of militaristic coercion eventually was overtaken by a symbolic rendition of ritual reenactment. As this constitutes yet a third of Kulke's five criteria for axiality, this early habituation of spiritual leaders into an increasingly literature *Hochkultur* required the priestly authority to learn more complex cognitive and critical capacities to mediate access to the original Sanskrit scriptures. The steady institutionalization of learning transitioned from an oral mode of transmission and exegesis gradually to the written accumulation of recorded interpretive precedent that began to attribute symbolical meaning to these quasi-historical narratives. The de-territorial appeal to texts as objects of joint attention upon which to construct patterns of social order also offered a new mode of legitimation for authority behind sheer military might and coercive power. The concrete self-sacrifices of clashing warriors on the battlefield were replaced by the higher-order purely ritual reenactment of these same practices as a common locus of culturally conferred and socially legitimated objects of mutual understanding.

This new elite-educated literate strata to the social order provided a cosmic dis-embedding of society through the reinterpretation of their original canon of sacred writings. By imbuing scripture with its mythic-historical rendering, a shared social order was continually redacted until the semi-historical battle sacrifices became purely symbolic through principled reasoning, competing schools of learning, and ritual reenactment by the priestly elite (Prbhupada 1997, pp. 55–59). While the third highest caste of political administrators still retained their pragmatic functions of this-worldly governance, the highest priestly caste that emerged—while not holding any this-worldly power—nonetheless played a co-participant function in the rational legitimation of the ongoing ritualized recreation of the social order.

> What happened was that ultimate value and legitimation, as it was realized and activated in the warrior's sacrifice, was taken out of the mundane sphere. Henceforth ultimate legitimation could only come from the transcendent ritual that took the place of sacrifice. For that reason the whole of dharma had to rest on or even had to be contained in the *sruti*—a necessary fiction, but a fiction all the same. For the *sruti* is patently devoid of use or meaning in the world's affairs and it is so as a matter of principle. Closed upon itself it has no meaning other than the self-contained rationality of its system. (Heesterman 1986, p. 399–400)

Heesterman describes the beginning of a binary split to run from here forward in the Hindu canon of scripture as a necessary condition for the priesthood's new role in the ongoing ritualistic maintenance of *dharma*, or better, presumed cosmic balance as an objective social order for focusing our joint attention. What becomes known as the *sruti* compilation of mythic-historical scriptures carried a new politicized meaning that owed its narrative origin to Voegelin's 'cosmion': the shared participatory realm of the cosmic gods, society, and individual mediators of competing statuses. These hermeneutic assumptions entail a confessional commitment on the part of the priesthood to the lack of human authorship ascribed to the *sruti*. The role of the priesthood thereby derived the legitimacy of its expert authority from the second person comportment of a participant role—taken up in ritualistic reproductions of a revelatory reception directly from an initially transcendent source.

> The ideal brahmin, like the Veda, stands apart from the world and cultivates the Veda by himself. The world, on the other hand, could not remain unaffected. The brahmin's standing apart illustrates how the world was impaired by the withdrawl of ultimate value and legitimation. Especially the king and the web of power relations he represents stand in need of the brahmin's legitimizing services. But it is exactly the king who is singled out as the one whom the brahmin should utterly shun. The situation is the more contradictory for the fact that subsistence and survival would force the Brahmin to turn to the king for his support. (Heesterman, p. 401)

What thereby emerges requires an inherently social conferral of hierarchically differentiated social roles that places all affected in mutual ties of participatory interdependence. Unique to these legitimation structures would be the necessary function that the Brahmin-priest plays in the legitimation of authority. However, in sheer material and economic terms of the concrete conditions for such social legitimation would be the precarious co-dependence of the hierarchically superior Brahmin elite upon the lower-order function of the king-administrator-warrior caste. The equally necessary social role of the king-warrior—as mutual participant and subject in the wider social and cosmic orders—provided the administrative and material conditions for ongoing structural stability of Hindu societies from the bottom up to the top. By providing sacral legitimation of the coercive power kings held over the lower two caste groups, the servants and the laborers, the efficient functioning of social roles presumed shared species capacities for reflection upon the order manifest in the cosmic domain:

> Accordingly, the political ruler achieved a high level of sacral or semi-sacral status, distinction and honor. The king was often portrayed as "king of the universe," his rule extending to the four corners of the earth, his coronation ceremony and its accompanying horse sacrifice renewing his powers annually. The king's claim to universal sovereignty, as "lord of all lords," and the manifestation of his greatness through temples and monuments attested to the power and distinctiveness of political authority. The symbolic portrayal as king of the universe also reflected an ever-present desire to extend political domination and constant attempts to aggrandize mundane power, primarily through territorial expansion or, even more so, through the encompassing of loyalty of peoples in the area. Therefore, although the king's symbolic authority was in principle derived from the overall cultural-religious vision and was symbolized through religious rituals, some degree of authority seems to have been attributed to him independently of religious legitimation. Yet, given the basic orientation of Hindu civilization away from mundane affairs, the political arenas maintained a certain, even if only partial, detachment from the "other-worldly" religious arena. (Eisenstadt 2003a, pp. 333–334)

In the wider world-historical context, we can justifiably extend these reflections in an inter-axial dimension, as an initial support for the plausibility of multiple world histories. To undergird our abiding commitment to multiple modernities, we see here the Hindu response to the historically under-determined role of the Persian Empire that comprised a common periphery to each of the axial settings. In this case, the administrative-warrior function of the Indian king(s) eventually also provided a necessary defensive military buffer against the impending rise of the Persian Empire that had begun at the leadership of the Persian Achaemenids. In addition, the functional differentiation of tasks also freed up the priestly leadership from tainting their ritual purity from too active of engagement in the pollutants of finite, mundane, and worldly affairs. In this respect, we have thus satisfied four of the five functions Kulke attributed to Axial orders, as this fulfills the fourth: the direct context of an Axial order with one or more of the imperial states to arise in the Near East—in this case, the Persian empire.

2.5 Axial Breakthrough? Rationalization of Ritual Praxis

While it would seem that the general thrust of a sufficiently rational and universalistic axial breakthrough includes moving away from a ritualistic world-view, the Hindu rationalization of ritual offers us a unique case of the simultaneous preservation of ritual while also overcoming its mythic, revelatory, and enchanted functions. The nuances of the Hindu twofold distinction of its enormous canon of scripture into *sruti* (hearing) and *smrti* (remembrance) placed the Hindu priest in a setting that led to the ongoing rationalization of ritual practice, that for Heesterman, constitute the most defining quality of its Axial breakthrough.

> That the Veda nevertheless goes under the name of *sruti* suggests that the age of the ecstatic seers is over and the revelation complete. The only thing that remained to be done was the painfully precise transmission of the revealed knowledge by hearing and learning it by rote. From then on the Veda became a fixed and bound body of texts, like the scriptures of Buddhists or Jainas. The point to be retained is the break between the revelatory vision of the seers and the *sruti* that purports to be the content of their vision....There is, then, a decisive gap between the revelatory vision and its ritualistic substance. It is in this gap—and not in the preceding age of the seers—that the Axial turning point is situated. This turning point does not lead to the exploitation of the revelation but is aimed at overcoming it. It replaces vision and revelation with something entirely different, namely the rational order of ritualism that by itself constitutes ultimate truth and leaves no room for anything so unsettling as revelatory vision. (Heesterman 1986, p. 395)

The prophetic revelations constituting the content of the *sruti* are taken by priests to have ended in order to facilitate the rational ordering of scriptural content. But, nonetheless, the insight and interpretations remained open for the priest to overcome the non-rational realm of visionary revelation with a hermeneutic deriving its legitimacy from the complex layering of rational principles. The interpretive precedent was super-added upon the *sruti* scriptures as they were transformed into the canonical body of texts from which the rationalized ritual was derived.

In terms of social differentiation of roles, the constitution of the caste hierarchy with its attendant elite-educated *Hochkultur* at the top of the social strata thereby led to the ongoing proliferation of canonical texts. The rationalized layers of interpretive precedent transformed the initial revelations into a means by which to secure the legitimation of the social order through rites and proprieties tied to the initial *sruti*. The ongoing increase of ritualized precedent was likewise catalogued and subsequently passed through processes of differentiation with competing schools of interpretation dependent upon the particular social strata in need of ongoing legitimation.

2.6 The Out-worldly Role of the Ascetic Renouncer

As for the five initial criteria listed by Kulke as conditions for the conferral of inclusion among the great traditions of the Axial Age, the only one not yet addressed would be the last to emerge historically within the millennia of traditions comprising Hinduism: the eventual emergence of the intellectual at odds with the status, proprieties, and authoritative hierarchy of an elite-priesthood. Yes, dismissals of the Hindu tradition often point to the enduring relevance of the caste system as proof that its insights had not truly attained the species-ethical universality. Moreover, the moral egalitarianism conventionally associated with the requisites of impartial justice call for the eradication of structural domination to ensure legitimate conferral of an axial breakthrough. However, the entry of the social role of the Hindu ascetic renouncer serves as an overt attempt to undermine the achieved legitimation of the authority conferred upon the caste structure by its participants—especially the spiritual and political leaders that had the most to gain from its ongoing maintenance.

At approximately the same time period as the historical transition from pre-Vedic to post-Vedic scriptures, the ascetic renouncer emerges on the scene as yet a fifth social role to introduce as an outsider (thereby fittingly labeled as out-worldly) to the original caste division of labor. These social roles had already been differentiated into four other social roles (in decreasing order of hierarchical authority) of the priest, warrior-king, skilled laborer, and servant. As yet an additional stratification to include within the axial rubric of an emergent *Hochkultur* (as according to Kulke's opening criteria), instead of the elite-educated functions reserved for the priests, we find the emergence of another form of elite individual, perhaps closest to the axial breakthrough of the philosopher as critic of the prevailing social order. Despite the layers of hierarchy, the out-worldly status of the Hindu renouncer takes on the more universalistic role of primary orientation to the Weberian intellectual-spiritual pursuit of species salvation within the participants socialized into this new sect:

> At the end of our period we find, correlatively with the beginnings of caste, a full-fledged and peculiar social role outside of society proper: the renouncer, as an individual-outside-the-world, inventor or adept of a "discipline of salvation" and of its social concomitant, best called the Indian sect. These sects were religio-philosophical movements transcending the Hinduism of the man-in-the-world. They were to be perennial in India and acted powerfully on this Hinduism. (Dumont 1975, pp. 162–163)

Along with this new social role, outside the caste strata proper, came the perpetuation of this new mode of spiritual, moral, and philosophical discipline that thereby required the formation of hierarchical, but nonetheless second-personal, mentor-mentee relationships. These led to organization in disaggregated sects committed to overcoming the finite constraints imposed by the impure profane social order.

> Hinduism, most fully articulated in the Brahminic ideology and symbolism, was based on what was, among the Axial Age civilizations, the most radical recognition of the tension between the transcendent and mundane orders—derived from the perception that the mundane order is polluted in cosmic terms, because its very creation constituted a breach of the original cosmic harmony. This pollution can be overcome in two different ways, which are at the same time complementary and contradictory. One way is the faithful performance of the ritual and mundane activities ascriptively allocated to different groups—above all to caste and subcaste groups—which signify different degrees of social and ritual purity and pollution. Closely related is the arrangement of social ritual activities and nexuses in a hierarchical order that reflects an individual's standing in the cosmic order and the performance of his duty with respect to it. At the same time, however, the stress on the pollution of the world also gives rise to attempts to reach beyond it, to renounce it: the institution of the renouncer (*Sannyasa*) has been a complementary pole of the Brahmanic tradition at least since the post-classical period. (Eisenstadt 2003a, p. 331)

According to Eisenstadt, while the renouncer did offer an alternative to the status-hierarchy of the priestly mode of ritual purification, the intra-axial parallel competition between priest and renouncer remained enduring constants throughout the history and ongoing development of Hindu practices.

In addition, these differentiated modes of reciprocal role taking continued further into the bifurcation of the renouncer of the pollutants of worldly-engagement into two principle functionaries. On the one hand, that of the *jnana yogi* entailed reflective philosophical study upon the presumed principled unity of scriptures (with supreme reason as object of joint attention within a particular sect). On the other hand, the disciplined labor of the *bhakti yogi* called for renunciation oriented strictly to devotional service to a personalized supreme deity (with Krsna as object of joint attention in a practicing sect). In Hindu scriptural canon, the *Bhagavad-Gita* presents in dialogical and narrative form Krsna's allegorical advice to warrior-devotee Arjuna that '[Both t]he renunciation of work [*jnana* yoga] and work in devotion [*bhakti* yoga] are good for liberation. But, of the two, work in devotional service is better than renunciation of work' (Prabhupada 1997, p. 174). In decided preference for this second-personal devotion over third-personal contemplation of God as an object of intellect, the Weberian salvation impulse embodied in the *Bhagavad-Gita* expresses an inherently communicative, affective, and relational ideal for liberation:

> Therefore, *jnana* (or knowledge that one is not this material body but spirit soul) is not sufficient for liberation. One has to *act* in the status of spirit soul, otherwise there is no escape from material bondage….One who knows that everything is Krsna's property is always situated in renunciation. Since everything belongs to Krsna, everything should be employed in the service of Krsna. This perfect form of action in Krsna consciousness is far better than any amount of artificial renunciation by a *sunnyasi*. (Prabhupada 1997, pp. 175–176)

In this respect, in response to objections to its caste hierarchy as obstacle to axiality, Hinduism owes its species-universality to out-worldly liberation in a double sense. The renouncer role allows for freedom from the proprieties of status ultimately regarded as a shackle, pollutant, or hindrance. In addition, the renouncer as devotee calls for a positive form of liberation as a means for full realization of empathetic capacities for participation within and eradication of the suffering of another.

I would be fair to concede that in a tradition as enduring as Hinduism, the rendition of the devotee-renouncer offered in the *Bhagavad-Gita* does not carry the final verdict on the necessary and sufficient conditions for renouncer salvation. Since reflective, meditative, and work-orientation modes of renunciation still fall under continued sect schools as legitimate disciplined practices, for Eisenstadt, Hinduism evinces this unique quality of having retained perhaps an unrivaled internal core-to-periphery heterogeneity that he and other theorists of multiple modernities characteristically ascribe to all axial traditions. Of all of them, Hinduism perhaps manifests this core-periphery tension to its highest extremes, in particular, as it belies intellectual and historical attempts to reduce its multi-faceted traditions to a set core of basic principles common to all self-ascribed practitioners.

Nonetheless, while Eisenstadt would agree that any principled effort to exhaust the contents of the Hindu tradition would certainly falter, he does find that it still retains a basic common core focus of joint attention of practitioners upon out-worldliness. With a background justification and legal form quite distinct from its Western counterparts, the Hindu tradition offers a common normative commitment to the de-confessionalized state, since the political realm itself could corrupt the spiritual and cosmic order.

> Given this strong articulation of the tension between the cosmic and mundane orders, Hindu civilization, like all the Axial Age civilizations, developed a distinctive centre. The major

> centre of Hinduism was not, however, political. Louis Dumont, in *Homo Hierarchus* and other works, and Jan Heesterman have pointed out how Indian conceptions of the political realm differed from the European. They both stressed that in India the political realm was not seen as a major arena of 'salvation,' where the tension between the transcendental and mundane orders could be bridged fully. According to Dumont, it constituted a secondary arena in relation to the realm of the sacred, as represented by the Brahmin; Heesterman pointed out that it constituted one of the major manifestations of the degeneration of the given world of 'artha'—against the absolute state of Dharma. According to both interpretations, the political arena did not command a high degree of transcendental commitment, even though kings were often seen as having sacred or sacral attributes and although kingship constituted a central and necessary organ of society. (Eisenstadt 2003a, p. 332)

As retaining its core outside of the political realm, we could also qualify Hinduism as embracing the transcensus introduced in the opening chapter as a philosophical-practical constant running across each of the Axial traditions. This distinctive outworldly mode of Hindu transcensus would best be described as the salvific effort to overcome the finite, temporal, and fleeting nature of the profane world.

With an apolitical center to its shared social practices, either the priestly-route of purification through ritual praxis or the renouncer route of sanctification through concerted efforts at willful withdrawl, each lead to liberation from attachment to an inherently perishing world. Eisenstadt confirms this distinction as two fundamentally different orientations to the achievement of a singularly common axial goal of transcendence:

> The two approaches to the mundane were based on two distinct value orientations, on two 'axes of sacred value'—those of auspiciousness and purity. These two distinct value orientations were always closely interrelated; although purity was hierarchically higher, it could never be concretely realized without auspiciousness. The concrete working out of the tension between these two axes constituted one of the major motive forces of the dynamics of Indian ideologies, institutions, and history. (Eisenstadt 2003a, pp. 331–332)

At risk of over-generalization, given the inherent interconnectedness of the two values, the path of auspiciousness would be closer to the priestly role in performing rituals that carry the promise of most adeptly bringing one in accord with the pre-ordained but tragically lost cosmic balance. As for the renouncers, the path of purity would be the closer identification here insofar as conscious efforts, affective dispositions, and even meditative endeavors all would share the common aim of purity by willed withdrawal of oneself from the pollutants of the profane world to attain salvation.

2.7 Intra-Axial Center to Periphery Tension: The De-territorialized Polity

Even if one were to object to the caste hierarchy on strictly moral grounds, the attendant culture to constitute the axial social order serves as its civilizational constant and became an object of joint attention for all affected, even when from widely divergent social perspectives. The politicization of a shared understanding of how one might participate proved reflective of a hidden cosmic order. The socialized participation in the cosmic order deeply impacted the Indian region and owed much of its success to the relative ease of transmission of such proprieties independent of local confines.

> Whatever the special roles of the Brahminical intellectuals, whether they were priests or court-priests, chaplains and advisors, whether they were lay intellectuals, they did nevertheless provide the theological doctrine which turned their ethnically and occupationally extremely variegated societies into a more or less unitary caste-bound society. They did not do this through the power of the state but by their acknowledged monopoly of the power to promote correctness of ritual behavior. Brahminical Indian intellectuals created in India a society which withstood many centuries of foreign rule and of many small states. They did this by creating a culture which spread beyond the boundaries of any single India polity. (Shils 1986, p. 444)

Insofar as political rulers sought legitimation from Brahmin priests for both strategically instrumental and for sincerely moral aims, since the cultural praxis was a condition of legitimacy conferral, this led to the ongoing longevity of the Hindu tradition.

We could also say that the universal transferability, while not fully embodying modern norms of freedom and equality, could also hint at its axial universality in as much as the transmission of this cultural nexus need not presuppose any particular political form. Its other-worldly salvational impulse could tolerate any number of concrete political institutions.

> The major centre of Indian civilization was the religious-ritual one. In close relation to its other-worldly emphasis, its wide ecological spread, and its being strongly embedded in ascriptive primordial units, this centre was not organized in a homogeneous, unified, organizational setting. It rather consisted of a series of networks and organizational-ritual subcentres—pilgrimage shrines and networks, temples, sects, schools—spread throughout the continent and often cutting across political boundaries. (Eisenstadt 2003a, p. 333)

In potential response to critics too, given the ascribed statuses conferred with this complex hierarchical nexus, one might deflect claims to suggest that the ascription of particular statuses had any direct bearing as a reflection of the moral and salvation-oriented capacities of the participant.[4] The non-territorial conferral of particular social roles allowed for a great deal of flexibility that also contributed to ongoing political instability. In this manner, the reflexive interdependence of the priestly ritual code upon a stable social-political nexus seems to strengthen the need for the member(s) of the administrative-warrior caste to provide a this-worldly anchor to balance the other-worldly emphasis of the priests (and renouncers).

---

[4] In Prahhupada's commentary on the *Bhagavad-Gita*, he interprets the famous claim 'It is better to engage in one's own occupation, even though one may perform it imperfectly, than to accept another's occupation and perform it perfectly' (Chap. 18, line 47, p. 577) in a manner that reconciles the obligatory status of one's particular social role with the universal capacity for salvation by means of devotional sacrifice. In the context of the scriptural narrative and in light of Arjuna's duty to fight as a *ksatriya* (administrator-warrior), the prospect of harm brought to his fellow humans nonetheless need not be regarded as an affront against Krshna. In Prahhupada's words, 'Whether one is a *ksatriya*, a *vaisya*, or a *sudra* doesn't matter, if he serves, by his work, the Supreme Personality of the Godhead' (578).

> [T]he political arena was characterized by a relatively high degree of political instability and turnover, manifested among other things by the continual changing of boundaries and in the expansion and contraction of political units. Despite their political distinctiveness and the drive for civilizational expansion, few polities achieved anything near unity of the sub-continent. Although India knew states of different scope, from semi-imperial centres to small patrimonial ones, the overall Indian cultural tradition was never identified with any of them. Kingdoms of various sizes were in constant competition, especially in the fringe areas, resulting in an instability temporarily overcome only by exceptionally strong rulers who formed strong networks of personal ties and espionage. The segmental nature of the political collectivities fostered the fluidity and instability of the political structure. (Eisenstadt 2003a, pp. 335–336)

These circumstances also reinforce Voegelin's observation that one feature of the ecumenical longevity of Axial traditions over millennia and into the present would be the long and growing empirical record of constant failure in forcing potential species-wide universality into an imperialistic institutional form. However, Voegelin (as we will see frequently arise in this chapter and in the Abrahamic Axial traditions) resolves these tensions endemic to transcensus by his normative mandate that no Axial order ought coercively to ascribe to an imperialistic/bureaucratic model of expansion by coercion of subjects as though they were merely third-personal objects of administrative power. For Voegelin, the universal-spiritual versus political-particular conflict endemic to transcencus runs in the other direction too. Political orders imperial in potential scope must, for Voegelin, remain void of enforcing a particular cultural content, and only in doing so do they evade self-imposed institutional and spiritual corrosion. When institutional conditions become ripe for any one of the great Axial traditions to crystallize into an imperial core, the call to seek salvation in this-worldly terms leads invariably to their demise. However, since it is also true that distinct Axial traditions have experimented with providing the cultural content for one or more imperially-oriented institutional scheme—not only has that contributed to their ongoing longevity—but has also been the institutional condition to make possible their communicative transition to cultures far from their original lands, territories, and regions of initial axial breakthrough.

2.8 Conclusion: A Non-Subjective Genealogy of Hindu (and Modern) Individuality?

According to Dumont, there are inexplicable narrative gaps in the emergence of modern individuality in the West that cannot be exhaustively explained by the prevalent scholarly practice of tracing Western modernity back to strictly Hellenistic roots. On the one hand, socialization leading to individuality seems problematic when the Greek polis (and even Greek view of species) seems to err on the side of an overt focus on the common good of the aggregate at the cost of the individual. He also notes that the Western philosophical leap to the Christian notion of subjectivity as a narrative shift super-added to the Greek person also seems at best to provide only a patchwork account of the emergence of modern subjectivity. The Western self-understanding improves little by merely amending the earliest phases of Christianity as having already emerging in Judaic contexts also deeply influenced by Hellenistic practices and ideals. In addition, Dumont notes that *even if* the onset of Western individuality cannot fully be understood without also acknowledging our Western-centric reconstructions as informed by additional Stoic influences, this genealogical leap presupposes that the early Christian understanding of the subject had roughly the same referent for individual identity as its Stoic counterpart.

While he does not pretend to put to rest these historical quandaries, he does introduce an intriguing revisionist strand that would further complicate conventional reconstructions. In particular, the emergence of Western individuality from the conventional inter-Axial triangulated borrowing from Hebrew, Christian, and Greek sources seems, to Dumont, incomplete. While we need not drop the modern conception of healthy individuation proceeding through processes of socialization, the inter-axial and inter-civilizational may need to become more, rather than less, complex:

> Now is this not a case where we should remember that our civilizations do not live in perfect isolation? It is not unlikely that Indian renouncers would have had imitators, if not representatives, in the Near East, and Plato's reference to Gymnosophists can be interpreted that way. I do not mean to explain away the Greek development by influence or imitation; I mean that Greeks may have found on some Eastern Mediterranean shores otherworldly individuals of perhaps remote Indian ancestry who would have helped them to develop a category they were striving toward (as such an encounter is generally at the root of any meaningful "borrowing"). In that case, the category might have been invented only once (but for the Judeo-Christian question) under conditions that are relatively clear to us, and the boundaries of our classical triangle would have been significantly penetrated at an early date. (Dumont 1975, p. 168)

While even Jaspers concedes that resolving such complex reconstructions will likely defy what we could practically expect from historical, archeological, and anthropological evidence, Jaspers also predicted that improvements in the relevant sets of empirical data will more likely reinforce endemic philosophical and hermeneutic disputes rather than resolve them.

In grappling with the same historical reconstruction to suffice in accounting for modern subjectivity, Robert Bellah's recent genealogy of the sources of the Axial Age offers some contemporary emendations to Dumont's query. In beginning with the Paleolithic Era, Bellah's *Religion and Human Evolution* (2011) provides some helpful conceptual resources from placing the Indian ascetic renouncer at least within the same reconstructive Axial classification scheme of the Greek philosopher as quasi-renouncer. All that Dumont has called for would be an imaginative openness that the one (Hindu) could have—via concrete cultural lines of dissemination—informed the other (Greek). While this would belie many assumptions about differentiations between Eastern/non-Western traditions and 'Western' ones, Dumont convincingly argues it at least merits our imaginative energies as it allows for a more complete empirical explanation. Even independent of direct imitiation, he also reckons that the salvational impulse toward fulfillment beyond the mundane order lends credence to the attendant notion that we may be misguided to expect more from our mundane social orders than they can feasibly provide.

2.8.1 *Buddhism: The Species-Ethical Soteriology of Right Speech*

As essential to our emphasis on the philosophy of language feeding into the dialectical transformation Buddha called for of his followers, I will derive a discourse ethic from the mentor-pupil teachings of Buddhism. These distinctly ontological and practical proprieties are immersed in a hermeneutic that allows for moral-practical insight to transform every possible object of joint attention between mentor and pupil. As one proceeds along the socialization practices required for success on the eightfold path to Enlightenment, the narrative self-constitution of the practitioner immerses them into participation in the liminality originally described in our opening remarks on transcensus.

> Buddhism too (just like Vedic religion at the stage of moving forwards to the Upanishads) can be counted among the great creations of the Axial Age, whose transcendental vision was closely linked to a reflexive realization of the discursive as well as poetic, the metaphorical as well as the performative, role of language as a vehicle for relating the mundane to the transcendental. (Tambiah 1986, p. 456)

Successful completion of the rigors of these eight stages culminates in liberation from suffering and pain caused by cravings and attachments to impermanent bodies, feelings, thoughts, and reality. In so far as Buddha taught that 'all we are is an object of what we have thought,' the ritual socialization into our use of language and concepts must exercise extreme vigilance in not mistaking a mundane object of craving as capable of accomplishing the deliverance that cannot be satiated in the finite concrete order of existence.

2.9 Biographical Remarks: Caste Hierarchy to Radical Egalitarianism

In order to situate the historical context from which Buddhism emerged, we must first revisit the Hindu culture from which it was derived, and specifically the caste hierarchy that can tell us the historical and material conditions of India during this period. On Hindu doctrine, the caste into which one was born reflected the positive karmic energy one had built up in their previous life. Insofar as the caste reflects not only one's social status but also one's moral capabilities, it reflects one's social-political responsibilities. Siddarthra Gottama, later renamed Buddha upon reaching enlightenment, was born into the third highest of the four castes. The attendant proprieties entailed exercising the role of administrative ruler, including the warrior function of society. However, upon leaving his family and renouncing his hereditary claim to rule, his life's vocation most closely reflected the duties, capacities, and responsibilities reserved for the fourth and highest caste: the rare Hindu Brahmin elite teachers and spiritual guides of society (Obeyesekere 2012, pp. 126–129).

Here we find the rudimentary origins of Buddhist egalitarianism as a dialectical development out of Hinduism since Buddha violated the Hindu prohibition on caste jumping. In addition, at another layer of dialectical development, the liminal dimensions of the changing role that he and his followers played as the ritual teachers in the new Buddhist communities were closest to that held by Hindu Brahmin elite. While Buddha's radical moral egalitarianism eliminated hereditary, material, status, linguistic-ritual, and other-worldly oriented proprieties normally tied to the Hindu elite sacred teachers, it nonetheless required an elite *Hochkultur* for its continued development and dissemination.

Although one of the differentiations Buddha preached as a distinguishing marker from the Hindu elite was the elimination of ritual as a means for increasing one's karmic merit, such a disavowal of the prior ritual left a space for which new Buddhist ritual slowly became institutionalized over time. The most important of these would be the eightfold path as the requisite ritual transformation through which Siddharthra became Buddha, and later initiates pass through as they undergo the axial equivalent of internal transformation shaped by these new modes of socialization. Insofar as Buddha preached both caste hierarchy and elite Hindu rituals as fetters to the universal moral-practical transformation he taught, the alleviation of species suffering (*dukkha*) was of such immediate focus that any Hindu obstacles to this goal were to be eliminated, including the willful extension of the practical disciplines of competing schools and sects into the local common vernacular.

2.10 Right Speech: Language as Moral-Practical Ontology

As the third step of the eightfold path, right speech best characterizes the distinct practical demands of a hermeneutic intended to render one mindful of each and every linguistic thought and utterance made. As all speech, even private thoughts and utterances emanate positive and negative karma, the associated pragmatic and linguistic norms for liberation require the shared Hindu (post-Vedic *Upanishad*) and Buddhist assumption of karmic reflexivity. That is, pedagogical claims about the transitory nature of mundane existence, about the passing of the external world, and the fiction of ascribing an enduring soul to oneself and others, carry an inescapable karmic imprint upon the ontology of the speaker and hearer. As an initial summation of right speech, hyper-vigilant self-cultivation requires perfecting one's linguistic capacities, or, at least minimally not proliferating *dukkha* through one's thoughts and utterances. In this respect, for the practices of the Buddhist, every opportunity for linguistic communication builds upon positive or negative karmic merit that contributes to one's public ministry of bringing oneself and others to enlightenment:

> The Buddha approached truth more ontologically than morally; he considered deceit more foolish than evil. It is foolish because it reduces one's being. For why do we deceive? Behind the rationalizations, the motive is almost always fear of revealing to others or to ourselves what we really are. Each time we give in to this "protective tariff," the walls of our egos thicken to further imprison us. To expect that we can dispense with our defenses at

> a stroke would be unrealistic, but it is possible to become progressively aware of them and recognize the ways in which they hem us in. (Smith 1986, p. 107)

What Smith labels as tariff would be allegorical language for the necessary karmic debt that both further increases one's *dukkha*/suffering/unsatisfactory life and likewise prolongs the ultimate release from suffering by tying the ego/self to the limitless vagaries of this fleeting world. However, since speech acts for the Buddhist carry ontological weight, they shape not only the constitution of the self but also always already carry ramifications for our shared social ontology:

> The second direction in which our speech should move is toward charity. False witness, idle chatter, gossip, slander, and abuse are to be avoided, not only in their obvious forms but also in their covert ones. The covert forms—subtle belittling, "accidental" tactlessness, barbed wit—are often more vicious because their animus is veiled. (Smith 1986, p. 107)

Smith thus offers us a spectrum of capacities upon which we can assess one's ontological success at striking the mean of full ontological realization. As for the individual, a speaker could errantly reduce their true ontology through self-depreciating thoughts and claims. The same speaker could also falter by over-inflating their ontology beyond its true capacities by boastful feelings, thoughts, and claims. Applying the same spectrum to inter-personal discourse, belittling claims reflexively reduce the ontology of both speaker and hearer while flattery would falsely over-inflate the egos of both hearer and speaker to constitute a false reality that will thereby recirculate mutual debts of negative karmic energy.

If one were able to strike the respective means of truthfulness and charitable speech, the reflexive karmic imprint of the attendant feelings, thoughts, and deeds will exact a corporate shaping of oneself and community closer to enlightenment with the concomitant alleviation of the associated *dukkha*. Once the speaker moves along the next 5 steps that nonetheless also presume the mindful mastery of each and every linguistic thought and utterance, deliverance from suffering ensues in *nirvana*, or literally having burnt away all attachments and enticements that comprise the lure of remaining perpetually attached the finite realm. On the one hand, the negating side of liberation refers to the true satisfaction achieved when one relinquishes ties to the fleetingly impermanent. This negative side of liberation refers to freedom from attachments to objects in a world comprised materially of various impermanent entities. In short, according to the doctrine of impermanence as an indelible mark of all material existence for the Buddhist, prolonged attachment to that which is transitory can only lead to suffering and loss. On the other hand, at the positive side of the spectrum, liberation from attachment is the epistemic precondition for rational clarity. Such epistemic openness (somewhat misleadingly termed emptiness) allows not only for the fullest realization of one's rational capacities but also carries an interpersonal or affective element in establishing dharma, as a shared common good or socio-moral balance in the world, since the alleviation of one's personal suffering leads to the empathetic second-personal desire to alleviate the pain of all humanity in the most collective possible sense.

Bellah reinforces both these ontological and existential dimensions of right speech by emphasizing that fully grasping the epistemic doctrine of impermanence has a performative quality that cannot be reduced to veridical claims:

> And it is also recounted that while he [Buddha] was giving the sermon, one of his followers, the Venerable Kondanna, became fully awakened to their truth: "Whatever is subject to origination is all subject to cessation." Thus, understanding the words and their logical connection is only the first step; it is only when the teachings have penetrated deep into one's consciousness that they can be transforming...[A]lthough systematic thought has always been important in Buddhist teachings, it has also always been accompanied by narrative and symbolic thought. (Bellah 2011, pp. 540–541)

Such a reflective transformation characterizes the moral-practical universalism of Buddha's teaching. While one could take the eightfold path as a form of rational argumentation providing the necessary and sufficient conditions for *nirvana*, the narrative dimension to the teachings of Buddha often require that one undergo not just the dialogic progress mediated by teacher and student but fully become a participant in a social order narratively constituted by its founder as much as any sincerely transformed adherents.

> Buddhist religious and ethical teaching is often expressed in systematic propositional form, with premises leading to conclusions. For this reason it is easy to see Buddhism as an Axial religion, if one takes the presence of "theory" as a marker of axiality. But as in the other axial cases, the "logical" aspect of Buddhist teaching is intertwined with a variety of other kinds of discourse—symbols and narratives—in ways sometimes overlooked by its Western admirers. Further, Buddhist truths are to be understood logically in terms of what the words mean (that is, semantically), but to be "really" understood they must change the hearers in their practical stance toward themselves and the world (in the linguistic sense, pragmatically). (Bellah 2011, p. 540)

Therefore, while right speech can be interpreted literally as true words or valid speech, we must not lose sight of the second-person discursive and narrative dimensions of the eightfold path. Buddha's own disdain for ritual and for not ensconcing the tradition in a dead language (Sanskrit) avoided both the first-person instrumental attitude of purely self-seeking gain and the third-person mentality of mastering objectively true how-to steps that mechanistically deliver the correct logical outcome. For instance, practitioners are encouraged also to undergo other less argumentative exercises that allow for scriptural meditations whereby the reader enters into a discursive relationship with the text, imaginatively positing themselves—even if in reality centuries or millennia removed—as a student participant among the audience at Buddha's early teachings.

Construed as a path demarcated out for the interactive progress among practitioner and mentor, each speech act that one makes carries deep ontological significance for their progress (or lack thereof) along the path to the ultimate goal: the cessation of human suffering construed in its reflexive scope as simultaneously singular and aggregate. The contribution of right speech to a negative epistemology thus seeks to eradicate the incorrect use of language if it has become separated from the ultimate experiential/soteriological aim of alleviating suffering. Including among the classification of a pragmatic failure of the use of speech would be complex speculations concerning the eternity (or potential lack thereof) of the universe, the soul, and/or ultimate reality. The simple Buddhist critique, of which Hinduism elite and contorted Brahmin discourse were normally the object of rebuke, would be the empirical constraint of not making claims that cannot be directly substantiated by experiential and pragmatic verification. However, such epistemic humility ought not too hastily be perceived as a cognitive deficit in the capacities of the practitioner:

> His refusal to speak of these things [the eternity or finitude of the world, the afterlife, creation, other metaphysical questions], says Buddha, does not mean that he does not know them. The power of silence that played so large a part in Buddha's life is wonderfully effective in the communication of his thinking. By not touching on all these ultimate things, he leaves them open. His silence concerning them does not spirit them away but leaves them perceptible as a vast background. It is considered possible to find in the world the path by which the world would disappear. The knowledge connected with the traveling of this path is imparted. But we must humbly forgo the knowledge of being as a whole. (Bellah 2011, p. 531; see also Jaspers 1957, p. 33)

In elaboration beyond these recommendations of restraint over lofty metaphysical speculation, contemporary Buddhist philosophers of language provide a comprehensive four-step pragmatic test for reaching common understanding with a second person. This provides a practical verification test of all speech acts, divided in terms of content, purpose, ultimate purpose, and connectedness:

1. Content comprises the different aspects of the doctrine being taught;
2. Purpose entails the listener's understanding of the content;
3. Ultimate purpose/goal brings about the complete enlightenment that is the result of accustoming oneself to the realization born from the understanding of the content;
4. Connectedness delimits the relationship of content, purpose, and ultimate purpose so that in dependence on the content, the purpose is fulfilled and in dependence on the purpose the goal is fulfilled (Cabezon 1994, pp. 43–44).

In other words, in taking 1 and 2 together, the verification test for content would not be merely that the correct articulation of the teaching could be assessed from a third-person perspective of the logical entailment of the correct truth propositions. Once we take 2 into account, the veracity of 1 ties directly to the correct and efficacious communication of the content to the hearer that has met the abiding purpose of mutual understanding. As an instance of the radically egalitarian component of 1 and 2 together would be Buddha's commitment to reaching second-person mutual understanding by calling his followers to learn to teach in the common vernacular of the student and/or language of any and every potential audience. Another instance would be narrative reports that he might go about teaching the same steps 1 and 2 in unique ways to distinct students, tailored to their levels of apprehension and their second-person conferral or readiness or lack thereof to proceed further along with the efficacious learning of content. Both the commitment to vernacularization and the tutorial stylized teaching to a single adherent reinforce again the egalitarian plane of Buddhist communicative ethics:

> From the point of view of axial ethicization, perhaps the most fundamental innovation of Buddhism (though shared by other non-Brahminical renouncer sects) was the ethical necessity of making the teaching of liberation, Dharma in the Buddhist sense, available to all people, regardless of status or ethnicity. (Bellah 2011, p. 537)

Condition 3 continues forward this move into the moral-practical realm of axial universalization whereby the epistemic status of a given claim can never be divorced from its moral-ethical transformative effect on the hearer. Part of the practical test of real efficacious learning to have occurred would be the ontological truth of doctrine performatively displayed in action. Lastly, condition 4 shows that each prior condition rests in an interconnected web of relationships to the others. The spread of Buddhist teaching forges the creation of a new social order as mediated by the universal law of karma that necessitates the inescapable reciprocal mediation across and between practicing members of a given sect and its enduring imprint upon the localized community.

In brief summation, one can test whether the given speech act/teaching in step 3 of the eightfold path succeeds or fails in achieving mutual understanding insofar as it contributes to the alleviation or increase of overall human suffering as entailed in its connectedness (condition 4) to all other 7 steps of the path. For instance, since step 4—right conduct—calls for a commitment not to lie, steal, kill, intoxicate, or promote an unchaste life, in any sentient being, Buddhists are entreated to follow a robust set of ontological commitments, including the practice of a pacifist life, specifically by proliferating non-violent attitudes of *ahimsa*. Success along the seemingly individualist trek of alleviating one's ignorance about the impermanent world eventually yields its attendant social and political carryovers. For instance, if I cannot treat my own person in a manner beyond the instrumental service of my own cravings, my attitude to others will be aggressive and hostile insofar as I merely view them as an extension or hindrance to the fulfillment of my cravings. However, staving off the array of forms of self-alienation that can come with fixation upon particular finite desires also allows one to view the person of another non-instrumentally with a default comportment of non-violence. Progressing along the way to full empathetic participation in the alleviation of their suffering, allows me to regard it as if it were indistinguishable from my own.

> As human beings we need to keep the channels of existential dialogue open at all times. When an act of violence is in progress, for example, we need to constantly nourish the silent and passive nature of nonviolence inherent in all human relations. Though nonviolence cannot counter violence on the latter's terms, still, its nourished presence serves as a reminder of the brighter side of existence and may even open the violator's mind to common or normal human traits such as tolerance, kindness, and noninjury (*ahimsa*). Paradoxically and most unfortunately, acts of violence only emphasize the fact that peace and tranquility are the normal course of human existence. (Inada 2006, p. 141)

Therefore, given the fulfillment of the four conditions for bringing about right speech, the radically pervasive interconnections among the steps of the eightfold path issue forth in a comprehensive species-ethic. When mentor-pupil communicative transmission of doctrinal teaching succeeds, the affected communities are to collaborate together to ensure the transformative social, moral, and political dimensions disseminate more broadly. The propagation of valid truth claims that comprise the teaching ministry of a given Buddhist sect ideally will transform the human species *and* all other sentient beings as those pursuing liberation must conform with just moral and political ends that contribute to the aggregate cosmic alleviation of *dukkha*.

2.11 Buddhist Inter- and Intra-Axial Competition: Common Vernacular, Parallel Social Orders, and the Proliferation of Sects

The world-historical context of Buddhist hermeneutics that call for such an egalitarian and discursive rendering of dukkha also carries application to the dialectics of religion, specifically with Hinduism as the original target of critique with its growing precedent of Sanskrit as the official language of the Brahmin elite. The commitment to teaching in the common vernacular brought to fore the moral-practical shift from kinship units as the primary framework of social solidarity to the wider more universalistic nexus of political self-ascription into the community of Buddhist initiates. In this respect, early Buddhist communities 'don't attack the existing order, but in important respects they ignore it and attempt to build a society on other foundations' (Bellah 2011, p. 530). As an instance of widening the dialectical scope of an alternative non-hierarchical Indian society, Bellah appeals to Thapar's formulation of a 'parallel' (Bellah 2011, p. 530) social order to show that the emergent counter-cultures of practicing Buddhist communities did not outright negate Hindu doctrine or strive to instantiate a wide-scale revolutionary undertaking:

> Insofar as this [Buddhist] teaching disregards all distinctions of birth and proclaims the equality of all human beings in their capacity to follow the Path, the teaching is revolutionary relative to early Indian society with its heavy reliance on birth and lineage. But as Romila Thapar noted, the Buddha called for no revolutionary overthrow of existing institutions; rather he attempted to establish a parallel society, offering an alternative way of life, which would grow by attraction, not by conquest. (Bellah 2011, p. 542)

The reinforcement of the commitment to non-violence proceeds along two tracks, as the new teachers in these alternative communities take on the leadership roles reserved for the Hindu ruler-warrior caste and do so in such a manner where the public mission would be spread via rational justification and moral example. The practical effects that ensue from right speech and non-violent conduct would serve to attract adherents from proximal Hindu societies.

Jaspers comments on the world-historical initiation brought about by such a unique blending of the universal and particular. As for the particular, the commitment to teaching in the common vernacular made an epistemic virtue of multiple historically-embedded languages that in turn constituted new communities that traversed conventional social, cultural, and geo-graphic divisions. As for the universal, Jaspers champions Buddhism as perhaps world-historically the first species-ethic open to encompassing the fullness of humanity, irrespective of the confines of kinship and cultural networks.

> But the revelation is addressed to all who possess the vocation for it, and in principle to all men; did Buddha not ordain that each man should learn the doctrine in his own language? Thus for the first time in history the idea of humanity, of a religion for the whole world, became a reality. The barriers of caste, nationality, of all appurtenance to a historically grounded order of society were breached....To speak to all is to speak to each individual. Buddha's decision and the life which followed from it became a model: to depart from the laws of house, family, society....Buddha spoke to individuals and in small circles. Lessons

> and conversations prepared the way for the insight that each man must attain by his own action. There are many accounts of how the force of Buddha's words facilitated the task. (Jaspers 1957, p. 35; see also Bellah 2011, p. 552)

In radical contrast to the elitist prerequisites for Hindu salvation, the unique effect of blending the universal and particular breaks open the prospect that the individual, as specific manifestation of the species, simultaneously triumphs over and eliminates the need for division within the many particular linguistic-cultural divisions that comprise social orders. By allowing for the prospect of even the beggar and wandering denizen in a foreign community to attain salvation, Buddha addressed the individual as second-person with the familiar adage to 'practice your salvation with diligence' gaining greater force insofar as in a single lifetime anyone could merit salvation through the requisite karmic advances.

Although the widest chasm in reconstructing the secularization dialectic came early on between Buddhist egalitarian communities formed in opposition to the many Hindu sects, eventually the vernacularization thrust led to heterodox movements internal to Buddhist monastic orders.

> The activities of systematization and hermeneutics were pursued vigorously during the early centuries of Buddhism, and inevitably these activities were accompanied by the contrapuntal development of schisms and sectarianism. These sectarian fragmentations were the product of many factors, such as genuine interpretive disagreements, which were generated in groups or communities of monks geographically dispersed, and employing different dialects of Prakrit and different languages such as Sanskrit and Pali. Once certain schools were formed, they in turn spawned more schools, which inevitably produced their own *Abidharma* treatises that were subsequently preserved in their separate traditions. A lively sectarianism and adversarial fragmentation may be taken to be indices of vigorous intellectual and missionary activity. (Tambiah 1986, p. 458)

As a reinforcement of Eisenstadt's common observation, in the long term, internal heterodoxy may help ensure the enduring presence of axial movements over millennia of cultural transformation by providing many sites of ongoing innovation in adapting to new environs. In other words, not only do the array of competing internal movements offer distinct alternatives in the recruitment of new initiates, the internal competition within and among competing schools contributes to their perennial relevance and cognitive vitality. In addition, as Buddhist communities morphed to adapt to the common vernacular of their localized culture, they also spread to expose new possible adherents. Competing sects and their schisms could migrate along with their respective target communities in response to material, climatic, and inter-regional conflict that could pressure groups to trek great distances.

> While Sanskrit remained for the [Hindu] Vedic-Brahmanical tradition the only sacred language, the early Buddhist monk missionaries and propagandists adopted the vernacular and the local dialect of the regions in which they preached. And the linguistic choice was in accord with the fact that the early monastic communities multiplied as they dispersed. (Tambiah 1986, p. 462)

In addition to the enduring openness and flexibility that the common vernacular commitment contributed to its early proselytization, the diversity of competing schools brought about a proliferation of canonical oral and written scriptural precedent. In a subtly historical materialist casting, the division of labor that came with the oral and written preservation of sacred teachings and texts led to increased differentiation among the tasks of these early Buddhist communities:

> This flexibility in the choice of language or dialect for teaching and transmitting the doctrine surely aided the spread of Buddhism, and must certainly have contributed its share to the sectarian versions of the doctrine itself and its interpretation. However, this flexibility of the language medium, and its stimulation of variant oral texts, must be placed within the larger truth that the early Buddhist monks developed and exploited effective memorization and recitation techniques in the same way as they forged sophisticated discursive techniques of argumentation and proof. (Tambiah 1986, p. 463)

According to Tambiah, the differentiation of the increasingly complex hermeneutic division of labor, included but was not limited to specialized tasks of complex oral memorization of short enigmatic phrases to replace otherwise extended selections of canonical texts, the use of stock phrases recognizable within one's linguistic group, branch and section specialization, detailed inventories and taxonomies (see also Bellah 2011, on *sastras* p. 552), recitation ritualization carrying elocutionary and performative significance, and horizontal and vertical substitution systems for key phrases (Tambiah, pp. 462–465). After centuries of school specific oral and written textual transmission, interpretation, redaction, and critique, meta-level modes of hermeneutic specialization were also introduced, including written treatises on grammar for bridging differences between the language of oral traditions as it became more differentiated from the performative norms of contemporary speech (Bellah 2011, pp. 551–552).

In addition to the internal heterodoxy among schools, we also find a complex division of labor among the mendicant monks and the Buddhist lay communities for whom the celibate and property-less monks were materially dependent upon for their survival. In accord with the original egalitarian thrust of Buddha's teaching, the prospect of mutual discursive understanding entailed by right speech must always remain a real human potency for all in order for both mendicant and lay individuals to take ultimate responsibility for their own personal enlightenment. Without a doubt, the onus of responsibility for salvation rested disproportionately on the Sangha orders of monks, perhaps most acutely demonstrated by its own internal sanctions on right speech, whereby false boasting of one's progress along the trek of enlightenment and inflation of one's pedagogical abilities were grounds for permanent dismissal from one's monastic community (Tambiah 1986, p. 467). However, as entire polities adapted Buddhist moral, social, and cultural norms, the role of the laity increasingly contributed to the trends toward differentiation matched with reflexive interdependence between monastic and lay adherents. In turn, the prospects for the accrual of the karmic merit requisite for salvation necessarily extended to non-monastic members too:

> In keeping with autosoteriology, the primary function of the monastic rule was to protect the spiritual independence of each monk. The overriding aim was to provide optimum conditions for pursuit of the ultimate religious goal, not to enforce ecclesiastical unity. For the laity and secular society, the leadership of the Sangha developed a secondary soteriology based on a merit-making ethic oriented to the economic and political needs of the urban

> mercantile and artisan classes….The Buddhist laity were expected to make donations to the Sangha, but the soteriology stressed the autonomy of the self as the sacrificial agent. A central component of this transformation was a growing emphasis on the worship of the person and image of Buddha, as accessible to all adherents. (Eisenstadt 2003a, pp. 321–322; Tambiah 1986, p. 469)

These ties of reciprocal interdependence extended down to the bestowal of karmic merit to a lay community obliged to support mendicants called to live a material life supported by voluntary almsgiving. In turn, while Buddha originally resisted efforts to support his own deification, the axial trends of moral universality behind these new ritual practices of worship rendered Buddha directly accessible to all communal members, regardless of monk or lay status.

As the material, social, and cultural dimensions of the monastic communities developed, the sources of legitimation that originally began in the Hindu caste context of familial structure, began to shift moral and political justification to normative standards internal to monastic life. These developed with an eye toward material integration of sects into surrounding lay communities via the normative obligation to accept lay almsgiving as means of material sustenance. On the one hand, an essential feature of the early Buddhist monastic communities remained as they more deeply internalized the moral commitment to the egalitarian absence of political hierarchy:

> It is in this way that we have to understand the so-called 'republican' model (*gana sangha*) of the tribal federations (in contrast to the 'monarchical' model of the Magadha and Kosala Kingdoms) which the Buddha recommended to his disciples. This aspect of the monastic fellowship emerges in better relief if we compare it with the rules which early European monastic communities endorsed, such as the Role of St. Benedict. The Benedictine monk took a vow of obedience not only to God but also to his Abbot and undertook thus to submit himself to an institutional authority in a way no Buddhist renouncer did. (Tambiah 1986, p. 469)

Pervasive moral egalitarianism was reflected in a novel model of the absence of institutional hierarchy and resource egalitarianism since, again in contrast to Benedictine monks, the early Buddhist communities were not self-sustaining cells. As they were deeply dependent upon the almsgiving of lay supporters, the institutional division of labor included distinct roles for members of the sangha to mediate property donations from the lay community. This differentiation of roles thereby comprised the early normative framework of monastic and lay interaction, norms of which were often extensively recorded in their respective communal canonical works. The differentiated vocations of representative sect members included arranging feasts hosted by kings, merchants, and nobles whereby the acceptance or rejection of such alms provision reflexively bestowed legitimacy and karmic merit upon lay activities in the wider community. Insofar as the begging for alms was a communal process, early mendicant communities were typically led by wandering peripatetics. Resource egalitarianism remained a feasible ideal via internal regulation of goods whereby each member of the sangha was restricted to eight minimal articles of property. These conditions ultimately led to the construction of lavish monasteries through the collective alms scheme that accrued aggregate property at greater rates and in larger holdings than any single beggar could accrue alone. As communal property, the monasteries were passed along in accord with group ascription since celibate monasticism circumvented hereditary transmission.

The growing success, practice, and spread of the Buddhist mendicant life contributed to additional significant material differentiations between rival social orders, directly affecting the governance of international relations between dispersed Hindu householders, private Hindu ascetic priests, and Buddhist monks.

> This interrelation between the religious and political elites also had its impact on the nature of the Buddhist international system. Unlike Hinduism, this system was not confined to a single ecological setting, however wide and diversified. Yet despite Buddhism's strong tendency to expansion, no Buddhist political ecumene arose. Similarly, despite the international links among the different Sanghas, each was constituted on a national basis. No universal Buddhist polity was created. Hence the Buddhist in the (especially Theravada) civilizations of Southeast Asia coalesced into consciously compact yet fragile national polities in which the maintenance of their boundaries and even their expansion were motivated by combined political and religious motives. (Eisenstadt 2003a, p. 327)

The nomadic character of these communal groups, their open adaptation and doctrinal spread through the employment of common vernacular, and the absence of any explicit hierarchical leadership internal to the orders and externally between them all contributed to a highly adaptive institutional structure. These diverse sects tended to morph well with the immediate political contexts. In addition, the material dimensions of the lay almsgiving allowed these groups to interact with wider communities and to coalesce with each particular local, regional, and national subculture without accountability to any wide over-arching institutional hierarchy, sovereign leader, or ecumenic empire.

2.12 Conclusion: Towards the Buddhist Galactic Polity

As a concluding Habermasian assessment of these secularization dialectics, given the quasi-moral autonomy that the Buddhist communities enjoyed through their common spiritual and ethical mandates, did these parallel polities garner their political legitimacy from the enduring presence of a pre-political moral substrate? Eisenstadt seems to answer this query by parsing apart the respective spiritual and political domains, while holding certain moral constants as conditions for the efficient functioning of each:

> Rather [than calling for a new social-political vision], it implied the more stringent, elaborate and articulate upholding of the given order and of its religious (and moral) precepts. Accordingly the complaints and demands articulated were not usually conceived in terms of new principles of political action, but rather in terms of further articulation of the premises of legitimation inherent in the existing principles. However, at the same time, such religious groups could become the standard bearer of outcries against the failure of the authorities to uphold their duties, as well as important factors in the fermenting of popular rebellions or upheaval. They could help in the spread of different 'populistic' demands, of demands to change the concrete application of existing rules as well as policies of rulers, thus generating a new dimension of political activity. (Eisenstadt 2003a, pp. 236–237, 325–226)

The ambivalent trek of (a) instituting modes of overlapping consensus on moral norms already previously held while perhaps disagreeing on their proper structure and background justifications for legitimation, also (b) allowed for the differentiated creation of orders that offered alternative cosmic justifications for their adherents. In other words, while the trend seemed to allow for flexible adaption to the social and material conditions present prior to the introduction of a new wandering community, the Buddhist alternative soteriology did offer the prospect for critique and occasional transformational protest of the prevalent moral-political orders.

In brief summation from Eisenstadt, on the one hand, there seemed to be a strong degree of complicity with the general political organization of the mundane order.

> Their organizational autonomy was contingent on the acceptance of the basic rules of the political game established by the political elites….[T]hey evinced but very little autonomous, potentially critical participation in the political realm. Indeed they tended to legitimize any victorious ruler. Their intellectual activities were not oriented to such participation. In so far as they developed alternative conceptions of a social or cultural order, these have been oriented almost entirely to 'other-worldly' spheres, or to the moral improvement of the community without, however, generating very high potential restructuring of the political, social or economic spheres of activities. (Eisenstadt 2003a, p. 236)

The incredible degree of capacity to construct societies of an other-worldly orientation allows for non-confessional states housing parallel Buddhist communities that pose little to no threat to the prevailing mundane social and political institutions.

However, on the other hand, the heightened disembedding of social, cosmic, and individual domains suggests an axial breakthrough that, at most, offers and implied legitimation of the secular authorities by both the cosmic and moral demands of the Buddhist community. The respective secularization dialectics allowed for the absence of hierarchical authority in the monastic orders to permit prevailing political authorities to uphold their leadership roles with little to no threat to usurpation of their power:

> The very upholding of the [Weberian] criteria of salvation as bearing also on the political realm added here several additional dimensions to the structuring of the political realm, its legitimation in general and accountability of rulers in particular. First of all there developed a basically secular conception of kingship. The King was desacralized and his role defined largely—even if perhaps not entirely—in secular terms with a strong emphasis on the necessity to accept it in terms of the maintenance of social order. At the same time however demands were made on him to support the higher cosmic order and the concomitant moral order of the community to which in principle he is subordinate. Thus in principle Royalty was legitimized in terms of the predominant 'other-worldly' religious symbols. (Eisentadt 2003a, p. 236)

While the explicit endorsement of the legitimate presence of the Buddhist monastic order may not be required by the authoritative powers of the king, the reverse does seem to hold in at least a minimal sense. The maintenance of public order, even when interpreted as an instantiation of *dharma* in the cosmos by the monastic community, was at least a minimal necessity to ensure the material conditions for alms giving and a safe haven for the ongoing teaching of Buddhist groups.

In particular, the monastic context of study via mentor-pupil arrangements and ongoing praxis made the monastic community central to the early transmission of Buddhism into a civilizational form rooted on the peaceful co-existence of two or more competing cosmic visions:

> [T]hese elites [the Sangha] provided a new dimension in the construction and definition of the basic collectivities. First of all, given the strong orientations it was the 'civilizational' collectivities and frameworks that developed here as distinct and symbolically autonomous highly articulated frameworks. Secondly, these orientations certainly effected important changes in the construction and the definition of the 'local', 'national', or political communities. They added to the 'usual' primordial or territorial components of such definition a certain broader orientation which provided the basis and frameworks for the crystallization of new symbols and boundaries of political collective identity, of national political communities, first of all in the fact that the political realm was conceived as a reflection or representation of basis conceptions of the cosmic order—giving rise to what S.J. Tambiah has called the galactic polity. (Eisenstadt 2003a, p. 237, 324, 327)

While the explicit endorsement of the monastic community nor of the ruler in a given domain was not required, the moral dimensions of Buddhism gradually assimilated norms that posed no direct threat to the salvational impulse to continue proselytization through public teaching. The ensuing galactic polity would reinforce Voegelin's earlier Axial commitments to the constructions of variegated cosmions, whereby the social-political order is taken by its participants at least as a potential reflection of a deeper, more subtle, cosmic social order. However, the bonds of community were as much amoral (territory, language, culture, differentiated recitations, specialized tasks) as they were constituted by a shared Buddhist pre-political basis.

> [In such a galactic polity] The king was seen as the ideal protector of the (other-worldly) religion and as at least a partial embodiment of the cosmic order. The royal *dharma* (duty) involved a combination of transcendental and mundane orientations, which tended to minimize the tension between the sacred and primordial components of legitimation. (Eisenstadt 2003a, p. 324)

The final verdict on the question of any presumed pre-political moral substrate to a functional society seems to offer only an ambivalent response to the presumed primacy of a moral basis for the legitimacy of particular political orders. Yes, the Buddhist monastic communities and the lay adherents offering their alms certainly presumed the cosmic moral order of a dharmic balance upheld by the earning of and public conferral of merit. However, the early co-existence of Buddhist communities with both alternative Hindu norms and the impending introduction into contexts with no prior contact of a Hindu or Buddhist heritage also show the extreme ability of these monastic orders to initiate parallel galactic polities alongside otherwise arbitrary or contingent factors. The enduring presence of a Buddhist order across centuries thus need not necessarily require the explicit endorsement of the broader social and political manifold. The minimal threshold of transcendence as moral-practical in its Buddhist guise thus offers a vision of society embodying immanent transcendence. In the end, Buddha's original adherence to right speech as a refusal to speculate upon what surpasses his empirical experience gives Buddhists a form of axial universal transcendence without any express commitment to a personal

God, the prospect of an afterlife, or the existence of an ultimate ground/foundation to reality. In addition to the secular dialectics putting Buddhism at odds with Hindu trends, in the wider inter-Axial global context, Buddhism also offers a uniquely agnostic axial tradition, putting it directly at odds with its Abrahamic counterparts (Sen 1999, p. 245).

2.12.1 Confucianism and the Rectification of Names: A Normative Semantics

As perhaps the most comprehensive explicit articulation of a truly Eastern internal development of a discourse theory, Confucianism narrows its focus upon the socialization processes feeding into the correct use of language as a recipe for political stability. Jaspers elaborates in a passage on the social and communicative casting of freedom via normative constraint as the form Confucian proprieties and rites take: "In the practice of the forms, the essential is 'freedom and lightness,' but the freedom must be 'regulated by the rhythm of set rules'" (1957, p. 45). In turn, the degree to which a given linguistic propriety (*li*) becomes legitimately institutionalized via ritual must be determined (a) through the correct use of a term, (b) assessed in light of its aggregate social utility, (c) as a function of how well the rite or practice manifests and realizes our innate empathetic capacities for proper socialization. Again, according to Jaspers, "They [the *li*] guide men through something universal which is acquired by education and becomes second nature, so that the individual comes to experience the universal not as a constraint but as his own being. The forms give the individual firmness, assurance, and freedom" (1957, p. 45). Therefore, insofar as proper linguistic usage is taken as a socially conferred practice, the fullest realization of our communicative capabilities requires the willful appropriation of an array of normative constraints upon our formative practices.

2.13 The Historical and Materialist Dynamics to Confucian Axiality: The Period of Warring States (800 BCE to 300 BCE)

For Confucius, given the 500-year Period of Warring States that both preceded his birth and followed his death, the ultimate goal of his philosophy was always practical: reclaim the social stability of the Golden Age of China enjoyed under the Chou Dynasty (Schwartz 1975, p. 60). His primary means for bringing about this social stability bore directly on his vision of the exemplary role of the public intellectual in stimulating the type of critical historical reflection that Habermas and others find as distinctive to axial breakthroughs.

> This [work to instill a renewal of the past] implies a "critical" view of history; in examining the past, Confucius distinguishes between the good and the bad; he selects facts that

> are worth remembering as models to be emulated or examples to be avoided. Moreover, he knows that in restoring what was good in the past one should not try to make something outwardly identical…What he advocates is not imitation of the past but repetition of the eternally true. The eternal ideas are more discernible in antiquity. Now, in his own dark times, he wished to restore them in their old radiance by fulfilling himself through them… Confucius finds a living solution to the problem of *authority*, which for him is not merely a monopoly on the exercise of violence. Here for the first time in history a great philosopher shows how the new, merging with the tradition flowing from the source of eternal truth, becomes the substance of our existence. He points the way to a conservative form of life, made dynamic by a liberal open-mindedness. (Jaspers 1957, pp. 43–44)

According to Confucius, the study of the past Classics could be innovatively re-deployed in order to accomplish practical aims in the present. This educational strategy also grounds social organization increasingly in the life of the autonomous individual and less in the realm of pre-theoretical myth (Cheng 2000, p. 202). With this move, Confucius had thus initiated his own secularization dialectic upon the spiritual traditions that he reoriented to the singular focus on social stability:

> [H]is [Kongzi's] insistence on the importance of "study," the mastery of texts by which the appropriate behavior defined in the past could be known. But this need to recover a pattern of conduct that had to some extent been lost already bespeaks the beginning of a critical and self-conscious separation from the present. And there was another, more important, break. In place of the old combination of religion and government, he put forward the conception of a state and society based on virtue in its own rights, without insisting on immediate validation by God or the gods in the form of success. In other words, he began to envisage the awakening of a purely moral determination in the individual. (Elvin 1986, pp. 332–333)

By melding the insights of Jaspers and Elvin, we see here a concession to the growing importance of a cosmic notion of eternal truth rendered this worldly as individual moral accountability (Cheng 2000, pp. 202–203), as again characteristic of our opening reflections on transcensus (Chap. 1, this volume). Confucius also recognizes the risk of subjectivity run rampant that characterized the individualism presumed by the emerging camps of strategic realist opponents he also sought to refute by restoring ritual proprieties (Cheng 2000, p. 207, 209).

Before going into the excessive individualism Confucius sought to restrain, we might benefit from a twofold historical and material attempt at giving more social content to the complex period of ongoing warfare that led to his critical appraisal of the past. Firstly, some of the contributing material factors included, but were not limited to: the growth in trade and institutionalized means of producing iron weaponry to facilitate the trans-continental distribution of arms, the use of horse drawn chariots that expanded the scope of travel, communication, trade, and conflict among dispersed states, and the concomitant increase in prospects for great wealth that also meant an increase in material disparity within and between competing polities organized along ever more complex divisions of labor. With the ongoing interaction, competition, and tension between previously isolated groups—and also given the growing differentiation within them—we must also add varied responses to the incursion of militaristic barbarians from the north. In Habermasian parlance, these gradual pluralizing trends moved forms of voluntary self-ascription from the first-person plural 'we' group identification to a growing strategic instrumental first-person singular 'I.'

Secondly, other important materialist social trends include the increasing need for differentiated specialization and a more complex division of labor, particularly as regards the enduring structural presence of liminality (here, taken to mean: the initiation of a crisis-prone phase requiring newly transformed variations upon old rites of passage). While some characterize the defining feature of the Axial Age as the historical emergence of schools of social-critique led by charismatic philosophers, the specific case of Confucianism shows the elite mobilization of social critique through the changing roles of the *shih* strata of diviners, scribes, and elite government advisors (Eisenstadt 2003a, pp. 249–264). In the Chou period of relative stability of ritual statuses under a unified kingdom, scribes and diviners were auxiliaries of the king and mostly focused on ritual procedures for sacrifices to departed ancestral spirits to mediate accord with the heavenly mandate of *Tian*. With the impending fall of the unified kingdom, and repeated failures in instituting increasingly corrupt hereditary monarchs, came a period of multiple feudal hierarchies whereby the advisory *shih* shifted their allegiance and counsel to the non-hereditary aristocratic succession of rulers. While these educated elite *shih* played dual functions of warrior-gentlemen and educated-advisors, we see an important shift in normative justification for their services. The rationale moves away from the strategic logic of sheer power to the moral-practical legitimacy of rulers via epistemic merits of virtue and greater technical efficacy.

As contributing historical factors to Confucian philosophical development, over the course of the Warring States Period, initial estimates of more than 20 feudal states declined to 7 major and 5 minor powers in an ongoing game of strategic elimination. As these various competing states encroached into new domains of ambassadorial trade, representation, and conflicting jurisdictional claims, the prior role of the *shih* as warrior-gentleman was subjected to two trends of even greater intensity of enhanced specialization. On the one hand, there was a need for a widened scope of conferring the warrant to fill new competencies of an evolving social order. With the multiplying division of labor, the educational functions of the *shih* now included military, educational, ambassadorial, cultural, and advisory functional innovation. On the other hand, as competing states eliminated rivals and affected families were dispersed by the ongoing warfare, more and more *shih* became master-less. Insofar as the number of master-less *shih* continued to grow, they began the gradual democratization of offering their tutoring services to a wider array of students that did not necessarily comprise the former aristocratic elite and also began stretching their tutelage outside the scope of their original cultural and/or provincial identification.

Thirdly, the gradual democratization of social roles offered by this genealogy of the increasingly nomadic elite advisor eventually fed directly into the biographical profile of Confucius as a master-less *shih* that eventually extended his services as far as taking on any student willing to learn and follow his teachings. What also undoubtedly contributed to the unique success and mission of Confucius was his relatively small and militarily weak home province of Lu that nonetheless boasted a culturally rich elite educational heritage that neighboring states had either already begun to adopt or were willing to take on once exposed to its superior practical, moral, technical, and cultural problem-solving innovations. These historical and material factors thus contributed significantly to the Confucian teaching of *wen*—the idealized moral-practical justification of successful competition between states and civilizations in moral-aesthetic terms of their highest cultural achievements—as an alternate to the strategic, instrumental, realist adage of 'might makes right.' The wider historical changes to the vocational role of the *shih* also spurred on Confucius's innovative axial universalization of aristocratic virtues as a species-ethic. The proselytization of *jen* as the ideal perfection of the human nature spread from the elite educated individual to any member of the species, or at minimum, anyone falling within the fluctuations of the territorial, cultural, and proprietary boundaries of the Middle Kingdom.

2.14 The Species-Ethics of Jen Rendered Communicative: The Universal Pragmatics of Name Rectification

Given an inherently dialogical spin, the exercise of a ritual role under liminal processes of ongoing transformation can be measured and assessed in terms of the highly abstract and universally moral-practical degree to which it embodies compassionate solidarity. In discourse-theoretic terms, the solidarity sought as an ideal extends performatively between a first person actor and second person recipient(s) through *jen*—literally interpreted as: human-to-humanness in an inherently second personal reflexive sense. Etymologically, we can construe *jen* in terms of the species-ethical practical ideal of inter-humanity, in light of the combined ideogrammatic terms for (a) human being and (b) two (Cheng 2000, p. 203). Consider the associated axial and communicative spin given in the illustration offered by Jaspers in his reflections on Confucius's view of human nature:

> The nature of man is called *jen*. Jen is humanity and morality in one. The ideogram means "man" and "two," that is to say: to be human means to be in communication. The question of the nature of man is answered, first in the elucidation of what he is and should be; second in an account of the diversity of his existence…[Firstly,] man is not like the animals which are as they are, whose instincts govern their existence without conscious thought; he is a task to himself. Men actively shape their life together and, transcending all instinct, build it on their human obligation…[Secondly,] Men resemble one another in essence—in *jen*. But they differ "in habits," individual character, age, stage of development, and knowledge. (Jaspers 1957, pp. 49–50)

Jen as a communicative ideal serves the dual role of (a) moral individuation—as responsibility for oneself and other while (b) also allowing for a tiered set of proprieties tailored to one's abilities, fluidity of social roles, and universal-rational conferral of justificatory advances in social mobility. Newly conferred statuses accrue in proportion to one's narrative realization of compassion in active service to others.

For Confucian study to carry these composite theoretical and pragmatic aims for concrete social transformation required his followers to redact society, ritual norms, and its foundational institutions through the aforementioned increase in moral learning. According to Jaspers, "With him the *mode of* learning and teaching becomes a fundamental problem. The aim of all learning is *practical efficacy*" (1957, p. 44). As a pragmatic illustration of the reflexive ties between moral individuation and collective processes of socialization, Confucian philosophy of language stimulated a distinct form of normative semantics oriented toward the mutual revision of concepts that must continually keep pace with the attendant cognitive social advances in behavioral proprieties. According to Cheng, we find a high degree of complicity between Confucian linguisitic practices and the pragmatic thrust of Habermasian discourse ethics. As an added insight, the procedural dimensions of Habermas's scheme that are often construed in terms of democratic institutionalization of society are given a ritual orientation through Cheng's emphasis on socialization as a broader phenomena than mere justificatory argumentation:

> [I]t is not far-reaching to say that Confucian ethics has been highly alerted to the process of communicative interaction which Habermas expounds in his theory of communicative interaction, and this process represents a larger process of socialization rather than a narrow process of argumentation. To know language is to engage in a communicative interaction with others and to be aware of the correct moral implications of our language, to socialize and integrate one's own reflective morality (moral sense and moral consciousness) with others so that one can determine what is right to do and what is right to say: it is to know a norm of morality by coming to an understanding of the universal moral principle which applies to everyone both descriptively and regulatively. This then is to know rituals (as parts of the social and moral norms) and to establish oneself (to be integrated with others both communicatively and interactively in a system of objective morality as represented by the system of Confucian *li*). (Cheng 2000, p. 219)

As support for Cheng's insight, Jaspers most clearly articulates this expanded discursive interpretation of Weber's axial salvation impulse behind both Confucian thought and universal pragmatics: 'Truth and reality are one. The mere idea is nothing. The root of human salvation lies in the "knowledge that influences reality," that is, in the truth of ideas that are translated into an inner, transforming action. What is true within takes form without' (Jaspers 1957, p. 51). In terms of honing our focus onto the micro-discourse philosophy of language, simply stated—'words must be set aright'—via the Confucian vigilance now applied to rectification of names:

> When asked, "What is the first thing to be done in order to promote renewal in disastrous circumstances?" Confucius gave a remarkable answer: Words must be set aright. What inheres in words should be brought out. The prince should be a prince, the father a father, the man a man. But language is constantly misused, words are employed for meanings that do not befit them. A separation arises between being and language. [Confucius said] "He who has the inner being also has the words; he who has the words does not always have the inner being." If language is in disorder, everything goes wrong. (Jaspers 1957, p. 52)

Therefore, in the parlance of Habermas's grammar of discourse, the correct second-person moral and practical fulfillment of a given social role would be closer to the truth of the name than merely an accurate third-person objective description of a particular position, or the first-person strategic self-assertion of coercive power without the requisite proprietary fulfillment. For a Confucian approach to language in which all philosophy is inherently social philosophy, the false use of a noun would be tantamount to forging false credentials in the exercise of a given social role (Li 1999, p. 73).

> Confucius has also advanced his doctrine of "rectifying names" (*zhengming*) where he requests that names must correctly conform and hold up to correct values and actuality of human relationships. By looking and recognizing the hidden moral requirement of our language we would be able to require our conduct to accord with these requirements. "Thus a ruler must be rulerlike and a father be fatherlike." This is indeed both a linguistic and a moral insight: by looking into our use of names we see that moral values and moral consciousness has already imbued itself with our moral common sense and an overlapping consensus on moral values. This suggests that a process of communication and interaction among people has already created this result and it is important to apply our moral consciousness to individual usage of language so that we shall guard the process from deterioration. (Cheng 2000, p. 219)

Confucian philosophy of language thus carries a performative component that directly aids in redefining the role of the public intellectual in the universalistic dimension as a means to accomplish a public ministry where social stability reflects cosmic, moral, and social dynamics constituting order in the species. Applied to inter-Axial discourse, while we see the legal institutionalization of norms and background justifications broadly differ in the Confucian and Habermasian schemes, nonetheless, we can achieve overlapping consensus on moral values (in both the species-ethical sense of Confucianism and the rational universalizability [U] of Habermas).

For Confucian linguistic analysis, one finds both strongly discursive and pragmatic elements, as social stability proved most likely when general names are used properly. For example, as an exemplary *chun tzu*—literally, superior person that most fully realizes the human capacity for *jen*—the Confucian public intellectual must engage in active social critique with a practical purchase on morally transforming the hearts and minds of both rulers and ruled.

> More important [than moralizing politics], in a broad cultural perspective, was their great contribution to the development of a political language, or more precisely, a grammar of action [name rectification] for all players in the political arena, including the members of the ruling minority. Remarkably, they managed to accomplish this without gaining direct access to the center of power. (Wei-Ming 1986, p. 366)

In order to remain in such a critical position as those responsible for the vigilant monitoring, redacting, and sanctioning of linguistic proprieties, Confucians taught from the ever-porous proprietary fences of the cultural, political, and territorial bounds of their civilizational matrix. In order to straddle the participant-observer perspective, they were thus dissuaded from becoming too enamored with the very power they sought to reshape. Akin to the inter-Axial observations of Eisenstadt, when most effective, these social elites tended to act upon institutions from periphery to core rather than monopolizing the third-person objective perspective of bureaucratic social engineers or first-person participant role of self-acclaimed philosopher kings.

In this respect, Confucius thereby initiated a dialectical inter-Axial approach not only to naming but the entire hermeneutic tradition feeding into the renaissance in study of the Classics. Confucian hermeneutics differentiated his scholarly activity from competing schools while also openly learning from their perceived failures and successes:

> Unlike the Taoists who tried to transcend the written word, or the Legalists who tried to confine it to the letters of the law, or the Moists who tried to use it as an ideological weapon, or the Yin-Yang cosmologists who tried to manipulate it as magic code, the Confucians embraced the entire literature and took it upon themselves, as a divine mission, to breathe vitality into it through the art of interpretation. Their hermeneutical efforts created one of the most comprehensive literary traditions in human history….[Therefore,] the most significant impact of Confucian education on Chinese political culture lies not in civil bureaucracy but in its definition of the intellectual's role in politics. (Wei-Ming 1986, p. 364)

Rather than for the particular forms of bureaucratic power that Confucian social thought brought about, one could uphold Confucian society as perhaps the most enduring political philosophy the post-axial world has ever seen because of the distinct insider-outsider/participant-observer role its practitioners must constantly maintain (Smith 1991, p. 187).

2.15 The Five Constant Relations: Ecumenic Social-Political Order or an Ethics of Kinship?

Based on the micro-level discourse reconstructions provided above, we can attempt an application to the macro-level construction of legitimate institutional procedures in proposing the Habermasian question that runs throughout his reflections on *Dialectics of Secularization*: whether Confucian political society, given a discursive basis, requires any moral pre-political core as the basis for a legitimate polity. The intuitive Confucian response would seemingly be to differ with Habermas on this point and say that, yes, the state does require *jen, li, wen*, and the near perfected moral sentiments of the *chun tzu* in order to serve as the pre-political basis. Even the most fitting of Confucian terms for this query, *te* (literally: political power), translates as leadership by moral example. Jaspers concurs with this verdict in the following remarks:

> Confucius has innumerable maxims about government. All are of a general ethical nature. For example: "Do nothing overhastily; that will not succeed. Do not consider the small advantage, for no great work can prosper in this way." In all these reflections he has in mind a statesman selected by the prince and governing with his consent and understanding. A great statesman proves himself by restoring and reinforcing the ethical-political edifice as a whole. (Jaspers 1957, p. 48)

However, placing Habermas's dialectics of secularization within the wider corpus of his aforementioned works, we should be careful not to impose the limited historical context of the bureaucratic state upon the much wider axial-scope of his reflections on world-historical transfers of legitimation. In other words, we should not apply the same empirical and historical data behind the first Habermasian principle of the absence of a pre-political moral substrate of the state to the second principle that concerned the transfer of authority beyond kinship ties. The first principle he currently addresses to the legitimacy of the contemporary polity in light of the global spread of culture wars and their attendant values debates. In contrast, the second principle extends much more broadly in world-historical scope as addressed to the legitimacy of any polity in light of its much wider three millennia development.

For instance, in honing our focus on extending kinship ties of trust more broadly to a wider communal network, three Confucian proprieties deal with relations within the family and comprise three of the five Constant Relations (parent/child, husband/wife, elder sibling/younger sibling). Extension beyond kinship mentioned in the other two Constant Relations apply at the local level (elder friend/younger friend), and state and imperial levels (ruler/subject). In focusing on the socialization practices of extending solidarity beyong the family nexus, it may be unnecessary to postulate any pre-political moral substrate if indeed Habermas is right that individuation and socialization practices are co-original.

As one example, the proprieties taught for the ideal *jen* as the prevailing norm to guide name rectification between parent (whom expresses supreme compassion in their authority) and child (whom expresses supreme reverence in their subordination)—each still entails an ideal of *jen* in mutually disciplined subordination to another as the condition for the supreme realization of self (Smith 1986, pp. 175–176). The child must reverentially submit to the authority and jurisdiction of the parent while the parent must restrain the potentially limitless power to dominate the subordinate. While one might say the parent carries the upper hand in the hierarchical relationship, they also bear the onus of a greater responsibility that comes with their enhanced sway, age-conferred maturity, and higher stage of moral learning achieved in their ego-development socialization processes.

As a second example, while Confucius and Mencius are each known for postulating the family as the root of the state, they also agree that for proper family socialization to occur, there must be rulers in place that mold citizens in accord with virtue and the attendant proprieties that reflect the aforementioned model of the parent-child relation. From this perspective, very similar proprieties are called for in the ruler and subject relation—benevolence and loyalty, respectively—that are parallel expressions of the ideal parent-child normative standards. In this instance, the reflexivity is more pronounced as we proceed from state down to ensure the ideal fruition of family up to higher modes of socialization.

As a third and final illustration, this time from name rectification, the progressively dialectical approach of the conservative mixing of past success with liberal open-mindedness toward the future, applies also to the normative semantics of the name ancestor. Even given his extreme veneration of both the family and of social order that by Western standards borders on worship, when pressed whether he had secularized ancestry to such an extent that he had foreclosed any access to the spiritual realm altogether, Confucius also allowed for crossing the liminal border of the transcendent realm permeating the profane with the famous Analects 3 adage 'without due respect to the Gods, to whom would we pray?' Nonetheless, consistent with the dialectical and this-worldly overtone of Confucius's teaching, Confucians later sought to secularize the Shang Ti ideal (literally, supreme ancestor construed as the primordial source and focus of pre-axial, mythical ancestral worship) and refocus public emphasis on the mundane realm as an indication of one's worthiness for sainthood, particularly on one's perfect expression of *jen* in the living family as the most important of units in the social order. Hence came about the modern secularized and disenchanted practice of Confucian filial and civic piety that extends even to this day, granting greater veneration to persons in a degree proportionate to their age and family proximity, checked by *jen* as the supreme virtue subordinating even the upper ends of the hierarchies to constraint. In appeal to name rectification, an elder/superior does not merit the proprietary license worthy of their name if they are abusive in their exercise of authority. In stark contrast, the pre-axial mythical religion that Confucius inherited as the prevailing social context put pride of place on the worship of departed ancestors through ritual sacrifice as the means for gaining the favor of the gods. Confucian scholar M. Elvin best captures the historical approximation of this dialectical transformation and thereby seems to reinforces Jaspers' axial hypothesis in this Eastern Sino-context:

> From perhaps the eighth century B.C.E. onwards there was a definitive transition from a concern to please God and the gods by sacrifices, without making morality a primary consideration, to a belief that morally correct actions were in themselves the key to survival and success in the world. It was felt that Tian operated Its dispensations almost automatically and dependably, and that Its favours and those of the lesser gods were the natural consequence of good conduct. (Elvin 1986, p. 328)

Allowing for the inclusion of the Tian mandate of heaven into his dialectical reconstruction of name rectification, Confucius did not want to do away with worship of ancestors. However, insofar as the maintenance of social and cosmic order remained intertwined, when conferring naming powers upon the *shih* sage—Confucius reoriented their focus away from worship of the departed. Confucian modified the naming rites to emphasize righteous governance over this realm as directed by the presumed moral qualification of maintaining the proper functioning of the overall cosmic order (Clark 2005, p. 126).

Confucius and Mencius thus found *te*, the proper wielding of power via exemplary virtue, including teaching socially-enhancing normative practices of general naming, to be one of the key traits of the former Chou Dynasty that was able to unite all of China. According to Jaspers' interpretation of Confucius, 'Good government is possible only in a sound social condition, molded by the *li*, the right music, the right modes of human intercourse. Such a condition can only grow. But though it cannot be made, it can be fostered or impeded' (1957, p. 47). Thus, as one final example of name rectification, while it is the task of the ruler to inculcate virtue in the life of fellow citizens, it is the more impartial role of the *chun tzu* as public intellectual, whom must hold leaders to account for their disproportionate authority that carries with it an enhanced capacity to magnify vice:

> The Confucian intellectuals and, to a certain extent, the scholar-officials as a whole, assumed the role of watchdog, not only for the imperial household but also for the common people….[T]hey could represent the people in addressing their grievances to the higher authority. They could serve as critics and censors when they believed that the sins of the dynasty were still redeemable. They could also advocate the creation of a new dynasty, if they felt the course of the degeneration of the present could not be reversed. The Confucians did not see their emperors as sage-kings. They also noticed that, historically, sages did not necessarily become kings. Perhaps they were impelled by the sage-king [chun-tzu] ideal when they honored Confucius as the "uncrowned king" (su-wang). The logic of this is not difficult to see. (Wei-Ming 1986, p. 372)

As an initial screening test for the *chun tzu* to place upon prospective rulers, Mencius astutely warns that a ruler cannot be promoted to ruler if they fail in the governance of their own family. And, furthermore, even if the ruler does pass the initial pragmatic test, much more is still expected in order to exit the undesirable historical condition of the Warring States Period. As another criteria, the ruler must not only embody perfect benevolence. They must also plan ahead for regulation of resource distribution to ensure the necessary material dimensions behind family flourishing in potential circumstances of widespread scarcity. While sinologists concur that Mencius leans more toward a positive casting of human nature as compared to Confucius's middle-of-the-road/skeptical outlook, Mencius does concede that resource redistribution will be necessary to allow families and individuals to maintain a fixed heart over time. Some paternalistic regulation may be required so subjects will not be warped into strategic self-preservation by the constant threat of material scarcity or lapse into the habitual vice of consumerism as a product of enduring periods of abundance.

However, even given the idealizations for social order offered by the five Constant Relations, Confucians were not so naïve as to presume their periphery to core activity of public critique would always directly transform the centers of political power. If coercive rule manifests primarily in the ruler, rulers might at best aspire to have Confucian advisors, since Confucians concede that most leaders would prove ultimately incapable of fully committing themselves to the rigors of such practical ethics. As a historical observation of political realities in China even during the flourishing of Confucian schools, Wei Ming adds an honest touch of skeptical realism:

> In reality, Confucian ethics rarely touched the inner lives of the rulers. Often it was abused to serve as an ideological weapon of social control. The Son of Heaven may not have been personally committed to self-cultivation, but he could appreciate the political benefit of ensuring that his ministers were. While the scholar-officials in power might not put Confucian ethics into practice themselves, they could surely see that their task of maintaining stability in society would make it relatively easy if the common people did so. (Wei-Ming 1986, p. 371)

Once this practical capacity infiltrated the political process itself, the original transformation of society that Confucius sought in his own failed attempts to carry public office eventually became manifest through the educational institutions that fed into the training of civil leadership for millennia to come. In the end, his ideal of the *chun tzu* endured beyond his death, not through the monarchs but through the competing schools that spread and differentiated in direct proportion to prolonged periods of political stability.

2.16 The Internal Heterodoxy of Deliberate Tradition: Mohists, Realists, and the Classics

Insofar as the Confucian notion of name rectification did not achieve its primary goal of ending the warfare within his lifetime (or that of the later Mencius), the dialectical transformation of society carried on in a widely heterodox genealogical development. Rival schools elaborated upon, critiqued, and likewise redacted the linguistic teachings of Confucius (551–479 BCE), including that of the Mohists led by Mo Di (470–391 BCE). For example, what Confucius ascribes to the role of the *chun tzu* to set names aright, Mo Di applies more conservatively to the jurisdiction and authority of the emperor as the true Son of Heaven. In differentiation from Confucius, Mo Di mixed (a) the Mohist *jen* induced call to universal love with (b) a realist view of state power by means of a tradition-bound linguistic epistemic corporatism:

> [In the Mohist epistemic redaction of Confucian name rectification, I]t was vital to have uniformity of values, strict hierarchy, and perfect inter-communication between superiors and inferiors. Before the creation of government there had been chaos. Each man had had his own particular values for words. The head of each family, each community, and each state had had to unify the values of those beneath him. It was the duty of the emperor to do this for the world as a whole….[Therefore,] Mo Di envisaged a corporatism very different from the Western ideal of democracy. He was speaking from the point of view of a ruler when he said: "If many others assist one to hear and see, then one will be able to hear and see across vast distances." (Elvin 1986, pp. 334–335)

As constituting the dialectical basis for his normative semantics, Mo Di thus put the ruler in the discursive role of the ideal Confucian public intellectual, putting much stock into the direct communicative mediation between ruler and ruled. Mohism thus embraced a paradoxical position conceding enhanced authority to rulers acting under the ideological framework of the growing presence of realist power together with a decidedly charitable and more idealistic view of humanity's universal capacity for loving compassion. The compassionate trust on the Mohist rendition shows a degree of transitivity missing in the Confucian rendition that, when focused on the position of the subordinate, calls for loyal submission from the subject (Roetz 2012, pp. 164–266). The idealism of the Mohist view thus stretches beyond the Confucian skeptical calls for conferring authority only when first merited by proven acts of non-strategic moral-practical warrant.

On the other hand, the ambivalent conservative hermeneutic of the rival Mohists also put a greater deal of epistemic weight upon the textual and historical basis of past precedent, together with the attendant realist emphasis on the direct practical results of a more immediate stabilization of authority:

> Mo Di maintained that a proposition should "meet three criteria". It had to have "a scriptural basis". In other words, suitable precedents had to exist in the acts or words of the sage-kings of the past. It had to have a "derivation" from the evidence of the senses. And due regard had to be paid to its "practical effects". That is to say, when acted upon, did it bring benefit or harm to humanity? (Elvin 1986, p. 334)

While Mohism wrought its historical realization as a competing school slightly after the time of Confucius, Confucians tended to critique it as an apologist attempt to justify the status quo insofar as their optimism was waning—and the attendant desperate conciliation for a short-term fix—as the Warring States Period had not yet ended. According to the Mohists, the past precedent for greater trust in *Tian* and the Mandate of Heaven could be demonstrated by appeal to a less flexible hermeneutics applied to the *Classics* that came prior to Confucius. The second hermeneutic condition: derivation from the senses, kept the less robust normative ideals grounded in the material and social reality of the negative experiential and utilitarian calculus of continued warfare. Lastly, the similarly consequentialist practical effects would lead to the pragmatic test of whether the correct use of a term enhances social stability and helps society calculate the attendant risks of resisting or accepting the presiding rulers—weighing self-preservation above the punishment for public rebuke of a presiding ruler.

However, the ensuing heterodoxy of competing schools both (a) spoke to the Confucian commitment to moral-practical justification based on rational argumentation and (b) eventually led to the Confucian wisdom that the enduring presence of rival philosophical schools allowed for the dialectical assimilation of the most efficacious problem-solving as an epistemic filter on politicized spheres of joint attention. In this context of ongoing liminal uncertainty that Jaspers finds characteristic of all forms of modernity that owe their historical roots to the axial period, later Confucians were obligated by their own commitment to rational justification to offer a response to the competing Mohism and Realism/Legalism. Still in the general spirit of Confucius and Mencius, as a supplement to the axial breakthrough of reflective critique from the intellectual as critic, the Confucian cosmology executed a dialectical reversal on Mohist conservatism. By redeploying the Heavenly Mandate as a principle of rational justification, their calls for rational moral justification added to its arsenal a cosmic perspective for rebuke of corrupt authority:

> Contrary to the widely held interpretive position, Tung Chung-shu's [neo-Confucian critic of Legalism, 141–87 BCE] cosmology was not an ideological justification for the divinity of the emperor. His famous thesis, "the mutual responsiveness of Heaven and man," was not intended to assign transcendent importance to the throne. Rather, he wanted to make the emperor accountable for his actions to Heaven above as well as to the people below. Thus, in establishing the supremacy of Heaven as the final arbiter of human worth, Tung perceived the power of the emperor as relativized authority. Without the legitimizing functions of the cosmic process, the emperor's leadership remained questionable. (Wei-Ming 1986, p. 368)

Here, with its neo-Confucian formulation, we find the cosmic mandate of heaven rendered moral-practical insofar as the empirical proof for its bestowal of legitimate authority upon a ruler opens them to public critique from peripheral Confucian elites and from the broader public increasingly socialized into Confucian proprieties by the democratized teachings of quasi-nomadic *shih*.

2.17 Towards Some Contemporary Concluding Themes: The Mandate of Heaven and the Dialectics of Secularization

In summation, for all the Western stigmas attached to Confucianism as rigidly hierarchical and tradition-bound, it instead evinces one of the earliest expressions of a more forward-looking, dynamic, and reflective canon of thought. As perhaps the most extreme example, it also includes the right to protest on the part of the people insofar as a given ruler does not practically live up to the normative semantics attached to this social designation.

> [The aforementioned common misunderstanding of Confucianism as dissuading external protest] fails to account for the Confucian ability to mobilize massive psychic energy through direct appeal to the transcendental principle, be it the Mandate of Heaven or the dictates of one's moral will. The convergence of the most generalizable social relevance (the sentiments of the people) and the most universalizable, ethico-religious sanction (the decrees of heaven) has allowed the Confucian to perceive politics in terms of the ultimate meaning of life and as a basic fact of ordinary existence. (Wei-Ming 1986, pp. 365–366)

The ambivalent liminal thresholds between the transcendent and mundane split that never requited its tension, even post-axial breakthrough, carry over today into its more contemporary context as pertains to extending Habermas's secularization dialectics. At least in Western academia, the predominant institutional secularity has led to an overtly humanistic rendering of the Confucian Mandate of Heaven, leading many to argue that for the Confucian the sacred is the secular (Li 1999, p. 145; Clark 2005).

However, in maintaining their role at the periphery, in the long term, the primary role of Confucians was one of education rather than bureaucratic decision-making which thereby contributed to the enduring character of the Confucian legacy to the cultural renewal of the ever-scarce internal cognitive resources of ultimate meaning and purpose:

> While the Confucians never gained access to the decision-making body of the ruling minority during the Warring States (403–221 B.C.E.) Period, they did become a notable social force exerting powerful control over the cultural system. This was accomplished mainly through education. The Confucian monopoly on education may have been the single most important factor for the reemergence of Confucian intellectuals in the Han dynasty (206 B.C.E.-220 C.E.) as the meaning-givers in society and the authority-legitimizers in polity….This democratization of the education process released a great deal of energy from the lower echelons of society. The channel of upward social mobility, once opened to the literatus, significantly changed its character….[I]n short, to bring law and order to his [the king's] regime and to enhance its presence in "international" politics. (Wei-Ming 1986, p. 363)

Thus, as additional dialectical iterations of the secularization stages that sway between the axial poles of transcendent and mundane, there were even reform movements internal to these complex dialectical struggles over which literary resources would be conferred rightful status, particularly via the Old Text School that sought to expand the corpus of orthodox Classics and thus extend the transcendent scope of talk of Heaven [first century CE]. This enhanced competition between schools thereby acted as a check on the abuse of scholasticism as a means to influence and/or usurp political power via dubious claims of prognostication.

> The scholars who studied the ancient texts eventually could not shake off the concerns of discussing interactions between Man and Heaven, such as in the works written by Yang Hsiung. Generally speaking, however, the use of the Old Text School represents an effort to restore the original Confucianism. It can be regarded as a second separation of the sacred and the mundane after the Han Confucians once again blended the Heavenly will and Human action in their attempt to synthesize the Confucian humanism and the themes of other schools, especially those of Yin-Yang naturalists. (Hsu 1986, p. 321)

While perhaps muddying the waters as to what we shall accept as orthodox Confucian doctrine, the dialectical moves seem to affirm S.N. Eisenstadt's claim that comfort with internal heterodoxy rather than dogmatic orthodoxy, and liberal openness to reformation and revival in the face of inter-Axial competition, may be among the enigmatic secrets to the time-tested longevity of the great axial traditions. The lively hermeneutic debates among competing Confucian schools—and against Mohist, Legalist/Realist, and Taoists—over which texts to take as authoritative and over the more vexing issue of the extent of transcendental influence over the mundane order kept the sinological traditions alive. In doing so, we are placed in the uncomfortable position of conceding no single prevailing orthodox hermeneutic in exchange for the moral-practical and epistemic benefits of the disaggregation of heterodox movements that remain alive in their capacity still to address the problems of the present.

By virtue of its enduring practical capacity for the dialectical assimilation, redaction, and adoption of competing schools, over time, Confucian thought widened its scope over two millennia beyond merely the orthodox teachings of its two founding proponents. At yet another dialectical level, what one might call inter-Axial competition among schools (specifically, Confucian and Taoist thought), leads one away from the false perception of an intractable stalemate between culturally-ossified monoliths exercising commitments to mutual toleration:

> In the perspective of intellectual history, the Confucianism that eventually emerged as the predominant court philosophy was no longer the teachings of Confucius and Mencius. Rather, it was an amalgamation of Hsun Tzu's ritualism with Legalist concepts, Yin-Yang cosmological categories, Taoist ideas, and a host of other contemporary beliefs. (Wei-Ming 1986, p. 367)

Therefore, we will continue to follow the inter- and intra-Axial historical imprint of Confucian thought upon Asia from roughly the Golden Age period of the Chou Dynasty, to the establishment of the great Middle Kingdom, to the China of modern day by now turning to the role of Taoism in the dialectical shaping of yet another moral-practical ethic of axial universality.

2.17.1 The Disclosive Power of the Tao: Liminal Anonymity in Taoist Language and Ritual

For Lao Tzu [400BCE?], presumably accepted as the author behind the *Tao Te Ching*, (literally, The Way and Its Power) and Yang Zhu [500 or 400 BCE?] as the ascribed author of the *Zhuangzi*, the unique disclosing power of Taoist language gives this religion an undeniably enigmatic character. Readers of these texts are continually called to lose small, particular, limiting, and confining language in order to attain the great language of the dao (Xianglong 2004, p. 207).

In other words, (in statements that some Western philosophers have aligned with the views on language espoused by Wittgenstein and Heidegger), one finds within language 'something that mutually harmonizes, suits, and satisfies with dao, a preconceptual dimension of language, and through this, or in its very midst, dao tells (dao) us that which it says (dao)' (Xianglong 2004, p. 207). Since the prevailing Taoist assumption holds that humanity, and all living beings, are always already holistically immanent to the eternal Tao, we must not allow naming, describing, and prescribing to circumvent a natural harmony that already prevails. However, while carrying undeniably strong cosmic overtones, the Taoist species ethic to ensue still retains a sufficient level of disembedding between person, society, and cosmos to qualify as axial.

2.18 Enigmas of the *Tao Te Ching*: An Elite Hermeneutics for Humble Teachings

The aforementioned dialectic between Legalists, Mohists, and Confucians will continue with stronger emphasis on the Taoist linguistic strands of argument. Again, the Period of Warring States serves as a common locus of historical reference insofar as its final closure comes after the onset of Taoist, Confucian, Legalist, and Mohist schools. Followers of the communicative logics ascribed to Confucian and Legalist schools, in particular, are placed under the heaviest Taoist critique. Insofar as Confucianism seeks clear normative bounds between acceptable and unacceptable uses of naming, and Legalists follow suit with an even stricter logic based on sensory justification, Taoism casts skepticism on the presumed capacity of concepts to provide such sharp differentiations between shared aspects of the same cosmic manifold:

> Zhuang's metaphysics make it easier to understand his attack on logic. It begins with the assertion that the division of experience by words into distinct categories is already a radical falsification. 'The Dao has never had boundaries. Speech has never had norms. It is through "truth by definition" that frontiers are created.' The terminology itself prevents one from seeing that "things have neither development nor decay, but return into each other and interpenetrate to form a single whole." (Elvin 1986, p. 344)

The Taoist school and its skeptical critique on logic in general bares on the uniquely enigmatic hermeneutic one must apply to the *Tao Te Ching.* On the one hand, the scripture itself was originally written to the very elite strata of society that presumably possessed the cognitive capacities to construct complex counter-arguments that disclose the pragmatic inefficacy of conceptual distinctions. On the other hand, in a sharp dialectic turn, one of the critiques directly against Confucian and Legalist hierarchical proprieties would be the general incapacity, and thus impotence, of elite constructed terminological distinctions for a society lacking the requisite widespread educational institutions.

Adding to its obscurity, the *Tao Te Ching* was transmitted orally in short poetic chapters not intended for organization in any explicit developmental logic or written catalogues of critical commentary. The linguistic medium of expression itself carries layer upon layer of aphoristic content. In a move running dialectically counter to the trends at democratizing Confucian thought as a mode of instantiating cultural solidarity, each explicit statement made in this scripture brings with it deep layers of implied understanding originally oriented to elites, while comprising a small minority of the society they were orally trained in the esoteric contextual nuances of that target audience.

> When a person uses an aphorism, they are implicitly asserting the relevance of the image evoked to some given situation, and this assertion frequently implies some kind of judgment as to what kind of values are to be given prime consideration in this situation. What this suggests about *Tao-te-ching* interpretations is that we do not look for coherence or unity in it by comparing the explicit content of different sayings, looking for some logically articulated system of doctrines Rather, we ought to ask, about each saying, what value priorities would be implied in choosing to present this particular image as a corrective to this particular target mentality. (LaFarge 1998, p. 268)

In contrast to the systematic treatment of Confucian morality as reducible to generalized norms, such as the Silver Rule, the universality of jen, and the Five Constant Relations, the emphasis in Taoism would tend toward moral particularism—sometimes misleading characterized under the broad description of the relativity of values. Not to be mistaken with contemporary relativism, whereby any opinion carries equal merit as compared to any other, the relativity of values implies both the situational character of moral-ethical judgment and the mutual interdependence of apparently opposed valuation schemes.

By pressing the liminal borders that constitute enormous gaps in the overall flow of the scriptural content of the *Tao Te Ching*, the emptiness itself between both themes and modalities of expression thereby clears a negative space that could not merely be bridged by more chapters, content, and a more precise specification of rules. As one instance of the relativity of values, the spontaneous vacillations between flux and order give limitless potential to the flowing of the Tao. Nature in its myriad particular manifestations provides finite expressions of the Tao as cosmic ordering principles to the limitless manifold.

Moeller has even gone so far as to compare the ancient nuances of the *Tao Te Ching* to the contemporary hypertext qualities of the internet whereby each page and site of the web serves at an analogical level to each chapter of the sacred text. Traversing between the array of virtual sites would thus be akin to recitation and reflection upon the various chapters of prose that have each presupposed a unique target audience. Each site (akin to each chapter in the analogy) does not render explicit the limitless sets of assumptions necessary to convey their respective content. To fill out the analogy, the one traversing across the hypertext can only navigate it effectively if and only if they share the background assumptions of the target audience that each site by expedience cannot fully articulate as its basic assumptions:

> The humble expression of the limits of language carries both a hermeneutic and a doctrinal implication. If the chapters are read on their own, or the book is read linearly, the text remains hermetically closed. But is one adopts a different reading strategy and treats the *Laozi* as a kind of hypertext, as a collection of nonlinear but still tightly connected materials, then the "darkness" lightens and the *Laozi* indeed becomes a "gate of multiple subtleties." (Moeller 2006, p. 6)

In this manner, hypertext content as an analogue to the themes covered in the *Tao Te Ching* range as diverse as moral-practical conduct in warfare, human sexuality, ordering society in a context of material scarcity and excess, the pragmatic and mystical lessons of agrarian life, the nature and origin of the cosmos, and meditations on prolonging life perpetually. Yet another enigmatic quality of the Taoist scriptures would be that all this can be addressed in the terse scope of 81 poetic chapters. Thus, a common claim among those familiar with Taoist hermeneutics, upholds the paradox that the *Tao Te Ching* can be read in a half hour or its content can be contemplated for a lifetime.

The critical hermeneutic perspective offered by the *Tao Te Ching* as derived out of the Warring States Period allows it to attain its axial status as proposing an alternative to the moral, social, and technological (merely perceived) progress feeding into the endemic conflict. Akin to the Confucian context, we must assume as rival sources of the justification of political authority the predominant Realist/Legalist recommendations to cede power and legitimacy to the greatest respective wielders of third-personal objective coercion in the name of first-person strategic self-preservation. However, even the Confucian efforts to meld character in accord with the proprieties of the Five Constant Relations and the regulative norms of the *chun tzu* are regarded as clumsy efforts to super-impose coercive order upon an empire that has outstretched the capacities for linguistic translation of its extremely variegated contents:

> The *Scripture of the Way and Its Power* offered a vision of a society uncontaminated by progress, without labour-saving machinery, travel, the use of weapons, or books. But its main polemical thrust was against the exponents of statecraft who thought, in the words of *Lord Shang*, they could "use the death-penalty to effect a turn to virtue". The apparent realism of this approach was an illusion. The nature of the world could not be caught in legalistic verbal categories. Policies devised on their basis turned constantly awry. (Elvin 1986, pp. 353–354)

For the Taoist, with Confucians as the most common subject of openly polemical critique, Confucians share the realist assumption of a strategically instrumental and/or objectivigating approach to language. They each conflate the external nature of the world of objects subject to technical, market, and bureaucratic manipulation with the inner nature of humans that surpasses any ability for immediate warrant by rational justification through logic for moral-practical aims, decisions, and activities that defy all attempts at rigid classification.

2.19 The Taoist Sage: Namelessness, Silence, and Truth Disclosure

The Taoist proprietary role of the teacher/sage likewise differs not just from realist statecraft but also from its Confucian contemporaries by radicalizing the decentered critical distance of the *shih* advisor to press the bounds of impartiality to the point of namelessness. The democratization strategy of the Confucian sage's public ministry to spread aristocratic virtues to the masses seems to the Taoist to rest on two unwarranted assumptions. It presumes that elite discourses can (a) be translated downwards into the popular vernacular. The idea that elite naming can rectify social ills also assume such naming can (b) be communicated in a manner that itself does not in its success thereby become a new tool of ideological manipulation.

By default then, in skeptical response to the translation potential of elite learning to the masses and as a buffer against ideological manipulation, the Taoist sage must employ a different approach to language. Taoism retains its axial quality by still placing trust in the prospect of moral learning. However, the Taoist sage must teach by living in a manner that non-coercively calls others to relinquish desires for property, status, and honor to the point of supreme indifference. Such anti-elitism thereby pushes the master-less nomadic Confucian to a new liminal threshold of extreme periphery whereby Taoist rulers intentionally took on names (or the absence thereof) to communicate their renunciation of the claims to property, honors, and status of this world:

> By calling themselves the "orphaned," the "abandoned," or the one "without possession," rulers symbolically located themselves in the "social desert"…. That they had no specific family among humans, no father and son, made them the "son of heaven" (*tian zi*), which was another, more common designation for the regent. By being "orphaned" and "abandoned" among humans, the ruler signals that he is the mother and father of all—he has no specific relations and therefore is equally related to all. As with the Dao, his alone-ness paradoxically serves to establish all-one-ness, an all-one-ness that even includes "heaven and earth." (Moeller 2006, p. 70)

Therefore, in light of Habermas's original query into the legitimacy of the axial shift of authority from kinship bonds to an anonymous public, the unique forfeiture of kinship status, in this case, makes possible the rite of passage into steward of the Tao for the sake of the communal good.

Such a Tao flows through the hermetic Sage but ultimately from an ineffable albeit immanent source, without ritual propriety and complex linguistic and social mores that arrive too late. Only in this manner can the Taoist sage—again borrowing and redacting from the Confucian—claim to instantiate the Heavenly Mandate that the Tao confers upon organically constituted communities via the cosmic order sustained by an impersonal Tao:

> The nonpolitical ruler rules without ruling. Therefore he has "small" names. He is not glorified and does not take on grand titles that would designate him as a performer of great tasks. It is through the absence of names and tasks that he is given the greatest mandate, namely the "mandate of heaven." The Daoist ruler's mandate is to manifest the rule of the Tao within society. This mandate is not a mandate of or by the people, much less a mandate of or by some (or the majority) of the people. It is a mandate of "nature" that only the most impartial human being qualifies for. (Moeller 2006, p. 65)

We are thrust right back into the characteristically axial ubiquity of transcensus that renders uncertain not only the precise linguistic articulation of thresholds between the transcendent and mundane, or center and periphery. Also at stake is the rightful nature, pace, and scope through which one initiates ritual transformation through communal processes of social learning. With this unique Taoist variation on the mandate of heaven, the paradoxical goal is to comprise a moral and social order where the humble choice of limited speech and non-action reign supreme.

The abiding constant of the key hermeneutic and political differences with Confucian and Legalist schools respectively, led Lao-Tzu, in particular to differentiate his thought from the rigorous study and learning of proprieties associated with any particular formalized school. According to Jaspers' account, we are offered the following illustrative narrative of the precarious position of the Taoist teacher as pre-lingual facilitator of the Tao.

> Legend tells how a young man went to see the aged Lao-tzu. Lao-tzu did not approve of his activity of planning, advising, and studying. Books are questionable, they are but footprints of the ancient sages. They made the footprints, whereas people today only talk. Lao-tzu is reported to have said, "[you] are concerned with things that are no better than footprints in the dust." "What you are reading can be nothing but the lees and scum of bygone men.... All that was worth handing on, died with them; the rest, they put in their books." (Jaspers 1957, p. 58)

Insofar as civilizational crisis calls for structural change in the legitimate rites of passage to be communicated in a given social context, the Taoist wisdom behind such cynicism would be akin to fighting against a riptide that pulls even the strongest most able swimmer further out to sea. Linguistic attempts to recapture and emulate the thrust of the original transformation of mythical primordial society in an explicit theoretical doctrine to be canonized as an orthodox text will only add yet another ossified layer on rites that will soon again call for supersession.

In such an attack on the Confucian emphasis on study as the road to moral self-cultivation intended to provide foundational solidarity upon which to stabilize the polity, we are also back to the Habermasian axial problem that originally was raised in his *Dialectics of Secularization*: this time, with respect to Taoism. We ask for this final Eastern tradition what we have raised for each of the others: Does the Taoist communitarian, self-sufficient, agrarian—albeit, likewise cosmic—polity necessarily presuppose a pre-political moral foundation for its legitimacy?

For the rudiments of an initial Taoist response, we are immediately led to an assault on the linguistic ethical-moral proprieties tied to social stability under name rectification. As a turn toward negative dialectics, repeated references to the nameless, the ineffable, and unspeakable are meant to convey that in Confucian morality the threshold of non-elite and characteristically illiterate human understanding has been surpassed by a tradition rooted in literary study. As a precondition for the political stability so desired, we must concede the inability of mundane human language to articulate the perfect dao (literally, way or path) of cosmic and social harmony.

> All his [Zhuang Zhou's] arguments, however, are in the end a ruthless attack on the adequacy of existing human standards of judgment, whether of fact or of logic, or of ethical desirability. They are designed to lead the hearer to what still lies beyond when we have come to the limit of what can be rationally spoken of: 'Contingent truths come to an end. When they are at an end, it is that of which we do not know of It what is so that we call the Dao.' (Elvin 1986, p. 342)

This is not an outright denial of a relationship between the ethical-moral dimensions of language and the cosmic order of the dao. Akin to the riptide analogy given earlier, skilled ocean swimmers know the only possible successful overcoming of its pull further out to sea would be counter-intuitively to swim parallel to the shore and eventually move beyond the uneven coastal depths that constitute the unseen dynamic to the crisis.

Analogously, by an entirely different linguistic route this time, we are led again back to Habermas's assumption of the co-originality of individual and collective social roles, if indeed individuation only proceeds through processes of socialization. In other words, since the Tao itself as inherently relational, to speak of this application in the instance of human moral and political order would be to articulate a layer of sediment missing below a set of relations actually in no need of relational mediation. Perhaps the closest Western corollary would be the tradition of negative theology with the prime difference being that the Dao, although ultimate, does not carry the explicit traits associated with a personal God. The periodic reiteration of negative shapes like valleys, un-carved wood, and muddy water (Moeller 2006, p. 8) suggest the limitless void that transforms the Tao into a spontaneous reservoir of limitless relational potential—and in a moral-practical twist—inexhaustible power, strength, and efficacy:

> The Tao in its aspect of the ineffable eternal is nondeterminate and nameless. It cannot be identified with anything nameable. It is *wu* or nonbeing. I translate this word here with a term often used in Western writings on mysticism, since it seems to correspond accurately to its use in the translation of mystical literature in other cultures. *Wu* is a reality which corresponds to no determinate finite entity, relation, or process which can be named. Yet it is eminently "real" and the source of all finite reality. The neutral belief in such a reality would not constitute mysticism, but the *tao-te-ching* is indeed not neutral. (Schwartz 1998, p. 193)

The possible connotations that Schwartz above attributes to belief could be construed in the threefold grammar of communication, either as a first-person subjective state that I alone hold, a third-person conjecture about a state of affairs, or a second-person commitment to a relational trust.

In following Schwartz's advice that the *Tao Te Ching* does not take a merely neutral third-person stance, we can infer the sense of a volitional movement into a relational trust while maintaining the negative connotations of an unknown impersonal reality. This leads Taoism to a deconstructive notion of the language of axial transcendence as pure immanence. Such a paradoxical concession of insurmountable obstacles in the expression of any sort of concrete concept also positively affirms a transcendence presupposed in a moral, social, and political relationship of trust/solidarity with an absolute ulterior. In line with such a holistic picture of always already presumed relations of socialization, the complete circumscription of the shared totality of the collective experience of a universal reign of justice also falls beyond the scope of affirmative linguistic expression. For instance, in light of the emergence of this thought during the Warring States Period, the pronouncement of falling short of justice rather than positively affirming the truth of a means to ensure social stability would, for the Taoist, move transcendence away from the endemic warfare rather than perpetuate its cycle.

2.20 Micro-Level Discourse Politicized: Towards a Macro-Level Reconstruction of the Taoist Polity

As for some generalized linguistic lessons, at the communicative threshold of these negative dialectical claims rests undeniable assumptions that are the necessary pragmatic presuppositions for successful action oriented toward reaching mutual understanding:

> This [competence via sharing the same set of assumptions] suggests also a possible answer to the age old problem as to how the words of the *Tao-te-ching* can describe a way that is "nameless" (chs. 1, 14, 32, 37, 41), and is properly conveyed only by a "teaching without words" (chs. 2, 43). That is, the meaning is not *literally* in the words, in the sense that anyone with a literal understanding of the words would get it. The words of the text only convey their intended meaning for someone who engages with them in a certain spirit—as an answer to certain specific personal concerns, and against the background of certain specific personal experiences. For such a person, the words of the text are "easy to understand," but for others they are not (ch. 70). (LaFarge 1998, p. 260)

On the realist side of the dilemma, mutual understanding needs to retain an uncoerced character to uphold the integrity of the addressee of communication. On the Confucian side of the dilemma, if the requisite proprieties require layers of esoteric tradition for their communicative socialization then they may either exceed the limits of common vernacular or prove too far removed from the immediate novelty of the problem at hand. As yet a third related dilemma, according to Moeller, the historical presence of multiple schools in the Warring States Period thereby runs the risk that the Taoist leader may seem arbitrary in their partiality to a particular school as the professed doctrinal commitments behind their volition: 'Acting and speaking are parallel forms of behavior. The Daoist ruler remains silent because if he spoke he would have to say specific things and thus take on specific positions or opinions' (Moeller 2006, p. 61).

In the inherently historical frame presumed by all post-axial contexts, this negation of doctrinal orthodoxy aims to express both the impossible (a) reversal of history backwards in the vain hope to retrieve a primordial forlorn utopia and (b) institutionalized learning as the privy standpoint for critique of the continent-wide circumstantial particularities of the ongoing warfare of the present. In other words, the skeptical verdict on language and even upon orthodox teachings and texts does not thereby amount to complicity with the ongoing social and political climate:

> Many studies point out that, historically, ancient Chinese philosophy flourished in the period of the so-called "Warring States" and that recognizing this context is crucial for correctly grasping the philosophical issues at stake. This is also true with respect to the *Laozi*. It was a guidebook for political leaders in times of more or less continuous war, and therefore the topic of war is not only treated theoretically but also practically. (Moeller 2006, p. 76)

Consider, for example, as the corresponding hermeneutic perspective the fitting illustration of the Taoist sage portrayed in Verse 2 of Tao Te Ching that paradoxically leads best by 'teaching no speaking' since even simple language over-generalizes the particular in its attempts at offering grand-historical narratives of the 10,000 changing human behaviors and attitudes:

> [T]he sage goes about doing nothing, teaching no-talking.
> The ten thousand things rise and fall without cease.
> Creating, yet not.
> Working, yet not taking credit.

The obscure statement "To teach no talking" thus breaks through or discloses the linguistic and conceptual limits of the false classifications that hinder its stated ultimate goal: *wu wei* (given a gamut of translations, including but not limited to pure effectiveness, nonaction, active nonstriving, and action without intent, that compositely suggest the abiding theme of non-friction with the cosmic Tao). Moreover, when the sage teaches no talking, as a likely result of his political minimalism, the people say 'we did it,' thus presuming the sage refraining from political paternalism led those most immediately affected to accomplish the particular tasks they deem necessary with the specific resources, talents, and energy they have voluntarily chosen to expend (Schwartz 1975, pp. 65–66).

As further examples of *wu wei* rendered practical, Taoism contains a diverse array of cryptic but nonetheless normative lessons for critical self-reflection gleaned from simple observations of the natural world. As the most common instance, the consistent use of water as the exemplification of humility expresses the Taoist notion of passively conforming to one's holistically constituted environment rather than retroactively seeking to dominate it. Taoism seeks to overcome the reductionist character of language by dissuading attempts to force the descriptions of persons, social interaction, and even grand cosmic design into totalizing classification schemes. As a Taoist aphorism for the most effective model of ruling, the *Tao Te Ching* asks: 'How is it that the sea is the king of one hundred streams?' With non-imposing submission as the unifying strand to the implied cosmic, social, and moral-practical order presumed for the success of *wu wei* to achieve non-friction with the *Tao,* the text tersely answers its own riddle via the humble lesson on filling natural voids: 'By lying below them [the one hundred streams],' the sea reigns supreme.

As the initial building blocks for a normative ethic built upon the edifice of the Taoist preference for negative dialectics, we should likely not expect much confidence in concerted efforts by the elite strata to filter-down their wisdom nor expect large scale popular movements to generate solidarity among the masses. Consider at the simplest level what such a Taoist affront on language by the *Zhuangzi* says about the prospect of any type of collaborative discourse oriented to mutual understanding between two of more dialogical partners:

> There is a famous passage in which Zhuang asks: "If you and I have a disputation, and you defeat me…are you then really in the right? Or, if I win…am I really right and you really wrong?" He goes on to show that appealing to a third party to arbitrate solves nothing. How can we tell if his arbitration is correct? (Elvin 1986, p. 345)

The apparent shock value of denying the sort of efficacy of moral-practical discourse that most would regard as daily practice when disputes about competing directions are resolved, or a common framework for developing a new relationship is established, leads the listener to reflect on the endless contingencies that could thwart success and render plausible this case of limitless regress. Perhaps one of the three parties, including the arbitrator could have an inadequate competence, may lack the relevant experience, or may superimpose the wrong assumption of social roles upon the wrong parties. As a specific remedy to potential pathologies of language posed here by the problem of infinite regress, Confucian proprieties are the usual target of its own dialectical development. In contrast, a Taoist moral culture of humility, silent reserve, and absolute indifference is called upon to replace Confucian rituals, formalized linguistic proprieties, and the internal Old and New School ongoing conflicts over the Heavenly Mandate versus the *shih* advisor as supreme arbitrator.

> [T]he vision that forms the basis for Zhuang Zhou's dissatisfaction with the human world and human understanding is of a natural wholeness of life, sentiment, and thought that has somehow been fragmented by civilization, morality, and language. Institutions, beliefs, and rigorously formulated arguments are not so much wrong as grotesque deformations that embody in lopsided form small parts of what is good or true. (Elvin 1986, p. 347)

The skeptical and often apologetic tone of Taoist philosophy of language nonetheless remains fully within the realm of the axial period by virtue of rigorous critique levied toward all aspects of lived experience, particularly given the looming civilizational crisis for how to survive in the context of constant warfare. Taoism thus comes closest to positive proposals for active inaction when prescribing long hermetic periods of meditative withdrawing from society only thereafter to execute the unconscious channeling of one's internal peace when re-immersed among others in society on the brink of collapse.

Institutionalized measures to ensure such efficacy also border on excess, for instance, via the use of the *Tao Te Ching* as a conduit for private mysticism leading to the norm of 10,000 meditatively outward recitations of the *Tao Te Ching* as the requisite practice for extending one's *ch'i/qi* (literally, vital energy or living breath) to immortalized harmony with the eternal *dao*. However, these mystical and ritualistic means of willed self-renunciation are also coupled with calls for very practical political reform entailing the return to a propriety-less society that seeks to disenchant the theistic and/or potentially opportunistic heavenly mandates of Confucian ritual.

2.21 Why Jaspers? Why Reset Political Theory to the Onset of the Axial Age? Revisiting Habermas's Critique of Heidegger's History of Being

Despite the array of pitfalls that Taoist doctrine shows mutual understanding poses in all of its foreseen and unforeseen obstacles, we should be wary of taking the naturalistic analogies of a mere disclosure of being too far in the cynical direction. Most importantly, we should avoid the desire merely to fault Taoism as falling prey to the related pitfalls of Heideggarian ontology, deep ecology, and/or postmodern critiques of modernity. For, in doing so, we would lose the axial character that Habermas, Jaspers, Eisenstadt, and Bellah (among others) ascribe to Taoism as among the great traditions of the Axial Period. If we are to push the negative critique of language too far, we might also lose the reflexive perspective that Taoist critique offers and collapse back into pre-theoretical primordial myth that axial traditions purportedly replaced. In addition, if we are to collapse our positive endorsement of Taoism into exactly the domain of arbitrariness it attempted to shed as just another philosophical school, perhaps akin to the Legalism mentioned above, that takes a defeatist approach to the ongoing warfare by conceding strategic instrumental reason, and its attendant 'might makes right' bureaucratic state, as the hapless fate of deterministic cosmos devoid of any transcendent purpose. Habermas, taking Heidegger's personal, philosophical, and political failures as his illustrative case, appeals to the disastrous consequences of either dismissing or reversing the moral-practical commitment to the prospects for mutual learning made possible by the Axial Period:

> *Reason which disclaims itself* is easily tempted to merely borrow the authority, and the air, of a sacred that has been deprived of its core and become anonymous. With Heidegger, devotion [*andacht*] mutates to become remembrance [*Andenken*]. But there is no new insight to be gained by having the day of the Last Judgment evaporate to an undetermined event in the history of being. If posthumanism is to be fulfilled in by the return to the archaic beginnings *before* Christ and *before* Socrates, the hour of religious kitsch has come….*Profane* but *nondefeatist* reason, by contrast, has too much respect for the glowing embers, rekindled time and again by the issue of theodicy, to offend religion. It knows that the profanation of the sacred begins with those world religions which disenchanted magic, overcame myth, sublimated sacrifice, and disclosed the secret. Thus, it [philosophy] can keep its distances from religion without ignoring its perspective. (Habermas 2003, p. 113; Habermas 2008a, p. 141–142, 246–247)

Through the express acknowledgement of the inescapable limits of its own claims, as indeed Axial, Taoism never loses the axial dimensions of heterodox center to periphery critique, a radically decentered approach to political rule, and a forthright embrace of the reflective tensions between the transcendence and the mundane:

> One route by which a multidimensional reason that is not exclusively fixated on its reference to the objective world can achieve a self-critical awareness of its boundaries is through a reconstruction of its own genesis that enables it to catch up with itself, as it were, and to overcome fixations. In the process, post-metaphysical thinking does not restrict itself to the heritage of Western metaphysics but also reconfirms its internal relationship to those world religions whose origins, like those of ancient philosophy, date back to the middle of the first millennium before Christ, i.e. to what Jaspers called the "Axial Age." For the religions that have their roots in this period made the cognitive leap from mystical narratives to a logos that differentiates between essence and appearance in a very similar way to Greek philosophy…The complex web of inheritance cannot be disentangled solely along the lines of a history of being, as Heidegger claimed. (Habermas 2008a, pp. 141–142)

With the aforementioned passages as our guidelines for what constitutes axial status as a great world religion, Taoism maintains its axial character by retaining some political teaching (Bellah 2011, p. 439) even if ambivalent in its competing recommendations of bare concern for survival mixed with charges for absolute worldly indifference as its unique axial mode of offering a minimalist species-ethic still directed to universalized salvation. In the hermeneutic dimensions, the quasi-negative cosmology of the *Zhuangzi* and *Tao Te Ching* called into question every given reality whereas the hermeneutic rituals tied to the *Tao Te Ching* of repetitious oral meditations ultimately express a performative hope in yielding internalized moral-practical self-transformation. In light of the wider prevalence of inter-Axial heterodoxy within the Sino-context of vacillating scope of the Middle Kingdom, Taoism itself participates in the Axial Age as a heterodox and peripheral critique of the predominating Confucian, Legalist, and Mohist schools (Bellah 2011, p. 452). In addition, there are hints of the syncretic extension of axial universalization even in spite of the apparent quietism of *wu wei* which contains an activist component when the sage teaches no talking, the people must undergo the moral learning only fully achieved when transforming themselves.

As a possible instance of the inescapable sociality of human biology, the Taoist problematic loss of a primitive utopianism thus contains an inherently axial salvific impulse. By means of returning to self-sustaining individuals and internally closed agrarian subsistence communities, it does not run much risk of ecumenically global aspirations for concrete institutionalization. On the one hand, the normative order retains the primacy of self-preservation if we read the *Tao Te Ching* as a survival manual for the warring states period (Bellah 2011, p. 454). On the other hand, when sages teach-no-talking, we also presume the masses listen, even if as non-elites they never read, recite, or encounter the sacred corpus of texts, the charge to listen entails that nature could address us in a second-personal way as a text might. We thus radicalize axial universalism potentially even to extend to members of the non-linguistic community (Bellah 2011, p. 455). Therefore, the Taoist liminal position of regarding ritual as the onset/way of calamity retains its consistency. If elite contrivances are explicitly taken as the only means of species transcendence, we ought to hold little hope of translation into common vernacular (Bellah 2011, p. 454).

Since Taoism on multiple fronts retains it axial character, we thus ought to remain skeptical of the attempts of contemporary postmodernism to champion it (and any other purportedly non-humanist world religion, such as some questionable readings of Buddhism) as an ally of deep ecology, anti-humanism, and/or post-modern relativism. In addition, along such aberrant anti-humanist Taoist hermeneutics include other reductive schools. Treating social-scientific materialism or biologically determined naturalism as purportedly the only rational interpretation of the human species runs similar risks of grand-theoretical closure. With these alluringly comprehensive third-person exhaustive descriptions, each characterizes as triumphant the successes of the technological age.

Along these lines of argument, both Jaspers and Eisenstadt appeal to the pioneering work of the predominant evolutionary socio-biologists J.P. Wilson and A. Portmann of their respective ages, on the capacity for what Wilson terms meta-relations. While Eisensadt employs these references to highlight dimensions of species transcendence, Jaspers notes the relevant contribution to the historicity of our species self-understanding. As a twofold theory that evades third person reductionism, Wilson and Portmann (as referenced below by Eisenstadt) provide a socio-biological and evolutionary basis for Habermas's second-person performative attitude requisite for moral-practical universalization:

> [A]mong those primates that we call human beings the primary bond extends over a longer period of time among other primates; and the pair relation, possibly correlated with a different pattern of sexual receptivity, is also more extended and possibly more intense. While each relationship is biologically determined and displays adaptive advantages, their co-existence results in an unforeseen and non-biological factor—the relation between the two relations, which I call the meta-relation, or the relational design….[E]xistence in the meta-relation gives a man the knowledge of his own being by subjecting and conditioning his being to the being of others. This applies equally to man the individual and to man as society or community. (Eisenstadt 2003a, p. 167)

As the above statements echo the Habermasian discursive commitment to co-originality of individual and social autonomy via Mead's coined statement of 'individuation proceeding through processes of socialization,' we also find in Wilson the rudiments of a socio-biological basis to Habermas's unfailing commitment to the pragmatic presuppositions of discourse as the weakly transcendental conditions for successful communicative action:

> Man's knowledge of the meta-relation is embodied by him, and for him, in the forms of the imperative we now call the promise and the taboo. These are the objective knowledge or re-presentation of the meta-relational design. They constitute the "minimum shared presupposition" that allows isolated, individual, instinctive men to understand one another….With his reason he has a sense of being; without his reason he suffers from an absence of a sense of being. It is in this sense, surely that we understand Hobbesian man to have been living in a state of nature, a state to which we fear a return. For there is no suggestion that Hobbesian man was biologically unsound, only that he is socially unsound; no suggestion that his emotions are invalid, only that he has no reason. (Eisenstadt 2003a, p. 167)

Eisenstadt thus aligns Wilson's meta-relational critique of the Legalist/Hobbesian first-person strategic self-preservation with the ethical-moral achievement that, for Eisenstadt, initiates our capacity for axial reflection. The requisite boundaries are drawn between the descriptively given mundane as is and the prescriptively modal transcendent as it could be. In comparison, Jaspers associates these same precarious qualities tied to human embodiment and socialization that Portmann highlights as yet another variant on the 'individuation via processes of socialization' meta-relational view of human nature.

> [Portmann] draws attention to the following: The newborn infant is different from all other mammals: His sense organs are developed, his brain- and body-weight are much higher than is the case with apes—and yet, by comparison, he is a pre-mature birth in the sense of being completely helpless. The first year of life in the human requires the maturing of functions which, in other mammals, mature *before* birth. Man lives his first year in the world, although—measured against the newborn animal—he ought to be continuing his intra-uterine growth. For instance, his spine acquires its S-shape through sitting up and standing. How does this come about? As the result of an instinctive urge and the imitation of adults, fostered by the latter's interest and encouragement; in every case, the historically determined environment is a co-factor in inducing the first step toward physical maturity. The spirit is already operative, even in the biological realm itself. (Jaspers 1953, p. 38)

Therefore, what Portmann casts as unique to our species can lend credence to Jaspers' defense of the co-original emergence of our species biology with our irreducibly post-axial historical/spiritual self-understanding.

While Enlightenment confidence in the deliverance of the social and biological sciences is often viewed as leading to moral maturity in the face of an uncaring and/

or indifferent universe, the Taoist notion of epistemic humility reverses the framework of investigation. After all, since only humans can express indifference, would that capacity also entail that what we are really presented with are two options, or spins—one tending towards transcendence and one not—on what Charles Taylor calls Jamesian open space (2007, p. 551)? Taoist scholar H.G. Moeller, although he often moves precisely in the anti-humanist direction I want to reject, seems at least to concur this much:

> In social interaction people communicate with each other approvingly or disapprovingly—these are the two "poles" of talking to another. Of course they are different, but the two attitudes constitute the frame of social exchange. So, while they are certainly different from each other, they are not entirely separate. They are the necessary opposites that make it possible for language to *proceed*, for talk to go on...From the perspective of the sage, each of the two different communicational attitudes—acceptance and rejection—are equally important for communication to take place and continue. (Moeller 2006, p. 105)

On the Taoist view of the sage, the equal significance, or unity that occurs in the opposition between the two poles, requires the sage to remain impartial and indifferent in all matters of moral concern. Moeller, despite offering a whole chapter to support his anti-humanist reading of the *Tao Te Ching*, finds the human and nonhuman nature distinction unavoidable:

> In nonhuman nature there is no morality to be observed. Winter is not more "evil" than summer, it is just colder. In the human realm, however, moral distinctions can easily turn antagonistic. Thus, a complementary distinction can become adversarial. If the sage-rulers would be partial, they would violate the balance in society and become antagonistic themselves. Therefore they refrain from moral judgments. By not taking part in moral communication and communication about right and wrong, the rulers prevent these communications from turning violent. Their neutrality prevents a partisan struggle. (Moeller 2006, pp. 106–107)

Particularly in the context of the Warring States Period, partiality of judgment could be perceived on the part of the ruled as license for ongoing conflict. And, as Moeller concedes, we cannot help but read the *Tao Te Ching* in the appropriate context of the Warring States Period.

We can conclude with a potential application to both Habermas and Taylor's recent endorsement of our post-secular age that has come about in a pluralist context where most parties are likely to remain permanent minorities. Despite their very distinct philosophical aims and comportments, they agree that those that question the presence of a transcendent order are not the only 'rational' voices. To assume the opposed verdict that openness to transcendence is characterized as irrational would be to foreclose the framing conditions mentioned above. For communicative discourse to proceed, an unbiased framework for open argumentative justification must allow for either acceptance or rejection as a second-person unforced commitment from the other. To privilege one over the other in the name of avoiding childish immaturity is to fall prey to the false ideology of the self-deliverance of scientific materialism that merely falls into the dogmatic errors of which Taoists warned against. As an effective illustration of over-stretching the limits of language, a negative verdict on the mere possibility of relational transcendence contradicts itself performatively as it reasserts the framing conditions for reaching its own conclusions (Taylor 2007, pp. 561–566; Bowman 2009).

In brief summation, not only must we be wary of the avowedly rational way Western academics choose to recast Confucius as a secular humanist, we should also resist casting Lao Tzu (or Buddha) as among the earliest advocates of either deep ecology or post-modern rejections of humanism. Although such an immanently materialist, skeptical, and cynically anti-humanist frame for how one views the universalist extension of moral obligations beyond just the human community carries the appeal of radical human renunciation to the point of subordination to the wider ecological community, it also loses the species-historical frame that Jaspers, Habermas, and Eisenstadt defend as an indispensable dimension of the onset of the axial period. Therefore, according to Jaspers' recommendations, although he encourages heterodox movements as necessary for ongoing axial critique, we should also avoid tendencies to read off Confucian and Taoist schools in these fashionable overtly humanist or overtly anti-humanist manners of gross over-simplification:

> It is often held that Lao-Tzu conceived of the *tao* as beyond good and evil, while Confucius moralized the *tao*. But it is more accurate to say that when Confucius enters on the worldly task of creating order in the community through knowledge of good and evil, he leaves the realm beyond good and evil strictly intact. He does not take the community as absolute. For him the Encompassing is a background, not a theme to work with; it is the limit and foundation to be considered with awe, not the immediate task. The essential difference is the difference between Lao-Tzu's direct way to the *tao* and Confucius' detour by way of the human order, hence the divergent practical consequences of the same fundamental view.... Though the two philosophers look in opposite directions, they stand on the same common ground. Their unity has been embodied by great historic figures, not in a philosophy that systematically embraced both sets of teachings, but in the Chinese wisdom of a life illumined by thought. (Jaspers 1957, pp. 59–60)

Although the Taoist view on language therefore includes pointing towards a more primal affective, pre-linguistic, and instinctual foreground, with the important insight that linguistic expression cannot positively express the very background conditions of its own possibility, this is not to say that Confucius confined his thought strictly to a this-worldly mundane order. In addition, since they offer competing views of axial learning and collective species reflection, it would be foolish to write off Taoism as a pre-axial and pre-theoretic lapse back into mythological reflection. In accord with Jaspers' inclusion of Confucius and Lao Tzu among the great axial figures, they nonetheless remain committed to the priority of the philosophical life led in accord with the imperative of ongoing critical self-reflection.

2.22 Brief Speculative Conclusion for Inter-Axial Discourse: Breadth Versus Toleration?

Li notes that Chinese cultures often use the term breadth as a normative disposition offered as an alternative to the Western notion of tolerance. Breadth connotes genuine understanding that seeks common ground while preserving differences. In contrast, tolerance more minimally requires one to put up with differences they would likely prefer not to understand (1999, p. 159). Toleration also presumes that civilizations remain distinct entities rendered immune from the dialectical interpenetration. Any significant differences risk relativizing epistemic claims to truth when a tolerant attitude of epistemic neutrality entails full dismissal of the rational content to spiritual claims. Consider as an extreme the critiques made by Horkheimer upon toleration—as perhaps proving catastrophic for religion—according to his *Eclipse of Reason* (1974, p. 18):

> All the consequences [tied to the neutrality of formalized reason tending toward the death of speculative reason in its claims to epistemic truth] were contained in the bourgeois idea of tolerance, which is ambivalent. On the one hand, tolerance means freedom from the rule of dogmatic authority; on the other hand, it furthers an attitude of neutrality toward all spiritual content, which is thus surrendered to relativism. Each cultural domain preserves its 'sovereignty' with regard to universal truth. The pattern of the social division of labor is automatically transferred to the life of the spirit, and this division of the realm of culture is a corollary to the replacement of universal objective truth by formalized, inherently relativist reason. (Horkheimer 1974, p. 19)

In potential reply on behalf of Habermas, his recent procedural *and* epistemic amendments to his views on the proper public role of spiritual claims places the burden upon non-believers to aid in the translation of norms and concepts from the language particular to each Axial tradition into the language of public discourse. However, in light of the warnings against impartial neutrality issued by Horkheimer, it would seem hard to ignore the likelihood that taking the lessons of a distinct axial breakthrough seriously would invariably leave some stamp of reflexive shaping upon the non-believer (or discursive participant*s* engaged in inter-axial competition).

For example, lessons we can draw about transcivilizational discourse from each of Confucianism, Taoism, and Buddhism respectively include dialectical forms tending toward both a descriptive and prescriptive preference for breadth over toleration. We find breadth in the Realist, Mohist, and Classicist dynamics feeding into Confucian name rectification. We also find it in the dialectical interplay over the role of the Tao in Confucian and Taoist thought that leads Taoists into the humble concession of the sheer impossibility of holistic epistemic mastery of not just a cosmic vision but cosmic vision*s* in the plural. Lastly, the dialectic between Hindu and Buddhist perspectives upon the karmic reflexivity lead one likely to expect empathy to ensue as an appropriate affective imprint left upon those engaged in right speech.

Taking our lessons from S.N. Eisenstadt, the Great axial traditions have borne perennial witness to ongoing struggles for influence between core and periphery, often even shifting what would constitute the central axis over distinct periods. The axial frame of reference we turn to instead of a decided preference for methodological atheism would begin with a concession to Onuma Yasuaki that we now (and may always have) live in a multi-polar world wherein spiritual commitments constitute the core motives behind the expression of one's rational, social, political, spiritual, and material capacities.

For instance, in the spirit of Habermas's enhanced epistemic burdens upon the listener, we might seriously consider what it would be to make Chinese Mandarin the universal language of the species. Or, as stated by revered world religion scholar Huston Smith:

> As there is no measure by which to rank-order civilizations qualitatively, we shall content ourselves with quantity, where numbers do tell an objective story. Unlike Europe or even India, China held together, forging a political structure which at its height embraced a third of the human race. The Chinese Empire lasted under a succession of dynasties over two thousand years, a stretch of time that makes the empires of Alexander, Caesar, and Napolean look ephemeral. If we multiply the number of years that empire lasted by the number of people it embraced in an average year, it emerges quantitatively as the most impressive social institution that human beings have devised. (Smith 1986, p. 188)

Since we have experimentally extended Habermas's dialectic one step further to the tensions between the mundane and transcendent orders historically faced by Eastern philosophical account of discourse, what are Western philosophers to make of these trends? For starters, if a dialectical openness to Eastern contributions entails an openness to all spiritual contributions to the public sphere, Western societies might come to view Christophobia, Islamophobia, and Anti-Semitism as their own distinctive pathologies of reason by making the initial step (particularly in Europe) beyond the notion that religion is irrational whereas science will always reign as the harbinger of reason (Taylor 2007, pp. 556–566; Nemoianu 2006, p. 38; Habermas 2006, pp. 50–52). Moreover, insofar as the four Eastern traditions typically moved into some prevailing spiritual context and rarely ever interacted with subjects having no spiritual commitments, the secularism commonly associated with Enlightenment reason, with its highest expression in contemporary Europe, then can gain a critical perspective on itself as the historical exception to the rule rather than the only viable mode of social organization.[5]

In addition, each of the Eastern traditions has much to contribute in terms of debunking unchallenged (purported objectivity of the scientific materialism?) characteristics of the Western secular tradition. For starters, Confucianism questions the certitude of strategic mean-ends calculations characteristic of instrumental reason by reminding us that any viable normative semantics will always regard the objectivity of judgments as a socially conferred propriety. The Taoist offers a deconstruction of the objectivity of scientific framing by presenting the helpful insight that both natural and social sciences cannot provide the background conditions for their own justification. This is something it must presuppose as a matter that should not be hastily regarded as a foregone conclusion. And finally, Buddhist notions of right speech reminded us that epistemological truths carry with them an essential tie to existential and moral well-being, or more minimally, the desired alleviation of *dukkha*.

While the critical theory tradition with its self-proclaimed goal of human emancipation clearly has the renewal of humanity within its aspirations, the Eastern views also fared comparatively well on this humanistic norm. Confucianism seeks social order, Taoism harmony with the Tao via humble reserve, Hinduism with liberation from craving, and Buddhism the alleviation of aggregate human suffering. In the end, perhaps much to the chagrin of devout critical theorists, even Habermas

[5] Habermas notes "In Teheran, a colleague once said to me that the comparative study of cultures and religious sociology surely suggested that *European Secularization* was the odd one out among the various developments—and that it ought to be corrected" (2006, pp. 37–38). Ratzinger likewise refers to this as an intriguing thesis (2006, pp. 75–76).

now suggests that the transnational longing for a renewed sense of human solidarity would more likely come through a public openness to the expressively transformative potentials of discourses of axial transcendence than via the naïve ideological assumption of an impending secular cosmopolitanism. Therefore, in a plural and truly transnational public sphere, beyond just a dialectical interplay between secular and non-secular Western views, we might expect something closer to a gradual dialectical assimilation of *Axial traditions* (emphasis on the plural) rather than an outright upheaval in each or an overwhelming reformation into one.[6] It will be the task of the next chapter to consider how this inter-Axial dialectic continues to play out in the three major Abrahamic Axial traditions: Judaism, Christianity, and Islam.

References

Asad, Talal. 1993. *Formations of the secular: Christianity, Islam, modernity*. Stanford: Stanford University Press.

Bellah, Robert. 2011. *Religion and human evolution: From the paleolithic to the axial age*. Cambridge: Belknap Press of Harvard University Press.

Bowman, Jonathan. 2009. Extending Habermas and Ratzinger's dialectics of secularization: Non-western discursive influences on faith and reason in a postsecular age. *Forum Philosophicum* 16 (1): 39–56.

Buber, Martin. 1970/1923. *I and Thou*. Trans: Walter Kaufmann. New York: Scribner.

Cabezon, J. 1994. *Buddhism and language*. Albany: SUNY.

Cheng, Chung-ying. 2000. Confucian reflection on Habermasian approaches: Moral rationality and inter-humanity. In *Perspectives on Habermas,* ed. Lewis Hahn, 195–233. Chicago: Open Court.

Clark, Kelly. 2005. The gods of Abraham, Isaiah, and Confucius. *Dao: A Journal of Comparative Philosophy* 5 (1): 109–136.

Donald, Merlin. 2012. An evolutionary approach to culture: Implications for the study of the axial age. In *The axial age and its consequences,* ed. Robert H. Bellah and Hans Joas, 47–76. Cambridge: Belknap Press of Harvard University.

Dumont, Louis. 1975. On the comparative understanding of non-modern civilizations. *Daedelus: Special Issue on Wisdom Revelation and Doubt: Perspectives on the First Millennium B.C* 104 (2): 153–172.

Eisenstadt, S. N. 2003a. *Comparative civilizations and multiple modernities. Part I*. Leiden: Brill.

Eisenstadt, S. N. 2003b. *Comparative civilizations and multiple modernities. Part II*. Leiden: Brill.

Eisenstadt, S. N., 2006. *The great revolutions and the civilizations of modernity*. Leiden: Brill.

Elvin, Mark. 1986. Was there a transcendental breakthrough in China? In *The origins and diversity of axial age civilations,* ed. S. N. Eisenstadt, 325–359. Albany: State University of New York Press.

Gopnik, Alison. 2009. *The philosophical baby: What children's minds tell us about truth, love, and the meaning of life*. New York: Farrar, Strauss, and Giroux.

Habermas, J. 1979. *Communication and the evolution of society*. Trans: Thomas McCarthy. Boston: Beacon.

Habermas, J. 1987. *Theory of Communicative Action*, vol. 2. Lifeworld and system: a critique of functionalist reason. Trans: Thomas McCarthy. Boston: Beacon.

[6] Taylor calls this the nova effect in Western Christianity and admits that extending such an analysis beyond one national culture would be something more akin to a supernova effect (2007, p. 300).

Habermas, J. 2003. *The future of human nature*. Cambridge: Polity.

Habermas, Jurgen. 2008a. *Between naturalism and religion: Philosophical essays*. Trans: Ciarin Cronin. Cambridge: Polity

Habermas, J. 2008b. Notes on a post-secular society. *SignandSight,* June 18.

Habermas, J., and J. Ratzinger. 2006. *Dialectics of secularization: On reason and religion*. San Francisco: Ignatius.

Heesterman, J. C. 1986. Ritual, revelation, and the axial age. In *The origins and diversity of axial age civilations,* ed. S. N. Eisenstadt, 393–406. Albany: State University of New York Press.

Horkheimer, Max. 1974. *The eclipse of reason*. New York: Continuum Publishing Company.

Hsu, Cho-Yun. 1986. Historical conditions of the emergence and crystallization of the confucian system. In *The origins and diversity of axial age civilizations,* ed. S. N. Eisenstadt, 306–324. Albany: State University of New York Press.

Inada, Kenneth. 2006. *A Buddhist response to the nature of human rights*. In Applied ethics: a multicultural approach, eds. May, Collins-Chobanian, and Wong, 133–142. Upper Saddle River: Pearson.

Jaspers, K. 1953. *The origin and goal of history*. Trans: Michael Bullock. New Haven: Yale University Press.

Jaspers, K. 1957. Socrates, Buddha, Confucius, Jesus: The paradigmatic individuals. In *the great philosophers,* ed. Hannah Arendt, vol. I. Trans: Ralph Manheim. San Diego: Harcourt Brace Jovanovich.

Joas, Hans. 2012. *The axial age debate as religious discourse*. In The axial age and its consequences, eds. Robert Bellah and Hans Joas, 9–29. Cambridge: Belknap Press of Harvard University Press.

Kulke, Hermann. 1986. The historical background of India's axial age. In *The origins and diversity of axial age civilizations,* ed. S. N. Eisenstadt, 374–392. Albany: State University of New York Press.

LaFarge, Michael. 1998. Recovering the *Tao-te-ching's* original meaning: Some remarks on historical hermeneutics. In *Lao Tzu and the Tao-te-Ching,* ed. Livia Kohn and Michael LaFarge, 255–276. Albany: SUNY.

Laozui. 1997. *Tao te ching*. Trans: Gia-Fu Feng and Jane English. New York: Vintage Books.

Li, C. 1999. *The Tao encounters the west: Explorations in comparative philosophy*. Albany: SUNY.

Moeller, Hans-Georg. 2006. *The philosophy of the Daodejing*. New York: Columbia University Press.

Nemoianu, V. 2006. The church and the secular establishment: A philosophical dialogue between Joseph Ratzinger and Jurgen Habermas. *Logos* 9 (2): 17–42.

Obeyesekere, Gananath. 2012. The Buddha's meditative trance: Visionary knowledge, aphoristic thinking, and axial age rationality in early Buddhism. In *The axial age and its consequences,* ed. Robert H. Bellah and Hans Joas, 126–145. Cambridge: Belknap Press of Harvard University.

Pinsent, Andrew. 2012. *The second person perspective in aquinas's ethics: Virtues and gifts*. New York: Routledge.

Prabhupada, A.C. Bhaktivedanta Swami. 1997. *Bhagavad-Gita: As it is*. Los Angeles: The Bhaktivedanta Book Trust.

Roetz, Heiner. 2012. A challenge to historicism or an explanatory device of civilizational analysis? With a look at the normative discourse in axial age china. In *The axial age and its consequences,* ed. Robert H. Bellah and Hans Joas, 248–273. Cambridge: Belknap Press of Harvard University.

Schwartz, Benjamin. 1975. Transcendence in ancient China. *Daedelus: Special Issue on Wisdom Revelation and Doubt: Perspectives on the First Millennium B.C.* 104 (2): 57–68.

Schwartz, Benjamin. 1998. Thought of the Tao-te-Ching. In *Lao Tzu and the Tao-te-Ching,* ed. Livia Kohn and Michael LaFarge, 189–210. Albany: SUNY.

Sen, Amartya. 1999. *Development as freedom*. New York: Anchor Books.

Shils, Edward.1986. Some observations on the place of intellectuals in max weber's sociology, with special reference to Hinduism. In *The origins and diversity of axial age civilizations,* ed. S. N. Eisenstadt, 427–452. Albany: State University of New York Press.

Shulman, David.1986. Asvatthaman and Brhannada: Brahmin and kingly paradigms in the sanskrit epic. In *The origins and diversity of axial age civilations,* ed. S. N. Eisenstadt, 407–426. Albany: State University of New York Press.

Smith, Huston. 1986. *The world's religions: Our great wisdom traditions*. New York: HarperCollins.

Tambiah, Stanley J. 1986. The reflexive and institutional achievements of early Buddhism. In *The origins and diversity of axial age civilizations,* ed. S. N. Eisenstadt, 453–471. Albany: State University of New York Press.

Taylor, C. 2007. *A secular age*. Cambridge: Belknap.

Thapar, Romila. 1975. Ethics, religion, and social protest in the first millennium B.C. in northern India *Daedelus: Special Issue on Wisdom Revelation and Doubt: Perspectives on the First Millennium B.C.* 104 (2): 119–132.

Wei-Ming, Tu. 1986. The structure and function of the confucian intellectual in ancient China. In *The origins and diversity of axial age civilizations,* ed. S. N. Eisenstadt, 360–373. Albany: State University of New York Press.

Xianglong, Z. 2004. Heidegger's view of language and the Lao-Zhuang view of *Dao*-Language. In *Chinese philosophy in an era of globalization,* ed. R. Wang, 195–213. Albany: SUNY.

Chapter 3
Jasper's Axial Prophesy Fulfilled? The Origin and Return of Biblical Religion, Abrahamic Hermeneutics, and the Second Person

Abstract This chapter will focus on Jasper's prediction that post-WWII global secularization trends will soon be matched by a resurgence of Biblical religion. I focus first on the Hebrew tetragramaton YHWH and the associated experiential backdrop of the Sinai covenant and Exodus event. From there, I trace second person narratives back to the universal species-ethic of Hebrew Biblical genealogies. I frame Horkheimer and Adorno's appeal to the non-utterance of God's name as akin to their refusal to claim achievement of ultimate justice. Applied to the Christian case, Jaspers' will follow suit in his resistance to the doctrine of Christ's incarnation. In reply, I follow a non-Hellenistic reading of the logos that uses the accounts of the Sermon on the Mount to couch the logos in terms of second person promissory narratives. I adapt Habermas's method for critically appropriating traditionally Judeo-Christian theological concepts communicatively, highlighting three examples. Finally, in the Muslim case, I confer Islam axial status by virtue of its secondary breakthrough from originally Judaic and Christian origins. I recount Talal Asad's emphasis on the embodied *habitus* of ritual experience and look to the Muslim jurisprudence of Abdullah An-Naim as an instance of an inherently Islamic call for religious liberty. Lastly, I turn to Rawls for hints at how an overlapping consensus among Axial traditions could be applied to international jurisprudence, specifically focusing on Islam.

Keywords Theodore Adorno · Abdullah An-Naim · Talal Asad · Axial age · Biblical religion · Critical theory · Jurgen Habermas · Max Horkheimer · Karl Jaspers · Logos · John Rawls · Second person · Eric Voegelin · Yahweh

3.1 Introduction

As a way to continue to address the prospects for mutual understanding between all great axial traditions, we will offer an internal reconstruction of the distinct social imaginary comprising each Abrahamic one. Taylor's *A Secular Age* (2007) had taken on the enormous task of reconstructing such a narrative for the axial context

J. Bowman, *Cosmoipolitan Justice*, Studies in Global Justice 15,
DOI 10.1007/978-3-319-12709-5_3

of Latin Christendom. In comparison, the enterprise I undertake will carry motives of both grander and lesser scale. As for the bigger picture, I agree with the litany of critiques that the focus on Latin Christendom proves too limited. It misses the colonial dimensions of secularization, reads global secular dynamics as inherently tied to Christianity, and overlooks significant inter-axial dynamics of secularization processes.

As for the narrowing of focus, if Taylor's project took 874 pages, we must streamline our survey in a way that permits inclusion of secularizing movements outside of Latin Christendom without going into the degree of detail his seminal study provided. My interest on Abrahamic hermeneutics utilizes contemporary work on second person narrative perspectives as the limiting qualifier. This delimitation will thereby open space for the inter-Axial dynamics of boundless communication originally laid out by Jaspers under the rubric of what he terms Biblical religion.

While Taylor's *A Secular Age* has been both heralded and critiqued by commentators for its maverick style most acutely branded as existential historiography, we find close parallels and predecessors in Jaspers' *On the Origin and Goal of Human History* (1953) and Voegelin's multi-volume *Order and History* (1974). Not only does Taylor refer to the axial period as reference point quite frequently, like Jaspers and Voegelin, he admits his purpose to be more genealogical than sheer historical empiricism. Taylor evades Hegelian excesses of offering a grand historical narrative of the species in confining his analysis to Latin Christendom. Unnoticed by many readers, he also concedes in his "Preface" that the book would best be read as a set of inter-locking essays rather than as a tightly knit, analytic, step-by-step deductive argument (p. ix).

When read as existential historiography, the genesis, dialectical interplay, and subsequent transformations of civilizational ideals proceed in a non-linear progression that allows Taylor's openness to multiple modernities to reinforce Voegelin's broader experimentation with multiple world histories. As for the mediation proposed in the present chapter, Jaspers' concept of Biblical religion offers a more comprehensive scope than Latin Christendom at which to start. It serves as an effective bridge to the onset of multiple modernities and the concomitant globalizing trends to be surveyed in the remaining chapters of this project.

3.2 Jaspers on Biblical Religion

Jaspers insightfully predicted at the end of his *The Origin and Goal of History* that post–WWII atheist, existential, secular, and nihilistic trends would be supplanted by a resurgence of what he terms Biblical religion. This movement for him seemed plausible not just as a non-dogmatic return to the civilizational roots of Latin Christendom. Insofar as the emergent global interdependence produced greater philosophical interest and study of the major figures and ideals informing India and China as nascent global powers, the reflexive imprint upon Latin Christendom required making explicit to itself and others the rational basis for its own civilizational order.

In a non-confessional construal that he expressly differentiates from ritual practice and participation in an organized church setting, Jaspers speculates that the Bible will remain a significant locus for hope, inspiration, mourning, lamenting, and reconciliation in the aftermath of such a global civilizational crisis. Jaspers finds in the Abrahamic narratives a source of inter-Axial—ecumenically open—communication that reflected his own nominally Christian upbringing and his WWII experience of constantly protecting his Jewish wife from Nazi pursuers. In particular, as disclosed in personal letters, he found the prophetic writings of *Jeremiah* and the lamentations of the *Psalms* as great sources of consolation, strength, and inspiration during the social despair of the war period. Like Horkheimer, Adorno, and other leading intellectuals, the constant threat of persecution to himself and his family eventually led him to seek asylum outside Germany.

Honing in on the axial period of 800–200 BCE, Jaspers' initial focus was on the prophets and writings of Hebrew Second Temple period in the historical context of the Babylonian exiles. In locating the Hebrew axial breakthrough to universality in this crucial axial shift, I will amend his analyses by tracing out the historically wider communicative resources behind what I will call second person narratives within the Abrahamic traditions. We will follow a much broader Biblical hermeneutic that more substantively contextualizes Jaspers' axial dates. Nonetheless, we will concede to his period of emphasis an important scriptural rejuvenation given the wave of Babylonian exiles (597 BCE, 587 BCE, and 582 BCE) that stirred on transition from temple-mediated ritual sacrifice to enhanced proprietary competition over legitimate Biblical interpretation.

With the impending analysis of the Hebrew tradition from multiple symbolic centers—such as the Adamic covenant, Abrahamic covenant, Sinai covenant, Exodus event, and Davidic monarchy—superadded to the prophetic climax of the exile period, comes the biblical constant of the universalization of the discursive capacities to address God as a you/Thou in the second personal mode (Buber 1970/1923). As a critical theorist emendation of Jaspers' and Buber's original project, I will frame the underlying methodology behind a discursive rendering of Biblical religion as an extension of Horkheimer and Adorno's dialectical critique of the failures of Enlightenment reason (2002/1947).

As a further iteration of Jasper's Biblical religion, we will extend its proliferation of multiple symbolic centers to the particular Christian and Muslim permutations, while nonetheless seeking to trace the second person perspective as an abiding constant. In the Christian case, I constrain the focus to the hermeneutics of the Johannine tradition of Christ as logos in a distinctly non-Hellenistic reading. I also use the accounts of the Sermon on the Mount in the synoptic gospels to reinforce this relational view of the logos as an alternative to its construal as the objectively rational, third-personal, non-discursive, and metaphysical first principle governing the cosmos. I will follow Voegelin's commentaries that encourage rereading John in accord with the axial fulfillment of bridging the communicative gap between humanity and God. Moving into second-generation critical theory, I will recast Habermas's method for critically appropriating traditionally Judeo-Christian theological concepts communicatively within Jaspers' context of Biblical religion.

Finally, in the Muslim case, I agree with the relevant literature conferring Islam axial status, despite historically falling well outside the conventions of the 800–200 BC temporal rubric. By virtue of its secondary breakthrough from originally Judaic and Christian origins, I will lay out the hermeneutic tensions between Habermas's call to subject Islamic scripture to the historical-critical method of interpretation while nonetheless seeking to maintain the orthodox interpretation of the Koran as eternally divine speech (2009, p. 75). We will consider the important contributions of Talal Asad's emphasis on the embodied habitus of ritual experience as a performative dimension to the believers' communicative submission to Gods' call (2003). These lessons from Islam teach us to resist Western tendencies to over-emphasize cognitive and epistemological claims of belief at the expense of ritual practice and corporeal embodiment. In the domain of Muslim jurisprudence, I will look to the work of Abdullah An-Naim to present an instance of a micro-level pragmatic presupposition of religious liberty as derived from sources internal to the Koran (2008). Lastly, I will appeal to John Rawls' treatment of the hypothetical people of Kazanistan as exemplary of what he terms a distinctively Muslim decent consultation hierarchy as candidate for communicative participation in his *Law of Peoples* (1999). I amend Rawls' view drawing upon insights from Taylor that define the goal of inter-Axial communication as ultimately seeking overlapping consensus upon shared norms irrespective of their legal form or background justification (1999).

As for the inclusion of Islam in the loose generalization of Biblical religion, two final points of clarification should suffice. Firstly, while its temporal inception with Muhammad (622 CE for the last Qur'an revelation) far outdates the 800–200 BCE conventional axial dates, Islam retrospectively appropriates Abraham, Moses, Jesus, and the attendant axial prophets emphasized by Jaspers. Insofar as Jaspers aspired to author a non-Christocentric version of world history, we could even say the Muslim re-appropriation of the Abrahamic, Mosaic, and prophetic dimensions of Judaism, reflects the equivalent for Jaspers in the Arabian context what Christ eventually brought about in Latin Christendom. Secondly, growing Muslim scholarly comfort with looking at the Qur'an through critical historical lenses suggests compelling evidence for both Hebrew Biblical and Christian Biblical influences upon its narrative, historical, and doctrinal themes in both synergetic and oppositional second-personal apologetics. For instance, insofar as each axial period provides a salvific view of transcendence that offers the visionary and practical resources for the vast communication of comprehensive civilizational transformation, the Muslim case is unrivaled as the single fastest civilizational reordering of all the axial faiths.

3.2.1 Judaism as the Onset of Biblical Religion: Yahweh, Theopolity, and Second Personal Discourse

Jaspers initially derives what he terms Biblical Religion from the Hebrew canon of scriptures. From these narrative sources, Jaspers seeks to develop an impartial and communicative account of justice to supplant inter-Axial discourse. In the context of my defense of cosmoipolitan justice, we will meld the Judaic covenantal promises, scriptural study, and inter-generational reenactment, with the philosophical overtones of Jaspers' own existential commitments, for a vision of humanity that retains the very real prospect of responsible co-participation with God in shaping history. In evading the charge of an excessively subjective individualism distorting Jaspers' existential reconstruction of Axial Age achievements, he radicalizes individual responsibility in the direction of a robust humanism of species-ethical responsibility. However, given Jaspers' hesitance to ascribe to God first-personal traits, the potential for securing justice as impartial objectivity in judgments about the world, others, and oneself comes at the risk of an over-inflation of individual autonomy. Nonetheless, by freely rejecting or affirming the explicit terms of such covenants, just relations among one's fellow members of humanity retain an inherently communicative dimension of reciprocal responsibility. Since covenants require free volition for their legitimacy, Jaspers grapples with the precise role God will play in his presentation of philosophical faith without running to the other extreme of losing individual autonomy at the Hegelian cost of the unfolding Absolute.

> Jaspers is perfectly right in stressing the inner independence of either partner in personal communication and relationship. This independence is a constituent of true personal correlation; it adds to the latter's intensity rather than weakening it. It has one of its expressions in that (not impersonal, but impartial) *objectivity* only man can afford—in every regard. First 'with regard to' the world (which thus—and thus only—will be thrown into relief and appear as a self-contained context of being). The same holds true with regard to my fellow-being (who will be closer to me in due distance, i.e. when I release and respect him in the otherness of an *alter ego*); and finally even with regard to myself (who can thus become an object of my own concern and a product of my own making). This character of correlation is maintained and enhanced in the covenant of Biblical religion, where both distance and intimacy are given maximal values. (Kaufmann 1957, p. 247, 248)

Jaspers closes his great work *The Origin and Goal of History* with an appeal to the necessary rejuvenation of Biblical religion as among the most potent hopes for the future of global philosophy to secure impartial justice post-WWII. He also presents it as a reservoir of meaning from which one can derive moral norms consistent with the onset of modern subjectivity, responsible communicative interaction among the species, and presupposed reference to a shared world as common objective framing for performative acts of joint attention.

Jaspers' grander reconstructive project would be the extension of this communicative species-ethic also to include other great Axial traditions. In this manner, he evades the charge of Western dogmatism by appeal to hope in the prospect of truly impartial communication that takes the person of the other—specifically, when manifest in Eastern or non-Western guises—within the attendant framing of authentic responsibility and intimacy. As one source of the subjectivity associated with the universalizable achievements of modernity—along with the Indian and Chinese permutations already addressed—he finds in Judaic covenants and rituals a common object of joint attention mediated by respectful difference for the inalienable sovereignty of the alter ego. Jaspers portrays such an assumption as essential for justice to maintain its status as constituting legitimately binding norms in the communicative interaction with another.

We must therefore acknowledge a tension that pervades the communicative ethic of Jaspers by virtue of claiming its substantive roots in the Israelite notion of a personal God (that he ultimately rejects) and persons being created in the image of God as a means for the ascription of boundless species universality. Consider the following remarks of Uffenheimer and Nikiprowetzky as reinforcing the challenge against Jaspers that such an ethical-moral construal of the objective truth of judgments must presume God as a personal being:

> When it is Yahweh's sovereign energy that is working in the world, the authors of the Scriptures use the expression the "Spirit of God" to designate it. The Spirit of God is presented as personal, because it is the reflection of a personal God, although it is not separate from God as a hypostasis. The same can be said of the Word or the Wisdom, concepts that express the absolute reign of God in the world or that specify his rule. (Nikiprowetzky 1975, p. 84)

Such a position can be stated even more directly in terms that concede the anthropomorphic presentation of God as expressing characteristics typical of existentially responsible functioning persons as the basis for a communicative ethic, species morality, and vision of communal justice.

> [T]he anthropomorphic presentation of God is at the very core of *imitation Dei*, which is the basis of biblical ethics….In other words, *imitation Dei*, which is the basis of both individual and collective morality in the Bible and the Midrash, is preconditioned by the mythical and anthropomorphic presentation of God. (Uffenheimer 1986, p. 152)

The conferral of the status of assuming what we have termed a second-personal capacity for reciprocal role taking can also apply to the learned empathetic projections required for Axial traditions. Even those falling outside the scope of Biblical religion—nonetheless are owed these same communicative proprieties by virtue of their humanity.

The hypothetical construct of openness to the prospect of communicating with God from a second person perspective, while not necessarily required as the personal commitment of the reader in order to gain epistemic access to every Hebrew Axial insight, nonetheless must be taken as pragmatic presuppositions behind the authorship of particular texts and even participation in specific rituals. However, we should also heed caution that, in the Hebrew context—while even entertaining the prospect of an organic unity to the cosmos certainly belies the disenchantment characteristic of a post-metaphysical worldview—we also must not err to the opposite extreme. The normative assessment of just, true, or good verdicts from a participant perspective not only belies the outright dismissal of such practices as exercises in divination or as inherently irrational from the outset. In a performative sense, the epistemic license for the ultimate conferral of authority to affirm, to reject, or even to redact the achievements of Biblical religion presumes an active effort on the part of the participant in undertaking the effort to begin to master its complex symbolic themes. My project here is to layout merely sufficient conditions for the conferral of such hermeneutics capacities. Setting a stronger threshold of necessary conditions would likely seem arbitrary and exclusionary in casting judgment upon where precisely to set one's standards.

As an introduction to some of the sufficient conditions for the requisite hermeneutic sensitivity, consider the associated remarks of Uffenheimer on the second-personal qualities of Hebrew ritual. In order to evade likely charges from skeptics bent on rejecting a personal God for philosophical reasons, we must first offer a view of human freedom that evades divine determinism (Darwall 2006).[1] At the other extreme, we must also dissuade practicing adherents from efforts at divination in order to manipulate the divine will. Therefore, the hidden assumption behind responsible participation in co-creating a truly just order would be its constitution as a gift on the part of a free act of interpersonally conferred grace. In other words, hasty rejection of divine co-participation on grounds of overt irrationality, coerced participation, or strategic game-theoretic motives to action oriented to earning one's redemption, circumvent the authenticity of truly voluntary participation:

> Cultic ceremonies such as the sprinkling of blood upon the alter at the offering of certain sacrifices, or breaking the heifer's neck (*Deut.* 21:1–9), etc., aim to restore purity. The effectiveness of these ceremonies is based on the above-mentioned belief about the organic unity of the universe. On the other hand, there are no ceremonies, spells, charms, or magical techniques intended to manipulate divine decisions or to influence the divine will in any way. This is due to the underlying assumption that the pagan ontological continuum has been replaced by a dialogical, voluntary relationship between God and His world. Indeed, the few mantic customs which have survived, such as the priestly questioning of the Urim and Tummim (*Num.* 27:21; *Deut.* 33:8; *I Sam.* 28:30) or the belief that the prophet is able to foresee the future and to disclose hidden facts (*Deut.* 18:9–22; *I Sam.* 9:6, 9, 15) are conceived as a special Divine gift, as the expression of Divine grace to man, remote from any belief in the Promethean faculty of penetrating the divine sphere. (Uffenheimer 1986, p. 158)

While indeed uncharacteristic of the Weberian disenchantment usually associated with critical theory, in order to lend credence to a view of Biblical religion that (in contrast to Jaspers) allows for the prospect of God's co-participation in establishing cosmoipolitan justice, we might consider such a dialogical stance akin to that entertained by Habermas (2002). His characterization of Schwabish mysticism informed his early developments of discourse ethics by supplanting the interaction between first-person and God with a linguistified sacred of first-person and alter ego engaged in communicative action (see my next section on the Christian iteration of Biblical religion for a fuller exposition of this theme). In brief, Habermas rendered discursive and ultimately secularized the idea of a hidden God that reserves the capacity for self-restraint as the very condition for the free interchange of commu-

[1] Although Darwall has recently emerged as the leading authority on the second-person perspective, he has yet to engage in any direct or substantive consideration of the work of Habermas and critical theory in general. Since Darwall has deeply engaged the relevant historical philosophy of the likes of Kant, Fichte, Nietzsche, Buber, Heidegger, and others, this gap in the literature cannot merely be reduced to a caesura in the classical analytic versus continental divide. As for my project, Darwall's most insightful moments come from his historical appeals to Saurez, Grotius, and Pufendorf as potentially reconciling the second personal authority of a divine standpoint with the preservation of individual responsibility—a problem he views as unresolved in Aquinas and classical natural law theories (2013a, pp. 157–221, b, p. 6, 15–17, 84–86). For more on his relevant appeals to Pufendorf, see his earlier (2006, pp. 104–15; 249–52).

nicative agents. More recently, for the socialization of persons that ideally share and possess these same latent capacities, such ritual performances initiated by the Axial Age each offer the unique grounds for the eventual universalization of these species potentials (Habermas, manuscript in progress; Mendieta 2013).[2]

Before addressing the full implications of the inter-Axial dynamics of contemporary conditions of truly boundless potentials for communication, we shall see what would be required to produce a discourse ethics internal to the Hebrew tradition before testing its external applicability to the species as such. I will draw extensively on Eric Voegelin as he seeks to clarify the participatory ethics of the covenantal bond between Yahweh and the Israelites as detailed by his probing commentary on the relevant biblical canon. Insofar as the most frequently cited references to his commentaries stem from Martin Buber, it should also be no surprise that his characteristic agreement with the insights offered by Buber's numerous biblical commentaries and re-translation of the Bible into German will provide much ground for continuing our focus on the second-personal I-Thou dimensions of the Hebrew scriptural canon (Buber 1970). Voegelin's framing of the Israelite experience will also serve as an opportunity to present an inter-axial account of world histories that will both complement and challenge that offered so far by Jaspers and Taylor. Then, I will proceed in stages that draw heavily on the work of Horkheimer and Adorno for further developing a more fully secularized account of justice for those still skeptical of too overt of theological overtones within the wide-ranging philosophical space inhabited by Jaspers, Buber, Eisenstadt, and Voegelin.

Judaism and the Species-Ethical Dimensions to Naming

As we reenter the philosophical grounds for demonstrating the boundless communication requisite for Abrahamic and non-Abrahamic inter-Axial dynamics, we must now assess Hebrew claims to species-ethical universality. As the leading Hebrew voice in lending social-scientific credibility to the multiple modernities

[2] Mendieta, playing dual roles as English translator and leading scholarly authority on the works of Habermas on religion, provides a foretaste of the work in progress (2013). A five chapter outline of this immense project runs as follows: "Chapter 1 deals with the 'revitalization of the world religions as a challenge for the secular understanding of modernity'....Chapter 2 focuses on the 'sacred roots of the Axial Age traditions'....The next chapter [3] deals with the transformation of religious consciousness itself through the cognitive breakthroughs embodied in these universalistic axial religions....Chapter 4 offers a comparison among some of the Axial Age world pictures. There are analyses and discussions of Buddha's teachings, Confucianism and Daoism, Socrates's 'Natural Philosophy,' and Plato's doctrine of ideas. The fifth chapter closes, for the moment, on an analysis of the configuration of a distinct constellation of forces among faith and knowledge as a 'result of the convergence between Christianity and Platonism'" (406). I am grateful to Prof. Mendieta for his (a) ongoing discussions about how best to navigate the burgeoning background literature, from both the Habermasian corpus of works, including calling attention to crucial areas where Habermas has revised or further developed his prior position(s), and (b) pointing to the best relevant literature from other historical figures that have either critiqued or endorsed some variant of the Axial Age thesis.

thesis, S.N. Eisenstadt claims that one step along the way would be to undermine the *de facto* legitimacy of a rational secular modernity as the surest route to species universality. We return full circle to the important question considered in our introductory chapter, the intellectual query: 'Why Jaspers?' According to Eisenstadt, to consider Jaspers as a viable scholarly alternative to Weber entails undermining misconceptions about the endemic pariah status errantly attributed by Weber to the Hebrew tradition:

> It [Hebrew moral, ethical, and rational appeals to species universalism] exhibited strong tendencies to proselytization which often were in tension with the more particularistic primordial emphases and which the sages and sects tried to resolve through their own mode of rationalization of religious contact. Thus even later on, in the medieval period, the Jewish people were not just, as Weber put it, a religious pariah community or people... .[M]any of the characteristics of a pariah people were not peculiar in this period to the Jews....Unlike many other minority peoples, the Jews attempted not only to maintain some place for themselves in the tumultuous political reality of the period, but also developed and continued claims of the universal validity of their religion and tradition. (Eisenstadt 2003, p. 132)

Taking these remarks into account, I concede that appeals to the domain of the species-ethical are most likely to be associated by the reader with modernist philosophical origins from Hegelian-Marxist analysis—especially for readers coming to political theory out a distinctively European understanding of modernity. With respect to Marx, my appeal to Eisenstadt does not seek in Marx a corrective to Hegelian and Weberian Protestantism often employed in order to justify the perceived necessity of a secularized state. These may indeed seem the best resolutions to two related dilemmas: the conflation of state secularization with dubious state neutrality and the corresponding trend of a biased, merely purported impartiality, heavily-weighted in the Christian direction. Instead, my prime motive would be to agree with Eisenstadt that addressing the Jewish question differently than the default intellectual positions requires a radical readjustment to our understanding of the origins of modernity. As an alternative to Weberian state secularity, Hegelian Protestantism secularized, or the opposed Zionist extreme of a distinct Hebrew nation-state as the path to ongoing vitality, we will read a universal species-ethic as an enduring constant for grasping the full symbolic import of the narrative self-understanding of the Hebrew Biblical heritage (Weil 1975, pp. 26–27).

The Hebrew salvific message of truly species-wide import stretches back to the historiogensis detailed in the earliest writings that comprise the corpus of Biblical religion. One risk of missing the full existential import of the Judaic salvation impulse would be the hasty conflation of the moral-ethical dimensions of universality solely with Moses' symbolic reception of the Sinai covenant. We concede to historical-critical Biblical scholarship the notion that the first five books of the *Torah* were likely written from the retrospective standpoint of the Exodus event. However, putting too much emphasis on the culmination of the historical process without due recognition to the origination (historiogenesis) loses much of the narrative and symbolic import of the ensuing species-ethical universality originally conferred by a personal God.

> [T]he process of world-history reaches its highest level with the divine choice of individuals and groups for special instruction and the trusting response of the chosen individuals and

> groups. The special covenant between God and man is formalized through the covenants. The covenant, the berith, must therefore be ranked with *toroth* [divine commands] and *toldoth* [generations] as the third great symbol used in the expression of Israelite historical thought….[W]e must remain aware that when we try to determine the historiographic function of the symbol, we are dealing with a layer of meaning superimposed on the two others. (Voegelin 1974a, p. 171)

The toroth, as the more than 500 commands found in the collected canon of the Torah, was rooted in the concrete pragmatic experience of a particular historical group. The toldoth, in particular, overcame the solidaristic limits of kinship identification of clan into the wider federated arrangement of the genetically dispersed but symbolically related twelve tribes of Israel as united by the berith. Generations of symbolically reconstructed meaning served to constitute an ethical monotheism producing commands binding not just on the elect of Israel but upon the species as such. Yes, the Sinai Covenant carried this dual function of issuing a set of divine commands with a species-ethical component. However, the universality extended beyond the Israelites insofar as they were prefaced by the reminder of the historical trustworthiness of Yahweh to uphold the Abrahamic Covenant to ensuing generations. In taking the Sinai covenant as prior in symbolic import to the Abrahamic, conflates the symbolic import with a reversal of the historical conditions.

In order to clarify this latter move from a historical-critical perspective, we also need to reconsider from a historiogenetic standpoint the symbol of each covenantal promise. The symbolic import of the berith takes its origin from the king to suzerain relations of other Near Eastern peoples. What was unique to the Hebrew experience was replacing the symbolic role of the king with Yahweh. God's elect supplant the place of the suzerain subjects. However, when adding yet a third layer to the berith, the narrative placement of the earliest Adamic covenant prior to both the Abrahamic and the Sinai one carried the command of species procreation. The dual Adamic command and promise also plays the symbolic function in the Hebrew canon as an act of grace requisite for the ensuing exposition of the human will as free only insofar as we posit divine gifts as freely offered. The species-ethic constant traces its symbolic historiogenesis to the Adamic covenant mandating all humans so constituted would never relinquish their unique differentiation from the rest of creation as image bearers of the divine.

> [T]he act of creation is evidence of God's free, unrestricted will, an expression of His loving-kindness and concern for His world. The motif of creation ex nihilo which was to occupy Jewish and Christian thought is still far removed from the world picture of the Bible. The main point is that ontological detachment is accompanied by the voluntary relationship between God and His world, a fact witnessed by Israel through its own fate. This is the common ground of all creation traditions in the Bible. Israel's primaeval experience during the Exodus from Egypt, the wanderings through the desert, and the revelation of God on Mount Sinai are concrete expressions of this voluntary relationship. (Uffenheimer 1986, p. 163)

In light of the mention of creation *ex nihilo* as completely foreign to the original (and arguably proper) Hebrew hermeneutic, Uffenheimer warns that the second-personal symbolic overtones to the narrative construct of both the Hebrew account of creation and Hebrew symbolic genealogies of humanity must not be taken as third-person scientific postulations. We miss their symbolic import if taking them exhaustively to explain the origination of the material cosmos, such as in rivaling the explanatory power of Big Bang physics at the cost of slipping out of the participatory narrative mode into a textually unwarranted third-person perspective. Likewise, we miss the point if reading *Genesis* as offering us an epistemically valid third-person standpoint for describing the origins of the human species as a viable alternative to evolutionary theory or in putting our hopes in saving the credibility of the Hebrew canon with the scientific trump card of an Eve gene. Voegelin concurs with these category mistakes:

> [T]aking it for granted that the ancient symbolists were not as naïve as modern fundamentalists, the quality of trustworthiness must have been meant to attach not to the detail of the registers but to the symbolic meaning which they intended to convey. A clue to the meaning is furnished by Genesis 2: 4: "These are the generations [toldoth] of heaven and earth." The passage opens an account of the creation but uses the same phraseology as the genealogical registers. That is an odd usage; for the noun toldoth contains the verb yalad, "to bear," "to bring forth," and thus unmistakingly refers not to creation but to procreation. Hence, we must assume that the oddity was intended, precisely in order to reveal a deeper connection between creation and procreation. (Voegelin 1974a, p. 169)

Voegelin thus applies this etymological subtlety to his ensuing reconstruction of how best to interpret the import of Hebrew historiogenesis. When read from a participatory second-person narrative construct, we disclose the co-originality of the creation of the cosmos and the procreative impulse to the species imbibed in the symbolic Biblical conferral of naming:

> Beyond the tribes of the confederacy we enter the realm of legend, myth, and speculation. The great nodal point in the symbolism is the descent from Shem, "the father of all the children of Eber" [the origination of the term Hebrew] (Gen. 10: 21). The Hebrew word shem means "name." With Shem the register of names reaches the abstraction of the Name by which "all Israel" is distinguished from a symbolically anonymous naming. From Shem, finally, the register goes back to Adam. The Hebrew word adam means "man." The man with the Name ultimately descends from the generic Man. (Voegelin 1974a, p. 166)

The symbolic ties referenced earlier between toldoth (generation) and the toroth (divine commands and promises of the attendant covenants) carry their species-ethical universality by virtue of the common origin of humanity from Adam. The promise that adhering to the Abrahamic covenant will serve as a sign or symbol to the rest of the nations (literally Gentiles, or 'non-named,' non-Jews) symbolically points the reader in two narrative directions simultaneously. We find a dual fulfillment backward to the Adamic covenant as co-participants in species origination from Adam/mankind and forward in the reiteration of this original divine grace through the narratively later Exodus event as both a sign to the Israelites and world-historical symbol of species import.

On this symbolic reading of human progeny, humans thereby become co-participants in a process of creation with God, adding layered iterations of toldoth generations escalating in divine conferral of sacred import from creation, to humankind, to the elect.

> No modern translation can adequately render the innuendo of the Hebrew text that the first generation of creation, that is, the heavens and earth, become procreative and co-operative

> with Yahweh in the work of creation. From the fertilization of *ad* [mist] and *adamah* [soil] arises, under the forming and animating action of Yahweh, the second generation of *adam*, with the double meaning of man and Adam. (Voegelin 1974a, p. 170)

In this respect, we can begin to understand why Voegelin's employment of the social-scientific dimensions to his interpretation of Hebrew history nonetheless does not fall prey to lapsing into the third-person objective descriptions offered by those he labels as gnostic ideologues.

> With the linguistic structure of the text before him, the reader will not doubt that the *toldoth* of Adam continue the *toldoth* of heavens and earth. The authors intended the meanings of creation and procreation to merge in a co-operative process; the order of being is meant to arise from the creative initiation of God and the procreative response of creation. Hence, what is trustworthy about the registers is not the genealogical ascent from the presently living to some remote ancestor but the generative descent from God—generative understood in the double meaning of creative-procreative. The *adam* that was created by God with the procreative response of *ad* and *adamah* continues to generate himself in the likeness of God. To the presently living the registers authenticate their being *adam* in the likeness of God—that is, the human medium that is supposed to co-operate in generating the order of being through procreative submission to the creative will of God. (Voegelin 1974a, p. 170, 171)

On such a read of human freedom, Voegelin suggests that accounts of the creation of the cosmos and that of man within the context of Biblical religion must be read from the proper hermeneutic in order to avoid two misunderstandings. On the one hand, an overemphasis on a literal historical read misses the rich allegorical overtones. In addition, at the other ideological extreme, the text bears no license for beginning with the secular modernist assumption of the absolute autonomy of man as the rubric for assessment of the rational merits of a particular tradition, Hebrew or otherwise.

Voegelin concludes in a pragmatically open manner fully consistent with his repeated resistance to collapsing our hopes for universal justice into what cannot receive adequate species closure in the nation-state, regional empire, or global political order. One can easily trace the symbolic roots of this philosophical and political commitment to his interpretation of the universal versus particular tension endemic to Israelite history he regards as having no consummating concrete resolution:

> The relationship between the life of the spirit and life in the world is the problem that lies unresolved at the bottom of the Israelite difficulties. Let us hasten to say that the problem by its nature is not capable of a solution valid for all times. Balances that work for a while can be found and have been found. But habituation, institutionalization, and ritualization inevitably, by their finiteness, degenerate sooner or later into a captivity of the spirit that is infinite; and then the time has come for the spirit to break a balance that has become demonic imprisonment. Hence, no criticism is implied when the problem is characterized as unresolvable. But precisely because the problem is unsolvable on principle, an inestimable importance attaches to its historically specific states of irresolution. In the Israelite case, the problem is unresolved in so far as it is on the point of emergence from the compactness of the Mosaic period [we] into the Prophetic differentiation [species]. And the foundation of the Kingdom was, furthermore, the specific crisis that revealed the demonic derailment of the Mosaic foundation. Here we witness the interplay of experiences in the struggle of the spirit for its freedom from encasement in a particular historical organization. That struggle of truly world-historic importance has, by its experiential phases, determined the unique structure of the Biblical narrative as a literary work. (Voegelin, 1974a, p. 183)

For the skeptic of the work of Voegelin having overstepped the bounds of political theory proper by including spiritual entities and cosmic comportments into his framing of political participation with the cosmion, he does buffer these speculative components with some pragmatic lessons. While contemporary academic treatments of American pragmatism have generally taken political theory mostly in the opposed direction of an outright dismissal of such a widened view of the political, Voegelin found much solace in the cosmic speculations of Whitehead, James, and Pierce in his extensive studies of American pragmatism that, on his read, constituted a philosophical tradition immune from the third-personal excesses of the Austrian positivism of his early intellectual development. Once one submits to the second-person narrative construct of man, the Thou second-person plural of the species, and the cosmic domain as an experiential manifold of spirit and human co-participation, we are closer to assuming a compatibilist account of human freedom that nonetheless can offer an alternate to one(s) that are inherently secular. We can take license to call this Biblical narrative construct modern nonetheless since we have not pretended to replace the necessary pragmatic assumption of the ongoing subjection of our epistemic commitments from the critical scrutiny of the empirical sciences. Nor have we sacrificed the crucial moral-ethical assumption of authentic responsibility taken for one's creative capacities for reason, sociability, and political agency.

While Jaspers would endorse the symbolic meanings ascribed above to what he terms collectively experiential 'ciphers,' Jaspers consistently resists the ascription of first-personal qualities to the divine. In turn, he also argues that we have stretched the limits of both our linguistic and philosophical capacities once we allow persons to address the divine from the performative attitude of a first person I to a second person you. He resolves this tension reserving the postulation of an Encompassing as a species-constant experiential domain that nonetheless must retain a third person distance from the subjective consciousness.

As a compelling alternative to Jaspers' accounts of subjective individuation born from the crisis of individual culpability for owning the social fact of species interdependence, the adoption of a universal species-ethic need not entail an existential humanism bereft of a personal God. Perhaps put best in the probing prose of Buber's *I and Thou*:

> Man becomes an I through a You. What confronts us comes and vanishes, relational events take shape and scatter, and through these changes crystallizes, more and more each time, the consciousness of the constant partner, the I-consciousness. To be sure, for a long time it appears only woven into a relation to a You; but it comes closer and closer to the bursting point until one day the bonds are broken and the I confronts its detached self for a moment like a You—and then it takes possession of itself and henceforth enters into relations in full consciousness. (Buber 1970, p. 80)

One's responsible participation in the species and cosmic order—or citizenship, for lack of a better term—renders its ultimate conferral from the You/Thou that Buber takes as the fundamentally pan-relational context we are thrown into since birth (Buber 1970, pp. 75–79).[3] However, while such an account rooted in a narrative

[3] Buber describes such an urge that begins in infancy as 'the drive to turn everything into a You, the drive to pan-relation—and where it does not find a living, active being that confronts it but

order to human experience can easily concede the distinctly pragmatic notion that 'individuation is the product of socialization,' the priority ultimately rests on the relational quality of our personhood that only thereafter makes possible the articulation of first-person responsibility.

The Thornbush Episode: Origins to a Theopolity of Biblical Monotheism

Jaspers' references to the Hebrew influence upon the initiation of the Axial Age highlight the importance of key prophetic elites like Amos, Jeremiah, and Isaiah—not only at the expense of Yahweh as a personal God, but also at the expense of Abraham and Moses. These assumptions belie the pragmatic reality of the experience of a collective people. In a parallel construct, Taylor's existential historiography of Latin Christendom repeatedly appeals to what he terms the nova effect of civilizational transformation through elites as driving Axial Age breakthroughs. For Taylor, these reconstructions typically begin with civilizational crisis, met by an elite-initiated response. In events of successful mediation of crisis, the requisite elite insights then spill over to eventuate the gradual transformation of the masses.

One initial step of critical analysis from the pragmatic experience of the Hebrew tradition would be to challenge the necessity of elite figures stirring on civilizational transformation. Along the lines of the incredibly compact Hebrew breakthrough that fits Jaspers' original Axial Age dates, the ensuing ethical monotheism of the Hebrew tradition becomes associated with the 800–600 BC prophets Amos, Hosea, and Duetero-Isaiah. However, Hebrew scholarship on its own Axial qualities tends to resist such a straight-forward temporal climax owing its success to transformative leaders. According to Uffenheimer, Jaspers in particular may have fallen prey to conflating otherwise experientially disparate phenomena, particularly in collapsing the Greek experience into the Hebrew one:

> We contend that this is diametrically opposed to the historical reality reflected in the biblical sources, especially in those pertaining to the Sinai covenant. These sources disclose that monotheism, far from being the speculative, contemplative faith of a small, elitist group, was the result of an overwhelming historical event involving an entire nation. While this powerful historical experience is embedded in legend and myth, there is nevertheless no reason to doubt its essential historical reality, nor is it likely that the legend was the free invention of late writers. This experience was Israel's redemption from the house of bondage in Egypt, followed by the covenant made by the people with their divine redeemer, the so-called Sinai covenant. In other words, the nucleus of monotheism is a primaeval collective historical event, which was perceived as the encounter of an entire nation with Yahweh, their redeemer. This was an existential experience totally different from an intellectual acquisition of a small elitist group, like the ontological monism of the pre-classical Greek philosophers. (Uffenheimer 1986, p. 150)

Uffenheimer cites the historical backdrop to the Sinai covenant that pushes the relevant dates much earlier than the conventional framework of the more compact 800–200 BC axial setting. As support, and in agreement with the scriptural herme-

---

only an image or symbol of that, it supplies the living activity from its own fullness' (1970, p. 77).

neutics of Voegelin and Buber, he appeals to the close literary conventions of the Sinai covenant to the sorts of treaties documented as characteristic of those between 1400 and 1250 BCE Hittite kings and their vassals:

> *Israel accepted the exclusive suzerainty of its divine king.* The prohibition against worshipping any other god besides Him found its classical expression in the first commandment. Indeed, this is consonant with the prohibitions found in Hittite vassal treaties, where the vassal is warned against recognizing anybody besides his suzerain, "the Sun." This is a striking parallel to the Sinai covenant in which Israel, the vassal nation, pledges absolute and exclusive obedience to Him by an act of free commitment. Thus, the Sinai covenant was tantamount to the establishment of the kingdom of God. We may therefore assume that it was the radical response of Israel to the traumatic experience of Egypt, "the house of bondage," the symbol of human enslavement and tyranny. By contrast, the kingdom of God was meant to be free of any kind of human domination and oppression. Buber, in his book *Konigtum Gottes* (1936), already persuasively demonstrated that this theopolitical utopia may be traced within the most ancient political and narrative sources of the Bible (*Num.* 10:35–36; 23:21–23; *Judg.* 5, etc.). There, the idea of human kingship is repudiated as an offense and a sin against God, the true king of Israel (*Judg.* 8:22–23; *I Sam.* 8:7 ff.). In other words, the covenant between God and His people, which is the very core of biblical monotheism, is in a certain sense the transmission and reshaping of these ancient vassal treaties, in which Israel is conceived as the vassal of God. (Uffenheimer 1986, p. 151)

In addition, as an answer the positivist nineteenth century Germanic historical critical school of Julius Wellhausen (1844–1918) that still retains substantial impact upon Biblical scholarship to this day, Voegelin also shows a decided preference for describing the ideal form of political governance for the Israelites as the notion of a theopolity (which he also attributes to Buber: Voegelin, 1974a, p. 415). Since theocracy too closely conflates the spiritual and political orders, Voegelin's contrast of the terminological type signs theocracy and theopolity gives his best clarification for the attendant danger of collapsing the two distinct orders: "The compact symbol of the Chosen People could never be completely broken by the idea of a universal God and a universal mankind. Yet the problem of the church, however imperfectly differentiated, was inherent in the situation as soon as a temporal polity was built into the Yahwist theopolity, with the national monarchy. Hence, the monarchy of Saul, indeed, marked the beginning of the theocratic problem" (1974, 1974a, p. 248).

Voegelin's recasting of the thornbush episode of Moses elicits a pragmatic sensitivity to the original Hebrew audience to whom Moses must communicate his revelatory message—an audience three centuries removed from the Israelite desire to be like their neighbors and anoint Saul as the king of their theocracy. On the one hand, we must concede our earlier remarks that Voegelin posits the Hebrew corpus of scriptures as stretching across multiple authors, clearly demonstrative of historical redaction, and even intermeshing layers of interpretive precedent into type symbols such as kingship, just governance, and retrospective prophetic fulfillments. On the other hand, like Uffenheimer, Voegelin resists the idea that the concession to historical redaction of the narrative therefore places composite authorship—even in the case of 800–600 BCE composite tradition of scriptural experts charged with preserving the historical meaning of sacred texts—between Wellhausen's dates of about

800–300 BCE (Voegelin, 1974a, pp. 192–193).[4] Voegelin also explicitly rejects Wellhausen's quasi-Hegelian evolutionary vision of Israelite history proceeding from primitive animism, to henotheism, and culminating in a mature monotheism only through composite redactors that were temporally situated in close proximity to the key Axial prophets of the period of Babylonia exile (Voegelin, IR 1974, p. 199, 200; Dillard and Longman 1994, p. 45, 46). By situating the thornbush episode in the much earlier Egyptian historical context, Voegelin acknowledges the import of historical context without falling into the errors he attributes to the Wellhausen historical-critical schools that tend to miss the forest of meaning imbibed in comprehensive symbolic imagery for the trees of the historical-critical deconstruction of type symbols (Voegelin 1974a, pp. 192–202). For instance, the third person charge that the miraculous parting of the reed sea never factually occurred (and therefore undermines the integrity of the entire Hebrew corpus of scripture), disavows the more significant postulation that some major collectively experiential event(s) occurred for the Israelites to derive such symbolic import to an experience that could only be equated with the grace of divine deliverance:

> The parallel between the Yahwist and the Amon symbols is clear enough not to require elaboration. The tension between the hidden depth in God and his manifestations has been transposed, by the thornbush episode, from the form of cosmological myth to the form of revealed presence in history. Such a transposition could well have been the decisive work of Moses, if we consider the fundamental issue of his existence as it has emerged from the previous analysis, that is, the conflict between the orders of Yahweh and the Egyptian empire. It is highly probable that the revelation of the new order was couched in symbol which clearly abrogated the order of the Egyptian gods as it was understood at the time. It would be the same type of symbolic opposition that we observe in the Abram episode of Genesis 14. [Abram's refusal to profit from the Canannite worship of Melchizedik but nonetheless put his trust in the covenant revealed to him by God]. The revelation could break with the cosmological experience, but it could not be communicable unless it continued the symbols while changing their meaning. The God of Moses had to make himself intelligible to his people, not only as God of the fathers, but also as the God of the new historical dispensation in opposition to the Amon of the empire. Hence, we are inclined to attribute the symbolism of the thornbush episode to Moses; and since the Egyptian texts which supply the continuity are later than the Amarna period, a date for Moses will have to be assumed in the thirteenth century B.C. (Voegelin 1974a, p. 414)

Voegelin therefore regards the passage as most properly read from a theopolitical typology rather than a theocratic one since he mixes the sort of evidence valid for the historical-critical school with the transformative symbolic meaning that for him indubitably constitutes the collective experience of a people dated near the thirteenth century BCE.

[4] While a complete explanation of the tenets of the Wellhausen school extend outside the scope of this project, it should suffice to mention the schools and approximate dates given by historical-critical scholars. According to Voegelin, 'The Yahwist narrative [J] originated in the kingdom of Judah in the ninth century; the Elohist [E] in the kingdom of Israel in the 8th century….A third source is the Deuteronomist [D]…presumed to be identical with Josiah's reform code of 621….A fourth source, finally, is the sacerdotal or priestly document [P], which…goes back to the time of Ezekiel. The integration of the J-E-D into the P narrative took place in the fourth century, and the revisions in the sacerdotal spirit may have still been going on by 300 BC.' (1974a, pp. 192–193; see also Dillard and Longman 1994, pp. 40–46).

He therefore provides us with a set of pragmatic presuppositions for the Hebrew hermeneutic of these type concepts that still retain the postulation of a personal God while also carrying the potential for responsible self-transformative learning. On the one hand, he highlights the sensitivity of the authors to appeal to symbols within the range of the second-personal audience's experiential manifold: in this case, by appeal to the Amon Hymns of Dynasty XIX that carry many of the characteristics of the thornbush episode (413). He finds in these a reference to the mysterious qualities of Amon that came into being at an unknown date through an unknown source, whose divine qualities carry close parallels to those ascribed to the Israelite pragmatic experience of their new relationship with Yahweh. In parallel symbolism, the Egyptian Amon and Israelite Yahweh have the capacities to remain hidden, while nonetheless the potencies are capable of becoming manifest in a multitude of possible forms (413). On the other hand, despite these typological similitudes, Voegelin also highlights that the symbols have been subjected to a transformed meaning that sets them apart from their original Egyptian imperial context: specifically the radical transformation from cosmological myth to revelatory presence in human history (414).

Thus, invariably we are led into the murky debate concerning the hidden meanings of the famous "I am who am" second-personal revelation of God's name to Moses at the thornbush that confirms for the participant reader the veridical status of a divine calling. While Voegelin concedes that the richness of such a debate could take a separate manuscript in order adequately to present the array of positions stated on the proper exegesis, he outright dismisses the efficacy of purely etymological attempts:

> [T]he rich etymological debate concerning the name of Yahweh, with its variegated conjectures, some more plausible than others but none conclusive, must be excluded as irrelevant to our problem. The narrative itself does not refer to any meaning attached to the name of Yahweh that could have influenced the content of the revelation. On the contrary, it presents the name as one whose meaning is unknown, so that an exegesis is necessary in order to endow it with spiritual vitality. The exegesis, furthermore, is not intended as an etymology. As far as we know, the *ehyeh* has etymologically no more to do with *Yahweh*, than *mashah* and *mosheh*, that is, nothing at all. The exegesis plays with a phonetic allusion, but its meaning is autonomous. (Voegelin 1974a, p. 408)

In other words, by dismissing any straightforward etymological point of departure to his scriptural hermeneutic for this passage, he claims that the very lack of direct content to the name serves as a necessary condition for endowing the name with a more dynamic experiential vitality.

In addition, although ascribing to Yahweh the personal qualities requisite for having established a communicative relation through Moses to the Israelites, Voegelin allows the precise capacities and qualities of God—akin to the Egyptian Amon—to remain hidden and indeterminate. However, he posits Yahweh less as a theocratic hypostasis to behold from a third-person objectivigating perspective nor does he, like Jaspers, supplant the personal God with and impersonal mystery of the Encommpassing. Instead, he posits Yahweh as a theopolitical practical moral agent whose primary action is salvific as the consummate helper of his people:

> In the framing passages of the thornbush episode, 3: 12 and 4: 12, the *ehyeh* has the meaning "I will be with you"; and the Chicago translation justly paraphrases the *ehyeh* in 4: 12 as "I will help you"—though the paraphrase destroys the structure of the text. The meaning that God will be present as the helper, furthermore, is confirmed by the instruction to Moses to tell the people: "*Ehyeh* has sent me to you" (3:14). The passage would have to be paraphrased: "The one who is present as your helper has sent me to you." In light of this meaning, supported by the prophecy of Hosea, must be understood the central *ehyeh asher ehyeh*, usually translated as I AM WHO I AM. Unless we introduce extraneous "philosophical" categories, the text can only mean that God reveals himself as the one who is present as the helper. While the God himself is hidden (the first *ehyeh*) and, therefore, must reveal himself, he will be manifest whenever, and whatever form, he chooses (the second *ehyeh*). (Voegelin, 1974a, p. 413)

In his seemingly misplaced reference to the much later prophetic writing of Hosea (1:9) to explain an event potentially six or more centuries prior, he seems to provide support for the Wellhausen school he had earlier rejected. Since scholarly dating of Hosea places the book in the eighth century BCE, it might seem more plausible to support to the notion that the entire Biblical canon had undergone significant redaction precisely around the climatic Axial period celebrated by Jaspers. In response, Voegelin explains that during the later period of the destroyed Northern Kingdom (722 BCE), Hosea has Yahweh explicitly call the Israelites *Lo-ammi* (literally: not-my-people) and even takes on the self-designation of *lo-ehyeh* (literally: I not I-am to you). The significance of his inclusion of the later dating of the Hosea reference nonetheless contributed to his painstaking efforts to retain the theopolitical import of original thornbush episode.

On the one hand, in support of Voegelin's resistance to the Wellhausen postulation of Torah authorship and significant redaction during Jaspers' Axial Period, the prophet Hosea severely chastises the people for their forgetfulness of having forsaken the Sinai covenant. They had effectively undermined the second-personal relations of trust with Yahweh essential to the ongoing vitality of the theopolity. On the other hand, Voegelin adds yet another reason for skepticism cast on the Wellhausen thesis of the greater corpus of the Hebrew Bible having been written and redacted considerably by Hebrew scriptural schools dated near the historical periods of Amos, Hosea, Ezekiel, and Deutero-Isaiah. According to Voegelin, and his affinity for Buber's hermeneutics, the very act of such a harsh rebuke in Hosea necessarily presumes the pragmatic weight of centuries of experiential revelation for it to remain consistent with God's status as a just and good author of true promises. On this interpretation, the Israelites symbolically merit the justice meted out by God's punishment for having willfully forgotten what he presumes was a collective experience carried forward with the toldoth across the numerous generations (anywhere from 15 to 20 generations on the biblical rubric of 40 years comprising a generation) that continued the line of communicative relationship with God across the centuries. The same promise initiated at the Sinai event of the thirteenth century continued to resonate in the collective consciousness up into the sixth century and forward (412).

While Voegelin avoided the etymological route for the interpretation of YHWH in order to open its symbolic content to the collective memory of an entire people, that does not mean he dismisses the role of etymological symbolism as an important carrier of meaning in Biblical religion. In the case of some proper names, Voegelin actually follows the etymological read of Buber's in-depth understanding of Hebrew. For instance, again in support of his experiential—as opposed to historical factual—reading of the Exodus event, he follows Buber in associating the name Moses not with the popular notions of 'because I drew him out of the water' with the dual overtones of Moses' sparing from death by deliverance out of the river by the family of Pharoah and the more overt overtones of the great Exodus event of the parting of the sea. Instead, in a reading that both he and Buber find grammatically more precise would be a symbolic 'drawing of Israel from the floods' (394, 395). Voegelin cites similar references to the use of the same grammar in the Psalms amidst trials whereby David receives deliverance from his enemies. Firstly, he finds this reading helpful in evading an overly naturalistic reading of the miracle of the Red Sea parting that could thereby lose its symbolic import of deliverance from real historical bondage. Secondly, if the historical precedence behind the name did derive from the exegesis of the naming to read "the one who draws out" from the certain death and destruction characteristic of a tumultuous flood (as in David's symbolic usage) then that would lend greater credence to the historical prospect that there was an event of such experiential magnitude later to become the symbolic association attributed retrospectively to Moses (395).

In response to the possible charge of gerrymandering his hermeneutic commitments to fit best with his theoretical and exegetical aims, when Voegelin opts to extract the etymological depth of symbolic terms, he emphasizes these instances to call attention to the historical-critical skeptic that attempts to exploit apparent textual inconsistencies through a mix of lack of knowledge of the original Hebrew, an over literalizing of merely symbolic terms, and mistaking the rational unfolding of scriptural narratives as ones that best proceed along a linear axis of time. For example, one fitting instance of Voegelin's hermeneutic sensitivity would be to read the grammatical parallels between burning bush (*seneh*) along a hermeneutic sensitivity to the close etymology of the Sinai mountain.

> To see God is to die. Moses has hidden his face from the terrifying sensual presence, and he listens, with his soul, to whatever the voice had to say. And the voice tells him of the divine knowledge that is action. The revelation opens: "Seen I have, seen the oppression of my people who are in Egypt"; and it closes: "Lead my people, the sons of Israel, out of Egypt!" Here, for the first time, appears the theme of "my people [*ammi*]," firmly framing the promise of freedom in 3:8. As the *seneh* [bush] points forward to *Sinai*, so the *ammi* points forward to the Berith [covenant] through which the Hebrew clans, who as yet are ignorant of the fate in store for them, will be transformed into "my people." In the knowledge of God the action distended in historical time is complete. Moreover, the historical action has subtly begun with the revelation, for the knowledge of God has now become the knowledge of Moses who, in the course of his life, has grown to the point where he can hear the divine voice articulate its command. When Moses can hear the voice appoint him the servant of Yahweh, he has grown spiritually into the servant of Yahweh. The command could be rejected only by a man who could never hear it; the man who can hear cannot reject, as the will of God has entered him. When the consciousness of the divine will has reached the clarity of revelation, the historical action has begun. (Voegelin 1974a, p. 407)

In other words, as the bush (*seneh*) is to Sinai, this similar etymological construct leads the reader to draw the historical parallel between the thornbush episode and the Sinai covenant. The dispersed wandering clans had not formed a polity by the theocratic and heroic leadership of Moses into a single people but rather served a participatory role in the unfolding drama of the disclosure of a new type of order: the theopolity of Yahweh's divine governance.

The combined result of reading the burning bush 'I am who am' passage as symbolically pointing to Yahweh's performative action as helping savior via the Exodus, widens the original second-personal discourse between God and Moses to the establishment of a second-person plural relationship with the Israelites (you plural implied) as my people.

> As in the preceding scene the promise of freedom was framed by the introductory and concluding references to "my people," so now the supreme revelation of God's nature is framed by the "I will be [*ehyeh*] with you" of Exodus 3:12 and 4:12. In the exegesis at the center, the meaning of God is then revealed as "I am who I am [*ehyeh asher ehyeh*]." To the skeptical sons of Israel Moses will have to say: "*Ehyeh* has sent me to you" (3:14). The people thus will break the bondage of Egypt and enter the present under God, once they have responded to the revelation of God's presence with them. The mutual presence of God and Moses in the thornbush dialogue will then have expanded into the mutual presence of God and his people, through the Berith, in history. (Voegelin 1974a, p. 407)

Voegelin uses this hermeneutic to reinforce the point the Moses must again not be mistaken as the king of a Hebrew theocracy. In addition to the three centuries of removal from David's monarchy, insofar as the people freely assent to this call too, the second-personal act of divine revelation breaks through historically as the we-experience of an entire people under the theopolical kingship of Yahweh their divine deliverer.

Eschaton Revisited, Theopolity Secured: The Hebrew Second Temple Axial Breakthrough

Despite my resistance to confining the Hebrew axial breakthrough to Jaspers' dates, one may nonetheless associate a secondary Axial breakthrough around the time of the writings of Deutero-Isaiah, as a restoration and final consummation of the first breakthrough of the monotheism established by the Sinai covenant (Stone 1986). In this respect, Jaspers gains credence in his appeal to this period of major Hebrew prophets as justification for inclusion of the axial breakthrough of Judaism within his original axial timeframe of 800–200 BCE. For commentators like Nikiprowetzky defending Jaspers' axial preference for the later dates, the axial moment comes with the consummation of the gradual process of Yahweh as truly unique among the competing gods of the temporal context. The strong contrast would point to Yahweh not just the mightiest and most trustworthy among many—but eventually crystallizing into yet a more complete revelation of the universal God of ethical monotheism.

> Radical monotheism is unambiguously present, however, in the doctrine of he Second Isaiah, which represents a crystallization of the entire previous process. Isaiah of Babylon still

> uses formulas of incomparability but now gives them a definite monotheistic meaning.... Hebrew and Judaic literature will never again cease to affirm the belief in an only God and the non-existence of all the others, so that ethical monotheism, in Palestine and in the Diaspora, will become the characteristic of Jewish uniqueness and so that a text from the Talmud will be able to proclaim the following definition: "Anyone who denies the existence of other gods is called Jewish." (Nikiprowetzky 1975, p. 82)

As a mediating of the two camps, I follow Voegelin in presuming a reading of the Hebrew canon with multiple centers of symbolic meaning that resist reduction to a single event, symbol, or principle. The breakthrough brought about by the diaspora following the Babylonian exiles preserves the historical dimensions of a full restoration of the Sinai covenant begun with Moses, lost for centuries in the real pragmatics of the historical wavering of the chosen people, and finally redeemed again during the Second Temple Period.

> It [ethical monotheism] simply represents the culmination of a historical process belonging to Israel and Israel alone. Even if one forfeits the notion of the monotheistic 'vocation' of the Semites, one still cannot achieve precision if one assumes that Israel had its concept of God from the beginning, either by finding it ready-made in the great African or Asian Near East, from whom it could have merely borrowed, or by taking advantage of the external and gnostic revelations in the Patriarchs' dreams or the flames of Sinai. Despite the fervor and the moving depth of its piety, and the grandiose sublimity of its theological concepts, neither the religion of Babylonia nor that of Egypt offers anything that is truly comparable to Israel's monotheism. Neither the Patriarchs nor Moses were true monotheists. Ethical monotheism, in its complete expression, incontestably appears only during the prophesy of the exile period. (Nikiprowetzky, p. 69)

Nikiprowetsy's commentary thereby notes a consistency between the collective experiential content the Israelites ascribed to ethical monotheism and Buber's defense of the Hebrew theopolity. Active participation in such a hypothetical polity need not require an explicitly territorial theocracy whereby a Hebrew monarch plays dual role of residing over Jerusalem as the spiritual and political capital of the kingdom, especially during historical periods in which the Israelites are not in Canaan. The impetus follows to regard the God of ethical monotheism in truly axial universalistic terms that can more fully encompass the species when diaspora surreptitiously facilitates the presence of Judaic practices more centered on Biblical religion as the temple cedes its symbolic place at the center of worship to the synagogue. We thus find additional reasons to support Jasper's association of Hebrew axiality with Isaiah, Jeremiah, Amos, Hosea, and the prophetic writings falling in the range of his Axial Age timeframe:

> Subsequent to Amos, in a famous vision in the temple of Jerusalem, Isaiah has the Seraphim proclaim the glory of Yahweh fills the entire world. This constant exaltation of the image of Israel's god left less and less room for others. Religious thought evolved from the idea of the incomparability of Yahweh to that of his uniqueness. The feeling the prophet Elijah expressed by proclaiming that Yahweh is God (*haelohim*) meant, as we mentioned earlier, that Baal cannot be compared in power and in the capacity to do and to save to Yahweh, to whom no other god can be likened. Next to the living God, the gods of the nations are only idols literally, 'nothings' *elilim*), 'breaths of wind' (*hebel*), 'non-gods' (*lo-elohim*), lies, or abominations. (Nikiprowetzky, p. 81)

However, again for the sake of preserving the symbolic unity to prior stages in the Hebrew narrative, we can compare this predicament to Voegelin's earlier emphasis on the retrospective chastising of the Israelite people by Hosea, speaking on behalf of God as calling them literally: not-my-people. The experiential lack of a covenantal bond between Yahweh and Israel manifests itself in pragmatic history through their worship of idols among a competing spectrum of possible Gods need not therefore warrant positing a quasi-evolutionary progression from henotheism to monotheism. Yahweh's proclamation of Israel's repeated failures lead to an etymological self-ascription as lies and abominations (*lo-elohim*), presuming centuries of a monotheistic collective experience stretching back to the Sinai covenant. This again magnifies rather than detracts from the justice of God. The etymology of the contrast between the God of the Sinai covenant and the Second Temple period of estrangement from God reads literally: not-divine-beings *and* not in a privileged ancestral or family relation of affinity between a people and their God. We evade the reading of the Hebrew God as temperamental and arbitrary in the exacting of justice by adapting a Biblical context again that presumes the loss of a covenantal relation that had earlier been still intact.

Moreover, the earlier Abrahamic covenant to establish the toldoth of the Israelites in the promised land of Canaan, with the split between Israel and Judah also continues to receive greater symbolic meaning in the historical context of a geographically divided Hebrew polity. We can follow the lead of Buber and Voegelin and continue to read the narrative symbolically in contrast to a literal historical expectation of fulfillment:

> Monotheism made further progress after the Jeroboam Schism. The political split and the enmity that had built up between the two kingdoms did not prevent either of them from worshipping Yahweh. Yahweh was no longer the divine patron of ethnic groups or united territories; in spite of the memory of and the regret over the loss of former unity, he was the god over two opposed political entities. This was the first practical recognition of his universal character. A further stage was attained when the Assyrians were seen as the instrument of God's anger, and Cyrus as Yahweh's anointed. (Nikiprowetzky, p. 81)

We should thus qualify Nikiprowetzky's remarks to say that the practical recognition of Yahweh's universal character did *not* occur the first time with the Jeroboam schism but instead represents a period where what was forgotten has been re-established by Yahweh. The consummate helper-God reaffirmed the historical realization first laid out with the Abrahamic and Sinai covenantal experiences when showing that the Middite Egyptian suzerainty of the God-king and subjects must indeed not have the same theocratic idolization of king and kingdom relation repeated in historical terms. When even Cyrus plays the quasi-messianic role of theocratic leader and king providing Assyrian resistance against Babylonian expansion, for Voegelin and Buber, Cyrus also unknowingly participates in the theopolitical realization of God's plan for the Hebrew kingdom.

The Hebrew species-ethical import begun with Adam, and affirmed through Abraham and Moses, in the period of both intense turmoil and prophesy finds its full construal as not one of empire but rather one of universalistic, salvific, and spiritual, collective and individual self-transformation (Weinfeld 1986, pp. 181-82). The emphasis continues in expanding the reign of world-historical influence beyond Egypt, Israel, and Assyria out to the wider regional context eventually to achieve Jaspers' universal scope of boundless communication:

> Around 750 B.C. we find Amos emphatically stressing the grandeur of Yahweh, and the universality of his field of action and jurisdiction. The prophet of Teqoa sees Yahweh as creator of the world and Lord of the celestial legions. He sees him as the Judge, not only of Israel and Judah, but also of the Aramaeans, of the Philistines, of the Phoenicians, of Edom, of Ammon, and of Moab. The Israelites are in fact no more than the Coushites are for him. If Yahweh helped Israel to rise out of Egypt, did he not also help the Philistines out of Caphtor and the Aramaeans out of Qir? (Nikiprowetzky, p. 81)

Even when reading these reflections from a contemporary standpoint, we can affirm along with Voegelin (and what seemed to be the likewise prescient assessment of Arendt) that the *any* gnostic conflation of theopolity with a theocracy falls subject to pagan idolatry. On the one hand, the risk of pagan idolatry would be the attendant assumption that a foreign god would be the true source of deliverance, in its myriad forms (fertility, ecstatic enjoyment, abundance crop yields, military conquest, etc.) that only Yahweh as the helper-God of historical intervention could accomplish. On the other hand, at the other end of the spectrum, the substitution of national institutionalization of worship as a prerequisite for salvation also falls subject to the idolatry of concrete institutions (that are uncontestably, and paradoxically, finite in nature) as the ultimate source of the experiential fullness only to be satisfied in faithful trust and commitment to the promises of Yahweh.

A Multiperspectival Rendering of Hebrew Hermeneutics and Narrative Time

Running throughout the symbolic reconstructions provided above, we can agree with Eisenstadt's generalizable observation that one abiding feature of all the Axial traditions would be constant endemic tensions between center and periphery. We could read these observations in the literal sense of multiple geographical centers and/or world-historical movements that see the various Axial centers morph with respect to internal and external imperial threats. In addition, we could also take center to periphery tension in the metaphorical or symbolic sense of shifting sites of worship (temple versus synagogue) or even among the ideas propagated by competing scholarly traditions of interpretive precedent. For our present purposes, I would like to follow Voegelin's most insightful conclusions drawn from his multi-volume *Order and History* that ultimately led him to abort the original motives of his project upon prolonged scholarly impasses that came about with his 4th Volume of the 5 Volume study: *The Ecumenic Age* (1974b). We will thus shift our focus to the influence of center to periphery competition upon the methodological paucity of a linear conception of time (termed by others, perhaps more fittingly: stadial consciousness) that fails to satisfy the sufficient degree of complexity he associates not only with the Hebrew corpus of literature, but also the deeper historical dilemmas tied to a linear construction of world history. In lieu of the Hebrew case in particular, he finds that

> The historical narrative from the creation of the world to the fall of Jerusalem is neither a book, nor a collection of books, but a unique symbolism that has grown into its ultimate form through more than six centuries of historiographic work from the time of Solomon

> to *ca.* 300 B.C. Moreover, this written literary work has absorbed oral traditions which probably reach back as far as the first half of the second millennium B.C. Hence, it is possible to find a tradition from the seventeenth century [B.C.], side by side with an editorial interpolation of the fifth century, in a story that has received its literary form in the ninth century B.C. (Voegelin, 1974a, p. 145)

For lack of a better term, we could thus deem his historical sensitivity to the overlapping plural centers of narrative motivation multiperspectival.[5] However, this must not lead to the opposed error of regarding the composite canon of Hebrew biblical religion as if it comprised an arbitrary collective authorship:

> One may, furthermore, find that the odd composition is not a piece of clumsy patchwork but a well-knit story that conveys a fine point of nomad ethics, or spiritual responses to revelation, or diplomatic compromises with foreign divinities. And we may, finally, find that the story has an important function in a wider historical and speculative context which in turn reveals an equally complex composition. That is a disconcerting situation, as it appears impossible to identify the object of inquiry. Do we deal with the component ideas of the seventeenth, ninth, or fifth centuries; or with the idea conveyed by the composition, which does not seem to have a date at all; or with the meaning which the piece has by virtue of its position in the larger context? Certainly no simple answer will be possible, and in many instances no satisfactory one at all. We must recognize the difficulties presented by a symbolism that has absorbed primary traditions and records of more than a thousand years, and overlaid them with interpretations, with interpretations of interpretations, with redactions and interpolations, and subtle imposition of new meanings through integration in wider contexts. (Voegelin, 1974a, p. 145).

With in the above rendering of Voegelin's historicized hermeneutic as multiperspectival, we could also label the complexity of his social-scientific methodology as multiperspectival in the disciplinary sense and with respect to the delicate inter-penetration of first person (Biblical narrative of first person singular reports and first person plural accounts of Hebrew collective experience), second person (divine rebukes of individual kings and prophets and prophetic warnings to 'you' individuals, the Israelites, and/or the species), and third person (reports of events subjected to historical-critical analysis).

Therefore, also in opposition to those that would regard its unique narrative form as akin to the construction of a piece of literature, the symbolic significance Voegelin and Buber attribute to the ontologically-open call to second-personal imaginative participation includes granting the prospect of the real participation of God in the ongoing course of historical revelation still in the process of disclosure.

> The *telos* of the people's existence was ontologically real, and whoever participated sensitively and imaginatively in Israel's order was a potential participant in the creation of the historiographic symbol. The literary characteristics indicate no more than the common language of a group of persons, perhaps numerous over a period of time, who were occupied with the traditions concerning Israel's existence under God. We have arrived here at the basic philosophical weaknesses of literary criticism, that is, at the attempt to treat the Bibli-

[5] According to Voegelin: "The source criticism of the old type, we may say, is indeed dead. What has come into view through the labors of Old Testament students is the rich stratification of the narrative and the plurality of motivating centers. And that new freedom of critical exploration is about to repair much of the damage inflicted upon the meaning of the narrative by the literary conceits of the nineteenth century" (1974a, p. 206).

> cal narrative as if it were "literature" in the modern sense and the disregard for its nature as a symbolism which articulates the experience of a people's order—of the ontologically real order of Israel's existence in historical form. (Voegelin, 1974a, p. 156)

As implied in the nomenclature of his wider project of *Order and History*, the Hebrew conferral of meaning upon creation, the exodus event, and the ensuing deliverance into Canaan serves as much for Voegelin as the unique collective psychological experience of the Israelites as it also becomes, for him, the historically variegated ordering that each of the Axial traditions confer upon their historical experience in this same non-linear self and collective understanding.

While Voegelin's openness to the prospect of divine second-personal participation in human history may seem beyond the post-metaphysical commitments of contemporary critical theory, his steadfast commitment to the pragmatic qualities of lived experience continually reorients the focus of his analysis away from the misguided distractions of lapsing back into treating social science as a third-person observer somehow outside the set of events through which one ultimately cannot escape from status as a perpetual participant.

> Complexities in a structure of meanings cannot be dissolved by far-fetched explanations, but only by a clearer statement of the issue. We started from the observation that the world-history had absorbed variegated materials and merged them in the medium of the narrative. The narrative, with its content, was recognized as a symbolic form *sui generis*. It did not have a "subject matter"; its meaning had to be understood in terms of the experiences that motivated its construction. (Voegelin, 1974a, p. 179)

The utter absence of any capacity to regard the composite whole of history from the observer standpoint, fittingly, makes Hegelian closure upon the successful completion of a grand-historical narrative the exact opposite of his methodological aims.

In the final analysis, his unique employment of the multiperspectival mode of critical reconstruction led him to uncover three related but distinct historical fallacies attributed to the exegetical correctives he exercises upon the Hebrew canon of scripture.

> The literary genesis revealed the foundation of the Kingdom as the primary motive in chronological order; but the total construction, with its long posthumous work, made the historical present created by the Covenant, as well as the speculative origins and periods of history, the dominating principle of the content, though this motivation was secondary in chronological order. The order of motives in the content, thus, was the reverse of the order of motives in time. Moreover, to round out the problem, the order of motivations in time—first the Kingdom, second the Covenant—was the reverse order of events in time. The elements which account for the complexity of the historiographic work can, therefore, be summarized in the following three propositions: (1) In the sequence of historical events the Covenant precedes the Kingdom; (2) in the sequence of motivations of the narrative the Kingdom precedes the Covenant; (3) in the content of the narrative itself the Covenant dominated the Kingdom. Once the structure is recognized, its meaning is apparent. (Voegelin, 1974a, p. 179)

As a composite lesson to be drawn from the clarification of the complexity of the reversals in motives and sequences comes a corrective to how best to read the eschatological movement of the narrative itself as retaining its central focus upon the unresolvable tension between spiritual orders and their concrete institutionalization as political orders. Treating the concrete historical realization of a particular political kingdom (or state or any other polity) as if it were the ultimate telos of history supplants the central role to be played by both God and subject(s) in ongoing relations of trust. To do so would run counter to the original first-commandment prohibition on the construction of false idols, certainly endorsed by Buber's and Voegelin's emphasis on the You performative perspective of participant, as most effectively illustrated in the first generation critical theory of Horkheimer and Adorno.

Yahweh, Critical Theory, and Non-Idolatry: Justice and the Hebrew Unnamed God

Aptly summarizing their general aims for the sociological study and philosophical critique of modernity, Horkheimer and Adorno devoted their intellectual work to ending sources of domination in all of their historical forms. Their critical accounts of the emergence of the modern state saw it as carrying as much, if not more, potential for domination than for justice. They thus share with both Jaspers and Voegelin a fundamental suspicion toward political closure through the rational institutionalization of principles. Jaspers expressed this in his conclusions to *The Origin and Goal to History* that endorses a world order over a world empire (pp. 193–212). Voegelin showed similar pessimism in warning against the reduction of the political order to state activities that preclude considerations of participation in the wider cosmic order. Therefore, in an odd consensus among diverse philosophical schools, Horkheimer, Adorno, Jaspers, and Voegelin, respectively regard states and constitutional orders with a cautious eye as these could coercively impose transcendental categories of absolute ordering upon phenomena that belie administrative closure. However, in closer affinity to Jaspers' Encompassing as a more universalizable philosophical category than the species-ethical personal God of Israel (and humanity)—as defended by Voegelin and Buber, Horkheimer and Adorno call for strict adherence to the mutually reinforcing commandments of non-idolatry and prohibition on the use of the divine name.

Horkheimer and Adorno give a philosophical exposition of the long tradition behind the first commandment Hebrew prohibition on idolatry as a radical critique of the Enlightenment obsession with third-person objectivity. They acknowledge it as running the ideological risk of objectification of the divine. They pair together the theological ban on idols with the ritualistic practice of the non-utterance of God's holy name that runs throughout Hebrew history and finds its climax in Hebrew Kabala mysticism.

> Yahweh's essence will be relegated more and more to an ontological abyss completely separated from the world, and his name will be increasingly supplanted by the personal pronoun *hu'*, i.e. "Him," the "absolute Being," until it becomes totally unutterable, probably under the influence of Greek custom. But such a process did not make Yahweh either a *deus otiosus* or a pure intellectual abstraction. By a sort of paradoxical dialectic, which we encounter constantly in the doctrine of the monotheism of Israel, this transcendent God did not cease to be passionately concerned with this world and with its history. Yahweh also never ceased to be a Holy God. (Nikiprowetzky, p. 83)

Horkheimer and Adorno thus associate the inarticulate ordering of a reign of perfect justice demanded by an absolutely holy God with the aforementioned tradition of the unknown and inarticulate qualities increasingly ascribed to the tetragramaton (YHWH).

In contrast to the Enlightenment optimism of universal historical progress, they offer an alternate postmetaphysical first principle: the practical hope of bringing an end to the species-ethical existential constant of unspeakable suffering and loss. Like Jaspers and Voegelin, Adorno and Horkheimer thus leave history as an open narrative script seeking redemptive hope. Therefore, as a general locus of broad agreement, they each viewed neo-Hegelian idealism as carrying the latent risk of lapsing into either dogmatic institutionalization or gnostic withdrawal from pragmatic engagement with the world altogether. In light of a thoroughgoing secularization of Horkheimer and Adorno's shared Hebrew heritage, they associate an inarticulate longing for justice with the longstanding Hebrew prohibition of idols:

> A consciousness interpolating images, a third element, between itself and that which it thinks would unwittingly produce idealism. A body of ideas would substitute for the object of cognition, and the subjective arbitrariness of such ideas is that of the authorities. The materialist longing to grasp the thing aims at the opposite: it is only in the absence of images that the full object could be conceived. *Such absence concurs with the theological ban on images*. Materialism brought that ban into secular form by not permitting Utopia to be positively pictured; this is the substance of its negativity. At its most materialistic, materialism comes to agree with theology. Its great desire would be resurrection of the flesh, a desire utterly foreign to idealism, the realm of absolute spirit. The perspective vanishing point of historical materialism would be its self-sublimation, the spirit's liberation from the primacy of material needs in their state of fulfillment. Only if the physical urge were quenched would the spirit be reconciled and would become that which it only promises while the spell of material conditions will not let it satisfy material needs. (Adorno, 1973, pp. 207, 400, 401, 404)

Conceived in this light, Horkheimer and Adorno's appeal to the resurrection of the body as the ultimate satisfaction for historical injustice pushes directly against the potential tendency to associate the ineffability of the divine with an other-worldly rejection of human material needs or with mystical cognitive abstraction back into the elite academic realm of idealist concepts.

As support for what otherwise might seem to be an odd conflation of non-idolatry and an affirmation of a robust materialism, Uffenheimer affirms that the most accurate hermeneutic of the original Hebrew cannot even distinguish between justice as an ideal and its ensuing performative dimensions in concrete praxis. The historical tradition that outright rejects modern distinctions between the spiritual and material can apply to Hebrew biblical semantics in general and the proper understanding of a long litany of particular examples in light of their material and embodied manifestations. For instance, he ties the Hebrew noun *nefresh* (life, soul, spirit) to blood as the material manifestation of life or spirit, thus enhancing the meaning of blood wiping out the contaminants of the soul in addition to the prohibition against eating blood on the assumption of its material representation of divinely-endowed life. He also associates affective and intellectual experience with particular organs of the body, such as the link between the heart, emotive, and cognitive functions and the kidneys direct bearing on conscience. Uffenheimer shows how this association between biblical semantics and materiality applies as much to an organic understanding of the entire cosmos as to moral action and scriptural content:

> [T]he semantic field of the word *ruah* bears witness to the organic unity of the world, for it means both "spirit" and "wind" simultaneously. As to *mishpat, sedek, sedakah,* etc., they are no mere pneumatic-spiritual immaterial concepts. On the contrary, they are functional derivatives of concrete ways of behavior: thus *mishpat* and *sedakah* do not mean "justice" and "righteousness" as such, but "just deeds" or "righteous deeds." True, by a process of generalization these nouns slowly developed into abstract concepts, but the most important point is their originally concrete functional meaning. Last but not least, *davar* means "word," but the compound *devar YHVH* is not only the "word of God"; it is a concrete force of creative and destructive power: By the word God created the world (*Gen.* 1:3, etc.; *Ps.* 33:6). There is also something material in it, for God transmitted it to Jeremiah by physically touching his mouth (*Jer.* 1:9); on another occasion he coerced Ezekiel to eat a scroll which contained his words (*Ezek.* 3:1–4 ff.); it aroused a physiological reaction, for Ezekial relates its sweetness. Its destructive faculty comes to the fore in Jeremiah, where it is supposed to uproot, destroy, and overthrow kingdoms and nations (*Jer.* 1:10). (Uffenheimer 1986, p. 159}

In line with the second-person narrative approach I have ascribed to the Hebrew canon of scriptural exegesis so far, Uffenheimer posits such a holistic outlook upon creation, divine revelation, human action, and ritual prescriptions to an inherently dialogical, communicative, and free personal engagement between God and the world and between Yahweh and the Israelites individually and collectively (158).

In a thoroughly secularized application of these materialist overtones to basic Hebrew concepts, Horkheimer and Adorno embrace the pragmatic dimensions of justice by focusing on the ultimate redemption of the lived and embodied capacities of the body. Via appeal to the symbolism provided by the messianic longing and hope for bodily resurrection, they also strive to secure the institutional and material conditions beyond injustice as carrying mutually reinforcing material and moral dimensions. They find in dubious appeals to the institutional fetish of universal first principles of reason an aggressive affront against any perceived threat to ideologically driven civilizational universality. For Horkheimer and Adorno, the Enlightenment path to the hope of species self-deliverance ultimately unleashes the destructive powers of total warfare, culminating in the evil of genocide.

In an outright critique of Hegelian phenomenology (and therefore aligned with mutual opposition to Hegel shared with Voegelin) they apply this prohibitive restriction on attaining the absolute justice only ascertainable by a transcendently holy God to the idealist exaltation of the absolute truth of concepts. They project this fetish with absolute truth as an Enlightenment regression into the auspices of myth it purportedly had overcome and into an overt dismissal of the material conditions requisite for moral achievement of a just order. The utter confidence in Enlightenment reason above the material phenomena and practical engagements under purvey led to an unbridgeable disjunction between the language of philosophy taken as infallible truth in contrast to the non-categorical material phenomena informing language, finite embodiment, and the diverse particulars of every novel historical circumstance.

While Horkheimer and Adorno sought in their *Dialectics of Enlightenment* more directly to deduce the historical conditions for the possibility of the Holocaust to have happened in order best to prevent its re-occurrence, their justifiable skepticism toward the political institutionalization of justice leads them to seek out universalizable truth in the domain of their respective Hebrew—albeit secularized—upbringing.

> [I]f the possibility, however feeble and distant, of redemption in existence is cut off altogether, the human spirit would become an illusion, and the finite, conditioned, merely existing subject would eventually be deified as carrier of the spirit. An answer to this paradox of the transcendent was Rimbaud's vision of mankind freed from oppression as being the true deity. (Adorno, 1973, p. 400)

Adorno views this methodological commitment to philosophical truth as nonetheless ensconced in historical tradition and best approximated in the critical exegesis of sacred texts. He grapples directly with the question of losing the universality of truth to the historical specificity of a given philosophical tradition in his *Negative Dialectics*:

> [T]hat is the question how a thinking obliged to relinquish tradition might preserve and transform tradition.... Yet philosophy's methexis in tradition would only be a definite denial of tradition. Philosophy rests on the texts it criticizes. They are brought to it by the tradition they embody, and it is in dealing with them that the conduct of philosophy becomes commensurable with tradition. This justifies the move from philosophy to exegesis, which exalts neither the interpretation nor the symbol into an absolute but seeks the truth where thinking secularizes the irretrievable archetype of sacred texts. (Adorno, p. 54, 55)

His own biographical immersion in the Hebrew tradition brings this secularization of its Biblical canon to philosophy as a general norm for pragmatically transcendental truth in a manner widely consistent with Habermas's later critical theorist approach to the translation of religious concepts into the more rationally accessible domain of public reason. As an emendation to Habermas, the requisite warrant for engagement in truly fruitful inter-axial comparative philosophy presupposes the utmost effort on the part of disparate traditions not only to translate their claims into publically accessible language but also at least presumes the prospect that one could engage in the rigorous hermeneutic training necessary at least to approximate treating another Axial tradition from concepts and practices internal to its own self-understanding.

As an additional pragmatic presupposition, we must not mistake the conflation of the ban on idols with a cynical approbation of the utter impossibility of even seeking a reign of justice. Since we must not forget the necessary critical theorist tie between cognitive learning and material advancement in securing justice, we ought not to devalue the rhetorical dimensions of negative dialectics.

> Dialectics—literally: language as the organon of thought—would mean to attempt a critical rescue of the rhetorical element, a mutual approximation of thing and expression, to the point where the difference fades. Dialectics appropriates for the power of thought what historically seemed to be a flaw in thinking: its link with language, which nothing can wholly break. It was this link that inspired phenomenology to try—naively, as always—to make sure of truth by analyzing words. It is in the rhetorical quality that culture, society, and tradition animate the thought; a stern hostility to it is leagued with barbarism, in which bourgeois thinking ends. (Adorno 1973, p. 56)

In a performative twist, the emphasis upon this universal longing as pragmatically presupposed also to be a species-wide constant ultimately implies seeking to persuade others to engage in such rational justifications with performative import. In other words, Habermas's infamous 'unforced force of the better argument' would also presume that exemplary acts of justice derived from one or more of the great Axial traditions would carry an affective appeal that would invariably motivate attempts at redactive emulation.

However, in contrast to Habermas's tenor of optimism towards democratic proceduralism as perhaps the best means to overcome domination in all of its historical forms, there unmistakably resides a pessimistic strand to first generation critical theory. As adapted from perhaps the most understated influence upon first generation critical theory—in their appropriation of Shopenhauer's tragic view of the will, they resist overburdening reason beyond its localized capacities, yielding a starting point that posits a more romanticized reading of the human will. And as for constructing a grand-historical narrative to cover the aggregate human experience, their skeptical portrayal of reason as instrumental parlays at points on an outright collapse into thorough pessimism:

> Universal history must be construed and denied. After the catastrophes that have happened, and in view of the catastrophes to come, it would be cynical to say that a plan for a better world is manifested in history and unites it….No universal history leads from savagery to humanitarianism, but there is one leading from the slingshot to the megaton bomb….[T]he One and All that keeps rolling on to this day—with occasional breathing spells—would teleologically be the absolute of suffering. (Adorno 1973, p. 320, 323)

While critical theory indeed holds out the prospect of a hope for a better future for the species, their starting point would be to recognize the atrocities of the present as unjustifiable if one were to attempt a rational justification for such evils as the means to an aggregate progress to the history of humankind. In particular, Adorno's construal of negative dialectics plays two distinct functions in articulating a micro-level approach to communication action. Adorno's approach to a communicative ethics, in its disavowal of the prospect of constructing a systematically comprehensive theory makes an epistemic virtue out of this incompleteness: 'It lies in the definition of negative dialectics that it will not come to rest in itself, as if it were total. This is its form of hope' (Adorno 1973, p. 406). Such epistemic humility therefore serves as the motivational force seeking a perfect justice always to be unfulfilled in this world. Thus, in contrast to their more idealistic predecessors and later second-generation progeny, they are hesitant to offer a verdict of continual species moral maturation in light of trends globally that might rather bear testament to aggregate regress.

Since Horkheimer and Adorno were both Nazi-era German Jewish intellectuals forced to flee to the US for political asylum, and given that such a pragmatic and deeply historical style of philosophy emerged in the immediate context of the holocaust, critical theory in its practical orientation to social justice has since its origin held an ambivalent attitude toward religion and its impending secularization. On the one hand, in partial agreement with the likes of Freud and Nietzsche, they saw in religion, at its worst, ideological tendencies towards the highest forms of paranoia, neurosis, and politically charged resentment and oppression over alterity. However, on the other hand, in their 'Elements of Anti-Semitism: Limits of the Enlightenment' they characterized the pogrom as the climax of historical injustice through the German fascist totalitarian domination over the religious practices expressed by the European-wide Jewish diaspora of minority sub-cultures (Horkheimer and Adorno 1947, pp. 137–172). Therefore, they defended religious tolerance as a normative prerequisite of political justice, particularly in affirming their closing remarks to their seminal *Dialectics of Enlightenment* that recommend limiting and ultimately overcoming the 'rage against difference' often all too characteristic of Enlightenment secular modernity.

As for Adorno's position (which was typically a bit more optimistic than that of Horkheimer), he seems closest to Voegelin's biblical heritage of experiencing history as a manifold of textual interpretation, periodically disclosing aspects of the divine through communicative co-participation in a shared reality between humanity and God:

> How one should think instead has its distant and vague archetype in the various languages, in the names which do not categorically cover the thing, albeit at the cost of their cognitive function. …It is when things are read as a text of their becoming that idealistic and materialistic dialectics touch. But while idealism sees in the inner history of immediacy its vindication as a stage of the concept, materialism makes that inner history the measure, not just of the untruth of the concepts, but even more of the immediacy in being. The means employed in negative dialectics for the penetration of its hard objects is possibility—the possibility of which their reality has cheated the objects and which is nonetheless visible in each one. But no matter how hard we try for linguistic expression of such a history congealed in things, the words we use will remain concepts….To be known, the inwardness to which cognition clings in expression always needs its own outwardness as well. (Adorno 1973, p. 52, 53)

My own employment of alternative modernities as derived from the shared premises of a critical theorist micro-analysis of discursive communication will eventually lead to my casting of cosmoipolitan justice as the best rubric for realizing justice historically. Such an approach is amenable to attempts, for better and worse, to articulate the theopolitical species-ethical domains of each tradition as close as possible to its own hermeneutic self-understanding. As a project in comparative philosophy, competing Axial claims to species-ethical universality will be put to the pragmatic test of candidate rational discourses conducted in the characteristic mode of presupposed reason responsiveness to legitimate justificatory claims.

As a historical reconstruction of these Hebrew hermeneutic lessons from which Horkheimer and Adorno recognized deep indebtedness, Habermas comments on Adorno's warnings against 'reification as deification' or, rather, 'the distortion of something conditioned into the Unconditioned' (Habermas 2002, p. 158). The attendant Hebrew prohibition against images can be recast discursively as a critique of the 'reification of interpersonal relationships' that can employ the insights of philosophical school of first generation critical theory to inform Habermas's renewed interest in resetting the onset of modernity at the universalizing species-ethical achievements of the Axial Age (158):

> Adorno's work is guided by the intuition that a subjectivity run amok transforms everything around it into objects, elevating itself into an Absolute—against the unconditional right of each creature not to be overlooked, to be acknowledged for what it is. The rage of objectification ignores the essential core of the fully individuated Other, by which the creature is marked as having been made "in the image of God." Looked at philosophically, the powerful cognitive impulse behind the "Axial Age" [*Achsenzeit*] is captured in the First Commandment, namely emancipation from the chain of lineage and from the arbitrary will of mythic powers. At the time the world religions, as they developed a monotheistic or acosmic concept of the Absolute, pierced through the uniform, flat surface of narratively interwoven, contingent appearance, thus tearing open the gap between deep and surface structure, between essence and appearance, which first granted humanity the freedom of reflection and the power to distance itself from the abyss of immediacy. (Habermas 2002, p. 158)

Habermas's treats the contemporary exegesis of the philosophical import of the Hebrew first commandment as inseparable from the wider project of developing a discourse-theoretic account of reconstructing our second-person reflective capacities as annunciating the beginning of the discursively conferred freedom he now shifts to the Axial Age. As among the most unlikely of cohorts, Habermas thereby joins Jaspers, Voegelin, and Taylor in displacing both the conventional association between the rationality of a secular modernity and the concomitant necessity to disavow all ties to the inheritances of the axial transition.

3.2.2 The Promissory Narrative as a Composite Christian Hermeneutic? Reconciling John's Logos with the Synoptic Gospels' Sermon on the Mount

Turning now to the Christian context, we find both a continuation and a reversal of key narrative themes found in Judaism. The endemic tensions between the particular establishing of Israel, either symbolically or literally, as a new type of theopolity buttresses against the universalistic demands of justice to encompass the species. The universal versus particular tensions to be presumed as our comprehensive philosophical backdrop will test the limits of the practical realization of an order of justice. According to Voegelin,

> Further light will fall on the nature of the Israelite difficulty through a comparison with the inverse difficulty that beset the early Christians. In Christianity, the logia of Jesus, and especially the Sermon on the Mount, had effectively disengaged the meaning of faith, as well as of the life of the spirit, from the conditions of a particular civilizational order. The separation was so effective indeed that loss of understanding was a serious danger to many Christians. (Voegelin, 1974a, pp. 182, 183)

Voegelin places above emphasis upon the crucial differences stemming from the Sermon on the Mount not so much because it introduces any new tenets or commands to Hebrew political justice but because of the higher-order symbolic abstraction required to realize the theopolitical form taken in Christianity. As this teaching of Christ on the kingdom of heaven issues forth a litany of seven promises, we will interpret the Johannine view of the logos as inherently second-personal through what commentators term a promissory narrative concerning a social imaginary yet to come to full concrete fruition (Pinsent 2012, pp. 86–91). The abiding assumption of a promissory narrative remain consistent with the Hebrew postulation of God's goodness and justice, in addition to God's inability to make a false promise. However, the narrative parallelism among the seven distinct promises juxtaposes a beginning and current condition of the hypothetical participant addressed with a future assurance of a transformative fulfillment of a more desirable state of affairs yet to come. In addition, since John's gospel contains no straightforward equivalent to the Sermon on the Mount as clearly evidenced in each of the synoptic gospels (Matthew, Mark, and Luke), we will present the promissory narrative as comprising two distinct hermeneutic forms. Firstly, I will present the promissory narrative as the most fitting hermeneutic for disclosing the theopolitical character of the kingdom of heaven as elucidated in the three distinct synoptic iterations of the Sermon on the Mount. Secondly, as a defense of Voegelin's affinity for a non-Hellenistic reading of John's logos, although the author of John rarely refers to an explicit kingdom of heaven as such, we will argue that the distinct eschatological overtones presume the initiation of such a kingdom through the life and teachings of Christ.

Taken as a composite list of seven promissory narratives, the litany of promises in the Sermon on the Mount also evince a steady escalation from a lowest experiential plane that considers an array of undesirable practical exigencies to one's current condition in the world guaranteed as a mark of one's discipleship: depravity, sorrow, weakness, injustice, unwarranted persecution, emotional turmoil, and warfare. The promise of future redemption forged by spiritual endurance and maturation through these trials culminates in supreme individual fullness and a collective kingdom of profound blessedness. The narrative promissory not only alludes to a shift in narrative context from its symbolic parallel of Moses' reception of the law at Sinai to Christ's ensuing adaptation and redaction of Mosaic law. At a higher experiential plane, the Sermon annunciates the onset of an eschatological breakthrough that brings a sweeping temporal change of circumstances. Christ juxtaposes seven concrete assurances of turmoil with their attendant transformation of initial depravity into a kingdom that first welcomes the participation of those openly acknowledging their constant state of need. In the latter six promissory narrative constructs, we also find paradoxical assurances that willful acceptance of sorrow brings comfort, sincere humility secures inheritance of status in the world, hope in the onset of a reign of justice satiates that endless longing, acts of unmerited mercy reciprocate in a manner that goes well beyond fair merit, the gift of steadfast character in trial yields the reward of second-personal (strikingly Buberian) joint attention with the face of God, and the makers of peace further affirm a you-relationship of filiality with God as symbolically adopted progeny (Pinsent 2012, p. 88).

We ought momentarily to set aside obvious questions of utopian excess in promising an impossible state of affairs. Over-attention upon the pragmatic feasibility of such a reign clouds the most unique methodological nuance to the Sermon on the Mount: the subtlety of the co-participant temporal and spatial progressions taken up by Christ as the narrator. Common to each of the narrative depictions evinces a state of eschatological fulfillment to come in a double spatial and temporal sense.

While Christ addresses the audience to his teachings in a second-personal manner to describe the conditions for authentic discipleship, one could super-impose each of the trials annunciated in the seven promissory deliverances to narrative events that Christ had himself either already undergone or eventually would endure. Here, for the sake of contributing to the comprehensive scope to the narratives, we can take license to insert events described in John's Gospel to states of affairs presented in the narrative construct of the Sermon on the Mount. Firstly, he entered the human condition to experience the material and spiritual depravity that necessarily comes with spatial embodiment (John 1: 1–18). As for the latter six: he mourned the death of friends and wept (John 11: 1–44), humbly hid his divinity at times his detractors called for concrete proof of his power (John 18: 28–19: 16), purported to fulfill Isaiah's messianic promise of justice for the lowly (John 1: 23), extended mercy upon those labeled by the priestly elite as unworthy of God (John 7: 53–58: 11), performatively disavowed cultural proprieties when trumped by a higher law of unconditioned love (John 5: 1–18), and called his followers to turn the other cheek to aggressors (John 18: 11).

The multiperspectival overlays to modes of participation extend more broadly forward—as across the four Gospels, into the Book of Acts, to the Pauline and non-Pauline Epistles, and Book of Revelation—and backward, when providing another interpretive lens for reading the events, prophesies, and type symbols of the earlier Hebrew Bible. Specifically, from this more comprehensive hermeneutic standpoint, the trials as iterated would be ones that his disciples—akin to the characteristic social reaction to earlier Hebrew prophets—should expect to undergo if they are to serve as willing participants in the kingdom he has set forth for them imaginatively to consider. As yet a final layer, for those reflectively participating in the narrative as past, current, and future readers also are addressed as potential 'you' participants pressed to take a Kierkegaardian first-person affirmative or negative stance on the concomitant call to authentic discipleship. The enigmatic state of affairs presented contrasts the undeniable lure of participating in such a realm as matched by the second-person promise that the initial affective draw wanes when weighed against each of their concomitant escalation of costs. We could also take the diverse social standings of the disciples and the unlimited cultural settings of his prospective audiences as an indicator of their inherent species universality.

Jaspers and Christianity: Conflating Biblical Religion and the Axial Age Thesis?

Jaspers' positing of his Axial Age dates draws attention to the Hebrew step into universality in the broadest possible species-ethical sense. However, where Voegelin finds strong expressions of symbolic differentiation between Judaism and Christianity, Jaspers' contrary efforts attempt to cast similitude within his wider framing of Biblical religion. In the Hebrew period of Babylonian exiles, this diaspora context—for Jaspers—indicated the promise of a social and political order not limited to the particular confines of historical Israel as comprised of Canaan and Judah. The constant hope for deliverance into the promised land of the Abrahamic and Sinai covenants with numerous descendants transformed symbolically to a wider audience. What Voegelin and Buber called Yahweh's theopolity nonetheless embraced the tension between the Israelites as a particular people to bear the sign of species-wide import to non-Jews with Yahweh as their consummate deliverer.

However, in emphasis upon the requisite distinctions, Voegelin argues that the Christian appropriation of these same symbolic tensions differentiates itself from the theopolitical order of the Israelites once Christ adopts the role of supreme governance previously held by Yahweh:

> While the Prophets had to struggle for an understanding of Yahwism in opposition to the concrete social order of Israel, a long series of Christian statesmen, from St. Paul to St. Augustine, had to struggle for an understanding of the exigencies of world-immanent social and political order. The Prophets had to stress that status in the social order of Israel did not confer spiritual status on a man before God; the Christians thinkers had to stress that sacramental acceptance into the Mystical Body did not touch the social status of man—that masters were still masters, and slaves were slaves, that thieves were thieves, and magistrates were magistrates. The Prophets had to explain that social success was not proof of righteousness before God; the Christian thinkers had to explain that the Gospel was no social gospel, redemption no social remedy, and Christianity in general no insurance for individual or collective prosperity. (Voegelin, 1974a, pp. 182, 183)

In the Hebrew case, adherence to the Sinai covenant and the divinely-conferred membership among God's elect people ran up against the tension of the more universalistic call to be a sign to other nations as co-participants in the concrete unfolding of the world-historical just governance prescribed by Yahweh. In contrast, in the Christian case, by starting with the universalism of the kingdom of heaven of the Sermon on the Mount as a message of deliverance open to all humanity struggled with the opposite disjunction.

In other words, how ought one best render such a promise of species-ethical deliverance viable to any given civilizational context, social status, or material condition without the promised pay-off of a concrete transformation of the immanent world order? Framed in the Christian case by the initiation of a new type of kingdom detailed in the Sermon on the Mount, and the odd temporal perspective of realized eschatology of John's Gospel, each of the seven iterated promises require the internal transformation of one's dispositions matched by an intense hope in an order imaginatively portrayed but left hanging as to time, manner, and concreteness of impending disclosure. While Voegelin regards the Sermon on the Mount as reason for regarding Christianity as distinct from its Hebrew inheritance, Jaspers regards the consummate focus on hope in a transformative order to come as an abiding feature of Biblical religion.

However, what may seem a mere philosophical quibble has much to do with additional biographical and political reasons behind Jaspers' explicit rejection of perhaps the abiding feature of John's Gospel: the divinity of Christ. While unique in degree of self-proclamation offered in John, Jaspers' regards the forthright denial of these ascriptions as essential to supplanting the axis of world history away from Christ's birth and death (as in Hegel) in order to shift the turning point backward to the onset of the Axial Age. Scholarly commentary on these issues overlooks the autobiographical records Jaspers provides of citing Biblical scriptures as providing great consolation during the WWII Nazi era for both he and his wife of Hebrew heritage. However, in *The Perennial Scope of Philosophy*, while extolling the courage and vitriol of Kierkegaard against hypocrisy, Jaspers outright accepts Kierkegaard's call to make the existential choice concerning Christ, willfully and authentically choosing *not* to accept Christ's divinity. In his autobiographical remarks, he also reveals that his wife retained a much more sincere faith in her Judaic commitments than he having renounced Christ.

When considering the viability of granting Christianity Axial status, as assessed from this vantage of its potential conferral from Jaspers himself, we find ourselves in an awkward position. Although Jaspers' earlier pronouncement of the Exile prophets as the Hebrew figures that best characterize, for Jaspers, the climax of the Hebrew axial breakthrough as its strongest step into universality, we previously found that such a verdict risked relegating the import of earlier Hebrew hints at the species-ethical symbolic scope that comes with axial universality. However, when applied in this case of Christianity, the Exile prophets of Judaism celebrated by Jaspers as the breakthrough of Biblical religion offer what might actually provide Christianity with a more central axial hub, in temporal, spatial, and symbolic senses. In the temporal sense, Christians accepting Christ as fulfillment of the Second Temple messianic prophesies could concede the lack of inclusion of Christ within the climatic period labeled as the Axial Age, since these key prophetic figures also set this historical stage for the Jewish-born Christ prophet as the consummating fulfillment of temporal progression that also stretches back to include Moses, Abraham, and Adam. In the symbolically spatial sense, Christ becomes for the Christian the messianic fulfillment of the Exile prophetic promises of a deliver to come to restore the disarray brought about by the geographic Hebrew diaspora and their endemic persecution as consequent upon the aggressive imperialistic aspirations of its neighboring kingdoms.

However, in an odd hermeneutic twist, of all the Axial traditions under purview in this project, Jaspers could place Christianity as perhaps first upon his list for exclusion from legitimate axial status. Why? Jaspers stands firmly in agreement with his critical theorists predecessors Horkheimer and Adorno in explicitly rejecting much of Christian canonical doctrine, including the Incarnation, Christ as Messiah, and the Trinity. Taken the doctrinal effects into account, the rejection of the divinity of Christ puts him more in line with a longer tradition of Hebrew prophets that offers little reason for substantial differentiation with the prior Hebrew tradition (Hearsh 1957).

In addition, beyond mere philosophical differences, Jaspers' looked upon the confessional institutionalization of Christianity and church organized worship as running the grave risk of the ideological construal of its symbolic teachings as if they were a concrete political project ripe for backing by legal-juridical coercion. Insofar as Jaspers likewise retrospectively reads the Hebrew Axial Age prophets—Amos, Hosea, Isaiah, and Jeremiah—and their messianic messages of hope in purely symbolic terms, he nonetheless envelopes all of the sufficiently axial experiential content of Christian praxis into his wider rubric of Biblical religion. In claims to the exclusivity of the truth of Christian revelation, he finds the conflation of a particular type symbol of the divine with universal species applicability as another exercise of impertinence against the deity. In a manner surprisingly akin to Horkheimer and Adorno's critiques of Christianity, he likewise follows in their Hebrew tradition of opting for a nameless God of the Encompassing as an alternative to objectification of the divine into ideological dogmatism.

Epistemic Authoritarianism: Jaspers' Critique of the Divinity of Christ Continued

On the one hand, Jaspers rejects the doctrine of the incarnation (as does Horkheimer and Adorno) due to concerns over rendering the infinite transcendence of God in human form. Reiterated in Adorno's words in his *Negative Dialectics*:

> No absolute can be expressed otherwise than in topics and categories of immanence, although neither in its conditionality nor as its totality is immanence to be deified. According to its own concept, metaphysics cannot be a deductive context of judgments about things in being, and neither can it be conceived after the model of absolute otherness terribly defying thought. It would be possible only as a legible constellation of things in being. From those it would get the material about which it would not be; it would not transfigure the existence of its elements, however, but would bring them into a configuration in which the elements unite to form a script. To that end, metaphysics must know how to wish. (Adorno 1973, p. 407)

As for Adorno's appeal to read a post-metaphysical epistemology as a script, such an analogy can inform Jaspers' concept of Biblical religion as a post-metaphysical construal of hope rooted in the pragmatic experience of particular groups. What Adorno adds to the communicative dimensions of cosmoipolitan justice would be the species-ethical appeal to hope and wishing insofar as he sees this as the ultimate motivational factor behind our affective drives for thought leading into pragmatic discourse. For Adorno, along with Jaspers' existentialism, the danger of conferring one's hope upon Christ as Messiah would also entail a concomitant lapse in personal responsibility and a vain hope for establishing a communicative relationship with a transcendent divine that could only be met by a fellow member of the species. Moreover, in putting too much stock into what can be given proof by our deductive reasoning, one's confidence in Christian metaphysics as delivering truth could easily lapse into a coercive justification for force against those that do not submit to the rational force of communicating such arguments. On this note, Jaspers goes as far as to say acknowledging Christ as 'God incarnate' postulates an irreconcilable tension between the infinite and finite whose possible mediation fully escapes his comprehension and thereby falls beyond the threshold of what one can reasonably hope to communicate.

As far as Jaspers' characterization of biblical religion is concerned, in disavowing the divinity of Christ he nonetheless interprets what Christians characterize as the four gospels of the New Testament as composing a unified script of continuity with the Hebrew Bible. He thus views the writers of the four gospels as Jews in conversation with the tradition of Biblical religion in their incorporation of the intense drama of the world-historical changes brought about by the expansion of the Roman Empire. As for Jesus, Jaspers views Christ as a Hebrew teacher possessing supreme communicative skills in rendering the tenets of Biblical religion to diverse audience in manners fully consistent with the general moral-ethical teachings of Hebrew origin. While Jaspers includes Christ among a short book on the great communicative personalities of world history that also includes Socrates, Confucius, and Buddha (Jaspers 1957b)—and Jaspers was raised with a Protestant background—he finds in the teachings of Christ the full culmination of the axial breakthrough initiated by the Hebrew prophets contemporaneous with the Greek, Athenian, Chinese, and Indian steps into the universal prospect of boundless communication.

As for the political backdrop, we should recall that one of Jaspers' stated goals in defending the axial age thesis was to de-center world-history away from a Christocentric and Eurocentric focus. Jaspers disaggregates the various strands of relatively simultaneous cultural forms of the universalization of our communicative capacities in a manner that could not be construed in a Hegelian step-wise progression of Spirit. Although competing accounts differ over whether Jaspers did or did not derive his original use of the term axial age from Hegel on world history, Jaspers sought to defend a truly world philosophy that displaced Christ as central. Relegating Christ's status also allowed Jaspers to remain consistent in establishing a world philosophy of boundless communication that could truly take a broader, multi-centered Axis of history to extend all the way into the present, as not culminating in the retrospective progress of European achievements over those stemming from Asia and India. Jaspers thereby redacted Hegel's reference to Christ as the axis upon which world history turns in an overtly political attempt too to advance a multi-polar view of world-history as a better account for taking other major world powers as true communicative partners as emerging into world-historical post-WWII prominence—such as the Soviet Union, India, and China (Jaspers 1953).

Pairing Jaspers' rejection of Christ's divinity with his hermeneutic emphasis upon all of Jesus's apostles as Jews, we can begin to understand why he conflates Hebrew and Christian traditions (and sometimes adds Islam) as Biblical religions. This implicitly confers axial status on Christianity only vicariously through the major Hebrew prophets insofar as Christ is not read as the fulfillment of messianic prophesies. In turn, it allows for a reconstructive reading of both Judaism and Islam as permutations of Biblical religion to be read on more neutral terms by not seeing Judaism and Islam as somehow deficient to its more dubiously Western corollary. As an epistemic alternative to Habermas's similar efforts to revisit the Axial Age thesis, Jaspers takes significant steps beyond a methodologically atheist stance by postulating each tradition as a philosophical faith (Habermas 2001, pp. 41–44). Instead of Habermas's tendency to view the role of philosophy as facilitating the translation of originally religious concepts in a more abstract, rationally universal, and publically communicable language, Jaspers presents philosophical faith as rational only insofar as participants in a given Axial tradition view their attempts at communicating universality as an ultimately unfillable wish that concedes the limits of faith to render communicable an ineffable Encompassing as the ultimate type symbol and cipher. He sees the Encompassing as closer to Adorno's above recommendation of metaphysics to re-engage its capacity to wish in a more affective and romantic construal of the universal material urges that unite the deepest symbolic longings of each branch of Biblical religion along with the four other axial traditions of China and India respectively.

Despite the historical remark of Christ falling outside the crucial 800–200 BCE. Axial Age, Jaspers' reasons for qualifying Christianity within the rubric of biblical religion still require more explicit formulation. Secondary literature has since clarified at least three main criteria for a tradition to attain Axial status, specifically adapted here to our current assessment of Christianity within the framing rubric of the promissory narrative. The three criteria include (i) heeding a call to transcending the immanent world order, even if opting to remain within the mundane order by employing some degree of radical reflection. This retains the prospect of a higher-order philosophical 'reflection upon reflection' that nonetheless still retains concrete material ties to the immanent world order, as evidenced best in the opening Chap. 1 discourse on Patocka's 'transcensus.' In its Christian scriptural iterations, we could trace such efforts at an inherently relational interpretation of transcensus back to Christ's purported teachings concerning the onset of the Kingdom of Heaven in the passages on the Sermon on the Mount in the synoptic Gospels and for the eschatological hermeneutic of already initiated but not yet fulfilled tenor of John's Gospel on the logos.

Secondly, we can agree with Charles Taylor's emphasis upon the onset of an Axial breakthrough entailing (ii) the outright confirmation of the paramount triumph of the good over evil as part of what would constitute the objective assessment of a fulfilling life. In illustrating the Christian overtones to Taylor's understanding of goodness as relational fulfillment, I will follow his construal of fullness in the opening pages of his *A Secular Age* (2007) that he sets in stark contrast to a Kantian alternative picture of fullness.

Given the general terms of this contrast, we can also lay it out in terms of my thorough resistance to reading the Johannine logos in neo-Platonic terms that do not give due justice to the relational hermeneutic to Christianity as a Biblical religion comprised of promissory narratives. For instance, take Kant's own read in his *Metaphysics of Morals* of the famous Gospel passage of Christ's rebuke of a wealthy ruler calling Christ 'Good teacher' in the ruler's query concerning the necessary and sufficient conditions for the inheritance of eternal life and entry in the Kingdom of God. As it reads in Luke 18: 18–19 (and parallels across the synoptic Gospels that appear in Mark 10: 17–19; Matthew 19: 16–17): 'A certain ruler asked him, "Good teacher, what must I do to inherit eternal life? (18)" "Why do you call me good?" Jesus answered. "No one is good—except God alone (19)."' Kant then proceeds to interpret the passage in a manner that supports a neo-Platonic primacy of ideal *a priori* recognition of a concept of perfection on the part of the moral exemplar, independent of the patchwork morals that others attempt to derive by starting with concrete examples and then building up to transcendental principles. Kant explains:

> Even the Holy One of the gospel must first be compared with our ideal of moral perfection before he is recognized as such. Even he says of himself, "Why do you call me (whom you see) good? None is good (the archetype of good) except God only (whom you do not see)." But whence have we the concept of God as the highest good? Solely from the ideal of moral perfection, which reason frames a priori and connects inseparably with the concept of a free will. (Kant 1993, p. 22; original 1785 *MM*, p. 408, 409)

We could certainly concede that the primary purpose of Kant's example here serves not to provide accurate Biblical exegesis. He clearly seeks as an illustration for his rejection of deriving morality from examples, and the concomitant necessity to appeal to a priori principles of reason. However, we do find a long inheritance of construing a sufficiently modern depiction of the second person perspective as ultimately derived from a secular rendition of irrevocable personal autonomy. Taylor describes the abiding features of this vision as follows:

> For modern unbelievers…The power to reach fullness is within. There are very different variations of this [fullness]. One is that which centres on our nature as rational beings. The Kantian variant is the most upfront form of this. We have the power of rational agency to make the laws by which we live. This is something so greatly superior to the force of mere nature in us, in the form of desire, that when we contemplate it without distortion, we cannot but feel reverence (Achtung) for this power. The place of fullness is where we manage finally to give this power full reign, and so live by it….But this doesn't in the end mean that there is any reception from the outside; the power is within; and the more we realize this power, the more we become aware that it is within, that morality must be autonomous and not heteronomous. (Taylor 2007, p. 8)

Taylor begins his affront against a myopic understanding of a sufficiently rational vision of modernity as inherently secular (and Western) in providing a Buddhist counter-example of an alternate understanding of morality, sufficiently modern, but nonetheless not putting all emphasis on subjective autonomy: '[H]ere [in Buddhist 'fullness'] the personal relation might drop out as central. But the emphasis would be all the stronger on the direction of transcending the self, opening it out, receiving the power that goes beyond us' (8).

As yet a third variant upon modernity, Taylor finds in Christian conceptions of fullness an inherently relational component that more fully accords with the above presentations of promissory narratives as second person forfeitures of full autonomy that nonetheless, for Taylor, provide a richer account for the achievement of moral fullness:

> [T]he sense is that fullness comes to them, that it is something they receive; moreover, receive in something like a personal relation, from another capable of love and giving…. [A]nd they are aware of being very far from the condition of full devotion and giving; they are aware of being self-enclosed, bound to lesser things and goals, not able to open themselves and receive/give as they would at the place of fullness. So there is the notion of receiving power or fullness in a relation; but the receiver isn't simply empowered in his/her present condition; he/she needs to be opened, transformed, brought out of self. (Taylor 2007, p. 8)

If we contextualize the aforementioned passage of the rich man seeking eternal life in the hermeneutic offered by Biblical religion in its Christian permutations, we find a long litany of supporting textual clues that fit quite consistently with our framing narrative of the Sermon on the Mount providing the requisite support for a second person rendering (and not neo-Platonic) of the Christian logos. Examples include but are not limited to each of the seven promissory narratives of the Sermon on the Mount. Immediately before the rich man comes on the scene, Jesus rebukes disciples for their own attempts to censure him for tending to children. Christ's reply to enter the kingdom like children points to the open recognition of one's depravity and utter lack of pervasively mature autonomy as juxtaposed by Taylor on the two understandings of modernity. At the other end of the framing passages, the narrative follows the interchange with the wealthy man with the straightforward promise from Christ that he willingly must forsake his own life upon his impending reenty into Jerusalem with a guarantee of persecution by trial and death. Before suggesting to his own followers they must be willing to sacrifice their own life to enter the kingdom, Christ also advises the rich man humbly to forsake all of his material possessions. At the close of the interchange, Christ also suggests entry to the kingdom may require even leaving one's family in order to enter into a state of spiritual and filial adoption to membership in God kingdom. Suffice it to say, in searching the relevant context to the narrative, Kant's derivation of a priori transcendental ideals of perfection from the passage, as grounded in personal rational autonomy, seem to offer a hermeneutic that fundamentally disavows the replete references to conceding our relational dependence as a precondition for Taylor's portrayal of Christian fullness.

Lastly, as a third and final condition for conferral of axial status, (iii) we find some concession that the world order as it currently stands is incomplete. World history considered retrospectively may even seem chaotic or tragic, without the axial breakthrough disclosing an alternative vision for the world as it could be—even if remaining fully unrealized while within the mundane temporal order. On this tripartite rubric of assessment, through the continual references to the kingdom of heaven as set in stark opposition to worldly kingdoms and empires, we will concede to Christianity having fully met the major criteria for axial status even while sticking within its own internal resources, whether scriptural, prophetic, or doctrinal.

As for additional background political motives that may have been informing Jaspers' philosophical commitments, some commentators on Jaspers' overall picture of Biblical religion highlight his rejection of the dogmatic authority of institutionalized religion. On such a fully politicized rendering, Jaspers' open rejection of the Incarnation includes his view of dogmatic theology as one of the contributing factors he associates with WWII totalitarian regimes. In lieu of our earlier parallels noted between the post-WWII philosophical commitment of Jaspers and first generation critical theorists, Horkheimer and Adorno likewise lament the volatile mix of unhindered spiritual dogma and the totalitarian concentration of power in the hands of the state:

> The alliance between enlightenment and power has debarred from consciousness the moment of truth in religion while conserving its reified forms. Both circumstances finally benefit fascism: the unchanneled longing is guided into racial-nationalist rebellion, while the descendants of the evangelistic zealots are converted into conspirators of blood communities and elite guards, on the model of the Wagnerian knights of the Grail. In this way religion as an institution is partly meshed directly into the system and partly transposed into the pomp of mass culture and parades. (Horkheimer and Adorno 1947, p. 144)

To lend credence to this political and philosophical reconstruction, it would not only be the Germanic (and Voegelin as Austrian) critics and persecuted academics immediately affected by conditions leading to the Holocaust that made this tie between dogmatic religion and fascism. In the Anglo-American context, Rawls as a former combatant in WWII, draws similar conclusions in his *Law of Peoples* (1999):

> Great evils are sufficient unto themselves. But the evils of the Inquisition and the Holocaust are not unrelated. Indeed, it seems clear that without Christian anti-semitism over many centuries—especially harsh in Russia and Eastern Europe—the Holocaust would not have happened. That Hitler's "redemptive anti-semitism" strikes us as demonic madness—how could one believe such fantasies?—doesn't change this fact. Yet we must not allow these great evils of the past to undermine our hope for the future of our society as belonging to a Society of liberal and decent peoples around the world. (Rawls 22)

Although addressing different aims and overall themes than Taylor's *A Secular Age*, Rawls thereby takes a clearer position on the darker sides of the history of Latin Christendom—the Inquisition and Holocaust—that critics find curiously lacking in the otherwise more comprehensive, relevant, and lengthy themes taken up by Taylor's seminal work.

Horkheimer and Adorno, in their unsettling reflections on the historical experience of the rise of the Nazi Fuhrer, go farther than Rawls in the sheer description of the attendant demonic madness motivating the Holocaust. One practical interpretation of their complex *Dialectics of Enlightenment* sees the composite work as having attempted to provide a philosophical account of the genealogy of the paranoiac that gains political sway and persuasive authority over the masses:

> It is as if the serpent which told the first humans 'Ye shall be as gods" had kept his promise in the paranoiac. He creates everything in his own image. He seems to need no living thing yet demands that all serve him. His will permeates the whole universe; nothing may be unrelated to him. His systems know of no gaps. (Horhmeimer and Adorno 1947, p. 157)

Intentionally ascribing allegorical overtones to perhaps the prime motivator of the Biblical account of the Fall, Horkheimer and Adorno refer to the relevant framing narrative with the serpent attempting a rational justification of God not wanting Adam and Eve to have their eyes opened to wisdom as reason for the prohibition placed upon the fruit of the tree of knowledge of good and evil (Genesis 1: 4–6). Horkheimer and Adorno perceive as the failure of the Enlightenment obsession with reason would be the objectivigating turn in metaphysics, epistemology, and theology as spilling over eventually into political theory. When tied to dogmatic theology, the rechanneling of affective sentiments politicized opens the prospect of reducing human action solely to the steering of a third-person perspective. When practical action does not conform to reified social and political ideals it must ultimately resort to administratively backed coercion.

> Objectifying thought, like its pathological counterpart, has the arbitrariness of a subjective purpose extraneous to the matter itself and, in forgetting the matter, does to it in thought the violence which later will be done in practice. The unconditional realism of civilized humanity, which culminates in fascism, is a special case of paranoid delusion which depopulates nature and finally nations themselves. (Horkheimer and Adorno, p. 159)

Seen in this light, Horkheimer, Adorno, Jaspers', and even Kant's explicit rejection of the incarnation was likely as much, or even more of an indictment on church dogma than exclusively tied to the veridical status of Christ's teachings (Habermas 2009, p. 214).[6] The perceived dangers of dogmatism unchecked by the political

[6] Habermas even goes so far as to suggest that the Kantian emphasis on individual autonomy derives, at least in part, to the Protestant emphasis on the autonomous intellect, or 'God in our-

mobilization of masses thereby introduced a dangerous buffer against any skeptical epistemic judgment cast upon political authority. In concrete historical effects, Rawls cites leading German church authorities as not just complicit but actively endorsing the new German regime's April 1, 1933, boycott of the Jews (originally scheduled only to last five days; Rawls 1999, p. 22, n. 16).

As far as the aforementioned personal, political, and methodological backdrop bears on deriving a distinctly Christian discourse-ethical approach to axiality, one major concern that arises with critical theorists, including Habermas, would be unwarranted institutionalized dogma insulating spiritual claims from critical scrutiny. Insofar as discourse ethics subjects every possible epistemic claim to the normative demands of rational justification, the appeal to the dogma of tradition as the rationale for holding a discursive commitment cannot serve as a legitimate warrant for one's claim(s). In the specific context of extending Axial claims to the methodological demands of Habermas's discourse ethics, Maeve Cooke notes that Habermas (and we could here include both Jaspers and Voegelin) wants to evade a particular brand of epistemic authoritarianism. For Jaspers, the immediacy of institutionalized church complicity with the conditions leading up to the Holocaust provides him additional reasons for casting Biblical religion outside the domain of any particular institutional orthodoxy and calling explicitly for state regimes that promote religious tolerance (Jaspers 1953, p. 221).

While I earlier attempted to differentiate the symbolic import Voegelin ascribes to Christian redaction of Hebrew biblical themes, Voegelin nonetheless heeds similar warnings of the dangers in collapsing theological and political dogma. Voegelin's expansive notion of Gnosticism negatively categorizes any attempt to institutionalize a particular salvational impulse into concrete form. He thus raises similar concerns with the attendant dangers of insulating dogmatism from critique via the moral, ethical, and political fallacy of institutionalized political closure coercively backed by privy claims to untested authority:

> Considering the history of Gnosticism, with the great bulk of its manifestations belonging to, or deriving from, the Christian orbit, I am inclined to recognize in the epiphany of Christ the great catalyst that made eschatological consciousness an historical force, both in forming and deforming Christianity. (Voegelin, 1974b, p. 20)

In her similar reflections on the domineering effects of unchecked epistemic dogmatism in Habermasian critical theory, Maeve Cooke concurs with Voegelin, Jaspers, Horkeimer, and Adorno's concerns and offers a response to these and related challenges of Christian epistemic authoritarianism (Cooke 2013, pp. 249–274).

---

selves' as final authority on scriptural exegesis—thus fully insulated from heteronomous dependence upon ecclesiastical warrant (2009, p. 214). Although not explicitly cited in any secondary literature I am aware of to this point, Kant may even have for support in mind the Romans 2: 13–15 proclamation: 'For it is not those who hear the law that are righteous in God's sight, but it is those who obey the law who will be declared righteous. Indeed, when Gentiles, who do not have the law, do by nature things required by the law, they are a law for themselves, even though they do not have the law, since they show the requirements of the law are written on their hearts, their consciences also bearing witness, and their thought now accusing, now even defending them' (Witte 2014, p. 78).

Firstly, she notes that in Habermas's public discourse with Ratzinger in 2004, each had recognized the normative imperative for placing restraints upon dogmatism characteristic of our postsecular age. Habermas and Ratzinger agree that religion (and I would substitute here: any claims of authority from an Axial tradition as a more expansive rubric than the seventeenth century notion of religion) must also allow itself to the subjection if critique from natural sciences, social sciences, and the deliberation of a critically rational public. They also agreed that in addition to opening church authority to the scrutiny of the historical-critical method, scientific rationality must subject itself to critique from religious authority to thwart its own dubious claims to epistemic supremacy.

Cooke also notes that a religious claim (which I will from here forward take the broad license to substitute for the wider scope of Axial claim) may derive from equally substantive ethical sources that are often likewise surreptitiously linked to deliberative claims of a secular and/or agnostic character. In other words, Cooke judges that Habermas's decided preference for the rational legitimacy and universalizable consensus of moral claims—most likely, for him, of a secular and/or agnostic origin—cannot thereby impute de facto irrationality to both religious claims and any claims made from an ethical standpoint (individual or group specific; possibly agnostic, secular, or religious). Whether Habermas repeats the same mistake of classifying Axial claims as unwarranted remains dubious at best. Since the Axial traditions are deeply imbued in a particular tradition for the sources of their species-ethical universality (and not moral-rational), one wonders whether their merely unrealized ability to generate rational consensus would be enough to discount their latent potential for achieving universality. The hypothetical abstraction of claims achieving universality to the moral level seems, for Cooke, inherently to mask as secular neutrality merely the successful cases of universality that may have initially started their attempts at legitimation from the more restricted domain of the ethical.

As a proposed alternative to Habermas, in her association of revelation with the less innocuous classification of disclosure (since even secular reasons of a variety of types could have at some moment in their genealogy broken through into many iterated stages of conscious disclosure), Cooke questions whether Habermas has put too much stock into the ability of public reasons alone to bring about epistemic transformation that often comes from the experiential disclosure of a wider epistemic/perceptual openness. For instance, she argues that environmental social movements of the last few decades have achieved variegated forms of disclosure, at distinct stages, from many epistemic sources all oriented to overlapping consensus on attributing an enhanced moral standing to an array of ecological communities—perhaps even approaching a conferral of second person Thou standing. In addition, even if Habermas were to retain the lexical priority of public reason-giving as the privileged source of legitimacy for the validity tied to one's yes/no verdict of rational justification, Cooke also points out that the real pragmatics of lived discourses and practical decision-making likely include a complex confluence of rational claims, moral claims, ethical commitments, and mixed religious, secular, and agnostic shifts in perceptual openness. She thus places moral and ethical claims on an equal discursive plane by seeing either as brought about by an array of revelatory and non-revelatory forms of truth disclosure.

A Critique of Jaspers on the Impersonal Encompassing: Towards a Christian Universal Pragmatics of Communication

In order to derive a distinctively Christian pragmatics of communication that draws from the micro-level discourse of person-to-person interaction, we must return to the covenantal character of justice as initiated by God's communicative interaction with His elect. Kaufmann provides the initial set of assumptions by couching the covenantal nature of God's justice along the terms of a promissory narrative. His account has less to do with the concretization of specific legal-juridical forms and more with a relational and personal understanding of the nature of God.

> To the Jews, the covenant between God and man is itself a moral contract binding on either partner: they are defined by their positions in it. God is the God of the covenant and, thus, the God of man, just as man is—not the *animal rationale* or the *homo faber*, but—the man of God. '*Zedakah*' (justice seasoned by charity) of both God and man means their standing the test in a common trial, in a correlation (*b'rith*) of mutual responsiveness and responsibility. That to the Jews correspondence in co-operation belongs to the very nature of God as well as man is to be emphasized over against the Augustinian Neo-Platonism in the interpretation of God's name in Exodus 3:12 ff, the translation of *Eheye asher Eheye* by the *Sum qui Sum*....Suffice it to say that the promise that is implied in the name: "I shall be with you the way I shall decide to be with you whenever you seek me in your need" has completely disappeared in Philo as well as in its Latin version and, therefore, also in the English "I am that I am." The phrase is rendered in Latin not only in the tense of the eternal present to designate the Immutable Being (*Esse est nomen incommutabilitatis*); it is said to denote the self-sufficiency, self-containedness, the inner absoluteness of Being as such apart from any relations. (Kaufmann 1957, p. 261, 262)

According to Kaufmann, Jaspers' conception of God errs on two related fronts as they both bear on the current attempt to derive a communicative ethic from the context of Christian axial universality. Jaspers' aforementioned overt resistance to accept the personhood of Christ as the man-God was intended to avert the risk of objectifying God within the realm of the finite. The conferral of divinity upon the person of Christ also brought the historical risk of Church dogmatic authority operationalized for political motives. However, Jaspers' insulation of God from interpersonal mutuality came at the cost of communicative discourse between individual persons and the Encompassing.

For Jaspers' axial hypothesis to work—he must uphold the dual claim that all the axial religions are cryptic referents to the same Absolute and that none thereby can claim supreme epistemic authority over the others. However, what Jaspers' gains in the universalism and tolerant appeal of his overall project, Kaufmann thinks he sacrifices in forfeiting the capability to utilize resources internal to *both* Christian and Hebrew doctrine. Kaufman's cooperative portrayal of the b'rith as a shared trial offers precisely the immanent practices of a realized hope for the boundless communication that Jaspers nonetheless ascribed to the onset of the Axial Age. In the end, some of the onus of responsibility placed upon Jaspers could be lightened if we attribute these errors to the Hellenization of Judaic and Christian hermeneutic doctrine characteristic of traditions building upon Plotinus and Augustine. If Biblical religion was already led in philosophical directions not really true to the more pragmatic and originally non-elite communicative appeal to an elect aggregate, the more universal you plural address of the original Hebrew address to anyone heeding the call to enter into communion with a personal God opens space for the boundless communication Jaspers' originally sought.

Kaufman goes as far as suggesting that Jaspers' deflation of God into an impersonal being renders the prospect of second personal responsibility for one's claims obsolete. Jaspers might have taken the less extreme route of rejecting the divinity of Christ but accepting the prospect of a Hebrew covenantal God with whom one can enter into yes or no binding promissory narratives. According to Kaufmann, the absence of God's powers of sociality already fully present in the Hebrew biblical canon also renders impossible the responsible acceptance or rejection of his commands:

> Seen in this way [as an asocial being], God is no longer essentially the God of the Covenant. In Jaspers, "*Bezug*"—the being drawn of things toward one another and, thus, toward the ultimate ground—may have its reward, but it has no authorization, has no response and is none. In responsible action, we may answer for ourselves by answering the claims of our fellow beings; but 'in this respect,' i.e., in our respect for them, we do not answer a question of which they are the carriers rather than the authors….This is, indeed, what seems to follow from the "*Sum qui Sum.*" It threatens both the personal and creative nature of deity. A person belongs into a social context. In the social grammar it is a first, second, or third person. (Kaufmann 1957, pp. 261–263)

In the social grammar recommended by Kaufmann above, to turn the name and nature of God into an objective essence risks treating God as a third-person object devoid of personality and creative freedom. For Kaufmann, the original appeal of the work of Jaspers on the potential for boundless communication characteristic of the Axial Age was Jaspers' non-objectification of the conditional ground for the very prospect of communication. In addition, insofar as Jaspers is well aware of the Hebrew notion of persons as image-bearers of God, Kaufmann also judges that Jaspers cannot conceive of human subjectivity independent of its ultimate satisfaction remaining unrealized. While taking the existential maxim of 'bound to be free' as a species-ethic claim in lieu of the concretization of global ties of irrevocable interdependence, Kaufmann argues that an existential humanism without God as co-participant in the creative process of shaping human history balks at the identification of the creative source of that aspect of our nature in the very foundation of ultimate reality as inter-personal. The flip side of the same dilemma would be to lapse into a Hegelian participation in the unfolding of the Encompassing without authentic responsibility as co-participants in shaping the emergent world order.

In contrast to a more dialogical view, ultimately Jaspers' account of addressing or communicating with the divine as a second person replaces the skepticism of the first generation critical theory of Horkheimer and Adorno with the reward of a benign mystical contemplation of participation in a transcendence lacking communicative means to decode its ultimately cryptic ciphers and symbolically cloked meaning. Jaspers' thereby echoes Horkheimer and Adorno's preference for a silent, ineffable, and inarticulate transcendence without the full force of their felt, experienced, and affective urge longing for justice:

> Transcendence remains to him [Jaspers], as to Kant an *a-logon*, both ineffable and incommunicative,—the strictly unknown and silent God, the *Ain Soph* of Jewish mysticism. Its presence may be experienced; but it cannot be personally addressed and revered in its 'proper name'. And to this silence corresponds, at the bottom of the scale, even in the dark recesses of our own animal lives, the muteness of nature. Nature's physiognomic expression, eloquent and fascinating as it may prove, is not communicative language, it is not empirically controllable and neither responsive nor responsible in itself. (Kaufmann 1957, p. 229)

In his final analysis, Jaspers runs contrary to the genealogical optimism of Voegelin's earlier offering of a species-ethical and experiential narrative to explain the thornbush episode of the Sinai covenant. In light of a narrative account of the co-creation of man and nature through the anthropomorphic projections of generations of progeny stretching across the Biblical accounts of both human and non-human origins, Jaspers ultimately must concede the inability to address either God or nature as a Thou co-participant in communication. Jaspers concludes that absolute transcendence has no communicative promissory of its ultimate consummation. The divine can at best be approached at the limits of cryptic ciphers. In stripping away any personal attributes ascribed to God, he insulates his more universally abstract Encompassing from the perceived parochialism of Abrahamic renditions of the divine.

> All transcendental use of the logical categories, all attempts to submit Transcendence to the judgment of the finite are overstepping the bounds of rational communication. To Jaspers, even the sublime tautology of the *Eheye asher Eheye*, the *Sum qui Sum* ("I am that I am") is, in the use of the first person, as inadequate an expression of the All-Encompassing as is the *Est qua Est* (the Being *qua* Being) in the Greek tradition from Parmenides to Plotinus. The categories creep into the final tautology, whether it is pronounced in the mode of being an object ("it") or in that of a subject ("I")—whereas Transcendence proper thrones above the contrast between subject and object and, is, thus, beyond the grasp of human understanding, not to be couched in terms of human language and communication. God is Being itself (*ipsum esse*) "without any subjective admixture by way of human apprehension. That is why he is the *Being that is* when man fades away." (Kaufmann 1957, p. 223)

The philosophical risk, as perceived by Jaspers, would be to approach God firstly from the anthropocentric categories of the subjective consciousness that merely impose human categories upon the divine. Secondly, from the objectivigating third person perspective, to treat God as an object would be to reduce the infinite to merely finite human categories of apprehension. In stark contrast, Jaspers' exaltation of the divine also evinces an epistemic humility that disavows human capacities to instrumentalize their dogmatic claims for strategic purposes (Jaspers 1957a).

However, Kaufmann regards Jaspers' valid post WWII concerns as forfeiting too much of the creative powers of both God and persons by undermining the inherently interpersonal qualities of social recognition. He steers the debate into the domain of developing a sufficiently normative account of human freedom that elides the dual prospects of divine determinism or an over-inflation of human autonomy. Kaufmann advances something akin to a compatibilist conception of freedom that provides content to his reading of covenantal promises and places both parties under mutual trial and testing. Kaufman argues that *both* divine and human parties to the covenantal bond, by necessity, must freely undergo willing subjection to basic presuppositions behind the communicative process.

> The substantiality of a being would even be enhanced wherever it entertains a relation that implies an element of the creative, i.e. whenever it posits another being—either altogether or by giving it an entirely new role and status. A person, for instance, would not be its true Self, did it not give and were it not given recognition as a fellow being. Thanks to this relation it is not merely another subject or object. As to God, there is no competition of things with divine Transcendence since, in the ontological order, Transcendence would not be at par with the beings with which it deigns to communicate. They are not founded in and by themselves, but taken to owe their actuality to an act of communication of being, their nature to their calling in the distribution of parts within the whole, and even their freedom, perhaps, to a sort of divine self-restraint which entrusts the creature with an active and responsible function in the process of creation. (Kaufmann 1957, p. 263, 264)

Moreover, by appeal to the conception of freedom advanced by Schelling's speculative views on nature, God, and man, Kaufmann moves his communicative ethic quite close to the nascent origins of what later receives fuller exposition in the account developed by Habermas in his doctoral thesis on Schelling. As confirmation, a footnote to the above passage reads in close affinity to Habermas's dispersed comments on the initial substantive roots to his discourse ethics actually stemming from his dissertation work on the philosophy of Shelling:

> The self-containedness of God would thus be an act of supreme resignation rather than a spurning of all relations by virtue of absolute transcendence. In one of its aspects, his Transcendence would be a product of this abdication so that he appears absent thanks to the discretion of his presence and is present in the terror of his absence. (Kaufmann 1957, p. 263, 264)

In this manner, we can provide an alternative to Jaspers' reluctance to translate the achievements of Biblical religion into a univeralizable discourse open to the prospect of God taking on the covenantal role of co-participant in communicative action. Following Habermas, we will continue to reconstruct the rich genealogy to an originally Christian account of a communicative ethic to its truly inter-axial origins that stem from a Hebrew heritage it never completely left behind. We will reconstruct the wider Germanic heritage behind the first and second generation critical theory contexts of adapting the philosophical theology of Schelling, Fichte, and Hegel's Schwabish mysticism of their Lutheran seminary studies, eventually carried into the more universalizable pragmatics of communication espoused in Habermas's *Theory of Communicative Action* and its attendant linguistification of the sacred (Habermas 1987, pp. 46, 77–111).

While these sort of overtly theological and revelatory claims about the moral and ethical foundations of practical discourse could seem surprising to ongoing critical theorist attempts to develop a thoroughly secular—and self-avowed methodologically atheist—subjection of sacred texts and rituals to the historical-critical method, I will agree wholeheartedly that proper hermeneutic exegesis requires the utmost attention to historical context. So, while some excitement among believers has come about (and malcontent among those critical theorists of a secular disposition) given Habermas's continuing reflections on the significance of the Axial traditions to a revisionist understanding of ourselves as participants in modernity, we should not err to the opposite extreme of overstepping the bounds of critical philosophical reflection. In Habermas's own words:

> I would not object to the claim that my conception of language and of communicative interaction oriented toward mutual understanding nourishes itself from the legacy of

> Christianity. The "telos of reaching understanding"—the concept of discursively directed agreement which measures itself against the standard of intersubjective recognition, that is, the double negation of criticizable validity claims—may well nourish itself from the heritage of a *logos* understood as Christian, one that is indeed embodied (and not just with the Quakers) in the communicative practice of the religious congregation. Already the communicative-theoretical version of the concept of emancipation in *Knowledge and Human Interests* could be "unmasked" as the secularizing translation of the divine promise of salvation….I only want to say that the evidence of my relation to a theological heritage does not bother me, as long as one recognizes the *methodological difference* of the discourses; that is, as long as the philosophical discourse conforms to the distinctive demands of justificatory speech. In my view, a philosophy that oversteps the bounds of methodological atheism loses its philosophical seriousness. (Habermas 2002, p. 160)

As far as justificatory speech goes, Habermas continues along his consistent path of requiring that the transcendent claims made of revelatory traditions must nonetheless pass the critical scrutiny of a deliberating public. Conferring success upon practical discourses necessarily entails the capacity for translation of originally sacred claims into the vernacularized language of universalizable validity claims.

While Habermas's comments on the applicability of a theory of communicative action to Christian revelatory themes are few and far between, for some potential insights, we might continue our appeals to parallel themes addressed in the work of Voegelin. He appeals to Thomist thought to attempt to show that new philosophical categories are needed for adding import to what was predominately a concrete historical experience rendered symbolic by the narrative layers of meaning uniting an entire Hebrew people across millennia of history. He thus begins by returning to his prior hermeneutic queries on the Biblical revelation of the name of God. This time, he provides us with a more detailed exegesis on the prospects of deriving a communicative ethic from the Hebrew tetragramaton:

> If now we place the issue of the "philosophical proposition" in the context of the Thomist analysis, the *ehyeh* will no longer appear as an incomprehensible philosophical outburst, but rather as an effort to articulate a compact experience of divine presence so as to express the essential omnipresence with man of a substantially hidden God. The "I will be with you," we may say, does not reveal the substance of God but precisely when the frontier of divine presence has become luminous through revelation, man will become sensitive to the abyss extending beyond into the incommunicable substance of the Tetragrammaton. As a matter of fact, the revelation of the thornbush episode, once the divine presence had become an historical experience of the people through the Berith, had no noteworthy sequel in the history of Israelite symbols and certainly no philosophical consequences. The unrevealed depth, however, that was implied in the revelation, has caused the name of God to become the unpronounceable Tetragrammaton YHWH. Philosophy can touch no more than the being of the substance whose order flows through the world. (Voegelin 1974a, p. 411)

He later applies these same methodological and more pragmatically experiential insights to deriving a distinctively Christian communicative ethic. He offers a comparative genealogy of Hebrew hermeneutic norms that were eventually appropriated and redacted later by the authors of the Christian gospels. Applied to the present, these interpretive practices were continually reinterpreted by the Axial precedent established through the historical experiences of the Gospel writers, and then again re-appropriated by Thomist schools that continue to this day.

> Once we have recognized the exegesis of the thornbush episode as a compact symbolism in need of explication, not only will the philosophical interpretation appear well founded,

> but the labors of analysis bestowed by Christian thinkers on the episode in general can be accepted as an important aid for the understanding of the symbol. We shall use for this purpose the summary of the problem given by St. Thomas in the *Summa Theologiae*. Thomas considers the HE WHO IS the most proper name of God for three reasons: (a) because it signifies God according to his essence, that is, as being itself; (b) because it is universal and does not more closely determine the divine essence which is inaccessible to human intellect in this life; and (c) because it signifies being in the present which is appropriate to God, whose being has no past or future. Thomas, however, goes beyond mere implications which the *ehyeh* has for a philosophy of being and brings the other components of meaning into play. While the name HE WHO IS is the most appropriate one with regard to the mode of signifying the divine essence, the name *God* is more appropriate with regard to the object intended to be signified by the name; and even more appropriate is the name *tetragrammaton* for the purpose of signifying the singular, incommunicable substance of God. The three names which occur in the last section of the thornbush episode—*ehyeh, elohim, YHWH*—are co-ordinated by St. Thomas with the structure of the divine being in depth, leading from the philosophically communicable essence, through the proper name of the object, into the depth of the incommunicable substance. (Voegelin 1974a, pp. 410, 411)

As evidenced in the passage above, Voegelin's remarks border at the threshold of surpassing a distinctively post-metaphysical philosophy insofar as his own self-ascription primarily as a political theorist (as opposed to philosopher) nonetheless remains radically open to the prospect of treating revelatory approaches to the divine as indeed concrete instances of attempts to extend the experiential dimensions of human and social communication to include the divine.

Rather than dismissing his remarks outright, given his attribution of some dimensions of his politico-philosophical development to the appeal he found within the American pragmatist tradition as an alternative to, what he viewed, the paradoxical dogmatism of the Austrian positivism, we might see if his exegesis of biblical concepts might pass the hypothetic Habermasian test for translation into the universalizable language of public discourse. We can follow Kaufmann's earlier critiques of Jaspers and Kaufmann's resistance to Arendt's overly pragmatic casting of the species as 'homo faber.' Insofar as Habermas quite openly recognizes that his communicative ethic owes as much, if not more to American pragmatism as to first generation critical theory, Kaufmann's evocation of Pierce on Firstness should not seem too far out of place. The experiential turn offered by Voegelin's account of concrete revelatory experience as deeply personal also addresses our recurrent theme of 'Why Jaspers?' when posed as a contemporary social scientific alternative to the Weberian understanding of the disenchantment presumed as essential to any hope to achieve universality in reconstructing our secularization dialectics:

> In its scientific aspects ours is a "disenchanted world" of objects, leveled down and classified as mere specimens of species and genera, easy substitutes for one another—just as even individual man has become an easily replaceable and expendable commodity. But things as factors of our personal world are no mere manufactures, identical samples of the same make. To speak with Peirce, everyone of them has its "Firstness." Even without individual selfhood, they are individual creatures—to be told from each other the way the shepherd can tell his sheep apart. If the Leibnizian *omne individuum sua tota entitate individuatur* ("each individual is individuated through its own whole nature") is true—as I think it is—it would be so as the product of a unique art and a unique 'principle' through which it has its 'beginning'—"in the beginning was the Word,"—and through which it is endowed with its

entelechy, the individual law of its being. Now this is just what we understand by 'creation.' (Kaufmann 1957, p. 287, 288)

Johannine metaphors indubitably permeate the above passage. In an additional level of pertinence to the pragmatic tradition informing Voegelin's (and Aquinas's) experiential read of John's gospel as a species-ethical rendering of a parallel narrative structure to Genesis, we could also add to the species-ethical dialectic Taylor's insights of a Jamesian open space whereby exposure to some or most of the great Axial traditions would serve as a live option in most contemporary (2014 CE) post-secular societies with their great urban centers. In casting this experiential dimension into a pragmatics of discourse, Voegelin finds in the narrative depictions of Christ the uncanny capacity for drawing upon a heritage his interlocutor must always already invariably accept, but then super-imposing upon the prior understanding a layer the participant may not initially fully accept. In reconstructing these discourses, even when the interlocutor rejects the terms of questions posed that intentionally disclose performative contradictions, they (and the reader) nonetheless begin to reconsider their epistemic commitments in light of a more expansive set of live options.

The Johannine language can surprise as the discourse proceeds, because the author does not develop new language symbols to express new meanings but uses the same symbol continuously to cover the several meanings that emerge from the compact "I am" in the process of differentiation. I have distinguished already two components of the complex. There is, first, the self-revelation of the hidden god to Moses in Exodus 3. This is the stratum in the complex that moves Etienne Gilson to understand all Christian metaphysics of being as the metaphysics of Exodus. There is, second, the "I am" that becomes luminous, through its presence in Christ, for its participatory presence in every human being, even in the pre-Christian men of faith: "Your father Abraham rejoiced that he was to see my day; he saw it and was glad" (8: 56). This is the stratum that moves Thomas to say that Christ is the head, not of a limited *corpus mysticum*, but of all men from the creation of the world to its end. And there is, third, the eschatological meaning, terminologically not separate from the others, which dominates the Gospel through the famous "I am (*ergo eimi*)..." pronouncements. (Voegelin 1974b, p. 15)

On the one hand, we saw in Voegelin's species-ethical appeal to Hebrew historiogenesis the inherent tension between the particular, as the Hebrew elect owing their special covenantal status to the Sinai experience and even the precursor quasi-exodus event ascribed to Abram leaving Ur and his family and opting to pursue the promised land of his heavenly father. On the other hand, the universalistic symbolism of the genesis of humanity and the etymological overtones of the generations of creation also bearing anthropological weight, gave Voegelin license to call the Hebrew breakthrough truly axial in its universalistic appeal to the species as such. This time, according to Voegelin, the "I am" proclamation by Christ carries the first and second connotations from Judaism but adds a distinctive emphasis on the third eschatological symbolic meaning.

By emphasizing the super-addition of these unique categories of eschatological significance, Voegelin seeks to reinforce the notion that the Christian appropriation of the Hebrew "I am" recasts the Greek logos as an interpersonal and communicative turn. This distances some of the experiential dimensions of the life of Christ recorded in the Gospels from a literal-historical reading as they both borrow their ongoing pertinence from these inter-Axial sources while simultaneously creating a novel realization of heretofore untapped spiritual and communicative capacities. As one instance of such a distinctively Christocentric experiential breakthrough, Voegelin offers some critical exegesis concerning Christ's identification with the Hebrew "I am" while nonetheless appropriating it from the novel perspective of the doctrine of the Incarnation (of course, explicitly rejected by Jaspers as a paradox incomprehensible) as espousing claims of the divine fully present in a particular embodied man:

> The "I am" in Jesus, on the other hand, reveals itself as the living presence of the word in a man; it does not intend to establish a people in history but will, for every man who responds to its appeal, dissolve the darkness and absurdity of existence into the luminous consciousness of participating in the divine word. Inexorably the author lets the debate between Jesus and the Pharisees advance toward the point where the conflict between the earlier, more compact revelations to Israel and the luminous presence of the "I am" in Jesus breaks into the open. How can the deathless, immortalizing presence of the "I am" in the man Jesus be reconciled with the death of man bound to history, be he so venerable a figure as Abraham? This crucial question provokes the climactic deliberation, with its magnificent break in the sequence of tense: "Before Abraham was, I am" (8: 58). After this declaration, the infuriated audience wants to stone him [for apostasy, as in accord with Deut 13: 15]; but Jesus makes his escape (8: 59). (Voegelin 1974b, p. 15)

In the parlance of Gilson's 'metaphysics of Exodus,' Christ has begun his symbolic initiation of the quasi-exodus event of liberating not just the Israelites from bondage to pharaoh, but also bondage to their particularistic reading of their own narrative that also belies dimensions of their narrative that identified the outcaste, the wandering denizen, and the impoverished as also among the family of God (ironically too, also statuses historically that the Israelites had known all too well prior to their re-entry into Canaan and reconstruction of the Second Temple as the historical context of Christ's teaching).

Habermas on Kierkegaard's Contributions to a Communicative Species-Ethic: Towards a Post-Metaphysical (Non-Dogmatic?) Christianity

Moving into second generation critical theory, I will turn to Habermas's method for critically appropriating traditionally Judeo-Christian theological concepts communicatively, highlighting three examples of his recasting of Judeo-Christian themes into his philosophy of language. Specifically, I will first reconstruct his discursive rendition of the fall (rebellion) he interprets in accord with themes developed in his aforementioned doctoral dissertation that appropriates Schelling's Schwabish mysticism. Read in term of a negative theology, Habermas suggests even placing a necessary limit upon God's freedom and power insofar as Adam must retain the full capacity for taking a 'yes/no' position on God's commands in order for Adam to retain his full communicative responsibility. Secondly, I will highlight Habermas's reconstruction of the genealogy of human rights as having originally derived inalienable dignity from the notion of humanity bearing the relational image of the divine. This yields a theological kernel to his secularized co-originality thesis of private and public autonomy and the concomitant pragmatic maxim of individuation proceeding through processes of socialization. Thirdly, I will look at Habermas's democratization of his normative commitment that true freedom comes about via willing constraint to social norms, reflected in his repeated warning not to switch the role of Creator and created in his writings on recent innovations in genetic engineering. His associated moral and legal derivation of neo-Keirkegaardian species-ethical constraints on genetic engineering preserve the basic freedom and equality of potentially affected future generations.

Despite his rejection of a pre-political ethical core as the ground for shared social solidarity, he argues that there is a great need for the translation of spiritual insights into secular language—specifically given the havoc wrought by market forces and growing bureaucracy over the public sphere.[7] In the general corpus of Habermas's work, he argues that the logic of the market and state bureaucracy both follow strategic forms of communication. The former relentlessly seeks the increase of capital whereas the latter seeks the unrestrained wielding of power. Only in the public sphere do we find language that conforms to the performative attitude: that which is oriented to achieving common understanding with a second person.

> [T]he balance achieved in the modern period between the three great media of social integration is now at risk, because the markets and the power of the bureaucracy are expelling social solidarity (that is, a coordination of action based on values, norms, and a vocabulary intended to promote mutual understanding) from more and more spheres of life. Thus it is in the interest of the constitutional state to deal carefully with all the cultural sources that nourish its citizens' consciousness of norms and their solidarity. This awareness, which has become conservative, is reflected in the phrase: "postsecular society" (Habermas and Ratzinger 2006, pp. 45–46).

Spiritual insights thus yield an untapped reservoir of vocabulary that can bring shared meaning and values into the increasingly strategic colonization of the life-world by both the market and institutional bureaucracy. In addition to the functional contributions that religious fellowships bring to society in the currency of motivations and attitudes normally deemed socially desirable, Habermas also finds that these fellowships carry a current of reflexivity whereby both believing and non-believing citizens undergo a complementary learning process in taking up a performative attitude with respect to one another's reasons offered over controversial public issues (Habermas and Ratzinger 2006, pp. 45–46)

[7] In reaching his conclusions, Habermas adapts the goals and aims of traditional critical theory to use the latest innovations in democratic theory applied to our postsecular context. He agrees with Horkheimer and Adorno that the major goal of critical theory seeks human emancipation from any form of social and political domination. In reaching such an aim, critical theory takes comfort in utilizing and mixing both normative and empirical modes of analysis using the most recent social science research and also holds to a commitment that rationality can occur in a plurality of sometimes seemingly incommensurable voices. Critical theory also carries a pragmatic component agreeing with Marx that the task of philosophy is not merely to critique social ideology but to change society.

Scattered throughout various writings, Habermas offers three prime examples of the translation of the spiritual into the secular. The first and most common reference is to the familiar Judeo-Christian notion of man created in the image of God translated in the secular sphere to the notion of inalienable human dignity that serves as the moral basis of many modern defenses of human rights. With this first instance of translation that still salvages the substance of the original term, he provides a pragmatic test to assess the degree of success in executing such translations: "this goes beyond the borders of one particular religious fellowship and makes the substance of biblical concepts accessible to a deliberating public that also includes those who have other faiths and those who have none" (Habermas and Ratzinger 2006, pp. 45–46). In a move that demonstrates the ambivalence of a postsecular society, the very conditions for religious liberty that he derives from a Judeo-Christian context must extend more broadly to commitments to religious liberty for all Axial traditions in the contemporary context of increasing pluralism.

In a second instance, although a very brief reference in light of his grand corpus of writing, Habermas claims it nonetheless plays a formative role in the initial development his theory of communicative action. As part of the early philosophical views worked out in his first doctoral dissertation, he draws upon Schwabish mysticism to regard the self-limitation of God as the grounds for the post-Fall social freedom of the human subject. He regards such non-coerced self-legislation on the part of Adam as a necessary pragmatic presupposition for the legitimate functioning of modern democracies (Haberms 2002). In other words, God's initial treatment of Adam as free receives confirmation in a discursive sense whereby Adam must have the real ability to take a 'yes' or 'no' discursive position on God's commands (Mendieta 2013, p. 397, 398). While this may seem to limit God's power, it is nonetheless essential to their mutual status as communicatively free agents and also stands as a discursive precondition for the possibility of non-coercive solidarity.

Habermas's third and most recent example has been brought about as an attempt to apply the Kierkegaardian turn to individual authenticity to the species-ethical domain of problems introduced through recent innovations in genetic engineering. Before getting into the fuller development of such a species-ethic in the introductory sections of his *Future of Human Nature* (2003), I will turn instead to his most recent debate with J.M. Bernstein on the wider implications of Habermas's turn to religion. Habermas's most recent openness to religious contributions in public discourse is perceived by his critic as threatening the methodological atheism regarded as indispensable for the impartial neutrality of justice (Bernstein 2013, pp. 154–175).

Bernstein uses Kierkegaard's famous Abraham-Isaac narrative as an illustration of how Kierkegaard's purported suspension of the ethical for the higher calling of religious mandates leads us down the road of epistemic authoritarianism. In this new iteration, we see Habermas actually concur with some of the earlier clarifications made by Maeve Cooke in order to reply to the misguided interpretation of Kierkegarrd that Habermas attributes to Bernstein. On the one side, Bernstein argues that a morally universal commitment to methodological atheism leaves no room for the ethical particularity of the claims of revelation. On the other side, Habermas finds that Bernstein has misconstrued Kierkegaard's critique of the Kantian universality of moral legislation as if the alternative appeal to covenantal trust had no internally rational justification on the part of the believer.

> [A] Romantic spirit like Soren Kierkegaard immersed himself in Abraham's torn state of mind in an attempt to recover the dimension of the promise of salvation that was lost with the transition to a secular and purely rational morality. As in the doctrine of stages of *Either/Or*, in his interpretation of the story of Abraham in *Fear and Trembling*, Kierkegaard is concerned with the pivotal difference between moral consciousness and religious faith. The moralization of the demonic forces of good and evil and the move toward a transcendent deity overcame myth and magic, but did not dissolve into the binding power of mere morality that which forms the proper core of religious experience, namely, the ambivalent dread inspired by the immediate presence of the sacred. The complex idea of God's *redemptive* justice is a synthesis in which the impersonal justice of morality represents just *one of two* moments. *Law-abidingness* (*Gesetzestreue*)—obedience to the moral legislator—is founded on *devoutness* (*Glaubenstreue*): trust in and loyalty to the omnipotent savior. *But they are not identical*. Kierkegaard's point is that devoutness must not be absorbed entirely by law-abidingness, as it is in Kant. (Habermas 2013, p. 368, 369)

Habermas's criticizes Bernstein on the Abraham-Isaac narrative in Kierkegaard for overstating Kierkegaard's position as an outright denial of morality altogether for the lexically prior preference for divine mandates, irrespective of their moral content. What Kierkegaard attempts to retrieve through this Romantic existential twist would be the affective and motivational dimensions of faith. We could introduce a helpful distinction to clarify. The faith Habermas has in mind could not be reduced to mere blind obedience with a total disregard for morality. Instead, Habermas wants to show that, for Kierkegaard, the appeal to faith includes the wider hermeneutic construct of the trusting relationship that Abraham has already developed in his covenantal bond with God, including but not limited to experiential reasons for that relational trust begun with the quasi-exodus redemptive event of delivering on the promise to provide for Abram upon leaving the comforts of Ur into the unseen promised land, the establishment of the circumcision rite with Ishmael, and the concomitant promise that Abraham would have numerous descendants despite having at the point of the call to sacrifice Isaac having followed through on the command to follow the bidding of Sarah and let Hagar and Ishmael permanently depart into the desert.

In the parlance of Habermas's discourse ethics, in order to regard the symbolic character of Abraham's faith more than just a first-personal narrative of strategically instrumental calculation of self-interest, the content of Kierkegaard's account of duty must rather be construed as second-personal trust in God as the conditional fulfillment of Abraham's duty. We find all the way back to Genesis, an instance of a promissory narrative that I had more restrictively applied at its introduction to the Sermon on the Mount events of the synoptic gospels and the logos of the gospel of John. For clarification, in the case of Abraham letting Hagar and Ishmael depart into the desert, one could say it was in the immediate strategic self-interest of Abraham to appease his angry wife Sarah's bidding. However, Abraham gains nothing from a strategic vantage in the case of Isaac—unless construing the sacrifice event as carried out under the trust and faith that God, construed as both good and rational, and thereby incapable of making a lying covenantal promise.[8] Since the promise of numerous descendants could not at that point derive from the line of the now departed Ishmael, Abraham—even upon raising his knife over Isaac—must have still trusted that God's covenantal promise of many descendants would still be fulfilled. Employing the Hebrew account of YHWH established earlier, we could regard the account as not only consistent with the narrative symbol provided by the life of Abraham but also as consistent with the symbolic character of the Sinai covenant yet to occur in the revelatory experience of Moses later to be taken up by the Israelites as a composite people. In this respect, YHWH could be regarded once again from the second-personal standpoint of the hidden God that creatively wills self-revelation in the manner of "I am the helper God who is always with you" and who will reveal myself to you in ways and manners that you can trust in (but never from a third-personal grand historical objectivigating stance predict).

In other words, as a potential alternative to the moral and rational universality of his standard appeals to subjection of validity claims to the justificatory tribunal of universal consent, Habermas attempts to develop a distinctively secularized variant of Christological appeals to species ethic by replacing Kierkegaard's Other with the second person of communicative action. As an emendation to the insights advanced in Habermas's *Future of Human Nature* (2003), he sets the conceptual stage for a response to critics that charged him with sneaking teleological claims about the pursuit of the good life into his post-metaphysical philosophy. In this interpretation, the more species-ethical potencies gleaned from Biblical narrative, aid in his overall project of generating the communicative translation of such second personal bonds of trust into more morally neutral modern deontological commitments to universalistic norms of solidarity, moral freedom, and moral equality of all rational persons. Habermas reconstructs how such a translation could be brought about by again employing Kierkegaard's existential vocabulary:

> The despairing failure of the ultimate heroic feat—namely, a willing to be oneself that is entirely fixated on oneself—should lead the finite mind to transcend itself and hence also to recognize its dependence on an absolute other in which individual freedom is founded. This reversal marks a starting point, namely, the overcoming of the secularized self-understanding of modern reason: "in relating itself to itself in willing to be itself, the self rest transparently in the power that established it." This consciousness alone makes it possible to be oneself authentically. A reason reflecting on its deepest foundations discovers its origin in an other; and it must acknowledge the latter's ominous power if it is not to lose its orientation in the dead end of hybrid self-subjection. (Habermas 2008, p. 236, 237)

Tying the authentic life to the not-misspent life free from despair, Habermas attempts again effectually to neutralize substantive critiques of having couched this new communicative ethic in light of a theory of the good life by keeping his commitments within the confines of assuming the irrevocable deontic achievements of modernity in securing basic moral freedom and equality. In addition, Habermas

[8] I am also indebted to the work of *Eleonore Stump's Wandering in the Wilderness* (Oxford Press, Cambridge: 2001) for her second-personal reconstruction of the Abraham-Isaac account.

laments the postmodern trend that philosophy, for some, can no longer brings its long Axial history to bear on questions of the good life. He finds this predicament odd given the general trust social scientists put into psychology, with its comparatively much shorter history than philosophy, of leading subjects away from the not-misspent life. Perhaps even more paradoxically, the social-scientific treatment of psychology as an autonomous discipline likewise completely overlooks the greater portion of the history of both Western and non-Western Axial traditions to treat philosophical and psychological concerns under the same rubric of empirical, anthropological, *and* communicative rubrics of investigative inquiry.

Lastly, if one does opt for maintaining the functional differentiation between disciplinary methods and motives for the sake of greater epistemic quality, Habermas regards the role of the philosopher under the idealized constraints of second-personal justificatory reason-giving and responsiveness as the most appropriate medium for generating multi-perspectival conclusions to social problems (like genetic engineering and innumerable others) that cut across multiple disciplinary domains. No single expert-oriented discourses could claim an ultimate third-personal God's eye view of all facets of a problematic domain, particularly when even greater epistemic clarity may be gleaned by consulting (at least hypothetically) all those immediately affected. In the case of genetic engineering, Habermas would certainly concede rational disagreement over his specific conclusions. Moreover, in a performative commitment to his ideal of the unforced force of the better argument, he would not just concede but encourage the ongoing input of those affected. As in genetic engineering and other social problems truly global in species application, since the relevant technologies and empirical data exponentially increase, these cases by sheer scope warrant at least a thinly normative, negatively derived, species-ethical solidarity as universal concern for all humanity affected. For instance, in genetic engineering, insofar as the proposed intervention even into one individual has pragmatic spillover effects into the aggregate gene pool of the entire species, we have at least a pragmatically derived species solidarity by virtue of sharing common crisis and threats. It is here where Habermas takes license to translate the Kierkegaardian Other of a personal God and the Johannie logos in the overtly humanist direction of the 'you-plural' of the species: present, past, and future.

> The linguistic turn permits a deflationary interpretation of the "wholly Other." As historical and social beings we find ourselves always in a linguistically structured lifeworld….How speakers and hearers make use of their communicative freedom to take yes- or no-positions is not a matter of their subjective discretion. For they are free only in virtue of the binding force of the justifiable claims they raise toward one another. The *logos* of language embodies the power of the intersubjective, which precedes and grounds the subjectivity of speakers. This weak proceduralist reading of the "Other" preserves the fallibilist as well as the anti-skeptical meaning of the "unconditioned." The *logos* of language escapes our control, and yet we are the ones, the subjects capable of speech and action, who reach an understanding with one another in the medium. It remains "our" language. The unconditionedness of truth and freedom is a necessary presupposition of our practices, but beyond the constituents of "our" form of life they lack any ontological guarantee. Similarly, the "right" ethical self-understanding is neither revealed nor "given" in some other way. It can only be won in a common endeavor. From this perspective, what makes our being-ourselves possible appears more as a transsubjective power than an absolute one. (Habermas 2003, p. 10, 11)

Akin to the limitless you-plural character he ascribes to the ideal construct of a boundless communicative community, the fitting analogue for the case of the human genome seems, if not to spill over into the domain of metaphysics, at least to raise deep philosophical questions about the transsubjective character of our shared ontology as a necessary pragmatic presupposition behind our capacity for communicative action. In deontic terms, what we have would be both a vertical and horizontal extension of our inter-generational obligations to the species as the open-ended community of past, present, and future of which no individual group or person could claim ultimate imperialistic jurisdiction. Such a disaggregated species subject—whom he democratically argues ought best be addressed in these matters that affect the future of human nature—finds its normative defense in the universal moral freedom and equality owed to each real and potential person when conceived from the aggregate participant 'you' perspective.

He argues along the lines of a morally romantic cosmopolitanism that comprising the content of such a species-ethic within a secular public would require a translation of Biblical concepts concerning the irreversibility of Creator and created into a rational discourse convincing to all affected perspectives: believing, agnostic, and atheist. Habermas judges that most non-believers would seem compelled by moral reasons to reject 'man playing God' via new genetic technologies, for instance, found in the secular law of the German constitution and Article 3 the EU Fundamental Charter of Rights through their respective bans on human cloning and the non-instrumentalization of the person (Habermas 2003, pp. 21–23; 2002, p. 15, 16).

Reserving a role for philosophy and the philosopher as stand-in and participant interpreter seems well justified in the case of genetic engineering since even the conventional divisions of labor between the hard sciences and social sciences require the objective claims of the former as translatable into the participants affects upon the latter. We could nonetheless concede to both Habermas (and his critics) that revelatory claims from the great Axial traditions face even greater burdens as far as one might question the full efficacy of their translation potential. It is on this matter that Habermas ultimately admits that the unique domain of any truly species-ethical problematic creates new levels of tension between distinct sets of the particularistic groups potentially affected and the ultimate goal nonetheless to generate universal moral validity. While Habermas finds the existentialist philosophies of Kierkegaard and Jaspers helpful in this regard, he also grants the potential of a hypothetical 'clash of civilizations' as we may ultimately be led to competing claims to species-ethical universality that cannot fully derive the requisite rational consensus for moral and rational legitimation:

> [E]xistentialist philosophy also lays claim to the legacy of Kierkegaard. It follows him along the path to an ethics that attaches only *formal* value to the historical mode of a self-critical, conscious conduct of life. Karl Jaspers attempts to go further by rationally reconstructing the radical tension between transcendence and worldly existence from the secular standpoint of the "illumination of existence." He succeeds, however, only at the cost of assimilating the validity claim of philosophical assertion to the status of truths of faith. He generalizes Kant's concept of rational faith, which was tailored to the postulates of God and immortality, to philosophy as a whole that demarcates "philosophical faith" from scientific knowledge. This leads to a family resemblance between philosophical teachings

> and religious traditions as competing systems of belief. Philosophy can at best clarify the character of this conflict but cannot resolve it with arguments. (Habermas 2008, p. 238)

Once one follows Jaspers and relegates philosophy to a philosophical-faith that can at best raise species-ethical concerns as mere candidates competing with other species-ethical claims of an intra- or inter-Axial origin from disparate traditions, I agree with Habermas that philosophy cannot transcend its own participant status as ultimate adjudicator of conflicting claims.

At this point, we will not attempt to resolve this seeming impasse but should at least comment on one reason for optimism in light of these conclusions and one reason for skeptical pessimism. As for the pessimistic side first, if we do concede an insurmountable impasse, we could certainly foresee and historically document similar such cases in the past that thereby forsake second-personal communication as adjudicated by 'the unforced force of the better argument' and fall into the problematic irresolution proposed by the onset of the clash of civilizations either by sheer coercive force or by subtle manipulation. As for the optimistic side, we could also foresee circumstances, or likewise point to historical cases, whereby moral-ethical impasse eventually becomes superseded by the gradual formation of consensus in light of new data, mutual learning, and the reciprocal transformation of axial viewpoints. As yet another philosophical path for optimism, which I will argue in the next chapter as ultimately most convincing, we could even pursue the Rawlsian/Taylor model (of course, consistently critiqued by Habermas for not generating the right sort of universalistic moral consensus upon the same reasons) of an overlapping consensus. On such a model that demands much less of our political institutionalization of norms, we may opt to endorse convergent norms in light of accepting endemic conflict among rational justifications and/or legal forms for their adjudication. Why I find this last alternative most appealing should become clearer as we broaden our candidate background justifications for normative consensus to include Islam as yet a third candidate for Axial status within Jaspers' tradition of Biblical religion.

3.2.3 *Islam: The Axial Dynamics of Culture, Internal Transformation, and Universality*

The full extent of the Islam-West divide as the political challenge of the day will take me the remainder of the book and still would require fuller elucidation. However, of all the burgeoning attendant literature, I have yet to find direct engagement with the ambivalence Jaspers himself treats Islam, specifically concerning Axial status. These tensions can best be addressed by providing a critical exegesis of the statements directly addressing this issue throughout the corpus of Jaspers' writings. In the end, I agree with the relevant social scientific literature that confers upon Islam axial status outside the conventions of the 800–200 BC rubric by virtue of its secondary breakthrough from original Judaic and Christian origins.

I will focus on the hermeneutic tensions between Habermas's call to subject Islamic scripture to the historical-critical method of interpretation while nonetheless attempting reconciliation with the orthodox interpretation of the Koran as divine speech. I will consider the important contributions of Talal Asad's emphasis on bridging this divide through reference to the embodied habitus of ritual experience as shaping one's cosmic lens to accord with the mandates of the Koran. As a legal-juridical attempt to mediate the critical-historical method with eternal revelation, I will appeal to the pioneering work of Muslim political philosopher Abdullah An-Naim as derived from sources he finds internal to the Koran. His work discloses the micro-level pragmatic presuppositions that come with a secular public as a necessary condition for authentically responsible Muslim faith. On his view, he gives a communicative defense of an inherently Islamic call for religious liberty. He judges the absence of state coercion as the only legitimate grounds for un-coerced profession of faith as required by the Muslim First Pillar. Lastly, I will turn the Anglo-American jurisprudence of John Rawls' *Law of Peoples* and its active engagement with Islam as a decent non-liberal peoples. In accord with the political conclusions of Jaspers', Rawls presents the ideal of an overlapping consensus as an alternative to political cosmopolitanism. Throughout these sections, I develop a second-personal strand of micro-level discourse as an abiding constant to these very distinct philosophical reflections on the place of Islam in a globally interdependent social order. I interpret the Muslim account of second person communication as consistent with the account of Biblical religion developed in the earlier Jewish and Christian parts of the chapter.

Jaspers' Ambivalence on Islam's Axial Status

In order to begin our assessment of Islam as falling within or outside the classification scheme of Axial status, we will start with the dubious character of Islam as characterized best by S.N. Eisenstadt.

> Our discussion ends with a brief analysis of the last of the Axial Age—really beyond Axial Age—the last monotheistic religion—Islam. In some way Islam can be seen as yet another secondary breakthrough from Judaism and Christianity, in the sense that both these religions constitute its starting point and the encounter with these civilizations, but of course especially with the Christian world, constituted a continuous part the civilizational dynamics of Islam. Yet quite obviously this was a rather different type of breakthrough from the ones discussed above, because it did not originate within any of these civilizations, but rather through the encounter of tribal units in Arabia, with inter-civilizational dynamics that have been taking place in this period in the Near and Middle East. (Eisenstadt 1986, p. 475)

As an initial source for his arduous multi-volume social-scientific research required for substantiating the multiple modernities thesis, Eisenstadt concedes the aforementioned tensions, placing Islam *both* within (conceptually as a secondary breakthrough of Judaism and Christianity) and beyond (temporally) the grouping of the great Axial traditions.

However, by following both Eisenstadt and Jaspers' decentering of world history away from a Christological axis, the hope for a retrieval of a heritage of Biblical religion internal to Islam must counter the false sentiment of secularization dialectics owing their exclusive heritage to Latin Christendom. This sentiment belies the real inter-Axial heritage of the multi-faceted sources to European modernity, without granting Islam it proper due. For starters, Jaspers concurs in rearticulating his original Axial Age hypothesis in light of the reflexive self-understanding offered by engaging with India and China, thereby shifting the attendant concept of Biblical religion to comprise not just Judaism and Christianity, but also Islam:

> The historic Christian space contains all the West and more. We Westerners, formed in this space, animated, motivated, and determined by this background, filled with images and concepts derived from the Bible, are all Christians. It would be better—as we realize if we immerse ourselves for a while in the spiritual worlds of India and China, get some distance, and then, from afar, see what this whole biblically-based world has in common—to speak of 'biblical religion,' including not only Christians of every kind but Jews, and in a sense, though more distantly, even Muslims. (Jaspers 1967, p. 20)

The wider distance provided by historical reflexivity would also disclose the Hebrew *and* Muslim heritages that have influenced where Europe has come from and where he sees it headed in the future. In addition, Jaspers (like Voegelin) was all too wary of the extremist forms of secularism that led to Soviet totalitarianism, Germanic Nazi-influenced neo-paganism, and the shared Nietzsche/Kierkegaard pronouncement of the death of the Christian god no longer motivating European solidarity to act on behalf of one another. Therefore, one important component to these revisionist historical efforts would also be the pre-WWII, WWII, and post-WWII neo-colonial exploits of the Muslim world, Asia, and Africa in a more nuanced picture of both the achievements of modernity and its imperialistic excesses. From this vantage, we can gain insight into where similar imperial domination might receive reiteration in more contemporary differentiated forms.

Therefore, throughout these initial series of passages on the dubious status of Islamic scriptural revelation from *Philosophical Faith and Revelation*, Jaspers seems compelled to grant Islam axial status and even place it within his wider rubric along with Judaism and Christianity as an extension of Biblical religion. In addition, he proceeds further into the messy and potentially volatile contexts of competing claims to epistemic authority over the contents, methods, and means of the salvational impulse stirring on each competing narrative comprising the three distinct Biblical scriptural canons. Despite the variety of historical creeds and distinct ritual modes of practice, he moves in the universalistic dimension offered by his earlier symbolic archetype of the Encompassing.

> I prefer [instead of confessional concepts of religion] to speak of the 'biblical religion,' or the 'biblical faith.' Against this term it has been argued that there is no biblical faith, that people can only be of the Jewish, Protestant, Lutheran, Calvinist, Anglican, or Islamic faith. I take the contrary view expressed by Cusanus: *Una religio in rituum variete*. The historical guise of the creeds has power and meaning for those who were born into them; it is not without significance for their historicity; but neither is it the form in which to acknowledge the absolute truth they claim. What matters is the 'invisible Church'. The weight, the truth, the worth of the visible churches depends on their share in the invisible one which no man

can claim exclusivity for himself alone. Though the denominations are the diverse historic forms of the biblical faith, the identity of the one living content remains undefinable. It cannot be reduced to one denominator. (Jaspers 1967, p. 355)

This passage clearly states the universalistic quality of Jaspers' commitment to philosophical faith ultimately pointing to an ineffable source. As a preliminary presupposition behind inter- and intra-Axial micro-level discourse between his denominational casting of Biblical religion, he does not want to eliminate the capacity for axial traditions to make veridical claims despite their manifest plurality as lived traditions. However, he also wants to occupy a neutral stance intended to restrain epistemic authoritarianism as a stopgap upon the path leading to dogmatic political authoritarianism. Here, he even extends the notion of denominationalism that would be conventionally held internal to each one of the Axial traditions to biblical faith writ large as the invisible and hidden manifestation of truth, containing within it the major Abraham traditions as quasi-denominations.[9] However, insofar as he wants to grant this more extensive notion of truth, he also claims for philosophical faith the inability to vie for a single particular exclusivism whereby one tradition holds the final word on ultimate truth at the expense of the falsity of each of the others.

Jaspers concedes in his *On the Origin and Goal of History* that the universalistic quality of his version of biblical religion runs exactly counter to the sorts of exclusivism most characteristic of the Abrahamic faiths that comprise its heterogeneous content.

In contradiction to its liberty and infinite fluidity, the West now developed the opposite extreme in the shape of the *claim to exclusive truth* by the various Biblical religions, including Islam. In was only in the West that the totality of this claim appeared as a principle that ran without interruption through the whole further course of history. (Jaspers 1953, p. 64)

As an ironic twist, while he saw above that the trans-civilizational analysis would bring about awareness of the distinct biblical heritage of European civilization, the multi-faceted institutional variations have run up against their own performative contradictions. While religious liberty and openness to internal cultural modification have become marks of modernity, once epistemic claims to exclusivist truth arise, Jaspers regards them as performatively undermining the very commitment to religious liberty that must be presupposed for their openly public practice.[10]

Perhaps the greatest obstacle to his claim that each Axial tradition refers symbolically to an ultimate Encompassing, would be his observation that each

[9] While Jose Casanova, as a sociologist of religion, would not go as far as Jaspers speculative comments on the nature of the Encompassing, Casanova does ascribe to a similar notion of 'global denominationalism' that he finds characteristic of the growing global pluralism of the spiritual plane.

[10] Here Jaspers has come across an insight that has significantly contributed to the renaissance of interest in the work of Eisenstadt. Besides his important work on the multiple modernities thesis, Eisenstadt has provided the clearest articulation of the paradox of religious fundamentalism—particularly in its most contemporary forms. While fundamentalism typically claims a stringent orthodoxy that we must return to as the surviving remnants of a more austere past, the very conditions for attempts at the political, and at times coercive, institutionalization of fundamentalism are all distinctly modern in their forms.

nonetheless contains differentiated ciphers that must indeed be read in their cultural particularity. The common Axial tensions between universal species-ethical claims and particular limited communities of believers, nonetheless, for Jaspers, point to an ineffable Transcendence that escapes the purview of the biblical tradition's longing to maintain a stronghold on the exclusive absolute truth of their revelatory claims.

> Only a single group—the ones based on the Bible—will assert, by virtue of the kind of revelation they believe in, that theirs is the sole true faith, regarding the rest as false or, at best, as preliminary steps or parts of the one sole truth, of which they alone are the full and original bearers. These Biblically based religions include not only the Christian ones and the Jewish one, but Islam as well. The spirit of exclusiveness gives them all a common state of mind. They belong together as one group. From this point of view, the basic dividing line does not run between Christianity and the non-Christian religions, but between the monopolistic group, grown on the soil of the Biblical faith as one of its inherent possibilities—the Christian denominations, Judaism, and Islam—and all other religions. (Jaspers 1963, p. 144)

Here Jaspers foresees the all too familiar contemporary indictment on Islam as uniquely exclusivist in its rendering Allah as the revelatory Author of the Qur'an, whereby even Islamic internal concessions to Jews and Christians as 'Peoples of the Book' ultimately serves, for Western critics and observers, tantamount to saying they have merely incomplete stages of the revelation to which Islam provides the ultimate fulfillment. However, while religious exclusivism runs internal to the claims of the Qur'an, Jaspers wants to remind his predominately Western audience that exclusivism also has its equally assertive voice within and between Hebrew and Christian expressions of heterogeneity.

In addition, returning to one of the passages in his *Philosophical Faith and Revelation* that bodes closer to the trans-civilizational comparisons in *Origin and Goal of History,* he finds in Islam the common denominator with Judaism and Christianity as among the revelatory religions that grant the world utmost significance and resist calling for utter transcendence on the basis of the quite distinct Eastern (Hindu-Buddhist) revelatory notion of the world as illusory:

> Insofar as Nirvana turns all things illusory, [r]evelation, on the other hand, is first diverse among Jews, Christians, and Muslims, and secondly it acts upon the world, promising and demanding. It becomes a factor of utmost vitality and tension in mundane existence that is not a matter of indifference, not an illusion, but the site of eternal decisions. Nirvana cancels all embodiment. The road to it is marked by ciphers only. (Jaspers 1967, p. 102)

However, despite the tensions between the Abrahamic traditions wrought by religious exclusivism, the commonalities (the common heritage back to the major Hebrew prophets, similar revelatory affirmation of the world, shared believers' claims to epistemic exclusivity, etc.) offer reasons to include Islam along with Judaism and Christianity within the shared symbolic heritage of biblical religion.

The experimental immersion into the cultural nuances of the Eastern traditions also brings to light their breadth of cross-axial extension that can find commonality, on the one hand, with the thematic unity to Biblical religion despite its internal variability. On the other hand, among the Eastern traditions and their variant revelatory claims, he finds a common commitment to a shared de-personalized mandate of heaven. In contrast to the dogmatic proclamations to exclusive truth he regards as pitting the Biblical religions at odds with one another despite their shared Biblical heritage, he also notes that the Eastern traditions demonstrate a much greater comfort and acknowledgement of the complex cross-breeding involved in syncretic hybrids, particularly as has emerged historically in places like India and China.

The Eastern historical tendencies to resist institutionalizing their ecumenic species-ethical claims into world-enveloping imperial conquests contrast sharply with Biblical religions' inherent tendencies to collapse the political and the spiritual. As contributing factors, the concomitant appeals in Biblical religion to creation as a locus of historiogenesis and eschaton as the consummation of God's creative participation and sovereign jurisdiction over the mundane affairs of the world tend to drive the concrete attempts on the part of believing communities to exact political closure in forms of imperial conquest. Jaspers thereby judges that the Eastern traditions provide an effective buffer against the this-worldly emphasis of the Biblical religions in disclosing the hiddenness of the Encompassing he sees uniting not just biblical faith but *all* Axial traditions.

However, as final points of differentiation between Islam and the two other Biblical traditions, not only does Islam escape the widest rendering of the Axial Period as encompassing the first millennium BCE, Jaspers also questions whether it evinces the requisite degree of reflectivity to confer inclusion among biblical revelation. In placing the revelatory faith of Islam this time along with Hinduism and Confucianism, Jaspers is *not* suggesting a hidden commonality between Hindu, Confucian, and Muslim revelation but instead their shared radical distinction in form and content from the Judaic and Christian modes of personal revelation.

> Historically there are many forms of both revealed and philosophical faith. We find faith in revelation in its biblical forms, also in Islam, Hinduism, Confucianism. Is faith the general concept covering both philosophical and revealed faith, and revealed faith the general concept covering Christianity among others? (Jaspers 1967, p. 17)

In these introductory reflections on the unity of faith in revelation in the multiplicity of practices and institutionalized forms, Jaspers refers specifically to the comportment of the believer exposed to a particular set of revelations in all their historicity. In other words, here he suggests that from the standpoint of the Muslim participating in and receiving the revelatory verses of the *Qur'an*, the Muslim practitioner would not regard themselves as participating within the wider rubric of biblical religion, particularly if that would entail renouncing their claim on the exclusive truths of the unique revelation received. Also as a key distinction between Judeo-Christian versus Muslim revelation would be the personalized conception of God in the former contrasting with the Absolute and utter depersonalized transcendence of the latter.

Thus, while the following passage from *The Perennial Scope of Philosophy* seems to include Islam among the biblical faiths, not only does he qualify the inclusion with a 'perhaps' but he also identifies Muslims this time along the somewhat disparaging lines of 'Mohammedans':

> Moreover, we have spoken only of religion and religions, not of what represents and proclaims itself as a unique revealed truth and declines to be classified as one religion among

> many. This is the case in the churches and denominations deriving from the comprehensive Biblical religion to which all of us belong, Jews and Christians, Catholics and Protestants, and perhaps Mohammedans as well. (Jaspers 1949, p. 88)

So, as an additional pragmatic presupposition behind authentic inter-Axial discourse, what about the following remarks would incite skeptical resentment in a Muslim as not being met on terms internal to their revelatory self-understanding? First, would be the perceived slight of misunderstanding the Arabic form of original revelation from Allah to Gabriel to Muhammad with Allah as the original author and *not* Muhammad and his followers (Mohammedans). Such a unique claim to divinely authored revelation lends even more of a distinct quality to Islamic revelation to render it separate from the Biblical religion of Judaism and Christianity that concedes human authorship to the various stages of revelation. Even though Judaism and Christianity would recognize denominational differentiations that could attribute more or less of the authorship itself to the subtle hand of God steering the revelatory process and maintaining its overall unity of narrative despite a variety of author social roles, modes, forms, and historical personages, the abiding constant would be the recognition of the historical exigencies of human authorship versus Allah as the exclusive divine Author of the Qur'an.

Returning then to concerns of religious exclusivity as bearing on scriptural revelation, Jaspers shows an acute awareness of precisely this Muslim doctrine as pertains to the revelatory self-understanding of its sacred scripture as compared to the Hebrew and Christian Bibles:

> The claim to exclusivity is present in the Christian faith, in the Jewish doctrine of the law, in the various forms of national religion, in Islam. Biblical religion is the inclusive historical area from which, if we overlook other contents, each denomination derives its particular emphasis. The whole Bible, including the Old and New Testament, is the sacred book only of the Christian denominations. For the Jews the New Testament, which was produced by the Jews, is not regarded as part of the Bible; but in its ethical and monotheistic content it is no less important for the Jewish religion than for the Christian. Islam does not regard the Bible as sacred, although Islam sprang from the same religious foundation under the influence of Jews and Christians. (Jaspers 1949, p. 96)

Within this multi-layered quotation we see Jaspers grappling with what might best be termed as doubly-meta reflection, or rather, the reflection upon reflection. At the philosophical level of reflection upon reflection we are within the domain of what Donald, and more recently Bellah, has called the theoretical stage of religion within which all the axial traditions qualify as steps beyond prior cultural evolutionary developments of Mimetic religion and Mythic religion (Bellah 2011, pp. 117–138; 272–282). From this standpoint, he seems to suggest a weakness on the part of Islam, that unlike Judaic and Christian concessions to inter-Axial overlap in their sacred texts, the more vehement exclusivism of Islam refuses to acknowledge the biblical heritage that Jaspers from the meta-level of the Encompassing appears fully assured.

Communicatively, what would be at stake here concerns the manner of engagement with Islam within Jasper's idealized universal discourse. Jaspers treats Islam as shaped by the inherently historical mindset characteristic of the axial period that nonetheless also seeks to preclude approaching Biblical religion from the perspective of the historical-critical method of exegesis. Furthermore, the inter-axial dynamics of communication would differ significantly if Islam were, on its own revelatory terms, to hold the self-ascribed status of a Biblical religion, within the same revelatory matrix as the Hebrew and Christian Bibles. If a presupposition of conferred inclusion includes passing through the Westernized academically driven methodological subjection to the historical-critical school of scriptural interpretation, we also must concede to Islam internal tensions with its regard for the Koran as always already having been co-eternal with Allah.

However, rather than resolving the ambivalence of his treatment from the meta-historical level of a multi-polar universal history, in his most authoritative work on deriving an inter-Axial matrix of boundless communication for exploring these complex matters—*On the Origin and Goal of History*, he further complicates matters. This time, by placing Islam among the 'Eastern' sequence of the binary classification of the alter egos of the "West" as circumscribed by Latin Christendom, he seems to render suspect its inclusion among Biblical religion:

> The Greeks and the Persians, the division of the *Imperium Romanum* into the Western and Eastern Empires, Western and Eastern Christendom, the Western World and Islam, Europe and Asia, which was in turn split up into the Near, Middle and Far East, are the successive shapes taken by the antithesis, in which cultures and peoples simultaneously attract and repel one another. This antithesis has at all times been an element in the make-up of Europe, whereas the Orient merely took it over from Europe and understood it in a European sense. (Jaspers 1953, p. 68)

Insofar as Islam is here regarded as distinctly other as among the Eastern traditions, Jaspers then would be led to posit it on the other side of the world-historical opposition between West and non-West/Eastern that has shaped the iterations of stages of the Encompassing more through outright tension than Biblical commonality.[11]

On such a complexly layered analysis, the multi-polar remains in constant tension with the bi-polar, as earlier in the same *Origin and Goal of History* he affirms the constant reflexive mutual interaction between Islam and Europe that the Muslim anthropologist Talad Asad finds all-too-often denied by Western academia: "In the East the empire and culture of Constantinople persisted in unbroken continuity into the fifteenth century. There the present-day Orient of Hither Asia was formed by Islam, in constant touch with both Europe and India" (Jaspers 1953, p. 57). As now

[11] It could be the case that what we are witnessing here would be attributed less to ambivalence on the part of Jaspers and more to the factors that ultimately led Voegelin to abandon the aims he set to establish in his multi-volume Order and History. Once immersed in the burgeoning growth of empirical research upon the conditions surrounding the onset and closure of Jaspers' Axial Age period, Voegelin found in his famous Volume IV, The Ecumenical Age, that either world history proceeded along a dual axis divided by sinological and Semetic tongues, or was an even more complex manifold of more than two world histories (1974b). While Voegelin denounced the strangeness of thereby positing two or more distinct species of humanity, he was led to reject the notion that a linear reconstruction of world history was even possible. Following Voegelin's open-ended conclusion, his findings would be one of the sources of my task for cosmoipolitan justice to embrace both multiple world histories while retaining optimism about the prospect for boundless communication (thus, not viewing the multiple histories as communicatively incommensurable).

constituting a third verdict on where historically and conceptually to posit the Axial status of Islam, this time he places Islam as the dubious mediator between East and West. Although vacillating between treating it as its own distinct entity while at other times dividing its historical heritage among each of Europe, India, and China, this concluding concession to its Eastern imprint also aids in explaining the contemporary genealogical construct of Muslim demographics showing the greatest growth, percentages, and aggregate number in what would be treated by contemporary scholars as falling within the geographic bounds of Asia.

The Qur'an and the Historical-Critical Method: *Surah 55* as Warrant for Muslim Inclusion as Biblical Religion?

While the general trend within Islam has been to resist the critical-historical method for reasons already mentioned above and enumerated more comprehensively below, if one were able to find historical traces of continuity among texts, we could lend credence to Jaspers' notion that the ascription of Biblical religion to Islam carries at least some semblance of commonality by means of narrative transmission into the Qur'an. Contemporary critical theorists, and in particular Habermas, argue that if a religion[12] and/or Axial tradition desires to have its claims subjected to potential translation into meaningful contributions to debates in the public sphere, the necessary trade-off would be voluntary subjection to the critical scrutiny of the scientific method and the historical-critical mode of analysis to which Judaism and Christianity have been assessed for centuries.

However, some necessary hermeneutic clarifications about the Muslim understanding of the Qur'an must be mentioned before proceeding. For starters, on the Muslim understanding, neither Muhammad—nor the Uthman Commission tasked to organize the revelations shortly after his death—were the 'authors' of the Qur'an. The author was Allah, to which Muhammad and his followers were recipients of divine revelation. The lineage of revelation was from Allah, to Gabriel, to Muhammad, to the initial community of followers, and then eventually to the Written Qur'an as the closest finite approximation possible of the Eternal Qur'an that has/had no finite beginning in time.

---

[12] Talad Asad casts helpful skepticism upon the now commonplace Western academic, political, and even legal-juridical debates concerning what will and will not qualify as 'religion.' According to Asad: 'True, the "proper domain of religion" is distinguished from and separated by the state in modern secular constitutions. But formal constitutions never give the whole story. On the one hand objects, sites, practices, words, representations—even the minds and bodies of worshippers—cannot be confined in the exclusive space of what secularists name "religion." They have their own ways of being…On the other hand the nation-state requires clearly demarcated spaces that it can classify and regulate: religion, education, health, leisure, work, income, justice, and war. The space that religion may properly occupy in society has to be continually redefined by the law because the reproduction of secular life within and beyond the nation-state continually affects the discursive clarity of that space. The unceasing pursuit of the new in productive effort, aesthetic experience, and claims to knowledge, as well as the unending struggle to extend individual self-creation, undermines the stability of established boundaries' (Asad, 2003, pp. 200–201).

In addition, Qur'anic exegesis runs differently than the conventions of Judaic and Christian biblical interpretation that thereby have necessarily informed the practices and conventions of the historical-critical method with its original roots in the Wellhausen German historical school. Insofar as one assumes the Qur'an (literally, in Arabic: 'to recite'), although revealed, when recited carries the reciter into conformity with the original oral transmission from Allah, to Gabriel, to Muhammad, to Followers, to Written Qur'an, this participatory act in the cycle of revelation, while historically recited, merely reiterates the content of an eternal oral revelation of truth. In additional layers of complexity, the Qur'an has been organized into chapters (*surahs*) by length not following the general historical organization one finds in the Hebrew and Christian Bibles. Even when conceding the historical stages of revelation in the life of Muhammad, this order by length puts the reader in a precarious position insofar as the longest *surahs*, which do have a mix of historical and doctrinal content, tend to be from later in the life of Muhammad while he is presiding as ruler and spiritual teacher of a loose confederation of tribes in Medina. By default then, the historically earlier revelations of more doctrinal and less historical content to the remaining *surahs* were received while Muhammad was in Mecca and tend to be toward the end of the Qur'an.

As a final exegetic note, the original eternal status of the Qur'an as co-original with Allah, for Muslim scholars remains fully comfortable with the notion that the interpretation of the Qur'an could lead to competing accounts that vary widely across differentiated times, major historical schools, and changing social problems. In this respect, proper Qur'anic hermeneutics entails consultation of *hadiths* that have canonized the centuries of interpretive layers to the text and its ongoing applicability to the life of the believer in the here and now. Lastly, the combination of *hadith* interpretation, together with the moral doctrine, associated ritual practices, political guidance, salvific promises, stark prohibitive warnings, private and public affairs, regulation of family life, and deep speculations into the ultimate philosophical questions of human existence together constitute the historical precedent behind *shari'a* law. As the prior in-exhaustive list suggests, the notion of law employed here could be used more broadly to include religious mandates outside the purview of governance, cultural norms, dietary prohibitions, ritual proprieties, etc., that certainly comprise a 'theopolity' that goes beyond the scope of the purely legal-juridical narrower conception of constitutional law.

In the words of Muslim philosophical anthropologist Talal Asad, the above general outline of the basis of Islamic hermeneutics leads to a 'second-personal' notion of textual interpretation that allows for simultaneity on the part of the interpreter as discursive participant in taking account of the multi-perspectival history of past precedent, applying to the present, and leaving open the very real prospect of the necessity of ongoing future communicative redaction:

> The Arabic word *hadith*, incidentally, captures nicely the double sense of temporality usually separated in English: on the one hand it denotes anything that is new or modern, and on the other hand a tradition that makes the past—and future—reencountered in the present. For *hadith* means "discourse" in the general secular sense as well as the remembered discourse of the Prophet and his Companions that is actualized in the disciplined body/

> mind of the faithful Muslim—and thus becomes the tradition, the *sunna*….The participant's engagement with his tradition is in part involvement with its multiple temporalities, his selection, affirmation, and reproduction of its authoritative practices. (Asad 2003, p. 224, 225)

As one participates in the ongoing redaction and interpretation of the Qur'an, while the oral connotations of 'to recite' certainly carry overtones of ritualistic recitations of sections of the Qur'an as an act of prayerful worship, we could also give a more pragmatic construal of this second-personal 'you' mandate that thereby comprises one's active participation in the ongoing construction of additional layers to the precedential *hadith*. The recitation practice carries this twofold significance of symbolic participation in the initial revelatory experience of Muhammad and in the more practical and historical orientation of 'walking the Straight Path' in a manner that entails ongoing disciplinary praxis.

While the participant's submission to the mandates of the Qur'an could indeed carry overtones of epistemic authoritarianism ascribed to the textual exegesis, McAuliffe draws attention to the recurring theme of *jadal*, most accurately translated as engagement in disputation, as carrying both positive and negative connotations in Qur'anic hermeneutics. In accord with the micro-level Habermasian call to engage in communicative action oriented to the practical activity of giving and responding to reasons in process of practical norm-justification, one can derive something akin to such praxis internal to the resources of the Qur'an on the various manifestations of *jadal*:

> Taken together these reorientations [macro and historical] correlate with a bi-partite understanding of debate as both (1) intellectual contest and (2) structure of argumentation. One orientation would urge sensitivity to the latter, would recast the classical analysis of particular scenes and exchanges of disputation into a more comprehensive phenomenology of persuasive discourse as a dominant Qur'anic pattern. On the other hand, debate as intellectual contest connects well with revisionist historiography that has theorized the Qur'anic canon's emergence in an intellectual environment of interreligious polemic. While the historical specificity of this hypothesis remains undetermined, it does draw attention to what one might call the 'macro' aspect of Qur'anic *jadal*. (McAuliffe 1999, p. 187, 188)

On the one hand, upon one's first reading of the Qur'an, the inter-Axial quality of polemic debate internal to its structure seems to presuppose on the part of the reader at least a basic understanding of the general tenets of Hebrew and Christian doctrine. For instance, both groups all called 'Peoples of the Book' which would seem to offer at least a loose specification to characterize the Qur'an within the rubric of Jaspers' Biblical religion, even when the commentary on Hebrew and Christian commitments turns polemical and elicits sentiments of outright open disputation of claims rather than an overlapping consensus of doctrinal agreement. On the other hand, read in terms of its overall grand narrative, one could also interpret the Qur'an as a collective corpus of writing intended to employ *jadal* as disputation providing reasons and justifications to the reader as argumentative participation for why they ought to submit to its authoritative mandates.

The epistemic openness to disputation does include positive renditions of such a practice and, in those instances, also recommends various moral and ethical proprieties attached to the proper discourse etiquette to disputation.

> Ibn Hazm provides an initial list of verses that condemn particular forms of *jadal or jidal* (Q30: 15–16, 43: 58, 42: 35, 3: 20), and follows with multiple citations that both praise *jadal bi-l-haqq* and provide examples of its successful application (Q41: 33, 16: 125, 28: 49–50, 10: 68–69, 29: 46, 4: 82). Like Ibn Furak, he stresses *jadal*'s obligatory character and, as expected, Q.16: 125 stands as the key verse: "In this verse God has made *jidal* mandatory and has taught the entire etiquette and procedure (*adab*) of *jidal*, including courtesy, clarity, adherence to the truth and having recourse to whatever decisive argument requires." A consistent theme that Ibn Hazm sounds in his subsequent elaboration of obligatory *jidal* is the pre-eminence of proof…His last citation in this series leads nicely to this author's effective use of a Qur'anic model for proper *mujadalah*, the prophet Abraham. The exhortation in Q.3: 95 to "follow the *millah* of Abraham" is understood as a further injunction to praiseworthy disputation (*munazarah*). (McAuliffe 1999, p. 176)

In Habermas's parlance, the list of 'pragmatic presuppositions' required of the discursive practitioner, include but are not limited to: courtesy in consideration of the perspective of the other, striving for clarity in the articulation of claims, a presupposed mutual commitment to the truth of the matter on the part of disputers, and operating under a meta-level mutual understanding of what concession of the force of the better argument would entail for positing a procedural finality to determine the most convincing outcome.

However, despite the fairly comprehensive listing of pragmatic proprieties of ethical disputation, McAuliffe carefully notes that the overwhelming precedent of references to *jadal* view such practice negatively, conveying the sense that the Qur'an rests on its own authority that need not necessarily concord with the moral, political, social, or personal autonomy of the participant-reader as the final word on the rational and semantic authority of its claims.

> Out of these many occurrences of *jadal* and its cognates, a clear semantic pattern emerges. In the overwhelming majority of cases, debates and disputation are viewed negatively…. There are, it should be noted, some exceptions to this general pattern of negativity. On the Day of Resurrection, the individual soul—but no one else—will dispute on its own behalf. Abraham was permitted to debate with God about the people of Lot. There is even an etiquette (22: 67–68) expressed and an encouragement to "summon the way of your Lord with wisdom and fine exhortation and debate with them in the better way" (16: 125; 29: 46). Yet the predominant Qur'anic usage of *jadal* and its cognates is negative, as signaled by its very first textual occurrence. Therefore when the Qur'an, disclosing a key element of its anthropology states *wa-kana l-insanu akthara shay'in jadalan* (18: 54), it is not conveying a compliment or highlighting a human virtue. (McAuliffe 1999, p. 168)

In other words, while there are sets of proprieties attached to appropriate means, methods, and aims of disputation, the default setting should be one of discernment and submission, particularly in matters that have been stated by the Qur'an that abide by its own standards of an orientation toward clarity, truthfulness, and argumentative closure. Not mentioned above, but also meriting inclusion on the list would be the Qur'anic exhortation not to attempt to explain, clarify, or dispute a claim made in the Qur'an that one does not yet fully understand. The attendant risk could include the proliferation of untruth, as precluded in the passage above. The call for epistemic humility also presumes that it would be better for the disputant to profess ignorance in need of clarification than speculate upon a matter over which they have not yet themselves achieved clarity.

While disputation as *jadal* in both negative and positive connotations clearly has its support on both sides from justification internal to the Qur'an, McAuliffe also warns against the potential misreading of its proprietary demands as if the sacred text required an elite education, disciplined philosophical training in rhetorical persuasion, and a superior intellect for a grasp of its basic teachings. The appeal below to Muhammad carries the connotation that the intended audience would be those sharing the non-elitist common Arabic vernacular of Muhammad, whom himself—in the general consensus on biographical accounts—had no access to formal education.

> [N]othing of the intellectual sophistication for which *kalam* works became noted is absent from the Qur'an. The acts of ratiocination, such as definition (*tahdid*), division into constituent parts (*taqsim*), proof (*burhan*), and demonstration (*dalalah*), are fully, in his own view, articulated in the Book of God. They are not, however—and this is his second point—couched in the technical methods and terminology of the *mutakallimun*. God rather chose the ordinary language of the Arabs (*'adat al-arab*), as promised by Q. 14: 4: "We sent no messenger except with the tongue of his people so that he could make [the message] clear to them." Distinguishing between the human talent for precise, detailed argumentation and that for large-scale persuasive discourse, al-Zarkashi contends that the Qur'an's author is capable of both. The divine orations were issued "in the grandest form, inclusive of the most precise refinements" so that ordinary people could grasp them in their broad outlines and find them compelling, while educated people could explore their intricacies. Al-Zarkashi nicely describes the varieties of human receptive capability through the conventional pairings of *'aql* and *sama'*, of *tafkir* and *tadhakkur*. (McAuliffe 1999, p. 184, 185)

McAuliffe likewise concedes that the great Kalam schools did develop centuries of deep philosophical reflection on the content of the Qur'an, conducted in accord with the internal mandates on the proprieties of disputation as applied to the conduct of elite discourse. On her analysis, this allows the Qur'an effectively to address the rational capacities of the reader simultaneously to make clear for all the basis premises of its doctrinal core while also to permit the higher-order reflection necessary to probe its deepest mysteries and multi-layered narrative structure.

So far, the justification for inclusion of the Qur'an within the general classification scheme of what Jaspers has termed Biblical religion, include the shared employment of second-personal participant-oriented narrative constructs, evidence of inter-Axial points of both agreement and disagreement with the Hebrew and Christian Bibles, reiteration of Biblical themes into the common Arabic vernacular of its intended audience, and a comprehensive listing of communicative assumptions attached to both its internal warrants to truthfulness and norms for addressing and articulating external sources of critique. What has perhaps been understated, even in my prior treatments of the Hebrew and Christian Bibles, would be the frequent usage of poetic literary methods of communicating both straightforward and symbolic meanings.

Fortunately, our present purposes of at least lending credence to the treatment of the Qur'an as a Biblical religion will focus on a specific *surah* (chapter), *Surat-al-Rahman* (Qur'an, Surah 55) that both evinces strong symbolically poetic overtones and seems to owe scriptural heritage to Psalm 136 of the Hebrew Bible. As telling support, the hymnal repetition of the refrain 'O which of your lords bounties will you and you deny?'[13] 31 times in its 78 verses finds no parallel instances in the

[13] Other English translations vary but convey the same general message. For instance, the English version disseminated widely in the English speaking world as commissioned by Prince Al Waleed

comparative corpus of the other Meccan *surahs* in proximity to the second half of the Qur'an. Although these later *surahs* all are replete with similar second-personal 'you' modes of address—not only do the Meccan *surahs* lack any such poetic and hymnal parallel, there are none such to be found anywhere in the Qur'an (Neuwirth, p. 391, 392). However, by looking instead to the canonical scripture of the Qur'an as a continuation of themes, symbols, styles, and interpretive redaction up Hebrew and Christian themes, Neuwirth points to the striking parallels between *Surat-al Rahman* and Psalm 136. Specifically the hymnal refrain on Psalm 136 that opens with three proclamations: 'O give thanks unto the Lord; for he is good: for his mercy endureth forever,' replaces Lord with 'God of Gods' in the second verse, then places 'God of Gods' with 'Lord of Lords' in the third opening verse, thereby repeating 'for his mercy endureth forever' 23 times in the ensuing 23 verses. Given not just the methodological parallels but the striking symmetry in thematic content seems, to her, to place the Hebrew Bible as the most likely canonical source for the otherwise unorthodox refrain that evinces no Qur'anic stylistic corollary.

Neuwirth explains the rationale behind her use of Psalm 136 from its initial Hebrew context as a means both to place it within a wider biblical tradition while also highlighting key distinctions between Surah 55 that thereby detail significant symbolic meanings given to the narrative in its iterated stages of Hebrew, Christian, and then Muslim ritual and narrative contexts:

> I will rather limit my scope to a rapid examination of their similarity, in order to make use of the older, biblical, text as a screen to show more clearly the focus of the discourse of the contrasting qur'anic text. It should be stressed from the beginning, that *Surat-al-Rahman* is in no way a simple mimesis of the Psalm, it is undeniably a very different text; still, it appears to comment on that prominent prototype of monotheistic praise of the Lord. It should be noted that the Psalm has been celebrated as the Great Laudes, *ha-hallel ha-gadol*, in Jewish liturgy and been in widespread use as a thanksgiving prayer in Christian tradition. In view of the qur'anic affirmation of the revealed character of the Psalms (*zabur/zubur*) it is hardly surprising to meet with a qur'anic comment on this part of Scriptural heritage—not more surprising than to find any other Scriptural feature figuring in the Qur'an, the detailed narrative of the prophet *Yusuf* being perhaps the most prominent. Formulaic expressions, clearly related in style to the psalms have been frequently identified in the Qur'an, these, however, in no way exhaust the qur'anic traces of a close relation between both Scriptures. (Neuwirth 1998, p. 394, 395)

In addition to the Muslim-Hebrew parallels, by virtue of the Christian appropriation of the Hebrew Bible into its own Biblical canon, this single example can address the poetic dynamics of Biblical religions and vicariously include each of the three Axial traditions informing Jaspers' classification of Biblical religion. In light of his associated call for the prospect of its future rejuvenation as an enduring source of inspiration for a post-WWII Europe in civilization crisis and cultural disarray, we could also point to the inclusion of Islam within the rubric of Biblical religion as a source of cultural solidarity to buttress against the sensationalist portrayals of an insurmountable Islam-West divide.

---

bin Talal bin Abdul-Aziz Al Saud of Saudi Arabia reads: 'Then which of the Blessings of your Lord will you (jinn and men) deny?'

Beginning from the initial Hebrew, and then Christian appropriation of the symbolic meanings present in Psalm 136, Eric Voegelin likewise uses this Psalm as an illustration of the meaning ascribed to history from the Israelite perspective:

> Organized in three distinct parts the liturgical Psalm 136 gives something like a commentary on the governing principle of Israelite history…The drama of divine creation moves through the three great acts: the creation of the world, the rescue from Egypt, and the conquest of Canaan. Each of the three acts wrests meaning from the meaningless: the world emerges from Nothing, Israel from the Sheol of Egypt, and the promised land from the Desert. The acts thus interpret one another as works of divine creation and as the historical stages in which a realm of meaning grows: In history God continues his work of creation, and the creation of the world is the first event in history. To this conception the term "world-history" can be applied in the pregnant sense of a process that is world-creation and history at the same time. In its sweep the Old Testament narrative surveys the process from the creative solitude of God to its completion through the establishment of the servants of Yahweh in the land of promise. (Voegelin 1974a, pp. 134, 135)

As additional support then for the inclusion of the *Qur'an* within the wider hermeneutic and inter-Axial context of Biblical religion, Neuwirth in comparison cites not just the meaning of Surah 55 but its poetic function. She draws both upon the presumed setting of a common set of historical memories and the intentional psychological function of giving them unexpected new resonance. This juxtaposition of the readers' perceived expectations suggests for her that the *Qur'an* itself likely emerged from a common core nucleus of canonical texts.

> Since this paper studies the Qur'an as literature, indeed, the surahs as poetic texts, it is based on the assumption that the surahs do not primarily convey a semantic message—a widely held mistaken view that has enticed scholars to ignore the artistic side of the text and consider single texts as mere repetitions of others. On the contrary, the strongly poetic language of the Qur'an appears in its main function to be a reference to the communication itself, it therefore relies on mnemotechnic and psychagogic devices which reflect the expectations of particular recipients. Since these devices can be observed to change, indeed develop, from single texts to others, but continue to rely on a particular communicational setting, which makes up the indispensable framework of the texts, we feel entitled to assume an organic genesis of the qur'anic corpus as a whole that appears to result less from an intended composition than from a canonical process. The concept of a canonical process, developed in Scriptural studies, presupposes the growth of a text corpus from a *nucleus* of particular basic texts which remains present as a permanent context during the course of ongoing text-generating development. (Neuwirth 1998, p. 390)

In presuming this common core from which the canon was derived, the shared set of deeply ingrained cultural memories are endowed with additional layers of meaning over an ongoing process of historical redaction, assimilation, introduction of new literary figures and events, and modification of historiogenetic and eschatological symbolism.

While Neuwirth recognizes that the Islamic approach to salvation history shares relatively common structural features to both Hebrew and Christian exegetical reading of Psalm 136, she emphasizes that the Qur'an should not be read as providing merely another layer of commentary upon the univocal direction within which salvation history will unfold. In the previous language of Jan Potacka's transcensus, we can attempt to describe the Qur'anic text as proclaiming harmony between the profane and the transcendent via the symbolic entry of the textual participant into the eternal recitation of the Qur'an. In other words, while the Qur'an does offer an eschaton that includes both individual accountability for judgment and the ultimate consummation of Allah's redemptive activity in the world, Neuwirth claims that an accord of wills between participant and Allah can issue forth in transformed self-understanding. The learning potential imbibed in the textual hermeneutic allows for a concession of historical-critical redaction of themes that nonetheless accord with the Muslim commitment to the eternal Koran as inviting the reader to participate in Allah's eternity in the here and now.

> I would dare to formulate a provisory conclusion: qur'anic texts sometime allow to be read as commentary on earlier scriptures; this is not limited to those that explicitly present themselves as such. But—returning to *Surat al-Rahman*—there are essential differences: whereas the older scriptural text would claim for its account to be rooted in Salvation History, and thus apt to instill a vision of the future with the familiar pattern of divine interaction taken for granted, the Qur'an rather focuses on the communicational achievement brought about by the re-enactment of divine revelation. The opening up of a communication between the divine speaker and his human audience in the earlier surahs as a novel achievement, bestows on the 'here and now' the vision of an attainable *equilibrium* between the oppositions governing reality [hence, harmony, submission, peace, and accord of wills upon the Straight Path]. Two textual stratagems contribute to this breakthrough in the Qur'an: the self-referential technique of reflecting the narrated world through diverse layers of the textual structure, and the genre-transcending stratagem of introducing two strands of speech. We are confronted here with a unique kind of intrinsic qur'anic commentary, through self-reference and through exhortation, that is through inviting the listener to 'explain', to practice *bayan*, to make apparent the hidden dimensions of meaning. He does so by interpreting the informations conveyed in the narrative strand as tokens of divine faculties, divine promises, but also divine demands: that is, social rulings. The listener's exegetical semiotization of the words received, is, thus, an indispensible part of the text itself, its intrinsic exegesis. (Neuwirth 1998, p. 414)

On her polemical analysis, the unique communicative achievement of the Surah 55 over Psalm 136 would be that the activity of textual exegesis itself invites the participant to disclose and reveal the hidden nature of God, not merely within the process of redemptive history, but via intrinsic participation in the text itself as the ongoing recitation of an already complete breakthrough of divine revelation.

Although Neuwirth does comment upon the relative frequency of surahs in the Qur'an addressing the reciting participant in the communicative language of the second-person perspective, she claims the Surah 55 offers something much more significant to the interpreter. The participant, in what we might call participation in a majestic collectivity—second-person plural aggregate—of spiritual beings transcends the human realm.

> What becomes common in the more complexly built later Meccan surahs—that the texts are addressed immediately to a single receiver, marked by the continuously used pronoun *anta*, you, applies already to many of the more simply built ones—not, however to *Surat al-Rahman*....On the contrary, the permanent address, uniquely in the *Qur'an*, is directed to a rather imaginary group made up of men and spirits, a group not only transcending the human kind as such, but also reappearing in the narrative strand of the text as co-agents of the divine protagonist in overtly mythic interactions. *Surat al-Rahman* is therefore less the usual mirror of multiple communication process between a sender, a reciter and his

> listeners—anchored in a particular, vaguely identifiable social setting, and judgeable as to its success from the distribution of inclined and disinclined listeners, the allusions to problematic interactions, etc.—than a hymnic text transcending time and social setting, dealing with cosmic and eschatological visions. With this very loosely structured communication framework between speakers and listeners the suruh stands unique in the Qur'an. (Neuwirth 1998, p. 390)

To participate as a 'you' in this sort of divine interaction places the interpreter in the unique role of co-agent in symbolic interactions of a Muslim theopolity of both cosmic and eschatological import. With the participant structure still intact, the textual symbolism suggests that the paradise of deliverance into Canaan in the Hebrew narrative, or the deliverance into the yet unrealized Kingdom of Heaven with Christ as sovereign, has been overcome with the real participation in the Garden of heavenly Paradise. In comparison to the Hebrew and Christian eschatologies referring to the consummation of heavenly city as kingdom, the Koran frequently references concretely embodied participation in a Garden/Paradise consistent with its distinct historiogenetic read of Adam and Eve's immediate forgiveness by Allah upon their initial transgression. In this manner, the symbolic return to a Garden Paradise in Muslim eschatology renders fully consistent with a restoration to a state of affairs from which humanity always already had not been so tragically separated (as compared to the Hebrew and Christian accounts of the Fall/rebellion).[14]

Talal Asad's Anthropology of Muslim Jurisprudence: Habitus, Ritual, and Embodied Second-Person Communication

One of the consequences Jaspers foresees coming with taking up the demanding epistemic perspective of trans-civilizational analysis would be that full immersion in the strangeness of a new Axial perspective reflexively will grant us greater clarity on our own religious genealogy that he sees as so deeply shaping the Western immanent fame of reference. In addition, for Jaspers, the potential inclusion of Islam within his generalized rubric of Biblical religion might serve to acknowledge a shared Abrahamic heritage while also open up avenues for the boundless communication he viewed as characteristic of inter-Axial discourse. However, in contrast to Jaspers' optimistic tenor, Talad Asad casts a critical stance upon the seemingly innocent epistemic reasons for seeking enhanced Western self-understanding.

We will consider the important contributions of Talal Asad's emphasis on the embodied habitus of ritual experience as shaping one's senses and cosmic lens in thereby taking primacy over merely Western tendencies to over-emphasize cognitive epistemological indices of belief. He reconsiders regarding these as merely functional differentiations in conceptual analysis, since he views the intellectual partitions as part of a longer world-historical narrative of European colonialism.

---

[14] An adequate comparative study on what Western philosophers would call 'weakness of the will' would take a separate manuscript to explore in its necessary depth. Since none such work, to my knowledge, has yet been composed, my most likely future project would be to develop a separate manuscript to provide such a comprehensively comparative thematic.

Even in newer neo-colonial forms, Asad sees the academic delineations as not reflective of the impartial stance of the objective social-scientific observer. Instead, he finds that the social-scientific conceptual manifold itself reinforces structural asymmetries of material, cultural, and racial divides. These distinctions thus serve the dual purpose of classifying Islam as a carrier civilization (for Europe, to serve Western aims and interests) and as Europe's perennially dark alter ego:

> There is a problem for any historian constructing a categorical boundary for "European civilization" because the populations designated by the label "Islam" are, in a great measure, the cultural heirs of the Hellenistic world—the very world in which "Europe" claims to have its roots. "Islamic civilization" must therefore be denied a vital link to the properties that define so much of what is essential to "Europe" if a civilizational difference is to be postulated between them. There appear to be two moves by which this is done. First, by denying that it has an essence of its own, "Islam" can be represented as a *carrier civilization* that helped to bring important elements into Europe from the outside, material and intellectual elements that were only contingently connected to Islam. Then, to this carrier civilization is attributed an essence: an *ingrained* hostility to all non-Muslims. That attribute constitutes Islam as Europe's primary alter. (Asad 2003, p. 168, 169)

While Asad also notes that much attention has been paid already to the contemporary demographic phenomena of more Muslims in the world presently residing in Asia than on any other continent, if we are to begin from the nascent origins of Islam as an Axial tradition, we also must consider its earliest impacts upon European civilization and the Near East. He takes us even farther in order to question the overall practical efficacy and ideological biases that are served by presuming an East and West divide. In addition, given the exponentially growing Muslim demographics in Europe, he likewise seeks to disclose the hidden dimensions of a continent-wide Islamophobia. Keeping these framing biases unchallenged has resulted in a skewed understanding of Europe's own path to secularization and reshapes even the inclusively optimistic tenor of its purported postsecular turn:

> What politics are promoted by the notion that the world is *not* divided into modern and nonmodern, into West and non-West? What practical options are opened up or closed by the notion that the world has *no* significant binary features, that it is, on the contrary, divided into overlapping, fragmented cultures, hybrid selves, continuously dissolving and emerging social states? As part of such an understanding I believe we must try to unpack the various assumptions on which secularism—a modern doctrine of the world in the world—is based. For it is precisely the process by which the conceptual binaries are established or subverted that tells us how people live the secular—how they vindicate the essential freedom and responsibility of the sovereign self in opposition to the constraints of that self by religious discourses. (Asad 2003, p. 15, 16)

Asad's skepticism towards the historical efficacy of the Western genealogical self-understanding as owing much to its Greek and Christian heritage must be critically reassessed, particularly in light of how they bear upon maintaining the conventional social-science efficacy of the secularization thesis that only until recently has begun receiving its due critical assessment.

> [I]f the secularization thesis seems increasingly implausible to some of us this is not simply because religion is now playing a vibrant part in the modern world of nations. In a sense what many would anachronistically call "religion" was *always* involved in the world

> of power. If the secularization thesis no longer carries the conviction it once did, this is because the categories of "politics" and "religion" turn out to implicate each other more profoundly than we thought, a discovery that has accompanied our growing understanding of the powers of the modern nation-state. The concept of the secular cannot do without the idea of religion. (Asad 2003, p. 200)

Couched behind the prized political autonomy to be retained by the secularization thesis would be a certain view of subjectivity as distinctly modern that belies the long-history of Muslim subjective interiority that nonetheless does not meet Western/European criteria:

> Perhaps more important is the mistaken assumption (gaining some popularity in Islamic studies) that modernity introduced subjective interiority into Islam, something that was previously absent. But subjective interiority has always been recognized in Islamic tradition—in ritual worship (*'ibadat*) as well as in mysticism (*tasawwuf*). What modernity does bring in is a new *kind* of subjectivity, one that is appropriate to ethical autonomy and aesthetic self-invention—a concept of "the subject" that has a new grammar. (Asad 2003, p. 225)

In addition to positing a distinctly Muslim conception of modernity that can be traced back to its very origins, he also takes on the laborious tasks of making explicit the undisclosed political, moral, and imperialistic reasons why we still hold dearly to these conceptual demarcations that more and more evade practical experience. One of these latent assumptions to challenge in what follows would be the assumption that European modernity has a univocal historical narrative that serves to unite its nonetheless highly distinct nation-states. Another assumption to critique would be the notion that we can properly dissect our Axial commitments into their respective private and public domains without biasing our assumptions about the secular genealogy of modernity in a way that best approximates only the gerrymandered history projected by Latin Christendom. On Asad's skeptical account, these biases can never adequately capture the unique nuances of the Muslim *umma* (de-territorialized community of faithful believers) as straddling the transcensus characteristic of the sacred-profane tensions to this theopolity.

Talal Asad's anthropology of jurisprudence requires stringent epistemic burdens that argue an ideally competent judge of these matters fully understand all the attendant Muslim ritual proprieties that lead into a particular course of action. Therefore, without mimetic and mythic spiritual training, it seems that he must adopt the apparently radical position that the secularist advancing a jurisprudential judgment from the purportedly impartial view from nowhere may have to refrain altogether from the debate until these epistemic conditions are met. As an interpretive minimum, the competent judge must at least be open to the prospect that demonstrative competence in the capacity to see actions as imbued with rational content requires the participant has undergone the intensive disciplined of cultivating embodied practices. In this manner, he rejects the Kantian assumption that one can glean the contents of the moral law from pure practical reason alone devoid of heteronomous desires and experiential content:

> The *shari'a*, in contrast, rejects the idea that the moral subject is completely sovereign ("Kant's conscience needs no guide; to have a conscience suffices"). Islamic jurists certainly recognized that a Muslim's relation to God (*fima baynahu wa bayn allah*) cannot

> be the object of a judge's (*qadi's*) verdict. But this is not because they thought this matter was practically inaccessible; it is simply that being set outside the jurisdiction of an earthly court of law, they regarded it as legally inviolable [thus no torture to exact evidence]. Nevertheless, they regard the individual's ability to judge which conduct is right and good (for oneself as well as for others) to be dependent not on inaccessible conscience but on embodied relationships—heavily so in the learning process of childhood, but also in adulthood where the intervention of authorities, relatives, and friends in particular situations may be critical for the exercise of that ability or for dealing with the consequences of its failure. Here body-mind is the object of moral discipline. In brief, I submit that although the *shari'a* does distinguish between "law" and "ethics," neither term should be understood in its modern, secular sense. (Asad 2003, p. 247, 248)

In other words, for Asad, responsibility, discipline, and punishment, always arise out of a context inherently social, embodied, and actively engaged with the ongoing cultural shaping of our sensory manifold stemming back to the earliest stages of infant and child development. Asad defines *habitus* as 'an embodied capacity that is more than physical ability in that it also includes cultivated sensibilities and passions, an orchestration of the senses' (2003, p. 95, 250–252). In this manner, even appeals to liberty of conscience as an inalienable international and/or global norm that have attained universal rational justification would appear to have overlooked the Muslim assumption that conscience presupposes an untenable separation between the individual-liberal-subjective-cognitive versus ethical-practical-social-affective modes of self-cultivation.

Asad finds this misconception easiest to demonstrate by a reconstruction of the assumptions that fed into the colonial incursion of European law into Muslim societies that invariably rested on assumptions utterly foreign to Muslim jurisprudence. He picks the apparently inviolable domain of family law in this history of colonial and neo-colonial jurisprudence as a case in point:

> The family is the unit of "society" in which the individual is physically and morally reproduced and has his or her primary formation as a "private" being. It is often assumed that colonial governments were reluctant to interfere with family law because it was the heart of religious doctrine and practice. I argue, on the contrary, that the *shari'a* thus defined is precisely a secular formula for privatizing "religion" and preparing the ground for the self-governing subject. (Asad 2003, p. 227, 228)

If one were to accept the colonial relegation of Muslim practices to the private domain of family life, Asad notes that this style of argumentation already presupposes the normative validity of the secularization thesis. We noted earlier that he finds although the secularization thesis of Western academia has only recently come under critique (post-1970s), its characteristic separations of private and public always already presupposed secularity as a foregone conclusion toward which the progressive society must evolve. He finds such a conclusion untenable and also tragically ironic for a mode of legislation ideally couching legitimacy only insofar as it has received the rational consent of all those immediately affected.

In yet another line of skeptical disclosure of untenable sets of assumptions, he also argues that within the construct of his anthropology of Muslim jurisprudence, legal judgment cannot strictly reside in the domain of mere access to cognitive truth.

> Thus the possibility is opened up of inquiring into the ways in which embodied practices (including language-in-use) form a precondition for varieties of religious (and secular) experience. The inability to "enter into communion with God" not only becomes a function of untaught bodies but it shifts the direction in which the authority for conduct can be sought. And authority itself comes to be understood not as an ideologically justified coercion but as a predisposition of the embodied self. (Asad 2003, p. 252)

On such an anthropological assumption, he goes so far as to suggest that all persons possess the latent capacities for socialization into relations of communion with God. However, if one has not undergone the rigors of this sort of embodied *habitus* from an early age, they also have forsaken their authority to make judgments upon matters of inherently spiritual import. Therefore, on his tradition-laden conception of legal legitimacy, all embodied and social action falls under the warranted province only of those whom have undergone such socialization.

As a last critique of the assumptions usually entertained by advocates of the secularization of society, he notes that even the Muslim use of the term faith has less to do with a consciously willed epistemic commitment or rational choice, and more to do with a cultivated second-personal disposition of trust and obedience developed over time.

> Conscious intentionality is here seen as important where inexperience or vice prevails, for it is in those conditions that the inertial resistance of the body, as well as its fragility, need to be addressed deliberately for responsible practice. Note that I speak here of the formation of virtues (*fada'il*) and sensibilities (*hisas*). Rites of worship (*'ibadat*)—whose regular practice is in fact necessary to the cultivation of the virtues and sensibilities required of a Muslim—always require the silent enunciation of one's intention (*niyya*) to perform a prayer (*salat*), and so forth, at the commencement of the rite. The *niyya* is therefore an integral part of the rite, a form of conscious commitment initiating acts of worship that must itself be cultivated as an aspect of one's continuous faith. *Iman*—usually translated into English as "faith"—is not a singular epistemological means that guarantees God's existence for the believer. It is better translated as the virtue of faithfulness toward God, an unquestioning habit of obedience that God requires of those faithful to him (*mu'minin*), a disposition that has to be cultivated like any other, and that links one to others who are faithful, through mutual trust and responsibility. (Asad 2003, p. 90)

With the above example of the embodied praxis of prayer typically coming prior to the initiation of any of the rituals that structure daily, yearly, and lifelong Muslim worship, even the faithful adherence to prayer must be construed as inseparable from the ritual which it precedes. In other words, the faithful engagement in prayer also amounts to proprietary socialization and not mere cognitive comportment of an individual consciously deciding to opt for or against belief.

In brief summation, Asad cannot accept the conventional split between law and morality, or the related distinction between the realm of the publically political and ethically private. As a supporting illustration, he argues that even Western forms of legal jurisprudence presuppose familiarity with entire sets of proprieties and traditions that thereby collapse the functional utility of the positivist law and ethics separation.

> [E]ven in the Western liberal scheme morality is connected to law in complicated ways. The authority of legal judgments is dependent on the ways justice, decency, reasonableness, and the like are culturally interpreted; the credibility of witnesses is linked to ways "good" and

"bad" character are culturally recognized, assessed, and responded to. Furthermore, there is the general sense that the laws in force should be consistent with the prevailing morality…. If traditionally embodied conceptions of justice and unconsciously assimilated experience are no longer relevant to the maintenance of law's authority, then that authority will depend entirely on the force of the state expressed through its codes. It might appear at first that I am making a familiar argument about the introduction of "foreign codes." But my concern here is neither with geographical origin of the law nor with codification as such. I argue that it is the power to make a strategic separation between law and morality that defines the colonial situation, because it is this separation that enables the legal work of educating subjects into the new public morality. (Asad 2003, p. 240)

In his final analysis, to accept the law and morality separation thereby entails implicit acceptance of the asymmetrical balance of power between the authority of colonial and neo-colonial liberal jurisprudence versus the, heretofore, coercive obedience of Muslim subjects to abide by a code inimical to ritual socialization. On his view, the true locus of the authority of any normative mandate, public or private, must fully reside within the tradition under which the subjects of the law reside.

An-Naim and the Oxymoron of Coerced 'Political Islam'

In an additional line of support with some of the symmetries we found running across each of the Axial traditions, Asad describes the Islamic *umma* as akin to the Hebrew (and Christian) conception of a theopolity endorsed by Voegelin earlier. The priority of the moral over the political and the self-governing submission to *shari'a* also lends credence to seeking our primary locus of community in the *umma* as not to be mistaken with the sovereign jurisdiction of the territorial nation-state—a construct for legal-political organization that Asad also finds adapted in the Muslim world from a previously coercive colonial project.

The Islamic *umma* in the classical theological view is thus not an imagined community on a par with the Arab nation waiting to be politically unified but a theologically defined space enabling Muslims to practice the disciplines of *din* [now translated as religion] in the world. Of course the word *umma* does also have the sense of "a people"—and "a community" in the Qur'an. But the members of every community imagine it to have a particular character, and relate to one another by virtue of it. The crucial point therefore is not that it is imagined but that what is imagined predicated distinctive modes of being and acting. The Islamic *umma* presupposes individuals who are self-governing but not autonomous. The *shari'a*, a system of practical reason morally binding on each faithful individual, exists independently of him or her. At the same time every Muslim has the psychological ability to discover its rules and to conform to them. (Asad 2003, p. 197)

The Arabic etymology of the '*slm*' tripartite consonant repetition in Muslim and Islam (and the Hebrew/Semitic *shalom*) entails for the believing practitioner a connotation of harmony or peace in submission to Allah's moral, social, personal, psychological, political, and familial mandates. What Asad means by self-governance without autonomy presumes the conception of a self, but one that can be cast as a member in Voegelin's theopolity that could also include God in addition to other persons within a particular Axial community. We could say that Allah addresses the participant with the normative mandates that 'you ought to X,' and fellow believing practitioners could address one another from a standpoint of second-person reciprocity. Therefore, one's relation to Allah relinquishes full autonomy in a manner by which even reference to Allah as a second-personal you runs the risk of anthropomorphicizing God, exalting humans too highly. Persons are not construed as the ultimate locus of the rationality of Allah's mandates. Likewise, the anthropomorphic turn in morality tends to treat persons as created in the image of God (which Islam, although saying human nature is fundmamentally good, does not follow in the Hebrew and Christian direction of putting humanity too closely on par with the absolute transcendence of Allah).

However, what would be shared with the Hebrew and Christian conceptions of humanity would be the species-ethical symbolic imagery of mankind owing a common origin to one another via Adam.

> The fact that the expression *umma 'arabiyya* is used today to denote the "Arab nation" represents a major conceptual transformation by which *umma* is cut off from the theological predicates that gave it its universalizing [species ethic] power, and is made to stand for an imagined community that is equivalent to a total political society, limited and sovereign like other limited and sovereign nations in a secular (social) world. The *umma-l-muslimin* (the Islamic *umma*) is ideologically not "a society" onto which *state*, *economy*, and *religion* can be mapped. It is neither limited nor sovereign, for unlike Arab nationalism's notion of *al-umma al-arabiyya*, it can and eventually should embrace all of humanity. It is therefore a mistake to regard it as an "archaic" (because "religious") community that predates the modern nation. The two are grammatically quite different. (Asad 2003, p. 197, 198)

In agreement with Voegelin, and also the introductory comments on cosmoipolitan justice as transcensus, Asad likewise avoids too hasty a conflation between the concrete mundane political realm and the ideal transcendence of a species-ethical community that could potentiality include all of humanity.

In his explicit efforts to derive a transcivilizational analysis devoid of a Western-centric bias, Onuma concedes that the universal call to proselytization all too familiar to Western colonialism and endemic warfare has also received its own distinct iteration in the Muslim world. Onuma finds that Muslim efforts to universalize the scope of their message outside the confines of Arabia also fell prey to the common Biblical religion conflation between this-worldly order and the ideal theopolity as an unrealized *eschaton* not yet to come.

> The teaching of sharia, as established during the expanding Abbisad dynasty [750–1258], sought to overcome ethnocentricism, which was common to most religions in those days. However, in the process of overcoming the ethnocentricity, it tended to regard Islam as the universal and absolute religion and to proselytize even by forceful means. The interpretation of Islam as dividing the world into the dar al-Islam [abode of Islam] and the dar al-harb [abode of war] reflected the aggressive and universalistic nature of the early Abbasid dynasty. (Onuma 2010, p. 190, 191)

Voegelin also recognized this tendency as a historical fact to Islam, as much as it lamentably has been a historical fact of the Hebrew and Christian traditions in variant phases of pushing universalism to the political limits of seeking imperial dominion.

> The Byzantine and Sassanian models of ecumenism which combined empire and church formed the horizon in which Mohammed conceived the new religion that would support its ecumenic ambition with the simultaneous development of imperial power. The case is of

special interest as there can be no doubt that Islam was primarily an ecumenic religion and only secondarily an imperial power. Hence it reveals in its extreme form the danger which beset all of the religions of the Ecumenic Age, the danger of impairing their universality by letting their ecumenic mission slide over into the acquisition of world-immanent, pragmatic power over a multitude of men which, however numerous, could never be mankind past, present, and future. (Voegelin 1974b, pp. 142, 143)

While characterized as a feature endemic to each of the axial traditions of what Voegelin termed *The Ecumenic Age*, this pragmatic thrust also led him to abandon the project of constructing a linear world-history of humankind insofar as axiological time proceeds instead in terms of experiential breakthroughs of symbolic meaning. His dauntingly complex study found that during simultaneous periods of history, one or more people may be jointly affected by potentially crossing and conflicting ecumenical visions of a historical closure—even if the purely symbolic imagery was never initially intended for their full concrete realization as an imperial project.

While in the exegesis of the Qur'an and the attendant obligations of the *shar'ia*—by virtue of disavowing any distinctively Muslim claim to autonomy—critics could certainly charge that it seems to risk lapsing back into precisely the same dogmatic calls to coercive enforcement into submission to Allah's law. From a Western mindset, Asad notes that the epistemic authority ascribed to the Qur'an tends to lead to the hasty conclusion that the sacred status of the text provides a major contributing factor to Muslim extremism:

The present discourse about the roots of "Islamic terrorism" in Islamic texts trails two intriguing assumptions: (a) that the Qur'anic text will force Muslims to be guided by it; and [in stark contrast] (b) that Christians and Jews are free to interpret the Bible as they please.….A magical quality is attributed to Islamic religious texts, for they are said to be essentially univocal (their meaning *cannot* be subject to dispute, just as "fundamentalists" insist) and infectious (except in relation to the orientalist, who is, fortunately for him, immune to this dangerous power). In fact in Islam as in Christianity there is a complicated history of shifting interpretations, and the distinction is recognized between the divine text and human approaches to it. (Asad 2003, p. 11)

Nonetheless, in reply, Asad still qualified the participant in the law as self-governing. He also questions: why it is that the Koran carries these mysteriously irrational powers of coercion? In contrast, similar acts in Christian and Hebrew history are more readily dismissed as mere exceptions to the norm. In addition the praxis of exercising judicious interpretive license in one's scriptural hermeneutic seems reserved only for Christians and Jews and not taken more widely to include Islam as among the shifting narrative exegetical traditions that are common to all three of the Biblical religions.

This seeming paradox of the eternal status of the Qur'an and its historicized this-worldly interpretation had already been partially debunked by Neurath's findings that *Surah* 55 carries layers of historicized collective memory presumed as a necessary backdrop for the alternative eschatology proposed in the *Surah* to retain its full argumentative force. While the poetic emphasis of her hermeneutic did not offer direct lessons for practical application, the same set of issues have been more fully articulated in the domain of Muslim jurisprudence by legal scholar Abdullah An'Naim. In this more practical domain, he argues that authentically responsible Muslim faith requires a secular state as its necessary condition for realization:

> By protecting my freedom to disbelieve, a secular state, as defined in this book, is necessary for my freedom to believe, which is the only way belief has any meaning and consequences. The claim of some Muslims to have the religious right and obligation to enforce Shari'a through state institutions must be forcefully blocked because it constitutes an immediate and total repudiation of the right of all citizens to believe in Islam or another religion or opinion. Paradoxically, the belief of some Muslims in the obligation to enforce Shari'a through state institutions repudiates their own ability to hold and advocate that view. Even those that believe in an Islamic state to enforce Shari'a need the freedom to hold and advocate that view, which will be lost to them if they achieve their objective, because the individual Muslims who control the institutions of the state will decide what Shari'a means and how to implement it. (An-Naim 2008, p. 279)

In addition, An-Naim regards all obedience or disobedience to the mandates of Islam as fundamentally derived from a multi-layered, historically indeterminate hermeneutic that must not become dogmatically ossified in any particular set of coercive institutions. According to An-Naim, in order of priority of hermeneutic authority, at the top would be the Qur'an, then the *hadiths* as scholarly interpretive precedent and authority on scriptural interpretation, then national customs and norms, and, finally, individual and collective efforts to realize these interpretive layers in concrete circumstances.

Although some fundamentalist readings of the Qur'an might errantly interpret the secularity of the state as license for corrupt irresponsibility, An-Naim argues the contrary maxim that only by virtue of a secular state can there be real responsibility. He finds this fully consistent with the Qur'an that advocates individual responsibility as one of its most repeated and significant claims about one of the prerequisites behind its salvation impulse:

> The premise of an Islamic discourse is that each and every Muslim is personally responsible for knowing and complying with what is required of him or her. The fundamental principle of individual responsibility that can never be abdicated or delegated is one of the recurring themes of the Qur'an (for example, 6: 164; 17: 15; 35: 18; 39: 7; 52: 21; 74: 38). (An-Naim 2008, p. 10)

An-Naim also reiterates the necessity of material conditions that ensure the requisite responsible exercise of human agency required for the complex hermeneutic practice of accurate context-sensitive interpretation:

> [W]henever Muslims consider these primary sources [the Qur'an and Sunna], they cannot avoid the layered filters of the experiences and interpretations of preceding generations of Muslims and the elaborate methodology that determines which texts are to be deemed to be relevant to any subject and how they should be understood. Human agency is therefore integral to any approach to the Qur'an and Sunna at multiple levels, ranging from centuries of accumulated experience and interpretation to the current context in which an Islamic frame of reference is invoked. [However, t]he state is not an entity that can feel, believe, or act by itself. (An-Naim 2008, p. 11)

Akin to Voegelin's multi-perspectival account of narrative history, the layers of interpretive precedent may require a delicate balance of centuries of practice, mixed with the novel introduction of a new practical problem not explicitly addressed in the Qur'an but nonetheless discerned from one or more most closely related chain of precedent as the background justification supplied for its normative warrant.

Rawls, Kazanistan, and the Decent Consultation Hierarchy: Overlapping Consensus as an Alternative to Political Cosmopolitanism?

While our earlier reflections on the prospective status of Islam as an Axial tradition and as Biblical religion have primarily emphasized the micro-level pragmatics of communication, the *Law of Peoples* of the late John Rawls moves the discourse concerning Muslim polities to the macro-level of the politics of international relations among peoples, as only briefly addressed above in the Islamic jurisprudence of Asad and An-Naim. For such a brief work, the complexity and breadth in scope, even when narrowed down to what Rawls has to say about the inclusion of Muslim peoples, exceeds the scope of what I can cover fully in this current investigation. However, since the wider focus of my project has been to develop an alternative to political cosmopolitanism, I want to streamline my attention to this theme as developed in Rawls' *Law of Peoples* (1999). In light of his overall rejection(s) of political cosmopolitanism, I will take up each of his objections to this macro-level institutional form, and proceed backwards from there to show how the institutional dynamics of his proposals inform my reflections on Islam.

I will organize Rawls' rejections of cosmopolitanism into four thematic critiques, and then briefly comment on how each of these impacts an analysis of Islam. His critiques include (1) the problem of soulless despotism, (2) the option for peoples rather than states, (3) the democratic peace hypothesis, and (4) the problem of cosmopolitan proposals for global resource redistribution.

Although even federative cosmopolitans draw their inspiration from Kant's *pacim foederis*, they tend to concede to Kant's charge of a 'soulless despotism' against the prospect of a world state that cosmopolitanism cannot be coercively imposed from above without tracking the interests of those subject to global policies nor without offering some sort of affective motive for persons to act on behalf of one another independent of any cultural, religious, national, regional, or state-mediated ties of solidarity. Those like Martha Nussbaum want to argue that supplanting the local, national, or regional with sets of obligations to the species as such need not necessarily be devoid of cultural, ethical, or moral motivational content. Nussbaum defends a romantic moral cosmopolitanism that can provide the content of motivations to act on behalf of a member of the same species by appeal to a rejuvenation of Stoic moral cosmopolitanism. Although drawing upon the Stoic tradition, she also claims that such a project need not be devoid of the feeling and sentimental attachments often solely reserved for patriotic appeals to a shared national history, language, culture, and substantive sets of shared praxis.

On the other hand, there are federative cosmopolitans like Jurgen Habermas that argue something akin to a global cosmopolitan regime offers the last best hope of preserving the many distinct forms of modernity. Habermas points primarily to the global spread of unregulated free-market flows of capital, that under the guise of a neo-liberal appeal to a general stance of non-interference in international and global markets, are actually undermining the multiple forms of modernity by the forced migrations of peoples to keep pace with the mobility of capital that tends to seek its base of employment in localities with the least labor protections, in the interest of the greatest short-term financial gains. Habermas finds continental regimes, like the European Union, as part of a multi-level federated cosmopolitanism, can aid in the prevention of neighboring and regionally-approximate nation-states from engaging in deregulatory 'races to the bottom'. Competitive regional austerity measures not only serve to undermine the protective measures of the most vulnerable but in the process encourage individuals to regard their decisions and actions increasingly on the modicum of an instrumental model of strategic rationality that thus undermines not only national sources of solidarity but also local and even familial. Part of his appeal to continental regimes would be to match economic ties of enhanced regional interdependence with democratic accountability to the wider scope of citizens most immediately affected, replacing at the level the sorts of social welfare measures lost at the national level.

In response to (1) soulless despotism and (2) the strategic behavior of states, Rawls finds a resolution to both in his construct of a peoples over a state. Although Rawls would agree with Habermas that (2) states tend to make strategically-rational decisions that serve their perceived institutional interests, Rawls' opting for peoples serves for him as an implicit response to (1) the problem of motivation for participation in the Society of Peoples. He presumes that peoples somewhat resemble nations in that there would be some shared sentiment of holding a common national history as the semi-patriotic but non-coercive motive for getting persons to act on behalf of one another. As applied to the hypothetical construct of Kazanistan as a decent consultation hierarchy, by opting for including this distinctively Muslim peoples (but albeit still tolerant of religious diversity), he recognizes that national ties of solidarity could be informed by religious modes of trust and motivation that might even super-cede or prove indistinguishable from political ties of moral solidarity. His opposition to political cosmopolitanism too, as applied to Kazanistan, carries the acknowledgement of neo-colonial skepticism likely harbored by Muslim peoples against the disproportionately Western powers that shape and influence the global order.

In light of (3) the democratic peace hypothesis, Rawls observes that historically, democratically organized polities tend not to engage in warfare with other democratic polities. This would also be associated with the aforementioned dilemma of historical resentment against colonial and neo-colonial pasts and present insofar as Rawls judged that inclusion of Kazanistan as a decent Muslim consultation hierarchy in the Society of Peoples would reinforce relations of trust between decent and liberal democratic peoples. Reinforced relations of trust over time, Rawls thinks, should tend to make Muslim decent peoples want to construct their consultation hierarchies in increasingly democratic directions. In addition, the non-coercive tolerance of liberal peoples toward decent peoples may also carry the spill-over effect of making the Muslim consultation hierarchy more tolerant internally over-time to those religious minorities within its immediate moral and political spheres of influence.

Lastly, with respect to his rejection of (4) strongly redistributive functions played by a cosmopolitan order, Rawls provides two layers of theoretical justification for his anti-cosmopolitan sentiments. On the one hand, since Rawls regards peoples as the primary subject of his hypothetical Society of Peoples, he thinks that a peoples' sovereign stewardship over its own land, resources, fiscal policy, and military expenditures serves as the best means to promote responsible moral and political governance that directly affects their immediate choices in how best to consume and/or distribute resources. As this bodes for Kazanistan, since Rawls leaves room for Islam as among the moral and political motivations that this consultation hierarchy utilizes as motivation for resource distribution to its own peoples, given the trek record in decent Muslim states for ensuring socio-economic rights as well as or even better than their liberal counterparts, he can draw on this heritage as the justification and/or distinct legal form for their realization of these obligations as a source of overlapping consensus that may differ widely from the background justification(s) and/or legal forms of enforcement used by their liberal and decent counterparts.

On the other hand, since Rawls cites instances whereby material rich peoples sometimes fair worse or even poorly (e.g. Brazil) in their aggregate and individual economic well-being as compared to resource thin peoples (e.g. Japan) that nonetheless utilize trade, innovation, and enhanced productivity most effectively, the Law of Peoples must not seek to redistribute wealth among or between peoples nor among individuals as distinct subjects of cosmopolitan law. In this respect, beyond an obligation within the Society of Peoples to aid systemically burdened peoples that cannot yet fully claim active agency in participating in the Society of Peoples due to supreme economic need, he does not see the warrant to institute any sort of global difference principle insofar as he also finds no magic economic threshold toward which this ideally should be calibrated. As far as these last material judgments bear upon Kazanistan as a decent Muslim peoples, we could also concede that internal to Islam there runs a consistent strand of responsible stewardship of one's resources, including but not limited to an obligatory charity tax to the most needy among one's people, complex laws of inheritance that presume redistribution of property between and among kinship networks prior to state-mediated forms of redistribution, and the annual month-long fasting period of Ramadan as a ritualistic reminder of divine provision of material needs.

3.2.4 Concluding Speculations: The Pragmatics of Biblical Religion in a Multi-polar World

As far as Judaism is concerned, one possible application of the insights of Jaspers and Voegelin above would be to the perpetual disputes over whether to take the symbolic Biblical role of Israel as a literal polity via a concretely institutionalized state with quasi-imperial exclusivist jurisdiction over that particular symbolic space. For instance, the pioneering work of Judith Butler has echoed the earlier concerns of Hannah Arendt on this same issue (Butler 2012). Butler has publically challenged the presumed necessity of a single state solution in Israel on its own internal Biblical grounds for the second-personal mistreatment of Palestinians (Butler 2011, pp. 70–91).

For Christianity, each of the major denominational branches of Christianity face efforts at internally reflexive redaction of their canonical self-understanding via species-ethical extensions into new cultural, geographic, socio-economic, and political contexts. For Protestantism, the ongoing diaspora to the global South has witnessed the greatest Christian demographic growth via Pentecostalism in Africa, Brazil, and parts of Central America. Some commentators on this phenomena note that these extensions of Christianity carry with them a new casting of Biblical religion. Since these new participants engage in the praxis of their scriptural hermeneutic and redactions without any assumptions of having culturally undergone the experiences of Europe, the United States, and others in the West. For instance, why presume an accurate rendering of the scriptures requires the experiential hermeneutic of the Protestant Reformation when it bears no similar cultural imprint in the experiential narratives of these new non-West contexts? In addition, Catholicism has most recently claimed its first South American pope and, in the process, seems to be acknowledging its new decentered non-European axes of new participants carrying with the democratic renaissance in interest in the social Gospel strands of economic and material precedent within Biblical religion. Eastern Orthodoxy has found itself immersed in a dubious relationship with re-emergent national sentiments throughout Russia and parts of the former Soviet Union while also facing tensions with the stated desire to reopen the great Orthodox seminaries of former Constantinople that have since been shut down by the dubiously secular regimes of post-Ataturk Turkey. In addition, the global spread of Mormonism has not only transformed American politics from the inside out with practitioners on both sides of the American political divide leading important representative roles in US governance but has also raised questions about granting Mormonism axial status as yet a fourth iterated strand of Abrahamic biblical religion. Lastly, the failure of Chinese authoritarianism to suppress religion has led to prognostications that by 2040 China will have the paradoxical mix of more Christians than any single country in the world and, simultaneously, more Muslims than any other country in what purportedly stands, at least on paper, as among the most secular and overtly repressive political regimes in the world.

With this last transition to Islam, as mentioned above, the emergent face of Asia as the real demographic presence of Islam far to outnumber the Near and Middle East, introduces novel syncretic and oppositional movements. In particular, while Jaspers and others have frequently noted the uniqueness of the Biblical religions to resist syncretizing with other Axial traditions, the Muslim presence in Asia cannot look beyond the genealogical heritage of the Asian Axial strands, particularly when considering China and others. While we might here only hint at emerging trends, the next chapter 4 will return to Rawls' and—more comprehensively—Taylor's attempts in their political theory to cast an overlapping consensus as an alternative to Habermas's constitutional patriotism. This immersion into the changing political contours of the United States and Europe will also address the association of

Judeo-Christianity (US) and rational-secular privatization of religion (Europe) with conflicting accounts of which ought to stand as the normative model for the future of democracy. On the one hand, Taylor's *A Secular Age* (2007) has much to inform a better understanding of Habermas's parallel but distinct proclamation of a post-secular age. On the other hand, we can also continue to assess the best mode of comparative analysis for realizing a second-person intra- and inter-Axial communicative ethics We compare how well Taylor's and Habermas's models fare on the discursive incorporation of increasing Muslim global demographics in assessing the relative merits of US versus European social-scientific claims to which will serve as the truly exceptionalist model for how best institutionally and politically to treat religion in an increasingly global public.

References

Adorno, Theodore W. 1966/1973. *Negative dialectics*. Trans: E. B. Ashton. New York: Continuum Publishing Company.

An-Na'im, Abdullah. 2008. *Islam and the secular state: Negotiating the future of Shari'a*. Cambridge: Harvard University Press.

Asad, Talal. 2003. *Formations of the secular: christianity, islam, modernity*. Stanford: Stanford University Press.

Bellah, Robert. 2011. *Religion and human evolution: From the paleolithic to the axial age*. Cambridge: Belknap Press of Harvard University.

Bernstein, J. M. 2013. Forgetting Isaac: Faith and the philosophical impossibility of a postsecular society. In *Habermas and religion,* eds. Mendieta Calhoun and Jonathan VanAntwerpen, 154–175. Cambridge: Polity Press.

Buber, Martin. 1970/1923. *I and Thou*. Trans: Walter Kaufmann. New York City: Scribner.

Butler, Judith. 2011. Is Judaism Zionism? In *The power of religion in the public sphere*, eds. Eduardo Mendieta and Jonathan VanAntwerpen, 70–91. New York: Columbia University Press.

Butler, Judith. 2012. *Parting ways: Jewishness and the critique of zionism*. New York: Columbia University Press.

Cooke, Maeve. 2013. Violating neutrality? Religious validity claims and democratic legitimacy. In *Habermas and religion,* eds. Mendieta Calhoun and Jonathan VanAntwerpen, 249–278. Cambridge: Polity Press.

Darwall, Stephen. 2006. *The second person standpoint: Morality, respect, and accountability*. Cambridge: Harvard University Press.

Darwall, Stephen. 2013a. *Morality, authority, and law: Essays in second personal ethics I*. Cambridge: Oxford University Press.

Darwall, Stephen. 2013b. *Honor, history, and relationship: Essays in second personal ethics II*. Cambridge: Oxford University Press.

Dillard, Raymond, and Tremper Longman. 1994. *An introduction to the old testament*. Grand Rapids: Zondervan Publishing House.

Eisenstadt, S. N., ed. 1986. *The origins and diversity of axial age civilizations*. Albany: State University of New York Press.

Eisenstadt, S. N. 2003. *Comparative civilizations and multiple modernities. Part I*. Leiden: Brill Publishers.

Eisenstadt, S. N. 2006. *The great revolutions and the civilizations of modernity*. Leiden: Brill Publishers.

Habermas, J. 1979. *Communication and the evolution of society*. Trans: Thomas McCarthy, Boston: Beacon Press.

Habermas, J. 1987. *The theory of communicative action*, vol. 2. Lifeworld and system: a critique of functionalist reason. Trans: Thomas McCarthy. Boston: Beacon Press.

Habermas, J. 2001. The conflict of beliefs: Karl Jaspers on the clash of cultures. In *The liberating power of symbols: Philosophical essays*, 30–45. Trans: Peter Dews. Cambridge: MIT Press.

Habermas, J. 2002. *"Conversations about God and the world," religion and rationality: Essays on reason, God, and modernity*. Cambridge: MIT Press.

Habermas, J. 2003. *The future of human nature*. Cambridge: Polity Press.

Habermas, J. 2008. *Between naturalism and reason*. Trans: Ciaran Cronin. Cambridge: Polity Press.

Habermas, J. 2009. What is meant by a 'post-secular society'? A discussion on Islam in Europe. In *Europe: The faltering project*, 59–77. Trans: Ciaran Cronin. Cambridge: Polity Press.

Habermas, J. 2013. Reply to critics. In *Habermas and religion*, 347–390. Trans: Ciarin Cronin. Cambridge: Polity Press.

Habermas, J., and J. Ratzinger. 2006. *Dialectics of secularization: On reason and religion*. San Francisco: Ignatius Press.

Hearsh, Jeanne. 1957. Jaspers' concept of tradition. In *The philosophy of Karl Jaspers: The library of living philosophers,* ed. Paul Arthur Schilpp, 593–610. LaSalle: Open Court Publishing Company.

Horkheimer, Max, and Theodore Adorno. 2002. *(1944, 1947, 1969). Dialectics of enlightenment*. Trans: Edmund Jephcott. Stanford: Stanford University Press.

Jaspers, K. 1949. *The perennial scope of philosophy*. Trans: Ralph Mannheim. New York: Philosophical Library.

Jaspers, K. 1953. *The origin and goal of history*. Trans: Michael Bullock. New Haven: Yale University Press.

Jaspers, K. 1957a. Reply to my critics. In *The philosophy of Karl Jaspers: The library of living philosophers,* ed. Paul Arthur Schilpp, 748–869. LaSalle: Open Court Publishing Company.

Jaspers, K. 1957b. Socrates, Buddha, Confucius, Jesus: The paradigmatic individuals. In *The great philosophers,* vol. I, ed. Hannah Arendt. Trans: Ralph Manheim. San Diego: Harcourt Brace Jovanovich Publishers.

Jaspers, K. 1963. *Philosophy and the world: Selected essays and lectures*. Trans: E. B. Ashton. Chicago: Regnery.

Jaspers, K. 1967. *Philosophical faith and revelation*. Trans: E. B. Ashton. New York: Harper and Row Publishers.

Kant, Immanuel. 1993/1785. *Grounding for the metaphysics of morals*. Trans: James Ellington. Indianapolis: Hackett Publishing Company.

Kaufmann, Fritz. 1957. Karl Jaspers and a philosophy of communication. In *The philosophy of Karl Jaspers: The library of living philosophers,* ed. Paul Arthur Schilpp, 407–436. LaSalle: Open Court Publishing Company.

McAuliffe, Jane Dammen. 1999. Debate with them in a better way: The construction of a qur'anic commonplace. In *Myths, historical archetyes and symbolic figures in arabic literature: Towards a new hermeneutic approach,* eds. A. Neuwirth, B. Embalo, S. Gunther, and M. Jarrar, 163–188. Stuttgart: Steiner.

Mendieta, Eduardo. 2013. Appendix: Religion in Habermas's work. In *Habermas and religion,* eds. Mendieta Calhoun and Jonathan VanAntwerpen, 391–407. Cambridge: Polity Press.

Neuwirth, Angelika. 1998. Quar'anic literary structure revisited: Surat-al-Rahman between mythic account and decodation of myth. In *Story-telling in the framework of non-fictional Arabic literature,* ed. Stefan Leder, 388–420. Wiesbaden: Harrassowitz Verlag.

Nikiprowetzky, V. 1975. Ethical monotheism. *Daedelus: Special Issue on Wisdom Revelation and Doubt: Perspectives on the First Millennium BC* 104 (2): 69–90.

Onuma, Yasuaki. 2010. *A Transcivilizational approach to international law*. Pocketbooks of the Hague Academy of International Law. Leiden: Martinus Nijhoff Publishers.

Pinsent, Andrew. 2012. *The second-person perspective in aquinas's ethics: Virtues and gifts*. New York: Routledge.

Rawls, John. 1999. *The law of peoples*. Cambridge: Harvard University Press.

Stone, Michael E. 1986. Eschatology, remythologization, and cosmic aporia. In *The origins and diversity of axial age civilizations,* ed. S. N. Eisenstadt, 360–373. Albany: State University of New York Press.

Taylor, C. 2007. *A secular age.* Cambridge: Belknap Press.

Uffenheimer, Benjaimin. 1986. Myth and reality in ancient Israel. In *The origins and diversity of axial age civilizations,* ed. S. N. Eisenstadt, 135–168. Albany: State University of New York Press.

Voegelin, Eric. 1974a. *Order and history: Volume two—Israel and revelation*. Baton Rouge: Louisiana State University Press.

Voegelin, Eric. 1974b. *Order and history: Volume four—The ecumenic age*. Baton Rouge: Louisiana State University Press.

Weil, Eric. 1975. What is a breakthrough in history? *Daedelus: Special Issue on Wisdom Revelation and Doubt: Perspectives on the First Millennium BC*. 104 (2): 21–36.

Weinfeld, Moshe. 1986. The protest against imperialism in ancient israelite prophesy. In *The origins and diversity of axial age civilizations,* ed. S. N. Eisenstadt, 163–82. Albany: State University of New York Press.

Witte, John. 2014. "God is hidden in the earthly kingdom:" The Lutheran two-kingdoms theory as foundation of Scandinavian secularity. In *Secular and sacred? The Scandinavian case of religion in human rights, law and public space,* eds. Rosemarie van der Breemer, Jose Casanova, and Trygve Wyller, 56–84. Bristol: Vandenhoeck and Ruprecht.

Part II
Axial Period Two—Multiple Modernities

Chapter 4
Whose Justice? Which Modernity? Taylor and Habermas on European versus American Exceptionalism

Abstract While Taylor and Habermas respectively follow communitarian versus cosmopolitan lines in their political theories, trends in each of their writings on religion in a global context have taken surprising turns toward convergence. However, what both views lack would be a further analytical and normative classification that better captures the pluralistic dimensions of this shared turn. I consider Taylor's critique of Habermas's appeals to constitutional patriotism that lead to recanting the exceptionalist thesis attributed to the US in order to own up to the exceptionalism of European secularity. I then take up the more pragmatic concern of the religion in a global public, using their writings on Islam in the US and in the EU as a litmus test for the epistemic scope of our respective degrees of Jamesian openness. By using Islam, we have an instance of an attempt on both sides of the Atlantic to widen the scope of moral and political solidarity from what Jaspers has termed Biblical religion as stemming from common Abrahamic roots. Assessing the inherent potentials for the integration of immigrants and minorities offers a practical test for the more encompassing inter-Axial communicative ethic characteristic of cosmoipolitan justice as a viable alternative to political cosmopolitanism. As a proposed mediation between Habermas and Taylor, I agree with Casanova that the unique framing conditions for secularity become, in a postsecular age, the very means of re-enchanting global public spaces, overcoming the injustices of Western colonialism, and conceding the presence (within Europe and globally) of multiple modernities.

Keywords Authenticity · Biblical religion · James Bohman · Jose Casanova · Cosmoipolitanism · S. N. Eisenstadt · Jurgen Habermas · Islam · Karl Jaspers · Multiple modernities · Post-secular · Secular · Charles Taylor

J. Bowman, *Cosmoipolitan Justice,* Studies in Global Justice 15,
DOI 10.1007/978-3-319-12709-5_4

4.1 Introduction

Taylor and Habermas respectively follow communitarian versus cosmopolitan lines that constitute substantive differences in their political theories.[1] Nonetheless, trends in each of their writings on religion in a global context have taken surprising turns toward communicative convergence. They find in the great Axial traditions rich resources for what could enhance species solidarity. This may not seem as surprising for Taylor given his earlier works on the ethical dimensions of authenticity. In *A Secular Age*, he extends this work as his concluding chapters propose a moral variant of cosmopolitanism, universal solidarity as a species ethic, and a Romantic dialogical view of revelatory language (Taylor 2007, pp. 694–695, 758–765; Kleingeld 1999, pp. 521–524). For Habermas, although a classical defender of neo-Kantian forms of political cosmopolitanism, his most recent writings bear the marks of a moral cosmopolitanism likewise of a romantic and expressive flare. Rather than following his more common politically revisionist recommendations for democratization of a robust set of regional and cosmopolitan institutional arrangements, his neo-Kierkegaardian species ethic draws upon an internal reconstruction of second-person discourse (Habermas 2003, pp. 37–44, 113–115, 2006, pp. 44–47, 2009, pp. 76–77).

On my reading, what both views lack would be a further analytical and normative classification that better captures the pluralistic dimensions of this shared expressive turn. Tracing the Axial roots to modernity moves the attendant communicative reconstructions from the political to the ethical characteristic of cosmoipolitan justice. In Karl Jaspers, Taylor and Habermas find a descriptive hermeneutic for the affective claims to moral universality deriving from the species ethic unique to each major world religion—including the expressive autonomy of secularists' background justifications. A discourse-theoretic rendition of the onset of the Axial Age also offers prescriptive norms for how public debate ought to proceed in a global context. Innovative justifications open new transnational public spheres as they proceed from expert discourse to real volitional commitments held by those believing and non-believing individuals uniquely affected. Highlighting ethical appeals to the variety of expressions of species universality inherent to the Axial traditions, need not presuppose that the sociological facts of interdependence necessarily lead to a secular political cosmopolitanism. Under conditions of multiple modernities, secular universality presents merely one among many options to be taken as morally and rationally justifiable for individuals (Taylor 2006b, pp. 143–158; Eisenstadt 2003; Bohman 2007b; Habermas 2008, pp. 312–352; Habermas 2009, pp. 60).[2]

[1] For an earlier version of this chapter in article form, see http://online.sagepub.com. The final, definitive version of this paper has been published in *Philosophy and Social Criticism*, 38 (2), February 2012 by SAGE Publications Ltd, All rights reserved. © Jonathan Bowman'.

[2] I am grateful to David Rasmussen for drawing my attention to the work on multiple modernities and to James Bohman for pointing to his work on the multiperspectival polity. My notion of cosmoipolitanism attempts to draw normative conclusions for democratic theory from the literature on multiple modernities derived from its predominantly descriptive bent and to differentiate my

We must hypothetically extend Taylor's descriptions of the nova effect of expert discourses becoming generalized to entire societies that Taylor traces out in his admittedly parochial narrative of secularization out of Latin Christendom. I will amend his brief reference to the 'supernova' of radical plurality by supplanting it with Jaspers' initiation of the Axial Age as more germane to the global perspective (Jaspers 1953; Taylor 2007, p. 300). In addition, we must further embellish Taylor's pragmatic endorsement of William James' concept of the openness of a volitional will to affective and relational comportments not reducible to the objectivigating discourses of scientific claims. We thus enter into the Jamesian open space that does not preclude an untested confidence in our secular stance as already obviously compelling for both self and others. Moving beyond a mere *modus vivendi*, we need to expand our scope beyond what Taylor labels as the subtraction narrative(s) of contemporary secularization. With a widened framing of our communicative ethic, we broaden what might constitute the domain of the rational. For example, Taylor's insightfully recasts the seemingly value-neutral proclaimed triumph of science itself as one among many types of ethical claims for how one might attain the fullness characteristic of contemporary searches for self-authenticating expression (Taylor 2007, p. 551; Habermas 2009, p. 67, 72). However, given the ensuing sorts of plural background justifications in a global public that constitute the moral and ethical substance of both basic rights and pragmatic solutions to shared problems, we ought then to adjust our normative semantics. We follow Jose Casanova in detailing one of the characteristics of the postsecular as the open prospect of a re-enchanted cosmos that might include pre-Axial, Axial, and post-Axial amendments. Simultaneously, by conceding what Casanova calls the emergence of global denominationalism, we will grant the sociological fact of the polyphonic complexity of Jamesian live options that drive the supernova of hybrid positions feeding into the richer epistemic reservoir best articulated by the semantic qualifier *cosmoi* (Habermas 2009, p. 76; Habermas and Ratzinger 2006, p. 79; Bowman 2009a).

Instead of the default stance of an overt focus on the traditions of Latin Christendom, by using Islam, we have an instance of an attempt on both sides of the Atlantic to widen the scope of moral and political solidarity from what Jaspers has termed Biblical religion stemming from common Abrahamic roots that include Islam (Jaspers 1948, p. 61). Assessing the inherent potentials for the integration of immigrants and minorities offers a practical test of the more encompassing inter-Axial communicative ethic characteristic of cosmoipolitan justice as a viable alternative to political cosmopolitanism (Habermas 2009, p. 71).

---

view from the multiperspectival polity in following Taylor's privileging of the moral over the political. See also Habermas's deferral to Taylor as reference to his remark that 'The many faces of the pluralist global society, or multiple modernities, do not fit well with a completely deregulated and politically neutralized world market society' (Habermas 2008, pp. 351–352).

4.2 Taylor's Evocative Classification of the Three Varieties of Secular

In his seminal work, *A Secular* Age, Taylor poses what he terms *the* most daunting problem for secularization theory: If European societies and the United States are so close in their comparative histories of liberal democratization, why are they so far apart in how they deal with religion in the public (Taylor 2007, p. 522, 530)? While Taylor proposes the conventional understanding to this query as something akin to the presumed triumph of the scientific worldview on the more rational European sense of modernity, he has a more complex narrative intended to disclose that the scientific worldview ultimately cannot be distinguished from its own tie to a particular view of ethical authenticity and moral fullness (Taylor 1989, 2007, p. 21).[3] To illustrate the notion that secularity cannot merely presuppose a rational and moral supremacy to religion, he proposed a tripartite genealogical reconstruction of three ways to characterize the concept, with a decided preference for the descriptive and prescriptive richness of the third classification.

For Taylor, secularity 1 refers most succinctly to God's displacement at the center of social life within a contemporary liberal democratic constitutional framework. While this is indeed an accurate description of the social world as we experience it—and state neutrality to religion seems an almost indisputable command of justice—only secularity 3 gives the genealogical account for how we got to this point. In addition, he also notes that much of secularization theory regards sociological evidence for his secularism 2, on the comparative data on declining indices of belief and practice, as leading to the hasty generalization that in a modern democratic (and cosmopolitan) republic, trends must thereby continue this way for the society to remain moral, just, and rational. Lastly, and perhaps most germane to my comparative analysis of how the EU vs. US comparison bodes for the global situation, Habermas and Taylor find much common ground in their mutual endorsement of secularity 3 as a sufficiently normative account. That is, they agree on the self-authenticating autonomy characteristic of modern societies (which Taylor deems the secularization of human flourishing and Habermas developed earlier via a communicative recasting of Kierkegaard on authenticity). In my comparison of the European and American respective claims to exceptionalism, I would like to address the hitherto unexplored implications of contemporary differences in secularism 1—that is, post-Age of Mobilization—as perhaps the real origin of the wide differences in *both* secularisms 2 and 3. This should thereby bring us to a *cosmoipolitan* norm of increasing differentiation as a better descriptive and prescriptive remedy than cosmopolitanism, particularly in noting the increased prevalence of religious organizations as national and international epistemic communities of interpretation for filtering out how best to address shared transnational social problems such as armed conflict and terrorism, and species ethic problems such as those made possible by

[3] See also footnote 20 for his reference to Schmuel Eisenstadt's copious works on multiple modernities (Taylor 2007, p. 781; Eisenstadt 2003a, b).

contemporary innovations in technologies associated with biomedical engineering (Habermas 2009, p. 64, 2003, pp. 101–115).

4.3 Taylor's Critique of Habermas's Constitutional Patriotism: Two False Exceptionalisms

Shifting the outlines of the debate over religion in the global public to moral and ethical differences constitutes a multi-perspectival task, since the modern notion of the self must fit within a socialization context that extends in potentially three directions, including communion with God (or lack thereof), membership in nation, and participation in global society. With respect to the first two of the three axes—God and nation—Robert Bellah points out that this offers one preliminary site of political differentiation between US and EU that starts the discussion immediately in the more familiar context of secularism 1 (the displacement of God from the center of public and social space):

> While America—perhaps uniquely in the Western world—seems able to keep God and nation together as predominant ideas together with Self, in Europe today neither God nor Nation musters deep loyalty among a significant majority. Instead we see the emergence of the individual Self as the primary moral focus. (Bellah 2008, pp. 15–21)

While Taylor's most intriguing remarks on this topic proposed by Bellah are buried in the footnotes of *A Secular Age* (2007, p. 831, n. 46), in his essay 'Religion and European Integration' (2006), Taylor finds that substantive differences between secularization in the US and EU boil down largely to questions of moral and political identity, which I will evaluate in terms of his discussion and critique of the array of available political forms for displacing God's role in the public domain (Taylor 2006a, pp. 1–22). Given what Taylor has termed the nova effect of the radical pluralization of believing and unbelieving positions (primarily placed in the domain of secularization 3), these differentiations are ultimately informed by the degree to which the cultural innovations of social elites spill over, disseminate socially, and then become challenged and/or adapted into the broader political public (secularization 1) at mutually reinforcing national and global levels.

One alternative response to the growing pluralization of religious forms that Taylor considers at length and attributes to the political theory of Habermas, has been to steer social integration via public law and its democratic institutionalization by means of moral constitutional patriotism (Bowman 2007). While I will generally agree with Taylor's critique of Habermas's position, Taylor does not fully articulate the implications of his critique of Habermas for answering the original question he raised, specifically as the analysis bears on the role of religion in a globalized domain. As an amendment to his proposals, I will provide an epistemic scorecard for what seems to work best in the competing accounts as we consider where secularization theory must go beyond the EU and US comparisons and into the more diverse global context offered by *cosmoipolitanism*. In this respect, I agree with Jose Casanova's observation that

> An impasse has been reached in the debate. The traditional theory of secularization works relatively well for Europe, but not for the United States. The American paradigm works relatively well for the U.S., but not for Europe. Neither can offer a plausible account of the internal variations within Europe. Most importantly, neither works well for other world religions and other parts of the world. (Casanova 2006a, p. 9)

Once I set up Taylor's critical remarks of moral constitutional patriotism as applied to both the US and EU, I will defend *cosmoipolitanism* as a better normative and epistemic model for fostering solidarity in an increasingly postsecular political environment via the Rawlsian notion of forming an overlapping consensus instead of Habermas's more typically international federative proposals (Taylor 2007, p. 532).[4]

Taylor initially defines the notion of constitutional-moral patriotism, as 'the reigning synthesis between nation, morality, and religion,' characterized most fully in the early secularization histories of the US—and to some extent Britain (Taylor 2007, p. 526). On such a view, which one could situate quite well in the domain of secularism 1, the constitution via its norms, principles, and schedule of inscribed rights offers citizens a focal point of political identity among many sources of moral solidarity and identity (Taylor 2007, p. 526, 2006a, p. 2, 9, 16). However, Taylor challenges the very basis of what he terms the Habermasian approach to political identity, since by circumscribing political inclusion and exclusion in terms of national citizenship, constitutions always contain the inherent philosophical tension of having universalist moral norms as inscribed within a particular political culture and a unique historical realization of these norms (Taylor 2006a, p. 9). Therefore, for Taylor, adhering strictly to the constitutional re-appropriation of moral norms and ethical principles as the primary locus of social identity runs the risk of masking religious forms of identity that might equally well be the true motivating moral (and perhaps non-political) source for commitment to universalistic norms we hold (Eisenstadt 2003a, pp. 399–433).[5]

In reply, as historical support for his *Verfassungspatriotismus* thesis, Habermas characteristically points to the translation of religious principles into constitutional

[4] I am grateful to David Rasmussen for pointing out that Taylor's position may present an advantage over Rawls' here insofar as Rawls' conception of the overlapping consensus draws upon the constitution as the institutional site of the convergence whereas Taylor's view remains independent of any particular legal form.

[5] While S.N. Eisenstadt commends Habermas for rejuvenating sociological discourse over civil society, he nonetheless finds Habermas has too hastily conflated the concepts of civil society and public sphere (Eisenstadt 2003a, pp. 399–400). More generally, Eisenstadt chastises the Western academic tendency to continue to misinterpret Muslim contemporary forms of modernity under significant misconceptions of the historical functioning of Islamic public spheres that characteristically function in ways that evade closing the sizable gap between rulers/legal orders and moral/theological commitments. In particular, Eisenstadt explains the larger misconception involved that follows the misconstrued view of civil is then errantly to regard Muslim rulers along the ideological framework of Oriental despots: 'the "political" weakness of many of the major organizations in the public sphere…is to be attributed not to the despotic tendencies of the ruler but to the absence of legal concepts and corporations. This decoupling of an autonomous and vibrant public sphere from the political arena…constituted one of the distinctive characteristics of Muslim civilization' (Eisenstadt 2003a, pp. 422–423).

norms. Classical examples include the person as created in the image of God recast as the inalienable dignity of the person enshrined in universal declarations of human rights (Habermas and Ratzinger 2006, p. 45). Or, he also considers the Pauline notion of universal solidarity translated into a common concern and compassion for all humankind. Most recently, he has even amended some of his early views that place the epistemic burden on non-believers to aid in the translation of religious insight into public language (Habermas 2008, pp. 130–140). However, even with this amended view that places the burden on the secularist to aid in the translation process by not presuming non-secular justifications as irrational and immoral from the outset, Taylor would not remain fully convinced given the tendency of what he terms ancestralism to lead to the problematic elision of one's national constitutional divide as 'the' proper threshold for secularization one (Taylor 2006a, p. 16).

While Taylor certainly would concede the aforementioned forms of translation as possible with notions like inalienable rights, his concluding remarks on Christian agape, incarnation, and resurrection in *A Secular Age* seem to agree with Martin (Taylor 2007, pp. 739–742), that the neo-Kantian fetish with moral rules and norms as viable candidates for politicization can only see particularistic expressions of moral fullness as an enemy and as a threat to political solidarity that must be reduced to a minimum:

> But the priority of faith, hope, and love—above all love—cannot be translated into civic and constitutional terms. Such priorities are laid on human beings by religious commitment in a manner that cannot be articulated as constitutive of the state or as a matter of policy in the public realm….How you treat that specificity and acknowledge it as a presence in the public realm is partly a matter of whether you view religion as archaic survival condemned to continuous erosion by social evolution, or as a constitutive language that is primordial in its way as reason, and with its own coherence and continuing relevance. (Martin 2006, p. 84)

In this manner, Taylor would seem to agree that the limits of the public encroachment into religious forms of self-authenticating expression cannot be breached without proclaiming the neo-Nietzschean death of God under the veiled language of 'our' constitutional tradition (Habermas 2010).

However, in reply, compare Taylor and Martin's pronouncements of the potential ideologies behind assuming secular autonomy as the golden road to self-authenticating fulfillment to similar remarks made by Habermas. His own revisions of prior positions seem to move his more recently pragmatic appeals to social solidarity out of the constitutional realm alone with his revised anthropological notion of a species ethic. In this respect, the politicized universalism of constitutional patriotism now seems to have been given a depoliticized and potentially more universal ethical counterpart via his introduction of species ethic inspired Kierkegaard's notion of the authentic life (Habermas 2003, pp. 5–15; Habermas 2009, pp. 22–30). In Habermas's words, he even regards religion as a check on the potential dogmas of Enlightenment rationalism:

> [S]omething can remain intact in the communal life of the religious fellowships—provided of course they avoid dogmatism and the coercion of people's consciences—something that has been lost elsewhere and cannot be restored by the professional knowledge of experts alone. I am referring to adequately differentiated possibilities of expression and to sensitivities with regard to lives that have gone astray, with regard to societal pathologies,

> with regard to the failure of individuals' plans for their lives, and with regard to the deformation and disfigurement of lives that people share with one another. (Habermas and Ratzinger 2006, pp. 43–44)

Both Taylor and Habermas pose the intriguing insight that increasing the range of possible epistemic influence of religious communities of interpretation over one's ethical self realization could at least negatively uncover truths about the nature of man that lead persons away from damaged forms of social solidarity that in turn threaten a more universally encompassing species ethic.

4.3.1 Constitutional Patriotism—Ideologically Construed as American Exceptionalism?

In his genealogical history of secularization as it moves past the Ancient Regime stage and into the Age of Mobilization, Taylor initially concedes to Habermas the relative historical successes of an American civic religion under a moral-constitutional patriotism. Taylor found that the US political culture, in seeking to maintain a neo-Durkheimian social imaginary, thereby led to an undeniably close psychological connection between faith and political identity.

> As far as the U.S.A. is concerned…there was a strong reaction against loosening the ties of religion, political identity and civilizational morality. Indeed, the mode of American patriotism which sees the country as essentially a nation under God, and certain 'family values' as essential to its greatness, remains very strong (Taylor 2007, p. 526).

Moving beyond the Age of Mobilization and into the radically interdependent world of the Age of Authenticity, he finds it increasingly dangerous to appeal to American exceptionalism as the basis to profess a unique sense of cosmic purpose. Therefore, Taylor finds the biggest area of concern for overemphasizing US constitutional patriotism is with mistaking successful cases of the political institutionalization of a thick overlapping consensus with the moral norms themselves that comprise such agreement (Taylor 2006a, pp. 16–17). In other words, back in the domain of secularization one, potentially mistaking the background justification for a particular norm with the particular legal basis from which the given norm derives, for Taylor, can be morally and politically disastrous. Since under an overlapping consensus, neither institutional forms nor background justifications need to hold as the sites of normative consensus, the same error of seeking consensus in the wrong places can also occur with respect to the moral-ethical justification of norms (Taylor 2007, p. 532, 693, 701; Taylor 2006b, pp. 143–158).

For instance, in a simple illustration, the worst possible form of constitutional patriotism would run as follows: we American (or, more recently, even more historically blind: 'we German') Judeo-Christians practice the mercy and compassion requisite for a strong basis of communal solidarity; therefore, for any political society to reach these ideals, they must become Judeo-Christian too (Habermas

2010).[6] To wed this error to the notion of cosmic purpose guiding one's constitutional patriotism would then add that it is God's will that we use whatever we find within our political capacities to ensure that others become merciful and compassionate Judeo-Christians too.

Of course, Habermas, as no stranger to such a dilemma and in the wake of the Iraq and Afghanistan wars, has devoted a great deal of attention to moral constitutional patriotism gone awry, which in the particular instance of the US, he deftly agrees with Taylor and terms hegemonic unilateralism. Such a political mentality assumes the moral uprightness of a hegemon can bypass the constraints of international institutions (Habermas 2006, p. 116). However, for Taylor, the irony in his solution is to make a fetish of political closure and to trade off one constitutional patriotism for another, whereby in good Kantian fashion, the higher level of political universalization trumps the lower. And not only does Habermas call for the constitutionalization of regional regimes like the EU across multiple iterations, he wants to embed these structures in a cosmopolitan constitution, given historical and cultural content via an emerging global civil society. However, in his more overt defenses of political cosmopolitanism as the necessary defense against the unrestrained American global market tendencies of neo-liberal capitalism, the precise role of religion Habermas has yet to articulate beyond a surprisingly Taylor-like appeal to the ensuring the political conditions for the authentic flourishing of multiple modernities (Taylor 2001; Taylor 2012a):

> The many faces of the pluralist global society, or multiple modernities, do not fit well with a completely deregulated and politically neutralized world market society. For this would rob the non-Western cultures that are shaped by other world religions of their freedom to assimilate the achievements of modernity with their own resources. (Habermas 2008, pp. 351–352)

On this line of argumentation, for Habermas—what began as American exceptionalism with respect to the role of religion in a global public—seems more akin to the norm (Habermas 2009, p. 60).

4.3.2 *European Exceptionalism: Ideologically Contrived as Euro-Secularity?*

In Taylor's genealogical reconstruction of secularization theory, the American exception has it own flipside that deals with another such claim often evoked in debates on the other side of the Atlantic.

[6] Habermas, in a rare entry to 'The Opinion Pages' of the *New York Times*, both critiques and laments the then rising predominance of public political platforms based on dubious appeals to a German 'Leitkultur': '[t]hat we are experiencing a relapse into this ethnic understanding of our liberal constitution is bad enough. It doesn't make things any better that today leitkultur is defined not by "German culture" but by religion. With an arrogant appropriation of Judaism—and an incredible disregard for the fate the Jews suffered in Germany—the apologists of the leitkultur now appeal to the "Judeo-Christian tradition," which distinguishes "us" from the foreigners.'

> Reference is often made to "American exceptionalism" (sometimes favorably, sometimes not so). America is undoubtedly exceptional in many ways, but *not* when it comes to religion. Most of the world is religious, as is America—*Europe is the exception*…and it is *that* exception which begs for explanation. (Berger 2006, p. 86)

As far as the European case goes, Taylor makes two general recommendations concerning the political dangers of this additional form of exceptionalism. First, he calls for a resolution of EU legitimacy deficits via the public articulation of an overlapping consensus rather than an appeal to Habermasian Euro-secularity as its own unique form of constitutional patriotism. Secondly, given the concomitant public acknowledgment of the increasing role of religious pluralism, since everyone's position in public matters become a minority viewpoint, he finds this as carrying an epistemic benefit of leveling 'an uneven but many-sided playing field' for all parties considered (Taylor 2007, p. 533; Bohman 2007, pp. 175–190).

With respect to the first, he observes the difficulty the EU has had in claiming some thick and substantive basis for social solidarity beyond a common market and currency. The most glaring of impasses on this front was the outright rejection of any explicit mention of a shared Judeo-Christian heritage as a basis for moral and political solidarity in the most recent drafts of its failed constitution:

> Up till now, we have been comparing the U.S. with European societies, but perhaps another aspect will emerge if we compare it with the European Union; because this, in its gradual self-definition, has taken steps of its own in the direction of secularity 1, most notable the refusal to integrate God in the new, highly contested constitution. (Taylor 2007, p. 831)

While Taylor does elsewhere unabashedly claim that 'Europe's roots are Christian and there is no way getting around it' (Taylor 2006a, p. 13), he would agree with Habermas that the constitutional enshrinement of such a recognition, to him, seems to be a violation of basic principles of justice in a plural society by 'not keeping an equal distance from different faith positions' (Taylor 2007, p. 532). However, if we are to maintain the epistemic constraints of a Jamesian open space, an outright rejection of any religious-moral constitutional patriotism in Europe he counterbalances with the simultaneous rejection of Eurosecularity as the converse form of a presumptive EU constitutional patriotism. Therefore, the EU also fails to this opposite end by falsely accepting the elite ideological contrivance of the purported Europeaness of secularization norms that must invariably abstract from national models that are themselves already radically plural (Habermas and Ratzinger, p. 79). The fallacy would run something as follows: For instance, we as French republicans hold to a norm of laicite given our history with French Catholicism. For any religious group to be dealt with adequately in a European wide public, they must adhere to this same Europeanized institutional norm (Taylor 2006a, pp. 9–10, 16).

In a foretaste to Taylor's endorsement of alternate modernities, while Taylor highlights the distinct heritage of Latin Christendom as lost to the auspices of the excessive European adoption of a master reform narrative, Karl Jaspers (yet 60 years prior to Taylor) read into Europe's multiple modernities diverse strands of secularization that each owe their substantive roots to Biblical religion:

> But if the question is put what, if anything, Europe could make of its pre-Biblical and pre-Greek origins, without the Bible, then it must be said again and again that what we are in virtue of Biblical religion and the secularizations which have sprung from this religion—from the basic principles of humanity to the motives of modern science and the impulses of our great philosophies. It is a simple fact that without the Bible we pass into nothing. (Jaspers 1948, p. 60)

While Jaspers does find constants to the tradition of Biblical religion such as an abiding current of hope in the face of tragic suffering and the narrative origins to a species-ethical solidarity to render communicative, he nonetheless also highlight an openness to change, self-authentication, and context-transcending adaptation as constants informing its revolutionary potentials.

> Only in indefinite terms is it possible to say that the Bible and the classical heritage are not sufficient in the form we have known them till now. Both must be transformed in a new appropriation. The vital problem for the coming age is how Biblical religion is to be metamorphosed. What can bring the transformation about? Only the primal faith out of which the Bible arose, the source which never *was* at any time but always *is*—the eternal truth of man and God, existence and transcendence. Everything else appears in the foreground to this, which is fundamental in Biblical religion for Jew and Christian, and also for Islam. Biblical religion can in fact continually change its appearance, as it were its clothes. (Jaspers 1948, p. 61)

In the immediate aftermath of the WWII atrocities, Jaspers viewed biblical religion as a potential source of solidarity and forgiveness that could only be conferred through unspeakable acts of grace—especially in the immediate German context—for Jews and Christians to seek reconciliation and for Islam to take on a new role with the huge influx of Turkish immigrants as crucial to post war reconstruction efforts.

However, Taylor's verdict on European cases concerning the failures of moral constitutional patriotism as either a rejection or confirmation of religion in a European public of publics seems, on his own epistemic scorecard, to indicate that Europe to this point is less mature in carrying out the last stage of what he terms the nova effect. What Jaspers had prognosticated as a necessary transformation for the rejuvenation of a lost Biblical heritage, has on Taylor's judgment, yet to come about and may likely never do so (Taylor 2012b). Taylor highlights the relative absence of the radical pluralization of buffered identities he finds characteristic of a secular age. He finds that Europe has successfully gone through the first two stages, including (1) buffered identities experiencing intense cross-pressures and (2) the civilizational crisis for Christianity as the presumed bedrock for social solidarity. However, he finds that the EU has not fully completed the third and last stage, in which (3) elite forms of novel moral and ethical expression spillover to the broader popular public that not only reproduce the elite forms but also begin introducing their own novel expressions.

> European societies have tended to follow along behind their elite cultures more than America, we said above. But this effect is magnified at the "European" level, where the running has been made entirely by these elites—with consequences which have emerged recently in referenda in various states on the Continent. (Taylor 2007, p. 831, n. 46)

Ultimately, for Taylor, it would beg the question to remedy the deficit in this last stage via political closure with the explicit constitutional reference to a shared locus of values in the absence of a European wide public articulation or outright rejection of the hegemony of the Eurosecularity narrative. Anything less would be to lapse back into an over-reliance on elite direction in EU affairs that has led to public outcries bemoaning the EU democratic and legitimacy deficits since Maastrict (Bowman 2006). While one of Habermas's recurrent solutions to such a legitimacy deficit has been the explicit founding of a European constitution, in the absence of a European-wide will to do so, and with the political concession to the Lisbon Treaty to resolve the constitution impasse, the democratic legitimation of such a transfer of authority must remain incomplete, only transferred second-hand via the elite direction of nationally-elected bureaucrats.

So the original question reemerges: why do Europe and the US differ so substantially on the role of religion in public, despite shared commitments to constitutional democracy? If we are to keep an epistemic scorecard as to the relative successes and failures of the EU vs. US in dealing with religion in the public, Taylor must tell us why Europe would seem less mature along the nova stage of secularization. Taylor argues that since within the formation of nation-states in the EU prior to the age of mobilization religion was often misused and maladapted to national-political aims, post-age of mobilization, the historical baggage of suspicion and/or apathy towards religion seems still to prevail, thus creating its own self-fulfilling prophesy given Europe's (and the EU's) greater comfort in following elite forms of unbelief (Taylor 2007, p. 525, 831). While he concedes this is not a sufficient blanket summary, as the unique cases of Poland and Ireland suggest, nonetheless it is certainly a general trend. For instance, despite a long and rich history of Judeo-Christian influences on European culture, the EU and its elitist structure tends to produce a cascade effect of reinforcing the relatively permanent entrenchment of secularity 1 by encouraging forms of unbelief in many, yet certainly not all, of its own internal member states.

> Comparing the two political structures, we can say that for many Americans the neo-Durkheimian link between God and nation is strong; whereas for Europeans, not only is the link discredited in individual countries, but on the continental level, the plurality of confessions in which the older patriotisms were embedded poses an additional obstacle. In this way, "God" can be seen to threaten European integration. (Taylor 2007, p 831)

As far as the comparative analyses of exceptionalisms go, even Habermas has now conceded that although the US was for a long time viewed as the exceptional case in secularization theory: 'Yet, in light of the globally extended perspective on other cultures and religions, it appears today more like the normal case' (Habermas 2009, p. 60). In the next section, I will examine the democratic features of such a concession by Habermas, leading to a further look at the status of Europe's growing immigrant and minority populations: those most potentially marginalized by the narrative social imaginary of Eurosecularity, applying the comparative analysis of the EU and US in order to draw some final conclusions.

4.4 Secularization and Integration of Religious Minorities: Islam as Litmus Test?

In brief summary, by including religion in the public articulation of an overlapping consensus, instead of via appeal to a moral constitutional patriotism, on the American side, Taylor can consistently maintain that religion will still play a crucial epistemic and political role in US policy debates without falling prey to the myopic conventions of its own ideological mantra: one nation under God. In addition, on the side of European exceptionalism, as diverse European voices continue to challenge the previous hegemony of secularization, the democratic articulation of a wider fusion of horizons might produce pacifying effects that counteract the political marginalization of its religious minorities and immigrants (Habermas 2006, p. 18; Bowman 2006). In this respect, we can take Roy at his word (and perhaps stay in the domain of Taylor's secularity three) in finding 'The religions of today are no longer the expression of cultures or societies. They are reconstructions made on individual and voluntary basis. Today, all religions are lived as minorities, even when they represent the majority'. (Roy 2006, p. 140) The question then of the best way to integrate these highly individualized epistemic communities of interpretation publically and democratically, in the absence of the cosmopolitan appeal to regional and/or global constitutionalization, will be tested in these American and European contexts (Rawls 1999, pp. 70, 75–78).

While Taylor offers differing specific recommendations for the US and EU concerning their respective Muslim minorities, he does see the general hope of including distinctly Muslim-based ideals in the future articulation of an overlapping consensus that, given its emphasis on a species universalization of secularity three, in the domain of secularity one looks much more like a moral *cosmoi*politanism than a cosmopolitanism (Taylor 2006a, pp. 19–20). As yet another illustration of the moral motivations behind the formation of identities produced as a byproduct of the nova effect, Taylor calls for continual reinterpretation and reappropriation of universal moral concepts within religious traditions themselves, such as his references to the constant invocation of the grace and mercy of Allah prior to almost every surah of the *Qur'an* (Tayor 2006b, p. 156). However, once exposed to the individualizing pressures of the nova effect, one might expect something akin to the American ('Judeo-Christian') historical experience with the concept of grace as it takes on various iterations that given the fragility of the concept may produce mutually incompatible social and political iterations.

> On top of that, these different pictures of grace and its substitutes are rivals. We can take our stand in one in order to reject the others. Because each of them is vulnerable, as we shall see later, because each can be brought to crisis, a complex interplay arises in which each can be at the same moment strengthened by the weakness exposed in the others. The belief in a unilateral process called 'secularization' is the belief that the crisis affects religious beliefs, and that the invariable beneficiaries are the secular ones. But this is not an adequate view of our situation. (Taylor 1989, p. 413)

Applying this example to the case of Islam, while one might in other contexts merely evoke images of pacifying divisions internal to Islam, in this context for a hypothetical Muslim nova-effect, in the context of pervasive fragilization, the attention to compassion and mercy can also be read as petitions for forgiveness from the inside and outside. Since his notion of overlapping consensus works towards a Gadamerian fusion of horizons from both ends, Taylor's general idea would *also* place some of the epistemic burden of transformation on repentant non-Muslims in American and European civil societies (Habermas 2006, p. 18). Granted the clear affronts against Islam by the US in the Iraq and Afghanistan wars, and the general European exclusion of Islam from a political voice in EU politics, there is also the reflexive challenge for Muslims of its diverse historical forms to undergo the simultaneous internal transformation of grace and its transformative effects upon their own religious-political identities in the direction of an expressive motivational source for the differentiated albeit nonetheless universal solidarity he calls for in the closing arguments of *A Secular Age* (2007, pp. 695–696, 701). In addition, applying such expressive transformation to other religious communities of interpretation suggests globally to the presence of a latent *cosmoipolitanism* even internal to competing moral universalities *within* Judaism, Christianity, and Islam.

4.4.1 United States: Stretching the Limits of a Civic Religion?

Given European secularity as the exception, we might be led to continue to mark points on our epistemic scorecard for the US model of approaching religion in the public in the context of secularity two (comparative indices), as Taylor continues with his more detailed expositions concerning some of the historical and political sources for religion to flourish (and continue to do so?) in the US, while it has waned in Europe. One genealogical source for the success was that in immigrant cultures, Taylor believes that religious identity often becomes a very important source of social and political solidarity. In addition, he finds that the US had parsed religion and race in such a way that immigrants could achieve solidaristic inclusion via their religious identities into the American civic religion when coming from otherwise marginalized races and ethnicities (Taylor 2007, p. 524; Casanova 2006b, p. 33). Given the two factors mentioned above, post-mobilization plus immigration leads to a context whereby Taylor believes the US has had much more comfort with something like a civic religion that has the ongoing capacity for internally reflexive expressive self-transformation.

From these general comments, given the additional relatively vast differences with respect to secularization one, the comparative US and EU narratives begin sharply to diverge in reference to the status of Muslim minorities in each. Although we can not overlook the immense differences in the domain of secularity two, that is, the differences in sheer numbers of Muslim minorities (US—between 1 and 3 %; EU—between 3 and 7 %), there is yet another generalized difference: the trend seems headed toward the increased incorporation of Muslims into political society in the US while moving toward greater exclusion in European contexts. However, for Taylor, since the United States, as compared to Europe, never held the real prospect of falling under the rubric of what he calls an ancient regime, Taylor finds that its origins post-Age of Mobilization present more fruitful possibilities for authentic religious expression of its current racial and religious minorities. For example, in the case of the US, Taylor finds that the US civic religion might be undergoing expansion with the most recent inclusion of Muslim imams at national prayer breakfasts and at public expressions of mourning post 9/11 (Taylor 2007, pp. 454, 524). In addition, although much attention has been given to the public debate of the New York mosque site and the Florida 'Burn a Qu'ran Day,' as just one of many counter-examples, public schools and universities in the US have recently begun setting a precedent of providing footbaths for the ritual observance of daily prayers to accommodate growing contingencies of Muslim immigrants. Given too, the market-like competitive culture of various religious communities of interpretation in the US, one might expect enhanced competition for congregates in any given community would reflexively modify the fragile internal structure of all denominations of a particular community or region, including Muslim communities. This might also be taken as an additional reason why comfort with religion in the political sphere has been higher in the US, since what one might see is constant competition from the beginning between many minorities leads to an overall regard for religion as enhancing the moral and social capital of society instead of falling from a past ancient regime history as evidenced in the history of many European nation-states (Asad 2003).

4.4.2 European Union: Immigrants as the 'Missing Nation' in an Ongoing Constitutionalization?

What was perhaps the greatest bane for the US case, in terms of the potential dangers of overemphasizing cosmic purpose, becomes the essential virtue of the European case. Given its long history of wars of religion, Taylor finds that European nations have completely severed any sort of implied connection between tighter moral bonds reinforced by plural expressions of religious solidarity and the generation of social capital that can be transformed from ethno-national into political solidarity, as were clear motivators behind US public justification for the Iraq and Afghanistan wars.

In a counterintuitive sense, for Taylor, the relative lack of public consensus over a sense of cosmic purpose in European societies can oddly bolster the democratizing potentials of including religious language to a greater degree in public discourse, that is, if democracy be construed in epistemic terms as a locus of diverse view points where varying degrees of problem-solving capacity emerge from an array of interpretive communities. In what James Bohman casts eloquently as an epistemic construal of Rawls' difference principle, Taylor observes that these minority religious voices in the EU, if construed in purely epistemic terms, may have reason for optimism since he finds it is often easier for a religious source of identity to become more vocal in its political activism when it has lapsed to a minority political position (Taylor 2007, p. 532; Bohman 2007a, b; Bowman 2009b, pp. 43–53; Eisenstadt 2003b, pp. 577–611).[7] Taylor cites in particular the increasingly vocal role of the Anglican Church in the UK which paradoxically had greater political clout under the Thatcher administration, or to put it in terms of Taylor's critical assessment of Habermas—post moral constitutional patriotism—once Anglicanism had become a minority voice in British society.

However, as applied to the Muslim case as litmus test, the optimism from Taylor only runs so far. In contrast to the greater trends of inclusion in the US public sphere, Muslim immigrants in the EU are triply characterized with otherness in many European societies (Asad 2003). Their otherness occurs with respect to race, religion, *and* cosmic vision for modernity, thus leading not just to deficits in social solidarity but to exponentially intense forms of democratic and political exclusion (Casanova 2006, p. 32).

> The core of the phenemenon of pluralization [due to immigration], clearly resides in the massive Islamic presence in several European countries, which is a common bond between European countries facing the problems of reciprocal acclimatization of quite separate religious and cultural worlds. At the same time, this necessitates the wholesale reassessment of the relationships between religion and culture in the societies concerned. (Hervieu-Leger 2006, p. 52)

With respect to this vastly growing immigrant population, Taylor argues that differentials in degree of access to public debate could only be rationally justifiable if hypothetically endorsed by those most epistemically disadvantaged—presumably immigrant and minority groups of religious persuasion as a subaltern public embedded with in a European 'public of publics' unified by its competing cosmic vision of Euro-secularity. The potential epistemic priority of a non-secular construal of alternative forms of modernity would be through their ongoing competition in vying for problem-solving efficacy in facing challenges that call into question the wider civilizational or cosmic vision as 'seeds of potential challenge—and transformation' (Eisenstadt 2006; Eisenstadt 2003a, p. 408). Taylor thereby advises that the EU draw upon its shared transnational institutional context and work to promote a pan-European Muslim identity as the basis of an initial overlapping consensus between diverse Muslim groups in various European publics fully consistent with my construal of cosmoipolitan justice. This seems to him to serve two mutually reinforcing purposes. On the one hand, he thinks it could lead to something akin to a Muslim humanism that might adapt a thin consensus developed across its diverse array of background justifications for moral universals such as socio-economic justice, mercy, and reciprocity to the schedule of basic norms/rights defended by EU courts and treaties (Taylor 2006a, p. 19). On the other hand, he also notes that an epistemic rendition of the

[7] S.N. Eisenstadt, in 'The Origins of the West in Recent Macrosociological Theory: The Protestant Ethic Reconsidered,' adds greater specificity and historical support for an epistemic rendition of the difference principle. He poses the intriguing insight that epistemic positions seem to fare best under conditions of heterogeneity when not acting merely as a tiny minority group nor as the state-endorsed religion, but most effectively when poised as the *secondary* voice in a given social milieu (2003b, p. 595).

difference principle could go some distance in resolving and pacifying democratic deficits not only suffered European-wide by religious minorities and immigrants, but also internally within various European national publics.

For instance, Taylor cites An-Na'im's insightful appeal to transformative immanence. Given the Muslim commitment to the Golden Rule internal to its traditions and Scriptures, this could be recast institutionally as a principle of reciprocity (An-Na'im 2006, p. 105; Taylor 2006b, p. 156). Or likewise, in the words of Parekh, this might even lead to a more expansive discourse concerning what it means to be 'European' that might extend eastward into Turkey and internally covering its growing contingency of first, second, and even third generation Muslim denizens:

> Islam has long been an important part of Europe and has shaped its cultural identity. Europe too has been a significant presence in Muslim societies, and has shaped their identity as well. Each has been the other's other, its cultural interlocutor. Their sometimes friendly and sometimes hostile relations have bonded them far more deeply that they realize or acknowledge. (Parekh 2006, p. 121)

Although there has been steadily growing numbers of Muslim immigrants to the European continent that comprise the largest constituency of some 30–60 million immigrants EU-wide, they have often not been particularly successful and in many cases seem to citizens of individual member states to lack the requisite political will to integrate into the given nation-state of residence since they are unwilling to drop their religious identities. As a way to challenge some of the ideological basis of its assumptions concerning the European-wide fiction of an absolutely uniform approach to secularity one, the best strategy would be to pursue available political channels of national and European-level political participation that might produce a pacifying effect as a wider overlapping consensus becomes articulated, in the absence of any vane hope for a final constitutionalized political closure, that now even Habermas has endorsed (Habermas 2009, pp. 63–66). Assuming that the ensuing nova effect would produce new plural and hybrid beliefs of Muslim expression, it would also be fair to expect that this could disclose hidden assumptions concerning the religious heritage of all Member States affected (Habermas 2009, p. 64). This would carry epistemic justifications of religious, cosmic, and ethical natures to the forefront of the public social imaginary, perhaps de-constitutionalizing political cultures instead of re-constitutionalization, finding potential sources of cosmoipolitan universality in diverse moral and ethical sources that preclude the assumption of a uniquely German 'Leitkultur' or an pre-formed essence of Europeaness waiting for disclosure (Habermas 2010).

For instance, Turkish minority and immigrant groups in the EU would have to draw on both legal juridical institutions and the emerging institutions of civil society to organize politically European-wide. Habermas articulates this step as follows: 'Muslim immigrants cannot be integrated into Western society in defiance of their religion, but only together with it' (Habermas 2009, p. 71). However, outside of political participation of any particular national form, Turkish minorities and immigrants in many cases have mobilized beyond the traditional networks recognized by Member State political cultures, forging the nascent origins of a transformed social imaginary via moral and ethical sources of motivation (Gole 2006, pp. 124–126;

Bowman 2009b). Reflexively, such a transformation would extend outward to a regional scale, while also radiating back to the individual actors that participate in this transformative perspective.

Gole even takes Taylor's individualization trend presumed by secularization 3 to the next extreme by postulating that often when Muslim immigrants come to Europe, there is relatively nothing remaining of the Islam they had left at home. For instance, they seek out and adapt into socially disembedded forms of religiosity that may even serve to de-constitutionalize their own national traditions 'in spite of the historical distinctions between spiritual Sufi and canonized Shariat Islam, Shia and Sunnite Islam, and conservative Saudi Arabia and revolutionary Iran' that constitute a newly formed horizontal social imaginary, tending towards Taylor's earlier call for the public articulation of a transnational Muslim humanism (Gole 2006, p. 124).

4.5 Concluding Recommendations: Towards Cosmoipolitan Justice

Although I attempted to provide a hypothetical scorecard, Taylor does not go so far as taking an explicit stance concerning which side of the Atlantic demonstrates a preferable model for dealing with religion in the public. However, it seems like at least in terms of advancing secularization theory, more positive points have been scored on his docket for the American side than the European one. As a principled defense of such a verdict, one could read the stages of the nova effect as a pragmatic test for secularization maturity, where the EU falls short on the plural transmission of elite novel forms of belief and unbelief to common citizens. However, according to Taylor, given the growing number of issues that tread at the bounds of religious concerns (for instance, non-traditional marriages and/or civil union, new bio-medical technologies, and a growing Muslim immigrant population), the EU's inability to accommodate religious perspectives into its elite discourse as adeptly as its US counter-part renders the EU so much the worst off morally, epistemically, and thereby democratically than its counterpart. Taylor comments that 'religious discourse will be very much in the public square [and] Democracy requires that each citizen or group of citizens speak the language in public debate that is most meaningful to them (Taylor 2007, p. 532). However, given the constantly changing historical matrix that goes into the supernova effects produced by secularization and desecularization movements, such a contemporary judgment would certainly not preclude that things will remain this way.

As a point of mediation between Habermas and Taylor, Jose Casanova extends his analysis beyond Taylor's limited focus on Latin Christendom and thus concedes to Habermas the latent potentials for neo-imperial domination without restraints on the prolonged narrative of colonial excesses of both the US and Europe. Casanova, however, concedes to Taylor the spiritual void left by Habermas's Weberian affinities for methodological atheism and the linguisitification of the sacred. Nonetheless, he finds his middle position in also ceding to Habermas distinctive features of modernity including the justificatory successes of modern science, market economies, individual rights, and democratic legitimacy. For Casanova, these abiding constants become the underlying structural similarities of multiple modernities:

> [N]ot only the so-called secular societies of the West but the entire globe is becoming increasingly more secular and "disenchanted" in the sense that the cosmic order is increasingly defined by modern science and technology; the social order is increasingly defined by the interlocking of "democratic" states, market economies, and mediatic public spheres; and the moral order is increasingly defined by the calculations of rights-bearing individual agents, claiming human dignity, liberty, equality, and the pursuit of happiness. Yet comparisons of secular Europe and religious America and the evidence of religious revivals around the world make clear that within the same secular immanent frame one can encounter very diverse religious dynamics. In this respect, the disenchantment of the world does not necessarily entail the disenchantment of consciousness, the decline of religion, or the end of magic. On the contrary, it is compatible with all forms of reenchantment. (Casanova 2012, p. 214)

In what Habermas called the onset of a postesecular age in Europe, Casanova agrees that the growing pluralization trend will increase rather than decrease the significance of religion in the global public (Casanova 2012, pp. 213–215). Perhaps in a counter-intuitive move though, in elaborating upon what Taylor only gestures at as a supernova effect of plugging world religions, new-age, and atheist/agnostic post-religion movements as re-enchanting the secularization narrative (Taylor 2007, p. 300), Casanova calls attention to novel forms of reenchantment to address the challenge of creating new forms of cosmoipolitan solidarity as prior forms of political identity undergo radical reconstruction (Taylor 2006a, p. 15).

While these remarks might seem to push the limits of future prognosis beyond any verifiable epistemic position, Jose Casanova details how such an identity construction might be expected to proceed reflexively, firstly, within the confines of the US, then spilling over into the new public spaces created by our global context:

> A complex process of mutual accommodation is taking place. Like Catholicism and Judaism before, other world religions, Islam, Hinduism, Buddhism are being 'Americanized' and in the process they are transforming American religion, while much as American Catholicism had an impact on world Catholicism and American Judaism has transformed world Judaism, the religious diasporas in America are serving as catalysts for the transformation of the old religions in their civilizational homes. (Casanova 2006b, pp. 34–35)

Moreover, we should be careful over-generalizing what can be gleaned from either the US or the European cases. The very achievements of modern secularization produce differentiated outcomes when rendered global (An-Na'im 2008). Particularly in post-colonial contexts, the same conditions for secularization reemerge as the social, moral, and political means for the potential resurgence of pre-Axial, Axial, and post-Axial traditions to comprise what Casanova has termed an emergent global denominationalism:

> Paradoxically, with its institutionalization first in the West and then globally, ensuing globalization, the secular immanent frame becomes the very guarantor of the post-axial secular/religious system which guarantees equal, non-hierarchic free exercise of religion to all forms of religion, pre-axial, axial and post-axial. The sacralisation of human rights and the sacralisation of the right of each and all individuals to religious freedom serves as the

> constitutive principle of such a post-axial global pluralist religious system….[T]he secular state management of religion is everywhere under siege, or at least in need of substantive revision, as it confronts the expansion of the principle of individual religious freedom, increasing religious pluralisation, and new transnational religious dynamics linked to immigration and globalization. (Casanova 2014, p. 32)

In a global society where newly dispersed immigrant communities will only increase, this mutual accommodation process, when supplanted by guarantees to religious liberty, would thereby be expected to transform religions and their internal and external epistemic communities of interpretation. The social fact of pluralism in its various forms transforms Axial traditions as they are experienced not only in the US and Europe, but as transnational movements that proceed not just politically but also ethically and morally as they reconstitute social orders from within (Eisenstadt 2003b, pp. 914–917).[8]

In drawing his concluding lessons, Casanova describes the ambivalence of a postsecular world that leads to two associated warnings for assessing the European case:

> [W]e should be cautious with this new fashionable discourse of European exceptionalism, for two main reasons. First, because when it comes to "religion" and its antonym, "the secular," there is no global rule. We must humbly recognize that many of our received categories, derived from our Christian-secular European developments, fail us when we try to understand developments in the rest of the world, in that rather than facilitating understanding these categories actually lead to a fundamental misunderstanding. (Casanova 2013, pp. 45–46)

As helpful reminders throughout his reflections on contemporary sociology of religion in a global context, Casanova continually reminds his readers that the very notions religion and secularization emerged in the context of Latin Christendom. For Casanova, exercises in extending these categories beyond the US and Europe often proliferate forms of neo-colonial domination that breed resentment and misunderstanding. However, in setting up broader themes I will address in the next chapter, Casanova most recently has explored in more detail the diverse forms of multiple modernities in Europe as its own experience with secularization trends evinces much more internal heterogeneity than uniformity:

> But, second, the discourse of European exceptionalism is also problematic because even within Europe there is no single European rule of secularization. It is the secular self-understanding of European modernization in its global colonial encounter with the other that has constructed such a rule of European secularization. The historical reality has been that of multiple and complex patterns of secularization and religious revivals across Europe, many

[8] S.N. Eisenstadt, in 'The Contemporary Scene: Beyond the Hegemony of the Nation and Revolutionary State Model' makes a virtue out of the epistemic novelty presented by new visions of modernity. He argues 'while the identities which are promulgated in these movements and settings are often very local and particularistic, they tend also to be broadly transnational and trans-state ones—often connected with broader civilizational or religious frameworks, often rooted in the great religions—Islam, Buddhism, and different branches of Christianity, but reconstructed in modern ways. In these settings and movements local dimensions were often brought together in new ways beyond the classical nation state, with transnational ones such as for instance the European Union' (Eisenstadt 2003b, p. 916).

> of them also intrinsically implicated with global colonial developments beyond Europe. (Casanova 2013, pp. 45–46)

While Taylor remains skeptical of Europe importing denominational models that have been successful in the US (Taylor 2007, p. 529), Casanova posits the opposite projection of what he terms the immanent prospect of global denominationalism (Casanova 2014, pp. 30–31). While a more intensive treatment of the cultural and religious factors at stake for both European citizens and immigrants throughout the globe will continue into the discussions to be taken up in Chapter 5 and Chapter 6, I will argue that more adaptable public standards of enforcement also do not immediately foreclose experimenting with moral motivations of a religious orientation entering into openly democratic debate, thus running directly counter to the predominant secularism of characteristically cosmopolitan justifications (Taylor 2006a, pp. 19–21; Gole 2006, pp. 125–126). Akin to normative proposals made in a different (albeit related) context by Charles Taylor—and what we have already seen comprehensively addressed in our preceding analysis of Rawls' *Law of Peoples*—in regimes oriented toward the expression of an overlapping consensus, background justifications might widely differ across cultures as well as their administrative implementation, which in the end, may enhance rather than detract from the epistemic and moral quality of our rights justification and implementation for immigrants (Taylor 2006b).

If we were to recast the Rawlsian difference principle in its epistemic variant to apply to the emergent conditions of global denominationalism, we might instead expect an internal process of expressive democratization whereby the religions themselves undergo change that reflexively guides their reintroduction and mutual adaption into new contexts. Such speculation carries us into what Taylor postulates as a Jamesian spin of the proposed future of secularization in the EU: 'we may be creating societies with an unprecedented degree of openness and inclusion' which is therefore why 'we follow the attempts of Europe to widen its boundaries even beyond the borders of former Christendom with fascination and excitement' (Taylor 2006a, p. 21). One thing seems to be certain, while the EU may have begun under the banner of Euro-secularity as an implied source of solidarity fueling its enhanced political integration, sheer demographics seem to suggest such a model over time is untenable:

> [T]oday, we seem to be set for a century of the Islam-West line. The political integration or incorporation of Muslims—remembering that there are more Muslims in the European Union than the combined populations of Finland, Ireland and Denmark—has not only become the most important goal of egalitarian multiculturalism, but is now pivotal in shaping the security, indeed the destiny, of many peoples across the globe. (Modood 2006, p. 110)

Given that Taylor believes shared institutional forms and common background justifications are non-essential in forming an overlapping consensus, we might agree also with Casanova and surprisingly expect international and cosmopolitan institutions in a global society to become more religious in character rather than less (Taylor 2006a, p. 22). Perhaps this trend has been reinforced even in EU institutions that are already suggesting hints among European elites of various stripes as having become postsecular (Taylor 2007, pp. 534, 831 n. 46; Habermas and Ratzinger 2006, p. 46). The goal of European and US citizens themselves in contributing to this move would be actively to participate in the ongoing pluralization of public forms of religious expression and simultaneously work towards the public articulation of the scope and extent of an overlapping consensus. As species-ethical justifications tending in universal directions, they may even surreptitiously provide civically derived sources of trust for closing European-wide legitimacy gaps, and thereby also bridge cosmopolitan democratic deficits along the way. If we are to remain empirically and normatively honest to the prevailing trends toward enhanced global integration, not only are we led to believe the European case is the true exceptionalism but that the cosmopolitan fantasy of a univocally secular modernity should instead be recast both normatively and descriptively as cosmoipolitanism. If this is not in order to be honest about the priority of the religious, the moral, and the ethical over the political in a good part of the world (Taylor's secularity one and two), we can at the minimum allow our normative threshold to include religious communities in reshaping the political. As we witness the increased interaction among alternative versions of modernity, the proposed epistemic recasting of the difference principle could restore our democratic considerations to the parity they warrant (secularity three).

In addition, if we therefore follow Habermas's most recent extension of a post-secular age as truly an emergent global shift in consciousness, beyond his original casting of this proclamation primarily to the uniquely advances processed of secularization experiencing their undoing in Europe, New Zealand, and Australia, then we must reconsider the secularization thesis in lieu of its exceptionalist application to the confines of a distinctly European model for modernity. If we were to continue to cast European modernity and its distinct secularity as the exception to the global norm of multiple modernities, then perhaps a radical alteration of the European model will call for sacrificing too much of what we elsewhere cherish as distinctive achievements of modernity. On such an understanding, the US would comprise an unfair comparison since it was Eisenstadt that originally pointed to the Central and North American contexts of the beginnings of colonial expansions as the first historical instance of the proliferation of multiple modernities (Eisenstadt 2003b, pp. 701-722). On this narrative to secularization, if the US and the post-colonial experiences of the rest of the globe evince much greater comfort and institutional flexibility in addressing a political public that always already integrated Axial and inter-Axial normative commitments, then perhaps we should not expect more from Europe.

However, if we can convincingly show that Europe too has always already been comprised of multiple modernities, then even if it currently serves as an exception to the global norm, we could at least attribute some of this real and perceived resistance to the political contributions of the Axial traditions as a false approbation of its own historical understanding. Only by disclosing the potential sources of error behind the attendant assumptions of a pervasive European secularity could we then more adequacy assess the prospects for extending cosmoipolitan justice as a truly global normative commitment. This will serve as the project to address in the next chapter 5, with specific emphasis upon how the prevalence of multiple modernities contributes to a flawed legal-juridical self-understanding of the European Union and its expressly secularized commitment to a principle of subsidiarity—a normative justification itself, perhaps ironically, owing its genealogical narrative to an inherently Christian intra- and inter-Axial origination.

References

An-Na'im, Abdullah. 2006. Islam, Islamic law, and the dilemma of cultural legitimacy for universal human rights. In *Applied ethics: A multicultural approach,* eds. Larry May, Collins Chobanian, and Kai Wong, 101–110. Upper Saddle River: Prentice Hall.

An-Na'im, Abdullah. 2008. *Islam and the secular state: Negotiating the future of shari'a.* Cambridge: Harvard University Press.

Asad, Talal. 2003. *Formations of the secular: Christianity, islam, modernity.* Stanford: Stanford University Press.

Bellah, Robert. 12 Sep 2008. The rules of engagement: Communion in a scientific age. *Commonweal,* 15–21.

Berger, Peter. 2006. Observations from America. In *Religion in the New Europe,* ed. Krzysztof Michalski, 85–93. Budapest: CEU Press.

Bohman, James. 2007a *Democracy across borders: From demos to demoi.* Cambridge: MIT Press.

Bohman, James. 2007b. The epistemic benefits of diversity. *Episteme* 3 (3): 175–190.

Bowman, Jonathan. 2006. The European Union democratic deficit: Federalists, skeptics, and revisionists. *The European Journal of Political Theory* 5 (2): 191–212.

Bowman, Jonathan. 2007. Challenging Habermas's response to the European Union democratic deficit. *Philosophy and Social Criticism* 33 (6): 736–755.

Bowman, Jonathan. 2009a. Extending habermas and ratzinger's *dialectics of secularization*: Non-western discursive influences on faith and reason in a postsecular age. *Forum Philosophicum* 16 (1): 39–56.

Bowman, Jonathan. 2009b. Immigrant rights and regional inclusion: Democratic experimentalism, the European Union, and immigration. *Theoria: A Journal of Social and Political Theory* (Special Issue on the Politics and Practice of Migration) 56 (121): 32–56.

Bowman, Jonathan. 2012 Why cosmoipolitan justice in a postsecular age? Taylor and Habermas on European versus American exceptionalism. *Philosophy and Social Criticism* 38 (2): 127–147.

Casanova, Jose. 2006a. Rethinking secularization: A global comparative perspective. *The Hedgehog Review*, pp. 7–22.

Casanova, Jose. 2006b. Religion, European secular identities and European integration. In *Religion in the New Europe,* ed. Krzysztof Michalski, 23–42. Budapest: Central European University Press.

Casanova, Jose. 2012. Religion, the axial age, and secular modernity in Bellah's theory of religious evolution. In *The axial age and its consequences,* eds. Robert Bellah and Hans Joas, 191–221. Cambridge: Belknap Press.

Casanova, Jose. 2013. Exploring the postsecular: three meanings of "the secular" and their possible transcendence. In *Habermas and Religion,* eds. Craig Calhoun, Eduardo Mendieta, and Jonathan VanAntwerpen, 27–48. Cambridge: Polity Press.

Casanova, Jose. 2014. The two dimensions, temporal and spatial, of the secular: Comparative reflections on the nordic protestant and southern catholic patterns from a global perspective. In *Secular and sacred? The Scandinavian case of religion in human rights, law and public space,* eds. Rosemarie Van den Breemer, Jose Casanova, and Trygve Wyller, 21–33. Bristol: Vandenhoeck and Ruprecht.

Eisenstadt, S. N. 2003a. *Comparative civilizations and multiple modernities, Part I.* Leiden: Brill Publishers.
Eisenstadt, S. N. 2003b. *Comparative civilizations and multiple modernities, Part II.* Leiden: Brill Publishers.
Eisenstadt, S. N. 2006. *The great revolutions and the civilizations of modernity*, Leiden: Brill Publishers.
Gole, Nilufer. Islam, European public space and civility. In *Religion in the New Europe,* ed. Krzysztof Michalski, 122–130. Budapest: Central European University Press.
Habermas, J. 2003. *The future of human nature*. Cambridge: Polity Press.
Habermas, J. 2006. *The divided west*. Trans: Ciaran Cronin. Cambridge: Polity Press.
Habermas, J. 2008. *Between naturalism and religion*. Trans: Ciaran Cronin. Cambridge: Polity Press.
Habermas, J. 2009. *Europe: The faltering project*. Trans: Ciaran Cronin. Cambridge: Polity Press.
Habermas, J. 2010. Leadership and leitkultur. *New York Times*. http://www.nytimes.com/2010/10/29/opinion/29Habermas.html?pagewanted=all&_r=0. Accessed 28 Oct 2010.
Habermas, J., and Ratzinger, J. 2006. *Dialectics of secularization: On reason and religion*. San Francisco: Ignatius Press.
Hervieu-Leger, Daniele. 2006. The role of religion in establishing social cohesion. In *Religion in the New Europe,* ed. Krzysztof Michalski, 45–63. Budapest: Central European University Press.
Jaspers, K. 1948. *The European spirit*. London: SCM Press, Ltd.
Jaspers, K. 1953. *The origin and goal of history*. Trans: Michael Bullock. New Haven: Yale University Press.
Kleingeld, Pauline. 1999. Six varieties of cosmopolitanism in late eighteenth century Germany. *Journal of the History of Ideas* 60 (3): 505–524.
Martin, David. 2006. Integration and fragmentation: Patterns of religion in Europe. In *Religion in the New Europe*, Ed. Krzysztof Michalski, 64–84. Budapest: CEU Press.
Modood, Tariq. 2006. In *Religion in the New Europe,* ed. Krzysztof Michalski, 97–110. Budapest: Central European University Press.
Parekh, Bhikh. 2006. Is islam a threat to Europe's multicultural democracies? In *Religion in the New Europe,* ed. Krzysztof Michalski, 111–121. Budapest: Central European University Press.
Rawls, John. 1999. *The law of peoples*. Cambridge: Harvard University Press.
Roy, Olivier. 2006. Islam in Europe: clash of religions or convergence of religiosities? In *Religion in the new Europe,* ed. Krzysztof Michalski, 131–144. Budapest: Central European University Press.
Taylor, C. 1989. *Sources of the self: The Making of modern identity*. Cambridge: Harvard University Press.
Taylor, C. 2001. Two theories of modernity. In *Alternative modernities,* ed. Dilip Gaonkar, 172–196. Duke: Duke University Press.
Taylor, C. 2006a. Religion and European integration. In *Religion in the New Europe,* ed. Krzysztof Michalski, 1–22. Budapest: Central European University Press.
Taylor, C. 2006b. Conditions of an unforced consensus on human rights. In *Applied ethics: A multicultural approach,* eds. Larry May, Collins Chobanian, and Kai Wong, 143–158. Upper Saddle River: Prentice Hall.
Taylor, C. 2007. *A Secular age*. Cambridge: Belknap Press.
Taylor, C. 2012a. Accommodating diversity: Received models under scrutiny: Interculturalism or multiculturalism? *Philosophy & Social Criticism* 38 (4–5): 413–423.
Taylor, C. 2012b. What was the axial revolution? In *The axial age and its consequences,* eds. Robert Bellah and Hans Joas, 30–46. Cambridge: Belknap Press.

Chapter 5
The Fiction of a European Secular Modernity: Rationalists, Romantics, and Multiple Modernists

Abstract Debates concerning the EU democratic deficit presuppose differing approaches to modernity and thereby, in turn, lead to conflicting interpretations of the principle of subsidiarity. Rationalists presume a conception of modernity whereby Europe sets the trend toward a rational secular regionalism for institutionalized progress via a neo-liberal principle of subsidiarity. Romantics are wedded to a view of modernity wherein the EU and/or its nation-states are the unique manifestation of a particular set of cultural narratives steeped in a deep commitment to economic social welfare that subsidiarity must preserve. Multiple modernists argue that there can be something like a common project of modernity without isolating its realization to the express confines of Europe or to rationalist/romantic straitjackets. In reconstructing the Scandinavian heritage of Nordic nation-states undergoing progressive de-confessionalization, I recast subsidiarity as a multiperspectival principle oriented to the common good of deepening networks of trust at mutually reinforcing political, cultural, and economic levels. In order best to treat the EU as the unique polity it has to come to be, including the cultural tensions that comprise its increasingly postsecular trends, I propose a future for the EU based on maximizing degrees of assurance in its democratic legitimacy. The major democratic successes to emulate include the Nordic sacralization of rights discourses and preservation of the unique European-wide commitment to social justice. The relative democratic successes of the Nordic region allow modernity to take multiple forms without strictly relying upon a common European identity, a shared neo-liberal common market, or an impending constitutional closure.

Keywords Democratic deficit · S. N. Eisenstadt · European Union · Andreas Follesdal · Jurgen Habermas · Lisbon Treaty · Multiperspectival principle · Multiple modernities · Postsecular · John Rawls · Stein Rokkan · Subsidiarity · Charles Taylor

J. Bowman, *Cosmoipolitan Justice*, Studies in Global Justice 15,
DOI 10.1007/978-3-319-12709-5_5

5.1 Introduction

Since the formal introduction of subsidiarity in the Maastrict Treaty (1992), the most promising efforts at addressing the European Union democratic deficit have sought to eliminate arbitrariness in the subjection of EU citizens to its ever-expanding laws (Bowman 2006, 2007, 2009b; Habermas 2011).[1] While notoriously abstruse, the undeniable public appeal to the subsidiarity principle presumes a commitment to disparage the raising of political decisions to a higher level (European Union) if they can be better solved at the more local level (Member State).[2] EU-level political norms bear the greater prospect of seeming foreign and alien to those they immediately affect—given the popular conception that they are derived frequently from political elites and administrative experts behind closed doors. Citizens of Member States seem rationally justified in advocating a democratized principle of subsidiarity as an aid in resisting structural forms of domination that lack accountability.

The democratic warrant behind movements of civic unrest challenging the EU comes from not only viewing its legal-juridical norms as arbitrary, but also for emotively expressive reasons of breeding political mistrust. When regarding EU laws as sources of political domination that create manifest social, moral, and financial uncertainties, the potential for additional subordination strikes at the indispensably moral core of modernity by threatening to stifle the very dignity of socially situated persons as such (Melish 2009, p. 218; Dashwood 2008, p. 6).

In order to maximize the democratic potentials inherent to the principle of subsidiarity, we need to trace the genealogy of the principle much further back than its legal-juridical introduction through Maastrict. By recognizing the rich heritage to the principle, not only do we immerse ourselves in the narrative of Latin Christendom that a purportedly more mature Europe had left behind, we also see that there are quasi-denominational influences that each belie the explicit constraints of

[1] This represents more of a set of necessary amendments in light of the burgeoning multiple modernities literature that has yet to be considered in European Union studies than a full scale overhaul of my previous views on the democratic deficit. One might point to Habermas's recent 'A Pact For or Against Europe' as the academic postponement of the enduring viability of the federalist dream for the EU, given that Habermas had previously been the foremost defender of a federated EU with its own constitution as the primary means to resolve its democratic deficits. Consider Habermas's claim in his recent 'A Pact For or Against Europe' that 'It was not inevitable that, after decades of widespread approval, support for European integration would significantly decline, even in Germany. The process of European integration, which has always taken place over the heads of the population, has now reached a dead end because it cannot go any further without switching from its usual administrative mode to one of greater public involvement. But political elites are burying their heads in the sand. They are doggedly persisting with their elitist project and the disenfranchisement of the European population.' (pp. 85–86).

[2] For the best overview of the genealogical basis of the European Union's principle of subsidiarity in five theoretical and historical variations, including Althusian/Calvinist, Confederalist, Fiscal Federalist, Catholic Personalist, and Liberal Contractualist, see Andreas Follesdal (1998). In other succinct definitions, Ales Gerloch emphasizes the ancillary aspects of its etymology (2008, p. 123). Daniel Halberstom, points to the notions of assistance, auxiliary Roman troops, *and* the presumed commitment to a common good shared between levels (2009, p. 34).

subsidiarity to the territorial confines of either the EU writ large or the modern achievement of the Westphalian nation-state. Firstly, by considering Anglican, Catholic, and Lutheran-Protestant iterations of the principle of subsidiarity, we will find that there are viable alternative modes to European modernity than an impartially rational and secular narrative of enhancing the common good for a predominately economic union of nation-states. If taking subsidiarity only within the narrowly secular rubric, its primary intent would be to adjudicate when European-wide market measures require political institutional backing and when state level interventions are required to keep national economies in accord with European standards (Taylor 2001, p. 181; Heidenrich 2006, pp. 1–3; Taylor 2007, p. 534, 535).

Secondly, by focusing upon the deep cultural and religious heritages of distinct variations on the principle as manifest across European history and into the present, we will challenge the presumed political neutrality to merely utilizing the proper political institutionalization of the principle as thereby producing the foregone conclusion of a more market competitive European continent. While raising a skeptical eye toward the presumed triumph of Euro-secularity, we will also seek to disclose the distinct European heritages to the principle that nonetheless are each intended to carry not only European but also species-wide import. Moreover, since institutions of modernity have historically fed upon the ongoing contestation characteristic of the deep cleavages between cultural cores and peripheries—we can also challenge the predominately secular read on subsidiarity by emphasizing sources of civic contestation reflexively drawing upon institutions of both church and polity tensions between core and periphery. Our focus bodes in particular on the historical reconstruction of the role(s) of the principle of subsidiarity in public discourse on the European Union, which has become a highly technical and legal term although beginning as (and in some variants of modernity—continues to remain) a deeply religious concept as emergent from the auspices of Latin Christendom (Rokkan 1999a, p. 170, 171, pp. 269–273). However, merely tracing out a simple bifurcation of secular and non-secular castings of subsidiarity would belie the richly embedded layers that comprise competing modernities, including the inter-civilizational strife (as evidenced in the last Chap. 4) driven by the great Axial traditions that constitute the backdrop to the ongoing redaction of European social imaginaries as we invariably seek to draw lessons of species-wide import from these historical experiments (Taylor 2007, pp. 549–551, 592,593; Bowman 2012).[3]

At the level of institutional design, an array of democratic revisionists seek to turn the ongoing agonistic debates characterizing EU politics into an epistemic virtue such as Besson and Muller's demoi-cracy (Paulus 2008, p. 199, note 24; Follesdal 2010a, p. 208), Bohman's shift from demos to demoi (Bohman 2007a), Cohen and Sabel's directly deliberative polyarchy (Sabel and Cohen 2004), Follesdal's multi-level federated polity, and Habermas's European public of publics (Habermas

[3] Thus, I agree with Charles Taylor's recommendations to regard our options in light of the civic presence of a Jamesian open space that can neither preclude religious conceptions as irrational from the outset nor overstep state neutrality toward religious worldviews as a prerequisite of social justice.

2001a; b). These are all steps in the right direction by drawing special attention to the institutional novelty required to break the conceptual confines of the sovereign nation-state, ensure the requisite levels of political trust, and still acknowledge the unprecedented overlapping levels of conflicting sovereignty in the EU.

In contrast, at the conceptual level of the history of political ideas, the resurgence of interest in the sociology of religion of Parsons (Rokkan 1999a, pp. 278–280; Habermas 1987, pp. 283–294), Rokkan (Rokkan 1981, pp. 70–95; 1999a, pp. 54–59, pp. 135–47; b, p. 30), and Eisenstadt (2003, pp. 94–107, 2006; Smith and Vaidyanathan 2011, pp. 250–266),—as initiated by the pioneering philosophical genealogy of Western secularity of Charles Taylor (2001, p. 195, 196, 2007, p. 21, pp. 594–617, p. 781; Smith and Vaidyanathan 2011, p. 252)—has shown great promise in providing more deeply social and anthropological reconstructions of the rich cultural sources of European modernity. Nonetheless, no one has yet proposed a serious engagement with the European Union democratic deficit that weds these revisionist theories of democratic institutional design with the empirically rich sociology of religion proposed by multiple modernists (Rasmussen 2010; Rasmussen 2012; Taylor 2006b, pp. 147–149).

While I did address the prospects of multiple modernities in Europe in the last chap. 4 given the huge influx of Muslim immigrants, this chapter will argue that if we are to understand the present and future of the European project, we must also delve more deeply into the past. Moreover, we can better read lessons for the future into European trends if we wed our analysis to the colonial heritages of Latin Christendom as played out differently in its Anglican, Catholic, and Lutheran-Protestant formations. A more differentiated narrative to European secularization will also help us better appreciate the wide differences between European and American experiences with secularization already laid out in Chap. 4 (Casanova 2014). For instance, I agree with Martin that while Britain does share some cultural, religious, and economic affinities with the U.S., when it come to European integration and delineations of subsidiarity, it is also helpful to think of Britain (Anglican) and Scandinavia (Luther-Protestant) as sharing common characteristics of peripheral divergence (also akin to the new Eastern Orthodox periphery) from the core of Continental Europe and its distinctive heritage with the Catholicism of Latin Christendom:

> England (and Scotland and Ulster) generated a style of evangelical Protestantism based on heartwork which, in the U.S., become a universal devotion to individual sincerity. However, the retention of an Anglican religious establishment meant that England also acted as a hinge turning, on the one hand, toward American inwardness, and, on the other, towards Scandinavian formality. If these distinctions seem rather marginal to European integration, I hope to illustrate how such cultural characteristics belong among others separating the Anglosphere from the European continent, as well as linking England to Scandinavia's cautious attitude toward European involvement. For a wide variety of cultural reasons, the national traditions of Britain and Scandinavia understand each other, while both regarding the mainland of Europe with suspicion. (Martin 2006, pp. 71–72)

In this respect, Martin also carries on the resurgence of interest in the sociology of religion that like Eisenstadt and Rokkan, cannot offer a fully adequate account of

European secularization processes without also conceding strong center to periphery cleavages that eventuate in the European characterization of modernity as inherently plural in geographic, conceptual, and cultural delineations.

In streamlining my focus on subsidiarity as bearing the most promising democratizing potential, I will emphasize these differences in how citizens actually take themselves to be participating in conflicting interpretations for what Eisenstadt and Habermas call the ongoing project of modernity as eventuating in the conflicting legal hermeneutics of subsidiarity within practical attempts to address varying permutations of the EU democratic deficit (MacCormick 1997, pp. 350–354; Habermas 1983; Taylor 2007; Eisenstadt 2003). In departing from standard democratic theory, I will not argue that the EU should be a democracy in the most robust sense of citizens equally subject to the law jointly serving as its authors (Dashwood 2008, p. 8; Paulus 2008). Instead, by pursuing a model of democracy focused on mutually reinforcing levels of facilitative assistance towards the common good (Melish 2009, pp. 218–222), I will highlight examples that suggest we need to take a more extensive philosophical step backwards and reconsider whether or not the diverse array of European publics even ever have shared basic assumptions concerning the project of modernity. In a context of widespread externalities in an expanded EU of 28 Members (Hix 2008, p. 9),[4] whereby single Member States are constantly affected by circumstances outside their national administrative influence (Halberstom 2009, p. 42, 43; Sabel and Cohen 2004; Eisenstadt 2003, p. 107),we ought to reject a single shared modernity without necessarily lapsing into the malaise of political relativism by instead seeking the path of overlapping consensus espoused by Rawls (1999), Taylor (2001, 2006b), Follesdal (2011), Rasmussen (2010, 2012), and others.

By bringing the multiple modernities thesis to bear on the institutions of the EU, I will demonstrate the need to shift away from a predominately rationalist and legal-juridical view of subsidiarity to a moral-ethical conception of democratic subsidiarity that can integrate *both* its more deeply culturally informed romantic-expressive non-secular sides along with learn from the successes and failures of its rational-juridical institutionalization (Gerloch 2008, p. 127; Dashwood 2008, p. 8;

---

[4] Professor Simon Hix characterizes subsidiarity as a principle designed to provide an institutional remedy to the various externalities that transnational governance brings about for Member States that hold heterogeneous sets of policies: '[O]ne of the other key issues to bear in mind [besides scale benefits], which I do not think is necessarily recognized in the legal work on subsidiarity but political scientists recognize it, is what we called externality. This is when you have a policy at a particular level of government such as immigration policy kept at the national level. Once you have a single market, there are negative effects upon your neighbors. We have seen classical examples of this with Sweden, for example, where Denmark introduced a more restrictive asylum seeking policy and it had an effect on asylum seekers in Sweden. These are externalities if you are having de-centralised policies, which then suggests that if there are these externalities you need to centralize that particular policy….if everyone shares the same opinions, then there is no problem with passing the policy up to the EU level….where there are clear differences in views, then you can see why there would be problems in passing it up to the central level…[Therefore,] I think it is nearly impossible to define in purely legal terms subsidiarity criteria and it is really ultimately a political question' (p. 9).

Hix 2008, p. 9; Rokkan 1999b, p. 107). By conceding to the likes of Stein Rokkan and S.M. Eisenstadt that Europe since its origins has always been constituted by competing cultural conceptions of modernity vying for influence over both center and periphery (Rokkan 1999b, pp. 134–147; Eisenstadt 2003a, pp. 94–107; Allhardt and Valen 1999, pp. 11–38)[5]—and taking the dichotomous tension between rationalism and romanticism as healthy for vibrant democratic cultures—in my final conclusion, I will reconstruct iterated stages of the historical emergence of subsidiarity as a multiperspectival principle (Bowman 2006; Paulus 2008, p. 212). These stages include reconstructing the steady evolution of the doctrine of subsidiarity in the courts that comprise its legal-constitutional framework, enhancing the role of national parliaments in checking the powers of both the European Commission and Council, introducing the practice of flexicurity that seeks to balance streamlining state bureaucracies without simultaneously vetting the array of safety nets provided by social welfare provisions, tracing out practices of subsidiarity by EU Member States that also affect non Member States via federal and confederated arrangements (Scandinavian cases), and even extending subsidiarity to the sacralization of basic rights.

In its longer form, this principle entails avoiding laws that can be traced back to a singular motivational perspective, by uncoupling competing Axial cosmic visions for what ought to comprise the original species-ethical extensions of Christendom from a single geographic, functional, or administrative site, and thus embracing the need for region-wide institutional reflexivity over balancing competing levels of proportionality as the best means for closing global democratic deficits (Gerloch 2008, p. 126). In the final analysis, a sufficiently normative account of subsidiarity must be guided by the common ideals of enhancing individual freedom, decreasing the threat of arbitrary rule, and parsing out variegated sources of mutual trust in establishing local, national, regional, and global normative consensus over common goods (Paulus 2008, p. 197, 200).

5.1.1 Three Narratives to Modernity, Three Social Imaginaries: Locked Iron Cage, Clash of Fanatic Affectations, or Multiple Modernities?

Before getting into the more detailed discussion of subsidiarity, we must first give a rough characterization of what Eisenstadt, Taylor, and others take to comprise contrasting visions of modernity. On the one hand, such a genealogy of the project of European modernity will not consist in offering a succinct historical delineation of

[5] According to Erik Allhardt and Henry Valen: 'Stein Rokkan might well be remembered as the cosmopolite from the periphery. Throughout his career his professional outlook was universal and internationalistic…Yet, his interest in the periphery was unmistakeable—a trait which clearly relates to his own personal background in northern Norway. His concern for the periphery was reflected through his research activities and became manifest in the center-periphery paradigm which represents a major contribution of his work' (p. 11).

when each civilizational rubric first emerged. Nor will I try to offer tight territorial jurisdictions over where precisely to delineate the geographic bounds of each manifestation of modernity. Nonetheless, on the other hand, we can still provide a loose specification of general features. In the tradition of the sociology of religion of Rokkan, I seek the rough construction of a multi-layered conceptual mapping of European modernities. The abiding features necessary to confer modernity include the onset of wide international networks of commerce, the questioning of heretofore presumed notions of cosmic purpose, the growth of individual autonomy, movements of political protest between core and peripheral civilization matrices, the rise of elite academic literati independent of states, and specifically, an overall expansion of reflectivity.

As a more succinct articulation of the practices that comprise modernity, Eisenstadt highlights as a characteristically determining factor: ongoing reflexivity cutting across all levels and cleavages within society. Reflexivity, according to Eisenstadt, becomes so culturally pervasive under conditions of modernity that it continually reshapes each one of the other above-mentioned criteria. In a dialectic fashion, tension and feedback loops of reflexivity between secular and sacred social imaginaries foster twofold sources of epistemic innovation. The two sides of reflexivity promote principled rationality and generate these principles in affectively romantic manners, to eventuate in what we had previously termed Axial Age 2.0 in our introductory Chap. 1:

> It is because of the fact that all such responses leave the problematic intact [the postulate that a divinely ordained and fated cosmos has had its decline], the reflectivity which developed in the program of modernity went beyond that which crystallized in the Axial Civilizations. The reflectivity that developed in the modern program focused not only on the possibility of different interpretations of the transcendental visions and basic ontological conceptions prevalent in society or societies but came to question the very givenness of such visions and the institutional patterns related to them. It gave rise to the awareness of the existence of multiplicity of such visions and patterns and of the possibility that such visions and conceptions can indeed be contested. (Eisenstadt 2003b, p. 495, 496)

European modernity expressed the aforementioned reflectivity as a definitively enigmatic feature, as an initial step leading those working in the tradition of Eisenstadt to posit modernity as inherently plural at more than one basic level. In other words, although not necessarily in order of lexical priority—given the reflective contestation of Axial Age 1.0 cosmic orientations—the presumed rational core to modernity (Axial 2.0) carries an equivocally romantic kernel via this ongoing triadic tension between the transcendent, mundane, and plural forms of transcendences. Once we lay out the conceptual terrain of Europe's modernities, we will be better placed to assess the origination of the postsecular turn (Axial 3.0 in Chap. 1) as it found its initial postulation in the wake of Europe's recent encounter with its growing waves of postcolonial immigration (Chap. 4; Habermas 2009, pp. 59–77).

In light of this general casting of modernity as inherently plural, there are three main social science traditions for characterizing what are more succinctly deemed European/Western tendencies. As classically formulated by various mainstream voices throughout political theory, these include: atomistic-universal-rationalists, communal-cultural-romantics, and multiple modernists (Allhardt 2005, pp. 468–491). In an analysis of 'Europe's Multiple Modernities,' Erik Allhardt provides a consistent narrative that we can hypothetically continue to extend to the present.

> There is in Western sociology a distinction that has appeared in many forms but that definitely records two entirely different cultural styles as typical for the Western civilization…a striving for a primordial social integration, on one hand, and the attempt to build a derived integration by rational means, on the other. This contrariness is expressed in many of the traditional dichotomies of the definitively Western attempts to sociological theory-building. As well-known examples we have the distinctions between Emile Durkheim's *mechanic* and *organic* solidarity, Ferdinand Tonnies' *Gemeinshaft* and *Gesellshaft*, and C. H. Cooley's *primary* and *secondary* groups…As an additional case, one may mention Ernest Gellner's fascinating description of the tensions between a *communal-cultural-romantic* vision and its counterpart, an *atomic-universalist-individualist* vision, typical of the tensions in the old Hapsburg empire. (Allhardt 2005, p. 486, 487)

Social scientists of the first sort loosely characterized as *rationalists* traditionally view modernity as an ongoing march to the further extension of an acultural Enlightened reason. Those that Gellner and Allhart associate with this tradition include Descartes, Kant, Ernst Mach, Max Weber, Bertrand Russell, and Talcot Parsons. These figures are often associated with empiricism, rationalism, positivism, *Gesellschaft*, economic markets, political liberalism, and market/economic cosmopolitanism followed by inevitable political spill over (Allhardt 2005, p. 487). The rational casting of European history also tends to assume what Casanova critiques as a stadial consciousness. This views the rationalizing tendencies of secularity as the necessary maturation of cultural forms to which the consummation of world history ultimately must lead. The democratic principle associated with this view requires that rational individuals affected by the stadial march of history subject themselves only to norms they could project as species universal for any similarly situated rational individual. As a means for achieving such universal scope, ethical and national differences are suppressed in the name of a more superior, moral, and rationally mature commitment to universal principles—especially those dropping the cultural baggage of some one or more permutation of Latin Christendom.

However, one problematic aspect of the rational-prudential view of European modernity applied to the institutions of the EU, would be addressing the question of competing views of reason as guiding assumptions for how best to steer the institutions of modernity. For instance, especially since the EU lacks an explicit constitutional founding to embody these principles in law, how ought the EU deal with competing rational principles, particularly balancing the principle of subsidiarity, with principles of proportionality (Murphy 2008),[6] sovereignty, fiscal responsibility, and legal supremacy?

[6] Under the auspices of the European Scrutiny Committee interviews and report produced by the British Parliament, Murphy provides a succinct definition for the guiding assumptions behind the principle of proportionality: 'there is a Commission/political (with a small "p") understanding of the sensitivity on better regulation, about proposals being proportionate to the nature of the problem, not trying to go further' (p. 31).

In addition, in spite of explicit attempts in the EU draft constitution and its prevailing treaty framework to disavow a unique heritage steeped in the traditions of Latin Christendon—the current bounds of the twenty-eight Member EU mirror almost precisely the confines of its prior Roman imperial Christianized polity. The most recent rounds of expansion have only served to reinforce and bring more directly to the fore the Eastern Orthodox heritage of three of its most recent members: Romania (2007), Bulgaria (2007), and Cyprus (2004), thus also bringing to the fore the growing self-identification of Greece (1981) with its own Eastern Orthodoxy.[7] In contrast, the EU treaty framework prefers the less contentious association of Greece with its great heritage steeped in Ancient Greek philosophical inquiry.

Likewise, the 2004 accession of Poland served for some political movements as an attempt to revitalize the Catholic heritage of its founding elites, including but not limited to Monet, Adenaur, and Delors. The Catholic heritage behind the successful integration of Europe owes much to the EU-friendly and anti-communist sentiments of both of the prior two holders of the Papacy—John Paul II (Poland) and Benedict (Germany). Lastly, famed "Rerum Novarum (1891)" Catholic heritage behind Social Democratic parties and politicians have provided the impetus for major transnational political movements to enshrine subsidiarity in the history of the EU with a strong legacy of promoting the European-wide commitment to building regional social-welfare institutions to buttress the excesses of an encroaching global neo-liberal capitalism.

Secondly, in line with the thrust of many of the critiques levied against rationalists above, *romantics* advocate deeply cultural reconstructions of modernity and present them as counter-proposals to the first view. Those associated with this vision include Hume, Burke, Rousseau, Herder, Fichte, Schelling, Hegel, Schmitt, and Milbank. Such thinkers tend to emphasize unreflective living, organicism, national populism, romantically conservative visions of historical and cosmic totality, systematicity, correctness, particularity, cultural specificity, close-rooted communitarianism, *Blut* and *Boden* (Milbank 2013a; Allhardt 2005, p. 487). In their many cultural manifestations, romantic religious and non-religious sources for European culture include but are nor limited to: Christianity (in each of its primary expressions: Orthodoxy,

[7] Leaders of the Eastern Orthodox Church initially lamented the lack of any mention of the distinct Christian heritage to Europe in the draft constitution. Moreover, Greece had ceded to EU pressure to eliminate the contentious practice of religious affiliation as a compulsory feature of national identification cards (Martin 2006, p. 74). As far as broader social issues, the Eastern Orthodox church sometimes tends to look upon rights to non-discrimination and non-traditional marriage as Western liberal intrusion into one's religious and cultural heritage as Eastern Orthodoxy tends to be even more publically opposed to homosexuality than the Catholic church. In terms of contemporary geo-political strife, the Russian Eastern Orthodox church has mobilized politically around this issue as a rallying cry against the pernicious side effects of the unchecked spread of US/Western/European ideals. In addition, strong ties develop between one's Eastern Orthodoxy and national politics insofar as the church appoints a locally immersed head of Eastern Orthodoxy to lead that particular national church. Lastly, the church tends to view salvation as a collective matter concerning the composite body of believers—construed both in terms of national identity and in terms of Eastern Orthodox identity—than strictly the private affair of the individual.

Catholicism, Anglicanism, Protestantism and its generalized expression via Latin Christendom), Roman imperialism, Ancient Greek philosophy, linguistically based forms of local and national identity, general pronouncements of upholding Judeo-Christian ideals, and most recently, the rising presence in Europe of both Islamic and Asian influences (Philpott and Shah 2006, pp. 34–64; Taylor 2001; Eisenstadt 2003, p. 104).

Romantic visions of European modernity applied to democratizing the EU appeal back to extending highly localized networks of mutual trust more broadly. Strategies include nostalgic calls for the return of Christian orthodoxy, the extension of familial/kinship bonds to be supplanted by national and/or transnational expressions of religious solidarity, and the self-reinforcing model of extending social-welfare measures across Europe as a middle-way between shrinking national welfare provisions and the common ties of reflexive interdependence and vulnerability produced by the global movements of capital.

However, what proves most surprising about romantic appeals to the construction of modernity in its variety of contemporary forms would be the risk of a performative contradiction in the varied projections of primordial social integration. Through these nostalgic appeals we run the threat of constructing narratives that skip over the reflective onset of modernity. The contradiction lies in calls effectively to mobilize these solidaristic bonds through manners that presuppose the social, civic, political, economic, and communicative features of modernity as key contributing factors to the endemic structural problems romantic social actors seek to escape.

For instance, for all of the striking differences between the resurgence of Eastern Orthodoxy as a key political player in Europe and the more contemporary (misleadingly named) Anglican movement derived from the UK called Radical Orthodoxy, each does carry a similar narrative resonance. The respective returns to ortho- (correct or true) doxy (belief or teachings) propose escaping the social ills of modernity by retrieving the virtue, piety, and social practices of Church Fathers and communities that predate the Protestant Reformation, American, French, and Industrial Revolutions, and the climax of rational reflection with the achievements of the Enlightenment. Again, despite all of the myriad differences, both Eastern and Radical Orthodoxy espouse robust social ontologies that border at the lines of the clash of civilizations in assuming theology as the queen of the sciences. Directly at odds with the modern postulation of religious liberty, and very much akin to both Protestant and Catholic (and Muslim) fundamentalisms—extreme forms of mobilization posit the subordination of any discourse concerning ideals of the just, true, and the good to a re-Christianized European political order as the last best hope for the species. In other words, such a robust social ontology rendered as a communicative species ethic would assume a neo-Burkean construal of goodness, justice, and truth as immune from the necessity of rational legitimation since only properly initiated elites can be expected to recognize such transcendently romantic ideals. Even if these competing sources of Christian solidarity profess potential extensions of species-ethical universality, they must receive their legitimation through an overlapping consensus on norms if they are to conform to the prevailing institutional realities posed by radical pluralism. European expansion together with growing immigration trends only serve to continue to make each politicized core of romantic socialization a minority political group in Europe with respect to the rest of the continent. Drastic underestimations from cultural romantics of the sheer magnitude and scope of an expanded EU thereby run the risk of coercion or overt violence in the politicization of their platforms if not directed toward the rational medium of justificatory discourse (Halberstam 2009, p. 45).

Lastly, as the third view, advocates of *multiple modernities* concede that the rational and romantic readings of modernity both have their comparative merits that justifiably warrant their inclusion in constructing plausible visions for European modernity. In accord with the tensions inherent to any pluralistic constitutional structure, the rationalist side to multiple modernists hold to a view of communicative idealism for humanity that can reason in an abstract and objective manner while the romantic side shows a decided preference for the social and emotional bonds among persons that ultimately serve as the political motivation for persons to act on behalf of one another. However, in contrast to rationalists, multiple modernists would contend that an acultural secularized reading of Europe—particularly in the realm of religious culture—belies its history including its postsecular and increasingly pluralistic present. According to Allhardt,

> [T]he importance and social value of the blend of rationality and affective social coherence has been expressed with different formulations by, for instance, Ulf Himmelstrand, Ernest Gellner, and Charles Taylor. They emphasize a different world than Max Weber and most of those who have developed theories about the nature of European modernity. They have rendered scientific descriptions of modern society, but they also advocate an ideal consisting of a blend of rationalism and romanticism….that blend has definitely assumed a special importance during the latter decades of the twentieth century. At least it seems permissible and telling to speak about a European multiple modernity. (Allhardt 2005, p. 490)

In other words, to espouse a theory of multiple modernities is less an attempt to posit rationalist views against romantic ones and more so an argument that, in agreement with Charles Taylor's preference for the label of alternative modernity, the rationalist view always already advocated particular unique visions of the good. In line with the grander themes of this project, we are again back to our introductory query that asked: why Jaspers as a plausible alternative to Weber?

According to Allhardt's critique of Weber, the acultural misreading of modernity overlooks how Europe came to this point via vast periods of cultural transformation that have now come to comprise some of the basic premises of modernity, particularly in light of the rich genealogical reconstructions provided by the likes of Eisenstadt, Taylor, Bellah, and Jaspers. As we continue to trace the postulation of multiple modernities into Europe's postsecular present, we can supplant Taylor's focus on Latin Christendom with Jaspers' wider casting of a non-dogmatic continuance of Europe's unique heritage of Biblical religion to include Catholic, Anglican, Nordic Lutheran Protestant, Eastern Orthodox, Hebrew, and Muslim influences on the ongoing construction of modernity (Taylor 2001, p. 189, 190).

Charles Taylor's brief, dense, but telling concluding section to *A Secular Age* (2007, pp. 773–776), his 'Epilogue: The Many Stories' critiques both ends of the extremist narratives presented respectively by the rational-universalist-secularist and the romantic-particularist-religious camps. Taylor associates the rationalist excesses of what he terms the Reform Master Narrative (RMN) to the greater bulk of the critical content of his major work, conceding that most of what we hold dearly as the pinnacle achievement of modernity would be the progressive impetus of reform that runs the grave risk of staving off the greater content of its rich heritage as if it had arrived there as a matter of an impartially objective rational self-understanding. It is here that Taylor keeps consistent with abiding themes that reinforce his postulation of alternative modernities in much earlier work:

> [t]he naturalistic account of the discovery of the kernel truths, implicit in the acultural theory, misses all these connections [between social, moral, historical, teleological, and background assumptions]. When the old metaphysical and religious beliefs crumble, we find as a matter of neutral fact that we are instrumental individuals, and we need to draw from elsewhere our values and acceptable grounds for association with others. In contrast, I want to describe the change as moving us from one dense constellation of background understanding and imaginary to another, both of which place us in relation to others and the good. There is never atomistic and neutral self-understanding; there is only a constellation (ours) which tends to throw up the myth of this self-understanding as part of its imaginary. This is the essence of a cultural theory of modernity. (Taylor 2001, pp. 195–196)

However, as one of the greatest surprises of *A Secular Age* would be the close association or family resemblance he ascribes to his position and that espoused by Milbank's radical orthodoxy (p. 774, 775). Taylor recast the narrative presented by radical orthodoxy as an Intellectual Deviation (ID) that in tracing its conceptual origins to the somewhat pre-modern nominalism of such figures as Ockham and Scotus in their justified critiqued of the metaphysical realism of Aquinas, nonetheless initiated a cascade effect that also leads to the derailed intellectual deviation from the robust social ontology that Milbank and others seek to retrieve in their neo-Platonic retrieval of the best insights of Anselm along with orthodox constants that run relatively uncontested across the Christian tradition. On my analysis, the merits of radical orthodoxy would be the peripheral critique provided by its Anglican roots that seek middle-ways between Catholicism and Protestantism on larger Christian doctrine and between Lutheran and Calvinist extremes on more contentious matters like pre-destination, the extent and nature of human depravity, church versus state jurisdiction, etc (Milbank 2013b). However, Taylor and I share the same concern with too robust of an emphasis on primordial social integration in radical orthodoxy that could be rendered as instrumental justification for the license of its romantically theological overtones to bypass the subjection of its claims to the public justificatory discourses characteristic of modernity. In a manner surprisingly congruent with Habermas' works in progress on these matters, Taylor articulates his critique in a manner that casts the achievements of modernity as bringing to fruition the original reformist breakthrough(s) brought about by Jasper's Axial Age:

> Now I believe that this story [radical orthodoxy] explicates some very important truths, and draws some crucial connections. But I don't think this can suffice as the main story behind secularity. There is another important piece, which deals with the thrust to complete the Axial revolution; I mean Reform, which strives to end the post-Axial equilibrium, that is, the balance and complementarity between pre- and post-Axial elements in all higher civilizations. (Taylor 2007, p. 774)

I have previously remarked that I endorse the model of overlapping consensus promulgated in the views of Rawls and Taylor. Here lies the most fruitful incorporation of radical orthodoxy as a competing rendition of European modernity, if only the product of consensus on norms could be reached through rational justification, albeit independent of a commitment to any single legal form or privy background justification.

However, the detailed assessment of Taylor's ties between reform and the Axial revolution requires more fine-tuned distinctions that endorse the merits of Taylor over Rawls. Taylor's critique of errantly collapsing the Reform Master Narrative into the secular-rational-universalist view could hold equally strong as a critique of Rawls on two related fronts. On the one hand, I cast my own construal of original position 3 in the opening chapter as suspicious of the neutrality claimed for Rawls' own variations on original position 1 and 2. In other words, by resetting the Axial Age as the default origination for original position 3, any variation on a legitimate claim to species-ethical universality must have originally always already borrowed its content from a long narrative of deeply cultural inter- and intra-Axial development. On the other hand, I agree with Habermas's own critique of Rawls (that would likewise agree with Taylor) that the purported neutrality of an acultural theory of Rawls sneaks teleological principles into its claim to offer a view not committed to any specific comprehensive doctrine. Habermas in particular critiques Rawls for building the set of primary goods into the original position that thereby has both bypassed the threshold for public rational justification and already undermined its commitment not to tailor principles of justice to one's own unique case. Specifically, by positing primary goods in this teleological manner, their ultimate pursuit must be secured through a strategically-rational disposition which runs directly against the non-strategic impartiality the original position was intended to offer (Habermas 1998, pp. 75–101; McCarthy 2013, pp. 115–131). For Habermas, the disagreement with Rawls rests not so much with the express content of the primary goods but rather with Habermas's unwavering commitment to truly legitimate justification as having proceeded from the argumentative process of giving and responding to reasons. In the end, Habermas finds Rawls' commitment to discursive justification via public reason potentially much more fruitful, thus rendering the original position unnecessary as merely a non-communicative hypothetical constraint that really cannot deliver the rationally universal impartiality it portends.

On the other end of the spectrum, in contrast to the growing predominance of conservative-leaning populist romantics espousing to recapture a common European, national, and/or local culture, Europe formed and continues to develop its highly differentiated centers and peripheries via ongoing communicative conflict more so than through internal agreement.[8] For instance, returning to the original social

[8] My project would be to apply the insights of Rasmussen's approach to alternative modernities at the global and international levels more explicitly to the multiple modernities that constitute contemporary Europe. Here, I agree with Rasmussen's (2010) thesis in 'Conflicted Modernity: Toleration as a Principle of Justice' that: 'Communication on the international level must be something like a public discourse which serve as a third kind of discourse, alongside religious discourses, on the one hand, and secular discourses, on the other. It presumably mediates the potential conflict

science literature supporting the multiple modernities thesis for Europe reminds us that stronger national integration originally formed in Europe in degrees directly commensurate with distance from various Catholic cores as carried over from its historical *ancien* regimes (Eisenstadt 2003, p. 103). The relatively homogenous Catholic core stretching along the city-belt from South to North via the median terrain of Western Europe thereby contributed to the reactionary peripheral forces that constitute the Protestant, Anglican, Eastern Orthodox, and Lutheran orientations that still permeate the constitutional structure of many EU periphery states—not to mention that the UK belies most characteristics typically ascribed to nation-states (Casanova 2014; Philpott and Shah 2006, p. 47). These multiple peripheries served as cleavage points of intense democratic differentiation by providing sites of moral extraterritoriality for both transcendent and profane cosmic visions that differed with the generally Catholic homogeneity. Although European states eventually allowed competing religious forces spaces for civic expression, this was promulgated in exchange for religious groups agreeing to refrain from having their leaders hold positions of public power, thereby encouraging reflexive commitments to twin toleration—from state to church and *vice versa*—in order to institutionalize and embed relatively permanent structural cleavages between these contradictory cosmic visions of modernity (Casanova 2014; Philpott and Shah 2006, p. 47).

5.1.2 Democratizing European Subsidiarity Under the Aegis of Multiple Modernities

As far as addressing the current state of the European Union democratic deficit, and in terms of assessing the relevant social science literature as it bears on proposals for how best to institutionalize a principle of subsidiarity, what are we to make of the aforementioned contrasting visions of European modernity? Allhardt, Himmelstrand, and Taylor argue that we are not faced with a zero sum trade-off of either multiple modernities with less democracy or secular modernity with more democracy (Taylor 2001). They each hold that we can best preserve these creative lines of reciprocal interpenetration democratically by embracing the rationally normative content of European modernity without loosing sight of the expressive cultural resources that give reinforcing layers of democratic assurance to our reasoned commitments (Himmelstrand 1960):

---

that the various alternative appropriations of modernity manifest. Whether or not we can call this public reason, or perhaps to use a term recently introduced by An-Naim, civic reason, on an international scale depends on whether it is possible to build an overlapping consensus on matters of international political concern. The achievement of some kind of overlapping consensus is our last best hope. The alternative is to conceive of politics as a continuing battle between them and us, which would lead, indeed, to a clash of civilizations….[T]he public reason view of politics takes with utmost seriousness the idea that conflict is at the center of the modern international political arena. However, the expression of that conflict is possible through the creation of a political discourse that has mutual understanding at its center. The result is not the elimination of difference but the expression of difference' (pp. 347–348).

> Without going into his lengthy methodological discussions, Himmelstrand's main findings can be summarized by saying that….strongly expressive individuals were the least democratic, and the strongly instrumental individuals were clearly less democratic than those who were both instrumental and expressive. (Allhardt 2005, p. 489)

The implications for subsidiarity would be to provide the richest possible democratic institutionalization of points of overlapping consensus even in spite of these enduring tensions and deep cleavages between higher and lower, core to periphery, rational and romantic. For starters, these multidimensional constituents of a post-secular Europe must overcome the notion that religious expressions of cultural and political salience can no longer be deemed inherently irrational under the aegis of the increasingly plural conditions of modernity (Rasmussen 2010, pp. 343–346).

However, as traditionally construed, *rationalist* proponents of an increasingly economically interdependent modernity defend a characteristically a-cultural view of market subsidiarity as a legal-juridical principle. This view of European integration is best protected and interpreted by seemingly neutral principled arguments in light of an unspoken strategic preservation of Euro-secularity supplanted by the market-oriented treaty framework of the European Union. This is a nuanced view that carries over from concerted attempts to alleviate ambiguity in the competing functional tasks and goals of the various institutional levels of economic, social, and political integration by seeking out a clear and concise logical delineation of competences and functional goals at as many local levels as possible but with the EU-level and Member States as the main actors (Paulus 2008, pp. 193, 194). The democratic principle here lies in insulating the competing levels of Member State governance from arbitrary seizures of power, often presuming a vision of the European Court of Justice that discourages judicial review of laws, thereby enhancing the economic integration that structures European-wide law and upholding the original market objectives of the European Community. In this respect, European-level judges are viewed as rational adjudicators of subsidiarity construed as a clear enumeration of powers in a vertically structured (non-horizontal) federation. Instead of taking subsidiarity as an interpretive guide and—by virtue of the principle of direct effect that secures the rational supremacy of European law—elites tend thereby to characterize the impartial market as the instrumentally rational adjudicator and preferential steering force behind integration to stave off the political biases of legislators and elected executives (Halberstam 2009, pp. 45–47).

On this model of what some have characterized as Anglo-Saxon subsidiarity (Kerr 2010; Veggeland 2007, pp. 98–100), the general tendency of the rationalist model tends to deal with issues of externality (that is, any circumstance outside the scope of the legislative jurisdiction of a given Member State that nonetheless affects that Member State) by shifting the competence downwards to the Member State level—or closer to the people as determined by their market preferences. Moves upwards to the European level receive their rational legitimation only when directly tied to the four freedoms of first pillar economic integration: goods, capital, services, and people (Davies 2008, p. 78, 90, 97, 98; Paulus 2008, pp. 209–211). In this somewhat ironic manner, although the rhetorical connotation of subsidiarity seems to point to the primacy of the local, critics of the rationalist approach see it as further entrenching the legal-juridical protection of the EU-wide open market policies. Insofar as Member States rarely carry the administrative capacity to deal with a growing array of externalities, the evolving precedent of subsidiarity appeals in the EU favor enhanced European social and economic integration, without the requisite political spillover needed to ensure harmonization of Member State commitments to the 1997 Growth and Stability Pact.[9] Therefore, the unhindered economic ties of interdependence have led to EU-wide political paralysis at the heavy cost of sacrifices in national *and* European accountability, widespread fiscal mistrust breeding instability, and huge deficits in local, national, and regional democratic legitimacy (Davies 2008, p. 79).

Critics also argue that rationalists are inclined to mask competition among universal legal principles under the veil of a deductively abstract logic that—when exposed—would disclose a complex set of competing variables that tend to vary on a case by case basis, surreptitiously gerrymandered to cover over otherwise conflicting objectives. Since the majority of financial transactions are transnational, cases are adjudicated on the basis of protecting the unassailable rationale behind the four basic market freedoms (Davies 2008, p. 81, 95; Gerloch 2008, p. 126, 127). In addition, while the prevailing logic of the principle of subsidiarity presumes the already questionable capacity for adjudicating Member State versus EU-level competence, the Anglo-Saxon model belies its own purported preference for the lower level over the higher European level insofar as the UK—while certainly an EU Member—does not at all meet the normal criteria ascribed to a nation-state. Since its own governance structure bears the semblance of a complex hybrid between a mixed commonwealth and a parliamentary democracy with a deeply entrenched imperial colonial history, appeals to subsidiarity in the name of democratic legitimacy would presuppose radical changes to the UK's own internal governance. These could include but are not limited to: the drafting of an explicit constitution, the end of any political, diplomatic, and administrative functions played by the monarchy, a stronger deconfessionalization of the Anglican church away from public services including schools, jurisdiction over family law, and ending the use of state and/or EU taxes for church provisions of social welfare services.

The second *romanticized* vision of a socially integrated European society could be advanced in order to catch up with and achieve the political closure elided by the Anglo-Saxon model that seeks to prise apart economic and political interdependence. What scholars characterize as Continental subsidiarity offers an either/or scenario for European modernity. On the one hand would be a nostalgic return to a more protectionist national constitutional culture in order to preserve the achievements of the social-welfare state, or, on the other hand, a forward-looking vision of a Europe that mimics the democratic and constitutional achievements of Continental states (particularly, France and Germany). The latter group also argues that the

[9] These would include maintaining less than a 60 % ratio of public debt to GDP, not exceeding a 3 % threshold of state deficit, and an inflation rate within 1.5 % of the average of the three best performing Member States (thus, typically below 3 % with the best performers usually around 1 % inflation).

EU might best halt continued expansion by keeping its borders consistent with the former outlines enjoyed under the Holy Roman Empire.

In a related, more extreme variant of the Continental vision for European integration, some such cultural romanticists also espouse Euro-secularity as the flip-side of stymied expansion in order to keep contemporary states 'European' by enacting protectionist policies in light of the EU's growing multiculturalism (thus blocking 'non-European' Muslim Candidate State Turkey and Potential Candidates: Kosovo, Albania, and Bosnia-Herzegovina).[10] In addition, on the Continental view of modernity, those seeking the benefits of enhanced economic integration would best forge ahead in creating a Europe of two tracks, one consisting of those not committed to greater political integration and another committed to an enhanced economic union matched by politico-legal integration. The Continental rendered regional could better hold Member States accountable to the original conditions set by the European Growth and Stability Pact (Veggeland 2007, pp. 98–100; Habermas 2001a).[11] This Continental mixing of the principles of proportionality and subsidiarity in the fiscal realm seeks to reconcile levels of economic integration with greater accountability via legislatively endorsed and judicially enforced constitutional procedures (Heidenreich 2006), introducing the expansion of the German constitutionalization of a 'debt brake' to potentially all Members of the Euro-Zone, as now being seriously considered by France, Spain, Italy, and others (Pogge 1997; Follesdal 1998b; Habermas 1998, 1999, 2001a, b, 2006).

---

[10] Due to his cosmopolitan and Kantian affinities, mixed with his deep commitments to preserving the social welfare state as a unique cultural achievement of Europe, most would characterize Habermas in the ensuing multiple modernities camp. In his (2008) 'A Political Constitution for the Pluralist World Society?' he seems to fall closest to the multiple modernities view in regarding the development of something akin to a cosmopolitan constitution as the best way to protect Europe's multiple modernities [citing Taylor's (1999) 'Two Theories of Modernity'] from the destructive tendencies of neo-liberal global capitalism (pp. 351–352). However, his many writings on the EU democratic deficit also seem to fall on both sides of the romantic spectrum. For instance, in his 2001 'Why Europe Needs a Constitution' he makes the substantive appeal to the need to preserve a common culture of social justice from global neo-liberal tendencies. Then, in his most recent view on the topic, 'A Pact for or Against Europe' (2011), he recommends that Germany concede the defeat of his hopes for a European federation that came with the last round of enlargement, Germany's overburdened position in staving off the Euro-zone financial crises, and the growing strategic importance of Asian and Middle Eastern economic-political policy. In light of Habermas's pronounced end to a European federation, he makes surprisingly romantic appeals to Germany to use these events as an opportunity to reassert its strategic, economic, and political importance on the global stage. At the same time, he seems to recommend excluding Turkey from EU membership in professing a romanticized vision of Europe as a geographic entity whose borders only contain a small portion of Turkey.

[11] As a concrete proposal to a more prolonged defense against the continually re-emerging European debt crisis, some within the Continental mold have suggested following the 2009 German measure legally to institutionalize the original 1997 EU Growth and Stability Pact threshold of the 60 % ceiling on public debt to GDP ratio as part of Member national constitutions. One might foresee something akin to such a constitutional measure as a proposed deciding factor for Member States seeking to forge ahead or stay behind in opting whether or not to proportion European economic and political integration with their national constitutions within an EU of two tracks.

Despite the wide variance of background conceptions feeding into cultural interpretations of European modernity, Continental romanticists seem to agree to the express commitment to dealing with the arbitrariness of the unhindered free market as a threat to political freedom. Romanticists are poised to solidify traditional social welfare provisions as European-wide common goods that insulate national and local sites of deep cultural solidarity from the destructive tendencies of the rampant individualism promoted by market-induced austerity pacts. Continental variants of subsidiarity critique the Anglo-Saxon model for introducing budget-cutting measures that induce races to the bottom, pitting EU-level, national level, and localized levels against one another as strategic competitors for scarce social, economic, and political capital (Dobson 2004; Bowman 2006).These romanticists associate the assurance of the legal-juridical dimensions of subsidiarity as a means to insulate both Member States and the EU from the neo-liberal threat of globalized unregulated capitalism leading to unwanted outside interference with the will of a sovereign people that shares a common politicized constitution or at least a clearly defined core of deep cultural commitments (Halberstam 2009, p. 46).

In contrast to the rationalist view, romantics deal with problems of externality as a way of constructing at least a differentiated—albeit unified—source of the requisite solidaristic affective bonds required for stronger commitments to economic redistribution. By making an epistemic virtue of the shared problem of the increased threats of European-wide austerity, romantics highlight the creation of distinctively European public sphere as a legitimating source for new constructions of wider social imaginaries built around the common good of securing social welfare. Romanticists also employ a positive view of expressive freedom insofar as democratic participation is cast in terms of a model of self-legislation usually secured through parliamentary means that can capitalize on empathetic extensions of the shared common threat of neo-liberalism unregulated that no individual should face alone. The construction of protectionist attitudes towards shared common cultural goods like language, religion (or lack thereof), and ethnicity thus are deemed legitimate insofar as they aid individuals in realizing their innately affective dispositions.

In lieu of the comparative strengths and weaknesses of the above visions for the future of European integration, *multiple modernists* propose to reconcile the more deeply cultural construal of subsidiarity with the proportionate balance of the relevant market and legal-juridical measures. On this view, arbitrariness leads to political domination in cases where market-oriented decisions and policies do not track the interests of each and every individual immediately affected, in ceasing to remain open to assurance appeals of affective, rational, and mixed orientations (Pettit 1997, p. 55). To make such a principle not seem overburdening, civic republicans of a romantic flare have also begun including more liberal social-contractarian dimensions in their views by pointing out that such a democratic principle would be 'modal' or counterfactual rather than historical (Pettit 1997, p. 186). In addition, in its contemporary manifestation as a political liberalism based more off of Habermas's endorsement of Rawls' public reason, neo-Rawlsian advocates (in particular, I am referring most directly to Andreas Follesdal—a former doctoral student of Rawls who studied and did his dissertation at Harvard under the tutelage of Rawls) integrating alternative modernities suggest why Rawls has begun to have such and appeal in the Nordic context. According to Follesdal,

> Political philosophy is typically called for in times of crises or fundamental social change. I therefore submit that we should expect Rawls's work to receive increasingly more attention in the Nordic countries. The features characteristic of the Nordic countries are changing, largely due to the multifaceted processes of Europeanisation. The legal and constitutional culture is changing, for at least three reasons. First, the role of parliament is being rethought. Both Sweden and Norway are reconsidering the role of the courts generally. International human rights courts—especially the European Court on Human Rights—pose fundamental challenges to the received conception of parliament as the site of legitimacy. Iceland included human rights in the constitution in 1994–95, and the new Finnish constitution includes a broad range of economic and social rights. Second, recent developments in the European Union (for Finland, Denmark and Sweden) and the European Economic Area (for Iceland and Norway) pose fundamental questions regarding sovereignty, due to the transfer and pooling of competences within the European Union. Third, the legal and constitutional ties to the Continent, combined with much scholarly exchange with the US, confront the Scandinavian Legal Realist tradition with other conceptions of constitutional democracy, including the widespread existence of Constitutional Courts. Such conceptions become harder to ignore. (Follesdal 2011, p. 186, 187)

Follesdal's ensuing appeal to guaranteeing *both* the rational and the affective dimensions of our capacity for trust in non-strategic modes, ultimately owes its conceptual roots to Rawls' initially innate subjective capacity for a sense of justice. In its Nordic recasting as a discourse ethic for multi-level political deliberation, we must communicatively secure the requisite degrees of second-personal deliberative assurance in the legitimacy of European-wide institutional change. Such an approach ensures that an overlapping consensus upon common norms will be upheld by the relevant parties affected even if drawing from distinct legal cultures and differing background justifications (Follesdal 2008, p. 200, 2011). Therefore, the modal capacity that one *could* communicatively contest decisions proves sufficient for the necessary social bond of political trust as assurance—with the realistic hope of overturning decisions and/or unforeseen externalities if found to be arbitrary—providing a less demanding democratic threshold than rational self-legislation that sees laws and directives as democratic only if they proceed through real historical acts of explicit willing.

However, in a summary point of difference with romantics, although the potential say of those affected by the growing array of externalities is important, institutional mediation of conflict and contestation will not always ensure autonomous collective control, or unanimously secured rational consent, over the final outcome of decisions. In this respect, also in some affinity with the liberal core of democratic institutions that presume the primacy of the individual, some forms of political interference against the polity even by individuals and minorities may be acceptable. Multiple modernists concede that the juridification of a romantic or rationalist legal guarantee of autonomous control over outcomes could itself become a source of political domination (Bohman 2004). In addition, Eisenstadt and Taylor both suggest that on this more agonistic model, the secondary and peripheral publics produced by openly democratic regimes must make the postsecular turn by allowing the mobilization of religious groups to exercise a creative force in public debates without necessarily running through the Habermasian filter of translating its reasons into rationally universalizable public claims (Taylor 2007, p. 532; Eisenstadt 2003, pp. 877–910). They find these epistemic minorities are often more productive in the long run than the center and/or majoritarian secular-humanist positions in a given political culture by, on the one hand, not being blinded by the various institutional biases they are often working against—either toward more secularity or the partial recognizing of the religious reasons of some groups as institutionally preferable over others' (Baum 2010, pp. 377–380; Bowman 2009a).[12] On the other hand, despite the differing array of background justifications for secular versus non-secular positions, rather than outright protesting against one another perpetually as characterized by the sensationalized culture wars—as far as shared moral norms go—they may serve to reinforce richer cultural foundations of differentiated trust as both sides pursue overlapping consensus upon the common good for perhaps different sources of background justification (Bohman 2007b). Ultimately, this last model of the complementary rational and expressive qualities of subsidiarity will fall closest to a model of democracy as facilitative assistance detailed more explicitly below—whereby common goods are reached through protest and contestation that collective willing might circumvent—thus departing from more conventional views couched in terms of republican popular sovereignty and/or the naïve projection of a neo-liberal consensus on the dubious efficiencies produced by policies of market non-interference (Melish 2009, p. 221).

5.1.3 Recasting Follesdal's Analysis of Subsidiarity for Multiple Modernities: Nordic/Scandinavian Subsidiarity as a Template for a More Liminal Europe?

Although constituting only piecemeal steps along the way to facing the EU's many democratic deficits, unfortunately, the earliest institutional replies to the democratic deficit fell into the conventional template of popular sovereignty as the minimal

[12] On this note, Ratzinger has even expressed openness to the idea of slowly phasing out the redistribution of state and federal taxes to religious institutions in Germany and elsewhere in Europe on the principle that allowing/forcing religious institutions to compete for congregational tithing as their primary means of support would thereby force religious institutions to play a more engaged/meaningful public role (Berger 2006, p. 91). Gregory Baum (2010) articulates this phenomenon well to reinforce that embracing the postsecular turn does not mean the naïve anticipation of the rejuvenated spiritual recovery of political majorities in modern societies: 'In the "back and forth" between religion and belief, religion remains, despite its minority status, a creative force. Because of this creativity, Taylor argues, there need not be opposition between faith and unbelief. I wish to add to this that in the present civilizational crisis, religious humanist and secular humanists must work together in defense of the common good and the integrity of the natural order. It is my impression that dialogue between believers and secular humanists is more difficult for the latter' (pp. 377–378). As an illustration of the 'back and forth' fostering mutually reflective epistemic creativity, he cites the 2004 public interchange between Habermas and Ratzinger (pp. 378–380).

threshold for democratic self-rule, employing the principle of subsidiarity under a naïve epistemic dualism to ensure that what is done at a more local level is not raised to a higher level. In addition, when decisions were actually raised to the EU-level, they were to be related to, at best, dubious European-wide objectives already laid out in its framework of treaties.

However, on the concession of multiple cores and peripheries in a Europe comprised of alternative modernities, the descriptive and prescriptive remedies lie in taking the singularity out of the often overly simplified, far from straight-forward appropriation of which side to choose between the presumably precise bifurcation separating EU and Member State levels (Follesdal 2010b, p. 13, 14). In initial agreement between multiple modernists and the tradition of classical republicanism, the oldest sort of political arbitrariness was that of the tyrant, requiring no rational justification for their decisions to those subject to their partisan mandates. While the tyrant unjustifiably placed himself as the privy object of his own will in the stead of the republic, the new arbitrary dominator can take innumerable forms that require a mutiperspectival analysis akin to the center-periphery social scientific tradition initiated by Stein Rokkan in its economic, political, and cultural dimensions (Flora 1999).[13] However, to understand these permutations in their present manifestations, we must not merely begin with the *sui generis* features of the EU that in many ways defy all conventional understanding of the shape and functioning of a polity. We must instead utilize Rokkan's insights to reconsider how the EU got this way by beginning with his lifelong efforts in devising a conceptual map for Europe:

> What needs to be emphasized is the *multidimensionality* of the model: at each stage it gives equal weight to economic/technological, political/territorial, and cultural/ethnic/religious dimensions. There is no economic determinism in the model, nor a geopolitical, nor a cultural: in this sense it seeks to combine the traditions of Karl Marx with those of Max Weber and Emile Durkheim….The central task for systematic macro-history is the analysis of the *dynamics of interaction* between the economic, the political, and the cultural systems: each system has its specific rhythm and its specific boundaries but the fate of a particular territory and its institutions is determined through processes of interaction among the systems, across their boundaries. (Rokkan 1999a, p. 140, 141)

Only by conceding the indeterminacy and dynamism of his initial model that—despite all its complexity still never went as far as attempting to explain the additional nuances of south-eastern Europe nor did it extend further eastward into what was then part of the Soviet bloc—can we thereafter address why the EU continues to resist popular sovereignty closure at *both* its highest and lowest institutional levels without conceding an impending resolution to greater market liberalization.

---

[13] Flora argues that Rokkan's approach can enrich our understanding and critical analysis of subsidiarity: 'Europe as a whole has the polycephalic structure of Central Europe, where the ideas of *federalism* and *subsidiarity* originated. Yet European-wide centre-periphery structures will form or solidify, and as they do so the 'city-belt' so central to Rokkan's theory may once again play a role…One might argue that as nation-states declined in significance, intensive research on their differences has also become less important. But I would counter that the process of European integration has given these differences a wholly new meaning. By looking back into the past, Rokkan points to the future' (p. 91).

As a good framework for assessing the democratizing potentials of subsidiarity, I will draw heavily the corpus of work of Andreas Follesdal whom has unarguably produced the most extensive contemporary work on the topic and also falls within Rokkan's Scandinavian tradition of creatively exploring the tensions and cleavages between center and periphery (Follesdal 1998a, 2000, 2006a, 2014). Given the track record of success in achieving consensus among neo-conservative and socialist parties in the Nordic/Scandinavian regions of Europe, this empirically-informed model would better aid in the democratic articulation of European-wide consensus among competing modernities via contractually-based consent as the normative threshold against forms of interference to be deemed as arbitrary versus acceptable (Veggeland 2007, pp. 97–114). Within the rubric of multiple modernities, Follesdal carefully develops a mixture of liberal and neo-republican insights to the problem of balancing trust and authority in a multi-leveled polity, pointing out that historically federalism has served as a structural response for institutionalizing measures for dispersing authority between center and periphery (Follesdal 2000, p. 86, 2007, pp. 383–394). Taken at face value then, Follesdal finds that in his historical surveys of EU treaties, the overt appeals to the principle of subsidiarity might get around the most troubling aspects of the EU democratic deficit by allowing local and national levels the autonomy to control matters closest to the immediate concerns of their constituents (Follesdal 2006a; Dashwood 2008, pp. 5, 6).

However, he takes an ambivalent approach to subsidiarity that, on the one hand, sees the potential for it to increase deliberative participation. On the other hand, he raises three crucial concerns over the status of subsidiarity as it stands in the present institutional design. These concerns I have taken the license to tailor/Taylor to my own purposes in order to align them with the three sub-sections to a workable notion of Nordic-Scandinavian subsidiarity. These respectively deal with (a) the accountability of administrators, (b) the appropriate sub-unit(s) of multi-level institutions, and (c) how best to employ federalism to foster the development of a political culture of trust *between* Member States rather than merely within them via a recursive appeal to subsidiarity rendered more consistent with standard normative criteria for enhanced political assurance (Follesdal 2000, p. 85, 2006a, p. 74, 77).

NSS [Nordic-Scandinavian Subsidiarity] (a): Plural Elites and Problems of Rationalism: The Yellow and Orange Card Methods

Follesdal finds appeals to subsidiarity paradoxically to increase the threat of arbitrary political domination at the EU-level when its administrative elites primarily seek to meet European-wide objectives in the name of strategic rationalist standards of market efficiency instead of by guaranteeing publicly accountable discretion to the affected Member States (Follesdal and Wind 2009, p. 133; Follesdal 2009a, p. 605, 606; Follesdal et al. 2007, p. 2; Halberstam 2009, p. 45). Follesdal also mentions that, even at the lower level, Member State administrators likewise often abuse subsidiarity to mask discretionary judgments that actually worsen the democratic deficit when instrumentally-motivated decisions would better be subjected to open public debate (Follesdal 2007, p. 2). Follesdal characterizes these instances of administrative discretion as arbitrary when appeals to overall efficiency are justified by dogmatic speculations over the merits of decentralized versus centralized decision-making (Follesdal 2000, p. 101). Unfortunately, while subsidiarity was originally taken as a measure to insulate citizens from unaccountable EU-level decisions, in its most perverse rationally instrumental forms it can also actually serve to promote undue centralization by insulating EU-level *and* national administrators from accountability to the growing diversity of European publics (Follesdal 2006a, p. 66, 67).

Although his analysis shows the weaknesses of the current institutionalization of a principle of subsidiarity that can circumvent prospects of further public deliberation, he does endorse the Lisbon protocols first presented in the proposed Constitutional Treaty of Europe (CTE), and then later passed as part of the Lisbon Treaty after the failed constitutional referendum. He describes the nuanced efforts to proceduralize its 'yellow card' method by formalizing the means by which national parliaments issue reasoned disputes against Commission legislative proposals deemed to violate a principle of subsidiarity. He finds that such measures actually enhance the degree of accountability of EU legislation and thereby lead to a *more* democratic form of multi-level subsidiarity (Paulus 2008, p. 210; Halberstam 2009, p. 47; Gerloch 2008, p. 125; Davies 2008, p. 96; Dashwood 2008, p. 6; Hix 2008, p. 9, 10). He fully endorses the special addendum including the yellow card method since it facilitates public deliberation about the means and ends of the EU by encouraging openness between EU and Member States and among Member States about comparative effectiveness. This measure would engender reflection by Member States about the ends of concerted actions. It encourages Member States to discuss how best to reach these ends of various directives in light of their unique national histories and administrative cultures (Follesdal 2006a, p. 65, 66; Cooper 2006). In addition, the non-uniform externalities of European interdependence can facilitate variegated epistemic communities. Since these typically traverse national borders, the addendum includes the provision that all new legislation proposed by the Commission must be sent to each national parliament in its given national language(s), followed by an eight week period whereby critical statements could be drafted and disseminated to other dissenting parliaments as additional frameworks for critical reference (Murphy 2008, p. 23; Dashwood 2008, p. 6).

While not explicitly mentioned by Follesdal as such, with twenty-eight monitors each representing distinct *demoi*, this multiperspectival form of contestation could better ensure the greater accountability and transparency of single-perspective administrative policy-making. This complements his theoretical recommendations to reach down to lower regional and local moral-ethical appeals to subsidiarity not just against EU-level initiatives, but also against one's own Member State government. If one finds that any higher level authority bypasses lower levels of governance in ways contrary to the will of those most immediately effected, local political movements could issue yellow-cards against potential dominators, with institutional patterns of precedent tracked and catalogued at the EU-level for comparative indices of best and worst practices (Murphy 2008, p. 29; Follesdal 2006a, p. 66; Halberstam

2009, p. 47; Davies 2008, p. 94; Bowman 2009b). It would also indubitably enhance the epistemic quality of new laws by enriching perspectives on the best practices and proposed means of implementation at Member State administrative levels and also at the EU committee levels. Mutual learning should be expected since each national parliament interprets subsidiarity differently—often due to fundamentally competing conceptions of what constitutes the project of shared and/or competing European projects of modernity (Dashwood 2008, p. 6).

Although an explicit 'red card' measure was considered, critics of such a procedure argued that such an extreme measure would thereby undermine the unique role of the Commission in its ability to initiate new legislation.[14] As a political conciliation, also included in the protocol was the median 'orange card' provision whereby Commission proposals subjected to reasoned objections from one-half of national parliaments would have to be suspended (Murphy 2008, p. 31). While critics of both the yellow and orange card procedures often hold that the one-third and one-half threshold of national parliaments sets the threshold for contestation too high, since Council proceedings ideally aspire to unanimity, responders to this critique highlight the rarity of legislative proposals passing when opposed by two or more Member States.

However, even when opting to reserve particular policies for the national level, a simplified nostalgic return to the nation-state via the Lisbon yellow and orange card methods ignores that the presence of the EU proceduralization of such means of contestation is itself a deliberative capacity ensured only by these newly introduced institutional preconditions. In an ironic twist, the presence of higher-level institutional orders might actually address local political poverty—that is, national and/or structural inequalities in the capacity to initiate new topics for public deliberation (Bohman 1996, pp. 107–149). In addition, even when yellow and orange card appeals to subsidiarity are not successful, once politicized by national and transnational media, such decisions have an EU-wide epistemic ripple-effect whereby broader patterns of domination are less likely to reemerge when subjected to the watchful eyes and catalogued written precedent of drafting reasoned objections. The potentials for collective learning intensify with twenty-eight national parliamentary and administrative interpretations of the newly politicized principle of subsidiarity. Therefore, we must take into account the critical insight from Gareth Davies that it is not so easy to parse areas of exclusive competence in the EU, whether economic, geo-political, institutional, militaristic, or social (Davies 2008, p. 79, 80; Gerloch 2008, pp. 127–128).[15] And in the concurring remarks from Simon

[14] The British European Scrutiny Committee, Concluding Recommendations, found that for subsidiarity to carry its original intent of enhancing national powers of democratic accountability over the EU-level Commission, the option of a 'red card' appeal still should have been permitted in the Lisbon protocol.

[15] In Davies' words, 'its [subsidiarity in EU treaties] talk of the goals of the proposed action' indicates a certain linguistic sneakiness. Actions have all the purposes possessed by those supporting them, which may be multiple, contradictory and even paradoxical. Speaking of the goal as if this was a simple and uncontested attribute suggests either that all participants have a level of unity and agreement which does not exist in the real world, or is a rhetorical trick to avoid thinking about real

Hix, the revamped threefold form of Rokkan's type of multidimensional competing economic/technical, political/territorial, and cultural/ethical/religious subsidiarity can aid in complementing the legal-juridical measures of the Court of Justice with a more politicized subsidiarity subject to parliamentary debate:

> [I]n a sense allowing national parliaments a say to police these kinds of competence boundaries—which is how I really interpret what this is about—is a sort of belt and braces approach. The Court of Justice already does it. There is no harm in letting national parliaments do it, too, and I think there are big transparency benefits in addition by allowing national parliaments to do exactly that job….It is like, in a sense, saying, where unanimity is required, "We keep them at the national level," because everyone has to agree. So sovereignty is not being transferred, sovereignty is being kept. So what you are doing is policing the use of unanimity versus the use of QMV and in a sense that is subsidiarity in another name, and that in a sense is how I can see where the Court of Justice already plays a role and national parliaments could play a secondary role. (Hix 2008, p. 9, 10)

While I agree with Hix that subsidiarity deals largely with delineating contested competence boundaries, he also seems nonetheless too quick to assume that these overlapping sovereignties and political identities can be separated so efficiently. With salience to the EU and subsidiarity, in the words of Gerald Ruggie, the ongoing formation of Member State identities in the EU 'endogenizes' the practices of what it means to be a Member State: to be a British, French, Dutch, and German citizen increasingly means to be a citizen that is part of the EU (Ruggie 1998). We could add onto these new deliberative capacities the mixing of the cultural, political, and religious levels too in order that the reality of invoking some religiously-oriented reasons may not always be an all-or-nothing affair, as merely one layer of a broader narrative incorporating a variety of rational justifications (Cooke 2013). For instance, while expert third-person administrator and politician accounts of the famous French headscarf affair decried the injustice of putting one's religious affiliation as prior to the republican ideal of being French, initially no members of academic, media, or career politicians thought to take the Habermasian participant-view of the second-person(s) most immediately affected. When the girls most affected were themselves consulted they produced a both/and response to what was initially foreseen errantly as an either/or rational-secular or religious-irrational justification. The girls as second-person participants in the public debate said that they voluntarily and authentically chose to wear the scarves at public school institutions to express their hybrid self-ascriptions as *both* French *and* Muslim (LaBorde 2001; Lavdas 2001).

In this multi-dimensional second-person light, EU institutions do not just merely add on another layer of political identity to replace and supersede national identity but instead carry a whole range of new communicative and institutional capacities—typically taken as a hallmark of the overall history of European forms of modernity—that make even local and regional citizenship more effective at ensuring

---

people and purposes at all, and elevate the action to a status of self-evident singularity of purpose which can only stifle discussion. These intellectual deficits are translated into concrete problems as a result of the relatively imprecise delimitation of Community competences' (p. 80).

participation in local, national, regional, and virtual forms for any multi-leveled EU policy context.

NSS (b): Inverting the Sub-Unit Question via Politicized Subsidiarity—The Species-Ethical Axial Orientation of Multiple Modernities and the Necessity of Trust

Follesdal also finds that the references to subsidiarity in the relevant EU treaty legislation often entrench Member States as the only sub-units of a European federation without providing the institutional assurances of mutual trust needed. Since such a complexly multi-leveled arrangement could easily lapse into administrative sclerosis, on his view, in order to promote the greatest possible ongoing flexibility, the EU need not necessarily derive moral legitimacy from an explicit constitution. Given Follesdal's recent work on other multi-level systems of governance that have become increasingly common under conditions of globality, akin to Simon Hix's earlier reference to the Lisbon protocol on parliaments resembling subsidiarity functions already exercised by the European Court of Justice, Follesdal also considers whether institutional assurances of trust can extend more affectively beyond national parliaments. On this matter, the treaty framework of the EU perhaps provides more hermeneutic flexibility than an explicit constitution. He makes this query without necessarily calling for political closure via the European Parliament in an explicit constitutional federation. He even welcomes the prospect of creating new institutional designs more amenable to deliberative input from those most affected by the burgeoning EU laws and policies that now guide the vast majority of legislative norms even internal to Member State affairs:

> We must also note that Europeans will continue to need mutual assurance when creating *new* institutions. In order to secure compliance over the long term, such changes and legal interpretations of rules must be accepted as legitimate expressions of equal respect among citizens of different Member States, rather than seen as dictated by expediency or arbitrary consensus alone. The institutional changes must be seen to be guided by more than principles of an existing constitution. Otherwise, such disagreements as about the proper division of competences between Member States and the Community institutions, may diminish support and compliance by citizens and government officials. Domestic politicians may for instance suspect civil servants sent to Brussels of developing inappropriate supranational loyalties. Shared conceptions of the roles of Member States and the Community, e.g. in the form of a suitably specified Principle of Subsidiarity, can serve to bolster trustworthiness and reduce such mistrust. (Follesdal 2009b, p. 19, 20)

He therefore finds mistrust problematic not just for nation-states facing externalities that are sometimes used as justification for having their voice bypassed in the name of the exclusive functional competences reserved for multi-leveled systems of governance. Mistrust becomes especially problematic for the most systemically marginalized persons affected by regulations and latent structural ties of global interdependence over which they have little input. These democratic deficits include not just those faced by migrant workers, undocumented migrants, and cultural minorities that continue to have their needs unmet, but even address the political reality of the lack of voice in the EU citizens facing the *ad hoc* emergency construction of new legal, economic, and social welfare institutions (Wyller 2014, p. 225, 226). For example, the 2010 ESM (European Stabilization Mechanism) was derived predominantly by European elites and was proposed as the only possible remedy to face the array of externalities that escape the jurisdiction of their own Member State, national central banks, and asymmetrically enforced fiscal policies over which they had no real voice (Follesdal 2000, p. 105, 2009b, pp. 19–21;).

Beyond such aforementioned parliamentary, legal-juridical, and cultural modes of procedural subsidiarity, Follesdal also briefly considers the prospects of other non-territorial and purely functional forms for organizing the principle of subsidiarity in accord with the modal threshold of contingent complier as test for democratic legitimacy (1998, p. 195; 2006a, p. 69; 2009b, pp. 94–98, p. 105). With more direct salience to extending the merits of the Nordic/Scandinavian cultural and legal hermeneutics of subsidiarity to apply outside the bounds of the EU:

> Within the Nordic context, it is interesting to study the territories which have attained the right to self-government and have been given law-making competence as well, which are the Faeroe Islands, Greenland and the Aaland Islands. They have subordinated agreement-based governance and, particularly in relation to the multi-federal model proposed above, these small states represent special forms of subsidiarity in practice today. (Veggeland 2007, p. 110)

As practical illustrations, the Faroe Islands and Greenland have a constitutional relationship with Denmark that renders them subject to continual influence by European law. However, in 1984 Greenland ended its membership in the EU that dated back to 1972 when Denmark initially joined. Applied to the present, although subject to EU law by vicarious ties back to Denmark, Greenland and the Faeroe Islands had never formally signed the Treaty of Rome. In the words of Veggeland, we see a unique instance of multi-level subsidiarity in practice whereby 'Constitutional power is, therefore, no longer vested solely in a nation-state mono-structure, but shared within a tripartite framework. The quasi-sovereign states are independent in certain areas of competence, while the motherland retains total sovereignty in the remaining areas' (Veggeland 2007, p. 110). As a secondary application of subsidiarity, issues of competing competence between Denmark, Greenland, and the Faroe Islands receive their ongoing legitimation primarily through the balances struck directly between these three polities most immediately tied in networks of reciprocal interdependence.

In another Scandinavian example, the case of the Aaland Islands with loose political ties to both Finland and Sweden acts as a predominantly independent state within the greater Finish territory. It has its own parliament, practices the language and culture of its Swedish traditions, controls its public finances, holds the status as a demilitarized zone, plans its own economic development, retains the right to veto international legislation affecting its own laws, while nonetheless does not hold the right to make its own fiscal policy (p. 112). And as a final unique multidimensional example from the extreme northern stretches of the Nordic nations, an indigenous group—the Lapps—have worked towards the creation of The Barents Euro-Artic

Council that runs akin to a Rawlsian decent consultation hierarchy (as perhaps do many of the merely consultative functions of the EU) on the basis of contractual institutional authority and represents delegates from all countries around the Barents Rim, including representatives from the EU and from the Saami indigenous people (pp. 113–114).

Outside the Nordic context, other examples include public spheres, associations, social sectors, and social functions exercised by non-state actors and institutions that protect privacy, cultural, and religious expression, and extend to various affected groups including family, church, and guild, such as the successes of Roma winning seats in the European Parliament, minority rights protections against racism and xenophobia offered by the Vienna Monitoring Center for Rights, the (unfortunately) disbanded Forum of Migrants, the Conference of European Churches (CEC) as a European-wide consortium of Protestant churches, and the changing political weight of Catholic and Orthodox churches in light of EU Eastern expansion (Philpot and Shah 2006; Vjekoslav 2006, p. 193, 194; Follesdal 1998a, p. 195). In addition, some EU Member States have drawn on basic rights to political participation in the EU Fundamental Charter of Rights to allow foreigners to vote in public elections (Connolly et al. 2006).

While Follesdal generally regards these novelties as exceptions to the rule, the fundamental dilemma to be perpetuated by the international precedent of arrangements set thus far for institutionalizing a principle of subsidiarity entails mediating EU-level versus Member State levels of political trust as the basis for both modes of politicization. Thus, he suggests modifications better attuned to the substantive moral-ethical commitment to a presumed species-wide modal sense of justice that must be shared by those whom he labels 'contingent compliers' as the minimal threshold for the legitimacy of participation in multi-level governance mechanisms (Follesdal 2009b, pp. 10–14). Drawing on the work of Rawls and on his reflections concerning our basic sense of justice as a presumed species-wide capacity, the assurance of the legal, political, juridical, ethical, and moral legitimacy of institutions presumes reference to joint objects of attention even when placed in the dynamic context of global interdependence. Follesdal argues for the democratic integration of both the rationalist and romantic strands of European modernity via the contractual constraints common to the unique Nordic cases of subsidiarity mentioned above:

> Contingent compliers are prepared to comply with common, fair rules as long as they believe others do so as well, for instance out of a sense of justice. Thus they would prefer to cooperate rather than free ride on existing practices….For contingently compliant citizens to have a normative duty to obey political rules and authorities two conditions must hold: firstly,
>
> a. that the commands, rulers and regime are normatively legitimate—by some defensible set of principles of legitimacy; and secondly, [rational modernity]
> b. that citizens also have reason to trust in the future compliance of other citizens and authorities with such command and regimes. [romantic modernity]
>
> To merit obedience by contingent compliers, institutions must address the assurance problems these actors face within complex structures of interdependence…Institutions can provide valuable assurance by mixes of positive laws, transparency, shared practices, and

> socialization. I venture that democratic rule, with constraints on legislatures in the form of judicial review may provide one important form of such assurance [my additions in brackets]. (Follesdal 2008, p. 200)

The modal test of complicit complier makes an epistemic virtue of our second-personal capacity to carry a basic sense of justice that applies both individually, collectively to group, and corporately to the species writ large. He applies this normative standard to shared problematic circumstances beyond just the Member State as presumed sub-unit, or, by default directly to the individual participant. He recognizes that insofar as cultural/indigenous specificities may or may not follow territorial jurisdiction, *and* may potentially envelop the species, he proposes at the lower end of the spectrum that other sub-units like those represented by Greenland, the Faeroe Islands, the Aaland Islands, the Barents Euro-Artic Council, and the EU Committee of Regions could be permitted to utilize the principle of subsidiarity to assert freedoms of self-ascription, voluntary entry, and exit (2000, p. 104, 105). And, at the higher end of the subsidiarity spectrum, contingent compliance may also be secured by subjecting individual rights to weak international and cosmopolitan judicial review, such as via the ECtHR, ECJ, or ICC or—as akin to Habermas's species-ethical concerns posed by genetic engineering—by extending the cultural dimensions of the great Axial traditions to their widest possible species-universality (Follesdal 2008, p. 200).[16] In this latter line of argument, some scholars have proposed the construction of a unique subsidiarity court reserved solely to address issues raised by yellow and orange card objections. Since the Nordic trends of strong parliamentary legitimation pair democratically well with the Lutheran genealogy to its unique secularization of human rights, this precedent offers best practice models in matters of social justice and public welfare that other non-Nordic states can nonetheless seek to emulate within their distinct administrative heritages (Casanova 2014, pp. 29–32). With the open prospect of multiple subsidiarity courts representing the various major ethnicities, religions, and unique cultural forms in Europe, these hybrid differentiations might also serve to protect and insulate familial law and kinship norms from the predominately secular bias and state-neutrality of EU-level and national courts.

As a more generalized casting of the deeply cultural and spiritual counter-currents in the context of European modernity, under the rubric of a multiple modernities analysis of a re-politicized subsidiarity, the cosmic and species dimensions of the

[16] For his distinction between weak versus strong judicial review, see (Follesdal and Wind 2009, p. 133). Alan Dashwood also appeals to the proceduralization of marginal (weak) review of the European Court of Justice over subsidiarity principles as enhancing democratic legitimacy (2008, p. 4). Simon Hix also suggests that with the Eastern enlargement of the EU, the inclusion of more integrationally-skeptic East European judges as part of the ECJ has shown some tendencies to use the EU-level institutions to resist the prior precedent of judgments reinforcing centralizing tendencies (2008, pp. 11–12). In yet a third perspective on the use of courts to enhance the democratic elements of subsidiarity, Hix also finds that EU precedent on dealing with human rights concerns has demonstrated a careful balance of subsidiarity together with the principle of proportionality whereby Member State national courts trump the European Court of Justice on human rights that are enshrined in their own national constitutions (2008, p. 11).

Axial traditions feeding into modernity belie territorial closure and often already receive protection via international laws and mandates external to the EU (Veggeland 2007, pp. 110–114). On the one hand, in its more communitarian casting, subsidiarity attempts to protect the lowest possible levels from domination by the Member State or European-level. On the other hand, since the Axial renditions of modernity and their counter-movements set views of social and political institutions within the wider context of fundamental assumptions about the place of humanity within the cosmos often under the implicit jurisdiction of *jus cogens*,[17] we are led to a hybridization of minority enclaves led by secondary elites. The expert authorities then set forth competing claims that carry not only European-wide epistemic potential but entail institutional support for the realized capacities for the entire species to engage in mutual learning when solving global problems (Bowman 2012; Eisenstadt 2006). As a case in point of what commentators say belies the standard secular construal of basic rights through the distinctive Nordic-Lutheran sacralization of human rights, European-wide prohibitions upon the use of the death penalty owe some of the genealogy of their legal-juridical precedent to the portions of its Judeo-Christian heritage that once regarded the individual in terms of the *imagio dei* (Witte 2014, pp. 77–81; Casanova 2014, p. 32). In a truly unique chain of informal Axial dispersion across the now virtual spaces uniting both continents and the globe, US Supreme Court justices overturned the jurisdiction of some American states practicing the death penalty on minors, issuing a legal brief citing as a best practice the European court prohibitions on the death penalty as supporting precedent for their final verdict against such a penalty exacted on minors (Sen 2010, pp. 403–407).

We assume with Eisenstadt and Taylor that one of the features of European modernity evinces a cadre of subaltern elites that typically utilize civil society networks in periods of great change, independent of the direct influence of state power. In addressing the attendant risks that come with uses and misuses of expert authority, Eisenstadt hones specifically on the delicate dimension of trust that always displays this romantic tension between species-universality and local-particularity. Given Follesdal's emphasis on trust in the context of wide-scale social change occurring in Europe, we could use the Nordic framework for contractual assurance as a means to assess the democratic potentials of Eisenstadt's broad recommendations below. Both Eisenstadt and Follesdal would agree that future institutional renditions of subsidiarity must be constructed that not only mediate regionally between international and national but also globally between universal/species and particular/local (Follesdal 2006b):

> [T]he autonomy and distinctiveness of different elites, the center, and various public arenas may be undermined in situations of intense change. Autonomous sectors of civil society

[17] Eisenstadt, argues 'Many of these movements [protests inherent in the program of modernity] constituted the transformation, in the modern setting, of the various heterodoxies of the Axial civilizations—especially those that sought to bring about by political action the realization and reconstruction of the Kingdom of God on Earth. Many of these movements epitomized the search for ways in which the concrete social and political order could become the embodiment of an ideal order, and that search constituted a central component, if certainly not the only one, of modern discourse and process. These movements in modern societies were one of the main bearers, and perhaps *the* main bearer, of utopian visions' (2003, p. 889).

> and public arenas may erode and impediments to restructuring the relations between civil society and the State may develop out of attempts to redefine the boundaries of the political—as, for instance, in demands for the extension of suffrage. In such cases, tensions can arise between, on the one hand, adherence to the existing rules of the game and the balance between State and civil society, and, on the other, the new demands of emerging social forces. Within all these sectors, old and new alike, there may develop tendencies to represent narrow or ascriptive settings, weakening whatever initial acceptance of the existence of such sectors was present in the newly emerging common frameworks and centers. In all such situations, those demanding such redefinition grow suspicious that the existing representative institutions do not serve the common good. (Eisenstadt 2003b, p. 906, 907)

Although intense social change experienced in the liminal context of multiple modernities constantly re-politicizies subsidiarity, contemporary actors can also draw upon the great epistemic resources from the millennia of tradition behind the Axial traditions. Since the cosmic and species dimensions of the Axial traditions feeding into modernity belie territorial closure given their shared historical commitments to vernacularize elite insights as universally translatable, the political mobilization of species universal claims can carry concrete Jacobin and revolutionary dimensions (Christoffersen 2014, p. 105, 106; Eisenstadt 2006). Despite their claims to moral universality, as conceded earlier by Voegelin citing the innumerable ecumenic cases of striving for truly universal expansion by coercively imperial means, they also carry immense capacities for inter-civilizational political strife and competition.

Although we could not expect to give any straight-forwardly quantitative model to assess the limits on contingent compliance in a vertical institutional structure comprised now by multiple Axial traditions vying for civilizational influence, we can at least set up two extremes on a continuous spectrum to aid in filtering how thick and also how flexible our networks of trust might be. As theoretical framing conditions for setting forth the social cleavages that subsidiarity attempts either to embrace or overcome, Rokkan's uses of the Dutch terms *vertzuiling* and *ontzuiling* should prove effective. On the one hand, *vertzuiling* connotes a high degree of mistrust and intolerance across cleavages within four distinct empirical axes (including mistrust between church vs. state groups, urban vs. rural, owners vs. workers, and majority vs. minority cultures). On the other hand, its contrary—*ontzuiling*—suggests higher indices of willful collaboration among opposed groups. Rokkan observes that the higher the forms of mistrust between opposed groups, the greater the ties of solidarity formed negatively around the primary sources of joint attention: sharing a common enemy.

> [T]hey use the term *ontzuiling* for reductions in the distinctiveness of each [vertical] segment and *verzuiling* for increases…In a high *ontzuild* system there is low *membership crystallization*; most of the participants tend to be tied to organizations and environments exposing them to *divergent* political pressures. By contrast in a highly *verzuild* system there is *high* membership crystallization; most of the participants tend to be exposed to messages and persuasive efforts in the *same* general direction in *all* their '24-hour, 7-day' environments. (Rokkan 1999a, p. 376, 377)

Both of these tendencies illustrate polar extremes of potential responses to what Charles Taylor respectively called the nova and super-nova effects that typically follow prolonged periods of civilization crisis. Eisenstadt would agree with Taylor's reconstruction of contemporary secular and postesecular trends in European-wide politics as what he highlights as the fragility of networks of trust the buffered self must balance against the growing pluralism faced by contemporary democracies (Eisenstadt 2003, p. 878, 879).The *verzuild* type of membership crystallization, while generating high degrees of compliance could also erupt into Jacobian revolutionary tendencies—even in cases where its motivational sources derive from one of the great Axial traditions. In contrast, the *ontzuiling* style of membership would entail a lower threshold of overlapping compliance to the norms of external groups given its less stringent demands that do not presume a relatively homogeneous group of common self-ascription. While conceding the reality of *both* types of membership carries a greater potential for democratic integration by balancing multiple indices of possible trust with a healthy degree of contestation and protest across diverse modes of self-ascription, it presumes from its subjects a porous sense of self that exhibits the capacity for reaching common understanding with potential adversaries, looking for win-win scenarios of overlapping consensus that presupposes second-person capacities for reciprocal role-taking. As the flip side of species-ethical bonds of universal solidarity come the particularity of group-specific identifications, specific when formed in contrast to other group-specific modes of self-understanding. In other words, we can agree with Habermas that the moral point of view, akin to Mead's generalized other, presumes the empathetic socialization of persons (likely secured within a particular Axial context of authentic self-identification as much as or even more so than a default secular humanist socialization) as at least potentially universal in order to carry capacities well beyond mere strategic attitudes of zero-sum calculation (Taylor 2007, p. 27, pp. 35–43, 549–551, p. 592). If Rokkan is right about the higher indices of *verzuild* trust, and Casanova's prognostication of global denominationalism holds true, the paradoxical side of negatively reinforced ties of solidarity rendered universal would be affective bonds of universal species vulnerability—whereby even Axial bonds of trust are experienced as minority enclaves when set against the diversity of primary networks of trust inhabited by the majoritarian remainder of the species.

NSS (c): Subsidiarity, Reflexivity, and the Nordic Sacralization of Basic Rights—Political Trust as an Object of Unforced Consensus?

Follesdal's final concern over subsidiarity deals with the unclear shared objectives of the EU as a federal arrangement (Davies 2008, p. 80),including such noteworthy issues of constitutional magnitude as considering whether there is a shared European cultural identity (Follesdal 2009b), the prospect of a Common Foreign and Security Policy, the contentious accession of predominately Muslim Candidate State Turkey and Potential Candidates Kosovo, Bosnia-Herzegovina, and Albania, and the doctrinaire claim that the EU has its basis for legitimacy in a fundamental respect for human rights (Williams 2004; Follesdal 2007, pp. 394–396).In more direct terms, what we have comprises competing attempts to take subsidiarity as both a rational principle of institutional design and also as a cultural, expressive, moral, and political principle. In addition, insofar as other regional, international, and even cosmopolitan legal orders are following suit by attempting to emulate the successes of the EU and learn from its failures in forging other multi-level institutional complexes, they tend in varying degrees also to show a decided preference for the rationalist instrumental views of subsidiarity. Here, they have also followed the EU in emphasizing market efficiency and principled rationality in order to bypass the more messy nuances of cultural specificity that come with complicit compliance as a rational and affective threshold for democratic accountability.

For example, in the EU cases, Follesdal finds that conventional channels for appeals to subsidiarity as they currently stand in the relevant treaty legislation all too often make *post hoc* references to framework law and questionable EU-level shared objectives, rendered no less subject to contestation in light of the Lisbon compromise in the wake of the European constitutional failure in an enlarged EU (2006a, p. 66, 67, 2009b, p. 14, 15). He therefore claims that while one day in the future we may get to the point where deliberative practices are able to generate the trust required for citizens to share common goals, until then the current appeals to shared values, or even the more enthusiastic claims to the EU as a harbinger of human rights protection, have little to substantiate them. Thus normative appeals by EU courts to its complex networks of treaties, legal precedent, and the *aquis communitaire* as a quasi-constitutional charter for the EU in order to resolve the democratic deficit beg the legitimacy question by envisioning the EU-wide eventual formation of shared objectives in the future as a possible justification for European-level exclusive domains of competencies already assumed by its framework law (Taylor 2006a; Follesdal 2009b, 2000, pp. 106–107).

Instead, to advocate the reflexivity associated with multi-level governance would agree with Follesdal and not be so quick to assume that projected future ends do not undergo radical transformation in the historical process of their more localized nova and supernova formulation and implementation, even with respect to such shared common goods as basic rights, material welfare, and political trust (Melish 2009, pp. 290–295; Gerloch 2008; Follesdal 2011).However, given the incredible complexity of institutional levels in protecting rights in the EU, the potential for obscurity could itself become a major source of domination. In light of the many forms of domination that may well come with a multi-leveled institutional scheme, I will focus on two that have direct salience to human rights. The first (1) takes up the problem of an apparent double standard: requiring Member States to adhere to conditions not demanded of the EU itself. In this manner, we could say that the EU itself might fall within the required threshold of membership in Rawls' *Law of Peoples* (1999) with the ironic result that the EU would have to be qualified as a decent peoples while its Member States pass the threshold for full status as liberal peoples. As a Rawlsian justification for the precarious state of affairs, we could say that inclusion of the EU in the Society of Peoples might produce the long-term effect of making it become more democratic in gradual transitions from a decent to liberal peoples. The second (2) addresses the risk of dogma: the assumption of agreement over human rights policy in light of a manifest plurality of rights protections within its Member States. Briefly, these include but are not limited to the regional particularity of Nordic-Lutheran rights that contrast sharply with the heritage to rights in the Catholic central core of Members down to the south and the ultra-conservative approach to rights defended toward the peripheral east by Eastern Orthodox Member and Candidate states (Follesdal 2011).

(1) The first paradox deals with one precondition for EU membership: signing onto the European Convention on Human Rights through the requisite membership in the Council of Europe. However, since the EU itself is not a signatory, this leads some critics to characterize EU human rights policy as arbitrary and hypocritical, or even worse, as 'a study in irony' (Williams 2004). Although the EU itself could accede to the ECtHR, and thus have its own internal human rights policy subject to the European Court of Human Rights, it has not chosen to do so.[18] Cases concerning rights abuses can be brought to the ECtHR—or, to the European Court of Justice—against Member States but not against the EU or EC itself. Such practices unchecked could lead to either unaccountable judges offering dynamic interpretations of human rights standards or to a two-track differentiation between its internal and external rights policies (Follesdal 2009a, p. 605, 606). Internally, the lack of institutional oversight on the rights policies of the EU could lead to disillusionment concerning its own rights standards; externally, it could become a source of domination over Candidate States seeking entry when they are held to more rigorous standards than those historically expected of the EU or its Member States.

(2) The second rights paradox, the risk of dogma in light of a manifest plurality of rights protections, deals with a specific subsidiarity claim made in the preamble of the Charter that it 'reaffirms the rights as they result, in particular, from the constitutional traditions and international obligations common to the Member States' (Claes 2006, p. 691). However, even given the fact that all Member States do indeed fall under the jurisdiction of the ECtHR, many still resist the assumption that there is anything like European-wide agreement on rights (Hix 2008, p. 11; Follesdal 2011; Casanova 2014). For example, Jose Casanova details the distinctive features to the genealogy of Nordic-Lutheran rights that owe their progressive character to their religious heritage that often is falsely interpreted as absent in light of the Lutheran deferral of political authority to since (almost fully) deconfessionalized national churches. In this unique secularization narrative, the progressive character owes its ultimate impetus to the ongoing reformist sacralization of the profane:

> A new dualism now emerges between the ecclesiastical institution, which as a visible church is just, part of the *saeculum* that falls under the law of the earthly kingdom, i.e., the state, and the invisible church of eschatological communion of the saints. In the process, the 'true religion', the Kingdom of God, of Love and of the Gospel, mutates into a religion of inwardness and migrates to the individual conscience, eventually giving birth to pietist movements on the margins of the ecclesiastical institution, which prepared the ground for the modern cult of the individual and the sacralisation of human rights. Secularisation or soft 'deconfessionalisation' in this [Nordic-Scandinavian-Lutheran] context

[18] Currently the European Court of Justice relies upon the precedent of the ECtHR and is legally bound never to provide a threshold for the defense of rights within its Member States lower than that set by the ECtHR.

> means: a) continued adherence to the national church, which remains under the jurisdiction of the national sovereign; b) a drastic decline in religious (ecclesiastical) beliefs (confessional faith) and practices (rituals); c) interiorisation of a modern, individual, spiritual realm which becomes the authentic space of the sacred. (Casanova 2014, p. 29)

In addition to this distinct Nordic heritage that runs quite contrary to the Catholic heritage of subordinating states to both an external authority in the Papacy and a normative justification steeped in natural law, extending the differentiations further into contentious second and third pillar issues like minority rights seem to demonstrate little to no hope for any impending European-wide consensus (Kymlicka 2006; Bowman 2009b). In addition, the institutional schemes themselves for protecting rights within Member States can vary significantly: the Netherlands, France, Belgium, and most recently, the UK, use the basic rights and the relevant case law of the ECtHR as their formal legal-juridical system for protecting rights while countries like Italy and Germany have constitutional courts with rights jurisdiction (Claes 2006, p. 691).

Such manifest plurality would certainly become even more pervasive if a Fundamental Charter of Rights in the EU were formalized, as some Member States (like Italy and Germany with constitutional courts) would face constitutional difficulties with the prospect of the formal adoption of the Charter into EU law. This sort of multi-leveled overlap of potential rights protections could leave Member States in the possible scenario that similar cases could put the supremacy of Community law in conflict with their ECtHR treaty obligations (Claes 2006, p. 705). Such potentials for conflict might enhance rather than eliminate potentials for domination when the overburdening complexity could lead to institutional paralysis. However, Monica Klaes suggests that interpreting the judicial framework both descriptively and normatively as an experimental ground for basic rights can embrace such complexity and make an epistemic virtue out of uncoupling rights from their more familiar national confines (Hix 2008, pp. 11–12; Bowman 2009b).

> It [the ECJ] does aim to follow the Human Rights Court in actual provisions, but for the rest, it can adopt a relatively open-ended and non-exhaustive approach, using the common constitutional traditions as 'an organic and living laboratory of rights protection' which case by case and in permanent dialogue with its national counterparts can be adopted and adapted for the European Union. (Claes 2006, p. 700; Weiler 2000, p. 96)

This experimental incorporation of the precedent established by the ECtHR takes on the semblance of the potentiality for the 'unbundling' functions of Ruggie's reflexive endogenization whereby the mutual learning entailed under a dynamic rendering of subsidiarity may not necessitate uniform interpretation (Ruggie 1998; Murphy 2008, p. 29),[19] again offering a democratic destabilizing effect on entrenched forms of authority that thereby strips even basic rights of potential biases.

Since the ECtHR has historically applied its judgments to Candidate and Member States alike in the absence of anything like a collective will shared by all of its signatories, such an experimental geographic unbundling of rights is thereby more

[19] EC Treaty, Protocol 30 says: 'subsidiarity is a dynamic concept and should be applied in the light of the objectives set out in the Treaty.'

likely also to stimulate democratizing reflexive institutional change than the dubious construction of European-wide shared values, particularly when the bounds of 'Europe' itself is a contested issue (Asad 2003, p. 168, 169; Taylor 2006a; Melish 2009, p. 280).This historical instance of applying these deeply cultural spatial novelties to democratization applies even to the most debated of candidates for entry into the EU: Turkey, Albania, Kosovo, and Bosnia-Herzegovina. These serve as cases of European legal-juridical institutions radicalizing non-territorial extensions of political rights by promoting the democratization of even Candidate States as these candidates engage in active benchmarking and are rendered increasingly subject to external monitoring (Bowman 2009b; Follesdal 2009b).

5.2 Conclusion: The Multiperspectival Principle and the Political Ethics of Global Subsidiarity

For democratization to succeed in ensuring the absence of arbitrariness in EU decision-making, we thus need a politicized principle of subsidiarity for democratizing the EU as a social order while seeking to preserve rather than overcome not only its deeply cultural sources of plurality but also the confounding administrative logic of its complex three-pillar structure. This manner of responding to the democratic deficit concedes that no single all-encompassing locus or uncontested conceptualization of democracy can adequately capture its diverse practices. The multiplicity inherent in the tentative principle introduced below both describes the social fact of power abuse from many possible sources and refers to the multi-leveled prescriptive correctives to domination that must be upheld to protect those affected:

> *Multiperspectival principle* (hereafter MPP): Democratization of the EU would ensue through the elimination of one-sided arbitrary authority, by creating institutional means whereby affected subjects could contest policies with the legitimate prospect of achieving reflexive amendment of the desired balances of functional proportionality between sites of decision-making activity.

On this principle, the remedies to all forms of power abuse are normatively imperative regardless of their typology. However, given the fact that domination can come from a myriad of sources, institutionalizing prescriptive remedies becomes particularly challenging, thus requiring three main areas of focus for democratizing decision-making in the EU in order to address threats of arbitrariness. In its longer form below, these are (a) eliminating singular perspectives, (b) recasting notions of political space and time, and (c) allowing for the reflexive readjustment of both norms and institutions:

a. Decision-making as deliberative inclusion must be open to contestation from a plural *demoi*, acknowledging that the potential for revision of decisions must extend beyond any singular subject to all those potentially dominated;

b. the modal (as opposed to historical) openness to contestability calls for a fundamental revision our categories for political space and time as cleavage structures take on regional, species, and inter- and intra-Axial cosmic dimensions (thus, *cosmoi*);
c. the multi-leveled institutions realizing the democratization process must remain open-ended in order that they can undergo reflexive revision towards a more public and locally amenable realization of political proportionality in the delineation of overlapping and conflicting competences.

Drawing from the above steps, this more politicized view of subsidiarity (as opposed to a strictly legal-juridical principle) shows the potential for a multiperspectival principle to inform an appropriate kind of descriptive and prescriptive program to respond to the democratic deficit, inasmuch as proposals that appeal to subsidiarity generally do so for the sake of democratization (Paulus 2008, p. 213). However, the aforementioned employment of the multiperspectival principle must address a final concern.

Given the recommendations already made above, advocates of more conventional accounts of democracy might claim a new form of arbitrariness has arisen since subsidiarity—on an interpretation of Europe as comprising multiple modernities—could surreptitiously allow fundamentalist anti-modern movements to undermine democratic legitimacy. It is actually here that the recent resurgence of interest in the work of Eisenstadt had initially come about eventually leading to the deeper investigations into his reflections upon developing Jaspers' Axial Age 1.0 construct into the more dynamic and culturally enriched multiple modernities thesis (Axial Age 2.0). His originally perplexing claim that fundamentalism in all its contemporary forms often employs premises fully consistent with modernity has now become a commonplace assumption among sociologists of religion and political philosophers alike. In his words,

> The basic ideology of fundamentalism is anti-modern—the negation of some of the basis tenets of modernity as a civilization—*although not necessarily its technological and organizational aspects.* These movements are radically oriented against some of the basic premises of the Enlightenment, especially against the change of the place of God in the construction of the cosmos and man, and of belief in God (or in some metaphysical principles) as constituting the starting point for the understanding of both man and cosmos, the sovereignty of reason, the exploration by reason of all the aspects of nature and society, and individual autonomy and freedom. They are also strongly against the pluralistic aspects of the political program of modernity. Yet, at the same time most fundamentalist ideologies exhibit some very distinct Jacobean characteristics. Accordingly, the anti-modern attitude that develops within the fundamentalist vision is not just a reaction of traditional groups to the encroachment of new ways of life, but a militant ideology which is basically couched in highly modern idiom. (Eisenstadt 2003, pp. 937–952)

Not just taking him at his word, an initial dilemma—as recently critiqued by Habermas in reflecting on *both* German and European-wide trends—would be the resurgence of populist claims of the purported Judeo-Christian roots to Europe and its individual nation-states along with the concomitant rise in neo-conservative, far-right, anti-immigration movements throughout Europe (Habermas 2010). Some of the proponents of a thick European identity required to forge greater political integration therefore want to keep the bounds of Europe as they stand and reinforce the perceived heritage of the continent steeped in Latin Christendom (Eisenstadt 2003, pp. 937–951; Eisenstadt 2006).[20]

In addition, at the advent of a postsecular age (Axial Age 3.0), alternative modernities will continue to proliferate via huge immigrant populations and lacking cultural and political integration into host societies may increase the perceived threat of their own forms of rising fundamentalism. For instance, sentiments of Islamophobia have been stoked in Europe through the prospect of an impending Turkish accession (estimated at 2020 at the earliest) that could be potentially followed by Albanian, Bosnian-Herzegovinan, and/or Kosovoan ones (no real perceived completion date on anyone's political policy horizon). This leads some alarmists to name the main ideological visions for the future of Europe to include a new regional vision for an impending Eurabia via its growing Muslim contingency (Kerr 2010, p. 323).

Along the same lines, and also with pejorative connotations would be the rise of Eurasia via the strategic importance of Russia, China, India and the increasing opportunities for forging economic, militaristic, and geo-political alliances between West and East (such as BRICS) rather than the former assumption of bowing Western to American hegemonic influence. These trends simultaneously bolster the importance of Europe on the geo-political landscape and aid in the challenge of the hegemonic grip of US foreign policy over both European and Asian regions, thus highlighting the strategic importance of Turkey, Russia, Afganistan, Syria, and others in the regional bloc termed Eurasia (Habermas 2011).

As replies to the aforementioned visions of alternative modernities in their romantic manifestations, yet a fourth vision of modernity often supported by Euro-secularists would regard the postsecular turn leading closer to Huntington's impending clash of civilizations (Rasmussen 2010, p. 348). In this light, detractors of the postsecular turn see in a prolonged secularization of the Europe Union the institutional precursors to a cosmopolitan federated order that would fare best by de-emphasizing culture and focus on secular principles for a more rational European *and* global order.

Finally, as a fifth vision of an even more anonymous European modernity would be the EU as proxy for all global cultures as universal translator (Delanty 2005).On this view, there is no substantive core of what it means to be European except to be

[20] Eisenstadt draws parallels between the utopian visions of the Great Revolutions and the messianic/eschatological visions of the fundamentalist strands of the Axial traditions: 'It is this new view of society, i.e., the view of society as an object of active construction by human beings—above all by political action—that constitutes one of the distinct characteristics of the cosmologies of these revolutions. They proclaimed the primacy of the political as being closely related to such visions in the process of the reconstruction of society. These dimensions of the Great Revolutions have become most fully manifest in Jacobian ideologies and movements—and they are shared, at least potentially, by many of the modern fundamentalist movements. The strong totalitarian, Jacobin-like component of these movements is visible…in the almost total conflation of center and periphery, negating the existence of intermediary institutions and association—of what can sometimes be called civil society, conflating civil society with the total community' (pp. 941–942).

the universal borrower, exchanger, redactor, and integrator of new cultural views from the outside in for a richer integration of many cultures that only find uniformity in their shared subjection to historical redaction and modification.

The question of what Europe would be best for a more just and democratic future may not necessarily be the same one as which empirical description of the sociological facts seems most convincing. However, on my proposal, in a Europe of multiple modernities that embraced the moral-ethical construal of subsidiarity as an alternative to the predominate legal-juridical view must include within its overlapping consensus its abiding commitment to social-welfare institutions to buttress against growing pressures toward global neo-liberalism. Here is where the Nordic-Scandinavian casting of subsidiarity has proven most successful, in positing a middle-way between Anglo-Saxon market and Continental bureaucratic excesses. While Follesdal concedes the new challenges posed by a growing multiculturalism, he does not see them as insurmountable:

> First, public discussions in the Nordic countries often center on whether multiculturalism threatens support for the welfare regimes. The experiences of the Netherlands and Belgium show that states can maintain high levels of universal welfare systems without homogeneity. However, the requisite bases of trust and the appropriate means for fostering such social capital are not yet sufficiently addressed. Moreover, homogeneity makes for simpler social policies, in that the same problems can be resolved by the same measures applied to all. Second, the increased variety of life plans requires renewed attention to how best to operationalise the state's commitment to equality whilst respecting diversity. Social reporting in the Nordic countries largely focuses on individuals' objective levels of resources—the things a person should have—should be secured as equally as possible, rather than for instance asking individuals about their subjective sense of well-being. The focus is on resources necessary to affect the capacity to satisfy one's basic needs, and that are under social influence. (Follesdal 2011, p. 187, 188)

While he does not deem it necessary to give precise speculations about where Europe is headed before getting there in the most just and democratic manner institutionally, he nonetheless regards the Nordic assurance of moral trust as inseparable from securing the economic and material capacities to exercise one's deliberative powers (Gerloch 2008, p. 129; Bohman 1996). His call for further investigation into the capability networks required to ensure the requisite social capital in a context of global economic interdependence will provide the material for my final chap. 6 that specifically centers on elaborating Amartya Sen's insights in this realm, thereby seeking to affirm Follesdal's ties between material and moral well-being.

If my empirical and normative evaluations are on track, the multiperspectical recasting of subsidiarity as the starting place seems not only best for the European case but also an ideal to strive for globally as we head into a *cosmoi*politan (rather than cosmopolitan) era (Bowman 2012). By embracing the romantic heritage of the principle of subsidiarity, the rational mediation of legal-juridical institutions conceding to multiple modernists the enduring sociological fact of Europe's many conflicting and competing cultures may (Bohman 2013), in the end, produce a pacifying effect leading to political *and* fiscal stability that imperial-like secularizing cosmopolitanism, despite all its austere motivations, might prove the worst route to pursue (Howse and Nicolaidis 2008).[21] In this *cosmoi*politan context—akin to the quasi-denizen status of the citizens of each Member State with respect to the rest of the citizens of the EU—each alternative form of modernity already shares in common with its Axial *and* secular competitors the epistemic status of permanent minority (Preuss 1996, p. 138).[22] This is not just in light of Europe's rich geneology but also if it might continue to serve as a novel order worthy of redactive emulation in an increasingly interdependent context of pervasive globality. With the growing array of externalities that stretch the jurisdiction of nation-states as a global and not just a regional problem, our best hope will be to draw upon the epistemic differentiation provided by the deep histories of each distinct social imaginary. The end to the plausibility of a univocal European narrative to secularity should also lay to rest the naïve ideology that the rational can and therefore must be interchangeable with the secular (Rasmussen 2012, p. 348).

References

Allhardt, Eric. 2005. Europe's multiple modernities. In *Comparing modernities: Pluralism versus homogeneity, essays in homage to S.N. Eisenstadt,* eds. E. Ban-Rafael and Y. Sternberg, 483–500. Boston: Brill Academic Publishers.

Allhardt, Eric, and Henry Valen. 1999. Stein Rokkan: An intellectual profile. In *Mobilization, center-periphery structures, and nation-building: A volume in honor of Stein Rokkan,* ed. Per Torsvik, 11–38. Oslo: Universitersforlaget.

Asad, Talal. 2003. *Formations of the Secular: Christianity, Islam, Modernity*. Stanford: Stanford University Press.

Baum, Gregory. 2010. The response of a theologian to Charles Taylor's a secular age. *Modern Theology* 26 (3): 363–381.

Bohman, James. 1996. *Public deliberation: Pluralism, complexity, and democracy*. Cambridge: MIT Press.

Bohman, James. 2004. Constitution making and democratic innovation: The European Union and transnational governance. *European Journal of Political Theory* 3 (3): 315–337.

Bohman, James. 2007a. *Democracy across borders: From demos to demoi*. Cambridge: MIT Press.

Bohman, James. 2007b. The epistemic benefits of diversity. *Episteme* 3 (3), pp. 175–190.

[21] In bringing the aforementioned insights of the European experience with the successes of the Nordic/Scandinavian subsidiarity as it might be integrated with the simultaneous commitment to a principle of political proportionality, Howse and Nicolaidis refer to what they term 'the political ethics of global subsidiarity: 'As an anchor for such a global political ethics, we come back to the spirit of subsidiarity, stripping the legal principle of its narrow meaning of the allocation of power. Instead we take it to mean that the transnational management of social conflict is more likely to be legitimate if addressed by the appropriate people in the appropriate 'space' of governance and in the appropriate way….[W]hile the transformation of insider network 'governance' by political ethics is unlikely to be rapid or easy, eventually the network will have to make itself open to this political ethics or it will simply continue to lose to other mechanisms of governance in the competition for legitimacy' (pp. 184–185).

[22] In the European context, Ulrich Preuss calls this entering into a state of permanent alienage (p. 138). I would like to preserve the original sense of its use in describing EU citizenship but adapt it to species membership in a postsecular and *cosmoi*politan age.

Bohman, James. 2013. A postsecular global order? The pluralism of forms of life and communicative freedom. In *Habermas and religion*, eds. C. Calhoun, E. Mendieta, and J. VanAntwerpen, 179–202. Cambridge: Polity Press.
Bowman, Jonathan. 2006. The European Union democratic deficit: Federalists, skeptics, and revisionists. *European Journal of Political Theory* 5 (2): 191–212.
Bowman, Jonathan. 2007. Challenging Habermas' response to the European Union democratic deficit. *Philosophy and Social Criticism* 33 (6): 736–755.
Bowman, Jonathan. 2009a. Extending Habermas and Ratzinger's *Dialectics of Secularization*: Non-western discursive influences on faith and reason in a postsecular age. *Forum Philosophicum* 16 (1): 39–56.
Bowman, Jonathan. 2009b. Immigrant rights and regional inclusion: Democratic experimentalism, the European Union, and immigration. *Theoria: A Journal of Social and Political Theory*, Special Issue on the Politics and Practice of Migration 121: 32–56.
Bowman, Jonathan. 2012. Why *Cosmoi*politan justice in a postsecular age? Taylor and Habermas on European versus American exceptionalism. *Philosophy and Social Criticism* 38 (2): 127–47.
Casanova, Jose. 2014. The two dimensions, temporal and spatial, of the secular: Comparative reflections on the Nordic Protestant and Southern Catholic patterns from a global perspective. In *Secular and sacred? The Scandinavian case of religion in human rights, law and public space,* eds. Rosemarie van der Breemer, Jose Casanova, and Trygve Wyller, 21–33. Bristol: Vandenhoeck and Ruprecht.
Christoffersen, Lisbet. 2014. Sacred spaces in secular (post)-Lutheran contexts: The summer 2009 case of Copenhagen 'church asylum' of 60 Iraqis. In *Secular and Sacred? The Scandinavian case of religion in human rights, law and public space*, eds. Rosemarie van der Breemer, Jose Casanova, and Trygve Wyller, 102–122. Bristol: Vandenhoeck and Ruprecht.
Claes, Monica. 2006. *The national courts' mandate in the European constitution.* Oxford: Hart Publishing.
Connolly, A., S. Day, and J. Shaw. 2006. The contested case of EU electoral rights. In *Making European citizens: Civic inclusion in a transnational process,* eds. R. Bellamy, D. Castiglione, and J. Shaw, 31–55. New York: Palgrave MacMillan.
Cooke, Maeve. 2013. Violating neutrality? Religious validity claims and democratic legitimacy. In *Habermas and Religion,* eds. Calhoun, Mendieta, and VanAntwerpen, 249–278. Cambridge: Polity Press.
Cooper, Ian. 2006. The watchdogs of subsidiarity: National parliaments and the logic of arguing in the European Union. *Journal of Common Market Studies* 44 (2): 281–304.
Dashwood, Alan. 2008. Subsidiarity, National Parliaments and the Lisbon Treaty. British House of Commons. European Scrutiny Committee, 33rd Report, Session 2007–08, pp. EV1-EV8. http://www.publications.parliament.uk/pa/cm200708/cmselect/cmeuleg/563/563.pdf. Accessed 12 Dec 2012
Davies, Gareth. 2008. Subsidiarity as a mode of policy centralization. In *The shifting allocation of authority in international law: Considering sovereignty, supremacy and subsidiarity,* eds. Tomer Broude and Yuval Shany. 79–98. Oxford: Hart Publishing.
Delanty, Gerard. 2005. Cultural translations and European modernity. In *Comparing modernities: Pluralism versus homogeneity, essays in homage to S.N. Eisenstadt,* eds. E. Ban-Rafael and Y. Sternberg, 443–460. Boston: Brill Academic Publishers.
Dobson, Lynn. 2004. Conceptions of freedom and the European constitution. In *Political theory and the European constitution,* eds. Andreas Follesdal and Lynn Dobson, 103–121. London: Routledge.
Eisenstadt, S. N. 2003a. *Comparative civilizations and multiple modernities*, part I. Leiden: Brill Publishers.
Eisenstadt, S. N. 2003b. *Comparative civilizations and multiple modernities*, part II. Leiden: Brill Publishers.
Eisenstadt, S. N. 2006. *The great revolutions and the civilizations of modernity*. Leiden: Brill Publishers.

Flora, Peter. 1999. Introduction and interpretation. In *State formation, nation-building and mass politics in Europe: The theory of Stein Rokkan based on his collected works,* eds. Peter Flora, Stein Kuhnle, and Derik Urwin, 1–91. New York: Oxford University Press.

Follesdal, Andreas. 1998a. Survey article: Subsidiarity. *Journal of Political Philosophy* 6 (2): 190–219.

Follesdal, Andreas. 1998b. Democracy, legitimacy, and majority rule in the European Union. In *Political theory and the European Union: Legitimacy, constitutional choice, and citizenship,* eds. A. Weale and M. Nentwich, 34–48. New York: Routledge.

Follesdal, Andreas. 2000. Subsidiarity and democratic deliberation. In *Democracy in the European Union: Integration through deliberation?,* eds. Erik Eriksen and John Fossum, 85–110. London: Routledge.

Follesdal, Andreas. 2006a. Subsidiarity, democracy, and human rights in the constitutional treaty of Europe. *Journal of Social Philosophy* 37 (1): 61–80.

Follesdal, Andreas. 2006b. Between petros and a hard place: Human rights to religious liberty or gender equality in Europe? In *Gender, religion, human rights in Europe,* eds. Kari Børresen and Sara Cabibbo, 63–83. Rome: Herder.

Follesdal, Andreas. 2007. Epilogue: Toward more legitimate multilevel regulation. *Multilevel regulation and the EU,* eds. Follesdal, Wessel, and Wouters, 377–398. Amsterdam: Koninklijke Brill.

Follesdal, Andreas. 2008. International judicial human rights review—effective, legitimate, or both? *Studies Across Disciplines in Humanities and Social Sciences* 4: 196–215.

Follesdal, Andreas. 2009a. The legitimacy of international human rights review: The case of the European Court of human rights. *Journal of Social Philosophy* 40 (4): 595–607.

Follesdal, Andreas. 2009b. If there is no common and unique European identity, should we create one? In *Multiculturalism and nationalism in a world of immigration,* eds. K. Lippert-Rasmussen, et al. 194–227. Basingstoke: Palgrave.

Follesdal, Andreas. 2010a. *Non-state oriented political theory: a critical assessment,* eds. J. Neyer and A. Wiener, 205–212. Oxford: Oxford University Press.

Follesdal, Andreas. 2010b. When 'common interests' are not common: Why the 'global basic structure' should be democratic. *Indiana Journal of Global Legal Studies* 16 (2): 1–23.

Follesdal, Andreas. 2011. Rawls in the Nordic countries. *European Journal of Political Theory* 1 (2): 181–198. Special issue on 'Rawls in Europe'.

Follesdal, Andreas. 2014. Competing conceptions of subsidiarity. In *Nomos LV: Federalism and subsidiarity,* eds. J.E. Fleming and J.T. Levy, 214–230. New York: New York University Press.

Follesdal, Andreas, and Marlene Wind. 2009. Introduction: Nordic reluctance toward judicial review under siege. *Nordisk Tidsskrift for Menneskerettigheter* 27 (2): 131–41.

Follesdal, Andreas, Ramses Wessel, and Jan Wouters. 2007. Multilevel regulation and the EU: A brief introduction. Multilevel regulation and the EU, eds. Follesdal, Wessel, and Wouters, 1–6. Amsterdam: Koninklijke Brill.

Gerloch, Ales. 2008. Some considerations about the application of the principle of subsidiarity upon the public execution of power. In *The process of constitutionalisation of the EU and related issues,* ed. Nadezda Siskova, 123–130. Groningen: Europa Law Publishing.

Habermas, J. 1983. Modernity: An incomplete project. In *The anti-aesthetic: Essays on postmodern culture,* ed. Hal Foster, 3–15. Seattle: Bay Press.

Habermas, J. 1987. *The theory of communicative action, volume two, lifeworld and system: A critique of functionalist reason*. Trans: Thomas McCarthy. Boston: Beacon Press.

Habermas, J. 1998. *The inclusion of the other*. Cambridge: MIT Press.

Habermas, J. 1999. The European nation-state and the pressures of globalization. *New Left Review* 235:46–54.

Habermas, J. 2001a. Why Europe needs a constitution. *New Left Review* 11:5–26.

Habermas, J. 2001b. *The postnational constellation: Political essays*. Trans: Max Pensky. Cambridge: MIT Press.

Habermas, J. 2006. *The divided west*. Trans: Ciaran Cronin. Cambridge: Polity Press.

Habermas, J. 2008. *Between naturalism and religion*. Trans: Ciaran Cronin. Cambridge: Polity Press.

Habermas, J. 2010. Leadership and Leitkultur. *New York Times*. http://www.nytimes.com/2010/10/29/opinion/29Habermas.html?pagewanted=all&_r=0. Accessed 28 Oct 2010

Habermas, J. 2011. *A pact for or against Europe. In What does Germany think about Europe?*, eds. Ulrike Guerot and Jacqueline Henard, 83–89 London: European Council on Foreign Relations. Text online at http://www.ecfr.eu/page/-/ECFR36_GERMANY.pdf. Accessed 18 Feb 2013

Habermas, J., J. Butler, C. Taylor, and C. West. 2011. *The power of religion in the public sphere*, (A Columbia/SSRC Book) eds Afterword by Craig Calhoun. Eduardo Mendieta and Jonathan VanAntwerpen. New York: Columbia University Press.

Halberstam, Daniel. 2009. Federal powers and the principle of subsidiarity. In *Global perspectives on constitutional law*, eds. Vikram D. Amar and Mark V. Tushnet, 34–47. Oxford University Press: Oxford.

Heidenreich, Martin. 2006. The Europeanization of solidarity: Between global markets, national institutions and European regulations. *Globality Studies Journal* 2:1–19.

Himmelstrand, Ulf. 1960. *Social pressures, attitudes, and democratic processes*. Stockholm: Almqvist and Wiksell.

Hix, Simon. 2008. Subsidiarity, National Parliaments and the Lisbon Treaty. British House of Commons. European Scrutiny Committee, 33rd Report, Session 2007–08, pp. EV9-EV16. http://www.publications.parliament.uk/pa/cm200708/cmselect/cmeuleg/563/563.pdf. Accessed 12 Dec 2012

Howse, Robert, and Kalypso Nicolaides. 2008. Democracy without sovereignty: The global vocation of political ethics. In *The shifting allocation of authority in international law: Considering sovereignty, supremacy, and subsidiarity*, eds. Tomer Broude and Yaval Shany, 163–191. Oxford: Hart Publishing.

Kerr, Fergus. 2010. How much can a philosopher do? *Modern Theology* 26 (3): 321–36.

Kymlicka, Will. 2006. The evolving basis of European norms of minority rights: Rights to culture, participation, and autonomy. In *European integration and the nationalities question*, eds. John McGarry and Michael Keating, 35–63. London: Routledge.

LaBorde, Cecile. 2001. The culture(s) of the republic: Nationalism and multiculturalism in French republican thought. *Political Theory* 29 (5): 716–735.

Lavdas, Kostas. 2001. Republican Europe and multicultural citizenship. *Politics* 21 (1): 1–10.

MacCormick, Neil. 1997. Democracy, subsidiarity, and citizenship in the 'European commonwealth'. *Law and Philosophy* 16:339–352.

Martin, David. 2006. Integration and fragmentation: Patterns of religion in Europe. In *Religion in the New Europe*, ed. Krzysztof Michalski, 64–84. Budapest: CEU Press.

McCarthy, Thomas. 2013. The burdens of modernized faith and postmetaphysical reason in public discourse. In *Habermas and religion*, eds. C. Calhoun, E. Mendieta, and J. VanAntwerpen, 115–131. Cambridge: Polity Press.

Melish, Tara. 2009. From paradox to subsidiarity: The United States and human rights treaty bodies. In *The sword and the scales: The United States and International Courts and Tribunals*, 210–296. Cambridge: Cambridge University Press.

Milbank, John. 2013a. What lacks is feeling: Human versus Kant and Habermas. In *Habermas and Religion*, eds. E. Mendieta and J Van Antwerpen, 322–346. Cambidge: Polity Press.

Milbank, John. 2013b. The Blue Labour dream. See online at http://richardsrobinson.org.uk/2013/07/the-blue-labour-dream-by-professor-john-millbank/. Accessed 07 Sep 2013

Murphy, Jim. 2008. Subsidiarity, national parliaments and the Lisbon treaty." British House of Commons. European Scrutiny Committee, 33rd Report, Session 2007–08, pp. EV25-EV35. http://www.publications.parliament.uk/pa/cm200708/cmselect/cmeuleg/563/563.pdf. Accessed 12 Dec 2012

Paulus, Andreas. 2008. Subsidiarity, fragmentation, and democracy: Towards the demise of general international law. In *The shifting allocation of authority in international law: Considering sovereignty, supremacy and subsidiarity*, eds. Tomer Broude and Yuval Shany, 193–216. Oxford: Hart Publishing.

Pettit, Philip. 1997. *Republicanism: A theory of freedom and government*. Oxford: Oxford University Press.

Philpott, Daniel, and Timothy Shah. 2006. Faith, freedom, and federation: The role of religious ideas and institutions in European political convergence. In *Religion in an expanding Europe,* eds. Timothy Byrnes and Peter Katzenstein, 34–64. Cambridge: Cambridge University Press.

Pogge, Thomas. 1997. Creating supra-national institutions democratically: Reflections on the European Union's democratic deficit. *Journal of Political Philosophy* 5:163–182.

Preuss, Ulrich. 1996. Two challenges to European citizenship. In *Constitutionalism in transformation: European and theoretical perspectives,* eds. Richard Bellamy and Dario Castiglione, 122–140. Oxford: Blackwell Publishers.

Rasmussen, David. 2010. Conflicted modernity: Toleration as a principle of justice. *Philosophy and Social Criticism* 36 (3–4): 339–352.

Rasmussen, David. 2012. The emerging domain of the political. *Philosophy and Social Criticism* 38 (4–5): 457–466.

Rawls, John. 1999. *The Law of peoples*. Cambridge: Harvard University Press.

Rokkan, Stein. 1981. Territories, nations, parties: Toward a geoeconomic-geopolitical model for the explanation of variations within Western Europe. In *From national development to global community: Essays in honor of Karl W. Deutsch,* eds. Richard Merritt and Bruce Russett, 70–95. Boston: G. Allen and Unwin.

Rokkan, Stein. 1999a. State formation, nation-building, and mass politics in Europe: the theory of Stein Rokkan, eds. Peter Flora, Stein Kuhnle, and Derek Urwin, Oxford: Oxford University Press.

Rokkan, Stein. 1999b. *Mobilization, center-periphery structures, and nation-building: A volume in honor of Stein Rokkan,* ed. Per Torsvik. Oslo: Universitersforlaget.

Ruggie, John G. 1998. *Constructing the world polity: Essays on international institutionalization.* New York: Routledge.

Sabel, Charles, and Joshua Cohen. 2004. Sovereignty and solidarity: EU and US. In *Public governance in the age of globalization,* ed. Karl-Heinz Ladeur, 157–175. London: Ashgate Publishing.

Sen, Amartya. 2010. *The idea of justice*. New York: Penguin Books.

Smith, Christian, and Brandon Vaidyanathan. 2011. Multiple modernities and religion. In *The Oxford handbook of religious diversity,* ed. Chad Meister. 250–265. Oxford: Oxford University Press.

Taylor, C. 1989. *Sources of the self: The making of modern identity*. Cambridge: Harvard University Press.

Taylor, C. 2001. Two theories of modernity. In *Alternative Modernities,* ed. Dilip Gaonkar, 172–196. Duke: Duke UP.

Taylor, C. 2006a. Religion and European integration. In *Religion in the New Europe,* ed. Krzysztof Michalski, 1–22. Budapest: CEU Press.

Taylor, C. 2006b. Conditions of an unforced consensus on human rights." In *Applied ethics: A multicultural approach,* eds. Larry May, Collins-Chobanian, and Kai Wong, 143–158. Upper Saddle River: Prentice Hall.

Taylor, C. 2007. *A secular age*. Cambridge: Belknap Press.

Taylor, C. 2012. Accommodating diversity: Received models under scrutiny: Interculturalism or multiculturalism? *Philosophy & Social Criticism* 38 (4–5): 413–423.

Veggeland, Noralv. 2007. *Paths of public innovation in the global age: Lessons from Scandinavia*. Northampton: Edward Elgar.

Vjekoslav, Perica. 2006. The politics of ambivalence: Europeanization and the Serbian orthodox church. In *Religion in an expanding Europe,* eds. Timothy Byrnes and Peter Katzenstein, 176–203. Cambridge: Cambridge University Press.

Weiler, Joseph. 2000. Editorial: Does the European Union need a charter of rights? *European Law Journal* 6 (2): 95–97.

Williams, Andrew. 2004. *EU human rights policies: A study in irony*. Oxford: Oxford University Press.

Witte, John. 2014. God is hidden in the earthly kingdom: The Lutheran tw-kingdoms theory as foundation of Scandinavian secularity. In *Secular and Sacred? The Scandinavian case of religion in human rights, law and public space,* eds. Rosemarie van der Breemer, Jose Casanova, and Trygve Wyller, 56–84. Bristol: Vandenhoeck and Ruprecht.

Wyller, Trygve. 2014. The undocumented embodied: Shaping the space where the sacred an secular intertwine. In *Secular and sacred? The Scandinavian case of religion in human rights, law and public space,* eds. Rosemarie van der Breemer, Jose Casanova, and Trygve Wyller, 221–235. Bristol: Vandenhoeck and Ruprecht.

Part III
Axial Period Three—The Postsecular Turn

Chapter 6
Conclusion—Western vs. Eastern Replies to the Inverse Economic Pyramid: Innovation, Development, and the Material Future of Cosmoipolitan Justice

Abstract Managerial, marketing, production, research, and human capital innovations in the emerging world—particularly in China and India—have led to a barrage of cleverly coined phrases such as 'reverse innovation,' 'inverse innovation pyramids,' 'frugal innovation,' and even 'disruptive innovation.' These trends in neo-innovation call for incremental improvement, collaborative exchange between suppliers and consumers, and markets targeting the middle and lower tiers of the global economic pyramid. Insofar as many of these models emphasize investment in human and cultural capital over sheer growth of economic capital, they also lead to an array of exotic corporate species that befuddle Western observers. Sen explains these best in terms of his conciliatory and dialectical assimilation of market efficiencies matched with the egalitarian assurance of democratic legitimation. In contrast, Lander privileges neo-liberal market approaches to the global economy as the unique achievement of the West, Europe, UK, and the USA as global template for future innovation. At the other extreme, Onuma offers a neo-Marxist critique of a long history of Eurocentric economic and moral exploitation of non-Western powers via the domineering imposition of an inherently biased and overly individualistic framework for international law. Once I lay out Sen's capability account as a viable middle way, I conclude with four non-Western economic and social innovations that lend credence to inter-Axial—East to West—moral, social, and technological learning. I commend their mutually reinforcing material and egalitarian efficacy at expanding the capability sets of those at the middle and bottom of the global inverse pyramid.

Keywords Capabilities · Development · Globalization · Guanxi · Human capital · Innovation · Inverse pyramid · Jugaad · Marc Lander · Yusuaki Onuma · Amartya Sen · Shanzhai · sacralized redistribution

J. Bowman, *Cosmoipolitan Justice*, Studies in Global Justice 15,
DOI 10.1007/978-3-319-12709-5_6

6.1 Introduction

The conventional Western model of economic innovation elicits images of transformative technological breakthroughs and revolutionary new inventions produced by strategic, entrepreneurial, self-assertive elites. These novelties are then graciously disseminated to the masses via centralized processes of manufacturing that thereby seek to maximize growth and economic capital. However, managerial, marketing, production, research, and human capital innovations in the emerging world—particularly in China and India—are turning these paradigmatic conceptions upside down, leading to a barrage of cleverly coined phrases such as reverse innovation, inverse innovation pyramids, frugal innovation, and even disruptive innovation. Diverse in the array of products and processes, these trends in neo-innovation call for incremental improvement, collaboratively dynamic exchange between suppliers and consumers, and markets targeting the billions of persons comprising the demographic of the middle and lower tiers of the global economic pyramid (Wooldridge 2010). Insofar as many of these models emphasize investment in human and cultural capital over sheer growth of income, they also lead to an array of exotic corporate species that befuddle Western observers.

It is my contention that the attendant shift in understanding of successful economic innovation will call for a radical reinterpretation of the nature, practices, and goals of economics as a social science in the West. Fortunately, I will not have to take up such a gestalt enterprise alone since much of the required work has already been done by Nobel Prize winning economist, professor, philosopher, and ethicist Amartya Sen. In his first major work, *Inequality Reexamined* (1992), he anticipates such a shift in social-welfare analysis from income comparison to measurements of aggregate social well-being and freedom:

> If the fundamental fact of human diversity and its far-reaching implications come to be recognized more widely in welfare-economic analysis and in public-policy assessment, then the approach would certainly need some radical transformation. The operations would have to move from the income space to the space of the constitutive elements of well-being and also of freedom, if the intrinsic importance of freedom, discussed earlier, is accepted. Social-welfare analysis would then take a different form, and the evaluation of inequality and of distributional badness would then have to reflect that foundational transformation. (Sen 1992, p. 101)

Sen calls for a return to the lost heritage of economics as an inherently moral and social discipline (that he notes, was indeed still present in Adam Smith). In treating economics in terms much grander than the strict domain of profit margins, supply and demand curves, and cold impersonal mathematics, he seeks to retrieve the necessary human element to this social science. As a representative from the largest democracy in the world, he also emphasizes dimensions from the Indian experience that reinforce essential ties between market efficiency and democratic accountability. While he concedes electoral politics alone do not constitute the benchmark for the substantive merits of democratic orders, he does gain credence both in counter critiques that democracy is a predominately Western phenomena and also critiques of questions of scale for the prospects of global democratization insofar as India boasts a functional democracy comprised of more than a billion persons organized into upwards of 200 distinct political parties (2013, p. 249).

> [C]ompared with the United States (an aspiring torch-bearer of democracy in the contemporary world), India fares better in many respects. For instance, India has much higher voter turnout rates (the United States has near the bottom of the international scale in that respect); it has more extensive provisions for the political representation of socially disadvantaged groups; and it is less vulnerable to the influence of 'big money' in electoral politics. There are fewer disputes on the outcome of elections in India than in the United States (the drama of 'hanging chads', as in the disputed election of 2000, and other counting battles seem to separate the American elections from their Indian counterparts). There is also far greater pluralism in Indian than in US politics. Dozens of political parties, from extreme left to extreme right, are represented in the Indian Parliament, in contrast with just two parties (with very similar positions on many issues) in the United States Congress. (Sen and Dreze 2013, p. 249)

By mixing the greatest insights of American, Chinese, and Indian political successes and failures, he also incorporates non-Western philosophies as they reaffirm or contrast with the Western classics written by Karl Marx and Adam Smith. In extending his conceptual genealogies of the Buddhist, Hindu, Confucian, and Ancient Greek traditions back to the historical context of Jaspers' initial Axial Age breakthrough, he also brings a neo-Aristotelian element to economics as a science devoted to enhancing well-being and the capability to function in social, morally, and rationally fulfilling manners. In his most recent work, *The Ideal of Justice*, he describes the enterprise as follows:

> The approach developed in this book is much influenced by the tradition of social choice theory…and concentrates, as the discipline of social choice does, one making evaluative comparisons over distinct social realizations. In this respect, the approach here also has important similarities with the works of Adam Smith, Jeremy Bentham, John Stuart Mill and Karl Marx, among others. While the roots of the approach go back to the Enlightenment, there is a significant contrast with another tradition particularly cultivated over that period—the discipline of reasoning about justice in terms of the idea of the social contract. (Sen 2010, pp. 410–411)

As an practical elucidation of the shift proposed above, in the relevant footnote to these claims, he demonstrates the layered heritage behind both his ability to engage in the history of economics as a moral practice in its Western heritage of intellectuals while also bringing to bare the cultural influence of his upbringing in India:

> I have also discussed earlier the similarity between the approach here and the long Indian tradition of seeking justice as *nyaya* (concentrating on comprehensive outcomes), rather than *niti* (focusing on arrangements and institutions). (Sen 2010, p. 411)

While the invocation of social choice theory might lead the uninitiated audience to presume the vestiges of a neo-liberal individualism permeating his ethical-moral approach, perhaps the crowning achievement of his *Development as Freedom* are his concluding insights that individual responsibility always already presupposes robust institutional conditions for its exercise as a functional capability (1999, p. 284). Akin to a slave that cannot responsibly opt for freedom, he finds that it would be naïve to suppose that the solution to dilemmas faced by developing nations rest upon sheer aggregate increases in income alone. He transforms both domestic and international rubrics of assessment of economic health away from sheer income growth of individuals and GDP/GNP of nation-states, into the more complexly rich domain of enhancing comparative indices that he respectively terms capability sets. As brief examples, the holistic range of these reflexive and mutually reinforcing capabilities to function with individual responsibility include: literacy and numeracy, low infant and adult mortality rates, gendered egalitarianism, social welfare safety nets, health care institutions, means to political participation in decision-making, market-steering legal mechanisms, cultural and religious liberties, famine prevention through democratic accountability of leaders, employment opportunities, and access to educational and job training institutions (Sen 1992, pp. 39–42, 1999, 2010, pp. 388–389).

In order to demonstrate the balanced tenor of Sen's neo-Aristotelian and/or neo-Buddhist middle way—or perhaps even neo-Confucian doctrine of the mean—I will first engage in a brief overview of two contemporary representatives of philosophical extremes that Sen both wants to concede some degree of truth without fully endorsing their radical excesses. On the one hand, I will use the work of contemporary Harvard social scientist M. Lander as something of a representative of Adam Smith's model of privileging neo-liberal market approaches to the global economy at the extreme of championing the unique achievement of the West, Europe, and the USA as the global template for future material innovation. On the other hand, I will employ the social scientific legal scholarship of Onuma Yasuaki as a neo-Marxist critique of a long history of Eurocentric economic and moral exploitation of non-Western powers. Onuma sees no impending end to neo-colonial forms of exploitation insofar as the domineering imposition of an inherently biased and overly individualistic framework for international law continues to predominate (Onuma 2010; Zakaria 2008).

Once I lay out these two alternative extremes of the spectrum, I will return to a further explanation of Sen's capability account of *Development as Freedom* (1999), specifically focusing on his views of globalization and culture. My contribution will be to connect his capability approach to economic science with the recent attention given globally to the role of the 'emerging economies'—particularly in India, China, and East Asia—in reshaping both Eastern and Western understandings of the role of innovation in navigating the complex benefits and harms of increased globalization, including the pronounced end of and hope for national insularity against global dynamics that thereby constitute a shared materialist species-ethic of interdependence.

> China has joined—and become a leader of—the world economy with stunning success, and from this India, like many other countries, has been learning a great deal, particularly in the recent years. The insularity of the earlier Indian approach to economic development needed to be replaced and here the experience of China has been profoundly important. There are great lessons also from China's early move to universalized health care and education. But the role of democratic participation in India suggests that some learning and understanding may go in the other direction as well. As it happens, India is the only country in the outside world to which scholars from ancient China went for education and training. The overcoming of cultural insularity that we can observe both in China and in India in the first millennium has continuing interest and practical usefulness in the world today…

> India and China learned a lot from each other in the first millennium, but the significance of that epistemic process has not dried up even at the beginning of the third millennium. (Sen 2005, pp. 189–190)

After doing the conceptual work needed to explain Sen's views in light of its multi-faceted Indian, Chinese, European, and American influences, I will further illustrate the changing dynamics between Eastern and Western approaches to a shared global economy by focusing on three Eastern forms of innovative novelty: firstly, Indian *jugaad*, secondly, Chinese *guanxi* and, thirdly, *shanzhai*. Lastly, I conclude with a specifically African case to seek to address the development economics of the growing North-South divide that is seeming to replace the old East vs. West dichotomy. The cases from Africa examine the conferral of authority upon various aid networks that produce a hybridization of pre-Axial local, Axial universalism, and post-Axial contemporary domains to constitute what I call—for sheer lack of a better concise terminology in the attendant literature—sacralized redistribution. Here I will attempt to apply some of the dynamics Casanova saw in the Nordic-Lutheran approach to basic rights to socio-economic rights as formulated in the unique hybridization of pre-Axial tribal forms and the post-Axial and post-colonial African re-appropriation of Abrahamic traditions.

While assuming moral learning through innovation cuts across a variety of business disciplines and takes on an array of institutional, technological, and scientific manifestations, we will not presume any one common cultural framework or the inherent superiority of a Western approach. Not only do I intend to hint at the historical and cultural successes of the Indian *jugaad* model of frugal engineering, the Chinese neo-Confucian model of *guanxi* as social networking, the Chinese practice of *shanzhai* as bandit/guerrilla innovation, and the African creative melding of pre-Axial and Axial models of authoritative trust through *sacralized redistribution*, but I will also conclude with some brief remarks on the implications of these novelties for challenging Western understandings of human nature and economics as a social science. I will follow Sen in presuming an inherent tie between market efficiencies and democratic participation in bringing these revisionist perspectives to bear on the cultural dynamics that drive participation in the global economy (Sen 1999; Bohman 1996).

6.1.1 Landes on the Historical Conditions for the European/British 'Invention of Invention'

In David Landes' *The Wealth and Poverty of Nations* (1998), the author's title intentionally plays off of Adam Smith's title *The Wealth of Nations* (1776). He intentionally insinuates exceptionalist roots to technological and material innovation that have a distinctly European, British, and free market origin. Landes wants to uphold the historical distinctiveness and incommensurable impact of European technological innovation. He describes European societies amidst the Middle Age period of 'the invention of invention' as follows:

> [T]hey entered during these centuries into an exciting world of innovation and emulation that challenged vested interests and rattled the forces of conservativism. Changes were cumulative; novelty spread fast. A new sense of progress replaced an older, effete reverence for authority. This intoxicating sense of freedom touched (infected) all domains. (Landes 1998, p. 57)

Since Landes wants to defend a European exceptionalist thesis, while technological and scientific conditions were indeed ripe for key world-transformative change in non-Western contexts (particularly China), he finds that historically the radical transformation affecting the West was long forestalled in the East.

Contributing factors to the comparatively slowed Eastern progress, according to Landes, include the sharp inequalities in gender relations that did not allow for industrial employment and a more widely differentiated division of labor. While paper was prevalent in China and Arabic societies for about 1000 years, Landes notes that it had been produced laboriously by hand and foot (46, 51–52) and the ideographic style of Chinese writing made the mass printing difficult for all texts other than canonical treatises (51). In contrast, he notes that the water wheel in the West was applied to the mechanized production of paper, thus paving the way for the later onset of mass printing via moveable type. In the context of smaller-scale technological innovation, eyeglasses perhaps doubled the productive career and magnified the expert skills of medieval craftsmen, including having led to the production of finely tuned small mechanical tools and instruments (46–47). Lastly, he claims that European free market exchange and private property also served as the necessary cultural backdrop for innovation to flourish (50).

As distinctly cultural contributions to European successes, he argues that religious resistance to centralized political control vastly aided technological and scientific maturation. He observes during this stretch of the late Middle Ages an ongoing spirit of inquiry and critique that eventually came to its climax in the Protestant Reformation (58).

> Important in all of this was the Church as custodian of knowledge and school for technicians. One might have expected otherwise: that organized spirituality, with its emphasis on prayer and contemplation, would have had little interest in technology….And yet everything worked in the opposite direction: the desire to free clerics from the time-consuming earthly tasks led to the introduction and diffusion of power machinery and, beginning with the Cisterians, to the hiring of lay brothers (*conversi*) to do the dirty work. Employment fostered in turn attention to time and productivity. All of this gave rise on monastic estates to remarkable assemblages of powered machinery. (Landes 1998, p. 58)

As other related cultural influences, he includes the Judeo-Christian tendency to look favorably on manual labor, the call to subdue nature, and a progressive narrative of overall historical progress in terms of the respective linear stages of creation, fall, redemption, and glory also stirred on technical innovation (58–59). He notes the epistemic advantages to the two kingdoms split between the mundane and transcendent that led clerical societies to employ technological innovations like the mechanical clock during the Middle Ages in order better to assess quantitative increases in output and thereby drive production efficiencies to free up time for regularized periods of contemplative prayer (Landes 1998, pp. 45, 58).

Also on the cultural-spiritual front, albeit in a dialectical contrast, Landes notes that the clock also served as a secularization force. Originally, the Middle Age Church kept track of time by the flow of nature (God's creation), dividing night and day hours into an equal number of parts thereby to produce irregular hours. However, the advent of clocks in the public space of the town square brought about a shift in authority and perspective on the regularized ordering of time toward mundane affairs (49) and led to the capacity not just to quantify and track labor output and productive increases but also to facilitate the temporal coordination of the increasingly complex differentiated modes of industrial production (50). Despites these gradual trends toward secularity, the Judeo-Christian linear sense of time also played a unique role in shaping an individual and collective consciousness oriented toward a quasi-Weberian conflation of moral-spiritual progress and discipline as facilitating ongoing materialistic innovative progress:

> Other societies thought of time as cyclical, returning to earlier stages and starting over again. Linear time is progressive and regressive, moving on to better things or declining from some earlier, happier state. For Europeans in our period, the progressive view prevailed. (Landes 1998, p. 59)

A sentiment of social progress in tandem with his predominate stress on the role of the free market led Landes to a view of Westernization as the major driver of global innovation even into the present. This main impetus to ongoing social transformation and progress leads to market-oriented social and economic reform that spread from England to Europe and then to the US. In endorsing this narrative of moral and social progress, he would like future trends to follow in the neo-liberal fashioning of a globalized free market that simultaneously spreads civilizing ideals of discipline, order, and collectively historical species-ethical progress.

6.1.2 *Onuma on the Transcivilizational Alternative to Eurocentric Imperialism*

In sharp contrast to Landes' endorsement of global free market competition as the template for organizing international society, Onuma Yasuaki's *A Transcivilizational Perspective on International Law* (2010) details a long narrative of Western imperial domination that he argues has strategically used international law to stifle economic, social, and cultural progress in both non-Western and developing nations. He explicitly points to the use of law intentionally to steer and gerrymander what will count as legitimate forms of innovation. Onuma argues that three Westernizing trends have historically destabilized the international order. The first two—(1) the enduring sense of victimization felt by many non-Western nations and (2) the imposition of a normative framework of a sovereign states order thereby conflict sharply with transnational economic interdependence. He argues that victimization and imposition are

> closely related to the third problem, i.e. the emerging discrepancies between the increasing substantive (economic and military) power of Asian nations, particularly China and India,

> and the persistent intellectual and informational hegemony of Western nations, especially the United States. (Onuma 2010, p. 57)

Therefore, Onuma advances a threefold legal realist and historical revisionist attack against the Western understanding of the triumphant successes of international law.

Primarily, in light of the first problem of perceived endemic victimization, Onuma argues that Western powers must not fuel the sense of victimization that has carried over from colonialism and must refrain from engaging in more covert forms of neo-colonialism. Onuma points to eradicating the double-standard of demanding external recognition from others and only, in rare cases, reciprocally conferring mutual recognition when in Western interests. He also laments Western trends of only having come to the conferral of communicative status to an interlocutor following the realization of a shift in power in the strategic engagement with a more formidable economic or military counterpart. In these cases, the legal conferral of statehood and international recognition must not merely contribute to Eurocentric national self-preservation, safety, and security with only second-hand coerced consent rendered legitimate by international laws and norms (268).

Secondly, in light of the problem of the sovereign states system in conflict with enhanced global economic integration, he treats the achievement of the current sovereign states system as actually a twofold failure (322–323). On the one hand, the US and Europe only conferred legitimacy on non-Western nations in many cases for economic reasons after having portioned large geographic regions into territorial borders that were drawn up more in light of other competing colonial claims to sovereign jurisdiction rather than via consultation with those indigenous peoples most affected (279–280; 286). Given a neo-Marxist spin, Onuma observes that post-colonial conferrals of state recognition typically took place after having already monopolized innumerable resources, including but not limited to: engaging in the global trade of slaves, decimating entire populations of undesirable indigenous persons, and in many cases, trading the conferral of citizenship status for compulsory military service.

Thirdly, as his proposed solution, for a twenty-first century world in which transnational economic interdependence has led to a multi-polar shift in power, he argues that we must follow his recommendation to develop and occupy the transcivilizational perspective. Only from this perspective can we begin to reconcile the growing economic and military presence of a multi-polar world with the requisite dispersal of intellectual and informational power in shaping the global order away from Eurocentric/Western prejudices:

> The perspective I call 'transcivilizational' can help to respond to these epistemological, normative and practical problems by expanding our concerns, questioning our self-evident or axiomatic assumptions, and enlarging our perspectives in a multi-layered manner. It is a perspective from which we see, recognize, interpret, assess, and seek to propose solutions to, ideas, activities, affairs and problems that transcend national boundaries, by developing a cognitive and evaluative framework based on the deliberate recognition of a plurality of civilizations that have long existed in human history. (Onuma 2010, p. 61)

Such a perspective will not only open up the prospect for revising both European and non-Western views for what will be taken as legitimate international law, but it also assumes an epistemic dimension conceding that no one civilization operating alone can adequately encounter the growing array of species crises that are truly global in magnitude and scope.[1]

Lastly, given Onuma's own Japanese/Asian heritage, he finds good reason to hold that the Chinese 'Middle Kingdom' has contributed as much, or more, to cultural, technological, and social innovation than its European counterpart. For instance, in direct contrast to Landes' view of Western world-historical progress, one need only compare the more than two millennia Confucian heritage of the Middle Kingdom in contrast to the concomitant brief world-historical imprint left by the mere centuries comprising the rise and fall of the Roman Empire. On this same note, Onuma finds the Chinese form of universality through the extension of *ren/jen* as a species-capacity has contributed and can continue to offer much more to the universalization impulses of humanistic morality than the Westernized dubious history of human rights protection (314–320; 361–362).

> In the imperial court of successive Chinese dynasties, various local princes, diplomats, agents of European chartered companies and other important persons were treated as tributary missions wishing to partake in Chinese civilization. Many of them acknowledged the universal authority of the Chinese emperor. Yet, we hardly think of treating such acknowledgement as evidence of the universality of Sinocentricism in those days. Sinocentricism might have been a universalistic notion, but not actually a universal notion that is valid to the whole cosmos or globe. Comparatively speaking, however, for the most of pre-nineteenth century human history, the *universalistic* claim of Sinocentricism had far more substantial basis than the *universalistic* claim of European natural law. It is only *through the uncritical projecting today's Eurocentric notion onto the past* that we are tempted to search for universality—not the universalistic claim—of natural law or European international law during the premodern period. (Onuma 2010, p. 363)

In addition, even if one were to follow the Western track along the purported progress of the greater unfolding of human rights, Onuma argues that much more emphasis needs to be placed on the socio-economic and cultural rights that comprise UN and Geneva conventions than merely the individual and political rights that carry a disproportionate amount of attention.

In summation, akin to advocates of the necessity for opening up cultural space for reverse/inverse innovation—particularly with China and India as emergent global powers—Onuma argues that the West must awake from its dogmatic legal-juridical slumber and concede the presence of a multi-polar world (59; 368; Zakaria 2008, pp. 1–3).[2] Given the end of the Cold War division of alliances down the USSR

[1] Onuma advises that we assess legal novelties derived to address a multi-polar world in light of the transcivilizational normative perspective: '[I]n considering theories of prominent thinkers, we must be careful how and to what extent they transcend their own cultural, religious and civilizational preconceptions. Great theorists and philosophers whose works are well read and influential are mostly Western thinkers. They may have produced ideas as general theory with universal applicability, but it must always be asked whether they transcend civilizational boundaries and demonstrate transcivilizationally valid reasoning and conclusions' (Onuma 449).

[2] Onuma highlights that criticism of Eurocentricism and/or West-centricism among intellectuals has at least begun slowly to emerge since the 1960s (187). However, he finds the prevailing intellectual climate still falling well short of his transcivilizational norm: 'West European intellectuals

and US axes, and given his skeptical attitude toward the US/West leading a unipolar order merely reflecting their own interests, he seeks to initiate the onset of an age of academic discourse also in line with his hope for the adaption of the transcivilizational perspective.

> [E]xperts have had insufficient knowledge on legal and other aspects of non-Western societies, cultures and civilizations, which should have a bearing on the concepts or frameworks of international law. In terms of representative legitimacy, most traditional concepts of international law—those of so-called "customary" international law—lack global legitimacy because they were not created and formulated in a manner representing humanity as a whole. More than 80 per cent of the world's population was not represented in the process where predominant notions and framework of "customary" international law were created and formulated.…The concepts or frameworks do not correspond to or represent realities of power constellation in the twenty-first-century world. (Onuma 2010, p. 178)

As yet an additional means for holding nation-states and the various multi-polar alliances to enhanced accountability, he also calls for a greater role to be played by NGOs (non-governmental organizations) in holding even their own home nation-states up to openly public criticism. As empirical support for this last charge, he highlights the success of Japenese NGOs in getting their own national leaders to sign on to and implement political *and* socio-economic human rights, specifically to minority groups holding little to no real political power in the Japanese national public sphere. Finally, in addition to treating socio-economic rights on the same par as political rights in this transcivilizational dialogue, his neo-Marxist affinities find a direct correlation between the material and spiritual capacities of civilizations that need not follow the neo-liberal preference of market growth at the necessary expense of the loss of a cultural and/or spiritual heritage that cannot be given an instrumental exchange value (Nussbaum 2011, note 35).

6.1.3 Sen on Capabilities: A Revisionist Understanding of Non-Western Contributions to Global Innovation

Amartya Sen's *Development as Freedom* (1999) offers an intermediate position based upon universal human capabilities to function that can be used to preserve culture while fostering innovation. Akin to Sen's mediation between the best insights of Smith and Marx—while avoiding the excesses of class disparity and

---

have generally been more willing that US intellectuals to understand cultures of others. However, many of them fundamentally lack interest in, and are ignorant of, non-European civilizations and cultures, as their US counterparts. For them, like those in the United States, the history of human ideas begins with Greek philosophy, moves to European medieval and natural law doctrines, then to the Enlightenment and social contract theory, and on to Hegel, Marx, and Nietzsche, to Jaspers, Heidegger and Foucault, although individual names may differ from one to the other. Confucianism, Islamic theology, Buddhism, Hinduism and any other great ideas or thoughts of the non-Western world have been virtually non-existent for them' (Onuma, 187–188).

totalitarian rule—Sen can also strike a mean between Landes' over-confidence in Western markets and Onuma's skeptical critique of Eurocentric neo-colonialism. In particular, Sen defends capability sets necessary for education as (a) the means to develop the new skills required in an interdependent world, (b) the way for cultures to have a voice in how they best seek to shape their preservation, and (c) the vehicle for inter-cultural exchange that can be mutually enriching in a globalized world.

Somewhat similar to Onuma, Sen's Asian/Indian heritage lends him the unique perspective to propose a revisionist historical approach to technological and scientific innovation that will unmask faulty biases contributing to the dogmatic belief in Western superiority.

> Western promoters of personal and political liberty in the non-Western world often see this as bringing Occidental values to Asia and Africa. The world is invited to join the club of "Western democracy" and to admire and endorse traditional "Western values." In all this, there is a substantial tendency to extrapolate *backward* from the present. Values that European Enlightenment and other relatively recent developments have made common and widespread cannot really be seen as part of the long-run Western heritage—experienced in the West over millennia. What we do find in the writings by particular Western classical authors (for example, Aristotle) is support for selected *components* of the comprehensive notion that makes up the contemporary idea of political liberty. But support for such components can be found in many writings in Asian traditions as well. (Sen 1999, p. 233)

Therefore, in contrast to Landes' Eurocentric reading of history in particular, Sen argues that non-Western histories will shift our perceptions of the major center(s) of civilizational progress. Sen instead judges that a more intellectually honest genealogy of innovation will not only disclose the non-Western heritage of many presumably 'Western' innovations but also enhance the objectivity of universal justice when construing the fact of global pluralism as an epistemic advantage for global democracy without a global state.

> [T]he demands of democracy can be (at least in one interpretation) seen as ways of enhancing the objectivity of the process. It can be asked, in this context, what the implications of these recognitions are for the demands of global justice and also for the nature and requirements of global democracy. The point is often made, with evident plausibility, that, for the foreseeable future, it is really impossible to have a global state, and therefore *a fortiori* a global democratic state. This is indeed so, and yet if democracy is seen in terms of public reasoning, then the practice of global democracy need not be in indefinite cold storage. Voices that can make a difference come from several sources, including global institutions as well as less formal communications and exchanges. (Sen 2010, p. 408)

Therefore, with a long litany of examples from non-Western contributions to essential innovations in mathematics (Sen 1999, 243–244), political science (235–238), literature (245–246), religion (234–235; 245–246), and philosophy (234/235; 245–246), Sen argues that scientific, technological, and economic innovation owes as much or even more of a true genealogy to non-Western than Western sources. In addition, he also shows that more complex historical reconstructions evince much more cross-cultural breeding and/or parallel developments that are too often cast through the myopic perspective of one civilization falsely claiming sole responsibility for what was really a dialectical process of transcivilizational innovation (242–244).

Sen therefore, again like Onuma, disagrees with the view of US and Eurocentric international law as a pacifying global force insofar as he cites 87 % of the global arms trade coming from the 'civilized' powers of the G-8 countries, 81 % from the current permanent members of the UN Security Council, and an overwhelming 50 % of arms trade in the world coming from the US—with more than two-thirds of that to developing nations. However, where Sen disagrees most directly with Onuma would be on the generally negative and pessimistic casting of global markets. Sen likewise disagrees for similar reasons with Landes' Eurocentric reading of the history of globalization as Westernization.

> [T]he confounding of globalization with Westernization is not only ahistorical, it also distracts attention from the many potential benefits of global integration…The very existence of large benefits makes the question of fairness in sharing the benefits of globalization so critically important. The central issue in contention is not globalization itself, nor is it the use of the market as an institution, but the inequity in the overall balance of the institutional arrangements—which produces very unequal sharing of the benefits of globalization. The question is not just whether the poor, too, gain something from globalization, but whether they get a fair share and a fair opportunity…Globalization deserves a reasoned defense, but it also needs reform. (Sen 2002, p. A6)

Since Sen advocates a multi-faceted local, state, national, regional, and global approach to the balance between markets, state, and social opportunities, he does not argue that a univocal extension of liberalized markets will solve every economic problem. While Sen does concede that we live in an interdependent global economy, the internal and external policies of each country and region of the world should demonstrate wide variations (Sen 1999, p. 127).

In an area of agreement, Sen concedes to both Landes and Onuma that a climate open to multiple avenues of dissent, protest, and outside participation should offer both epistemic and normative gains. According to Sen, subjecting market and governing institutions to critical scrutiny can not only enhance political liberties, but can also contribute to the effective regulation of markets, more equitable social welfare provisions, an aggregate overall increase in one's capability sets, and an effective voice in what aspects of one's culture are not worth trading away for the merely financial incentive of increased economic capital.

> [I]t is up to the society to determine what, if anything, it wants to do to preserve old forms of living, perhaps even at significant economic cost. Ways of life can be preserved if the society decides to do just that, and it is a question of balancing the costs of such preservation with the value that the society attaches to the objects and lifestyles preserved. There is, of course, no ready formula for this cost-benefit analysis, but what is crucial for a rational assessment of such choices is the ability of the people to participate in public discussions on the subject. We come back again to the perspective of capabilities: that different sections of the society (and not just the socially privileged) should be able to be active in the decisions regarding what to preserve and what to let go. (Sen 1999, pp. 241–242)

Sen goes on to argue that the ability to articulate one's views in public requires a robust range of capabilities including, but not limited to: remaining well-informed through a vibrant media, to have real opportunities for effective public participation, and to be able to read, write, and speak persuasively in public via access to basic education (Sen 1999, p. 242).

6.1.4 *Reverse Innovation, Human Nature, and a Renewal of Humanity: Four Non-Western Epistemic Contributions to Enhanced Global Material Justice*

Along with Sen's recommendation, by no means do I want to suggest that globalization occurs as an steady process that stretches all corners of the globe at an even pace, scope, and intensity. However, as pertains to global redistribution patterns of material, technological, and cognitive resources within a global market, I would like to focus most on the attendant reasons for both optimism and skepticism in light of global ideal toward promoting justice via greater moral and material equality. In particular, the three non-Western cases of innovation from India and China seem to affirm Sen's crucial economic variant of a Copernican Revolution whereby he recommends that in assessing comparative rubrics of social welfare and aggregate wellbeing

> What we are looking at here is not so much the social consequences of economic reforms, but the economic consequences of social reforms. The market economy flourishes on the foundations of such social development. (Sen 1999, p. 259)

Sen proposes his own rational justification for this gestalt shift on conventional wisdom concerning economic and technological innovation: enhancing overall capabilities sets proves the most effective means to stimulate ongoing economic and material progress. In other words, we must do away with Landes' false logic that one can have both: (a) wide-scale social progress through domestic and/or global market liberalization and at the same time (b) grant cultures an effective voice in how they adapt to the presumed primacy of economic over social and/or cultural capital.

In brief overview, on the conventional rendering of global distribution channels that Sen rejects, we can think figuratively in terms of a pyramid that has Western free market mavericks at the pinnacle, doling out ideas, innovations, and resources in trickle-down chains that move from West to East. Adapting this deceptively false pyramid trend would also include an errant focus on a target market of presumably consumer-oriented cultures to which one must court allegiance through the competitive spirit of the unrestrained market that must continually reinvent, market, and manufacture not just new products but fabricate the false perception of new 'necessities' requisite for participation in a globalized consumer society.

In contrast, Sen as a Nobel Prize winning economist has begun to highlight what might best be termed an inverse pyramid of reverse material, technological, and cognitive resource distribution with wellbeing as the consummate goal over aggregate increases in wealth. Following in the tradition of Sen, with this egalitarian reversal we might trace something akin to a greater emphasis on distributing the freedoms associated with enhanced capability sets more equitably to the lower and middle tiers of the global market pyramid. The non-Western twist of placing predominant focus on human capital (and not impersonal capital) as *both* the ends and means of production are making emerging markets, particularly in China and India, reshape the very assumptions one brings to debates concerning global development trends.

> [T]here is a general connection here [between positive unintended consequences and wide-scale social progress] that is quite close to the focus on capability in this work. The social changes under consideration (expansion of literacy, basic health care, and land reform) do enhance human capability to lead worthwhile and less vulnerable lives. But these capabilities are also associated with improving the productivity and employability of the people involved (expanding what is called their "human capital"). The interdependence between human capability in general and human capital in particular could be seen as being reasonably predictable…Anticipation of such social relations and causal connections helps us reason sensibly about social organization and about possible lines of social change and progress. (Sen 1999, p. 260)

One empirical dimension of the inverse pyramid would be the social fact of sheer demographic weight that these diverse emerging markets bring to global economic interdependence (Zakaria 2008). Here we can draw on the relevant data provided by Onuma:

> [T]oday's world is comprised of more than one billion Muslims, some 1.5 billion people whose way of thinking is more or less influenced by Confucianism, some 800 million Hindus and many other people whose world image is characterized not only by Eurocentric perspectives by also by some other perspectives. It is one thing to recognize the fact that Europeans dominated and unified the world. It is quite another to see the process of this European domination and unification solely from the perspective which Europeans have taken for granted. Such an attitude may well impoverish the academic undertakings, which should take diverse perspectives into account. (Onuma 2010, p. 368)

Given that these two populations of India and China number above a billion respectively, of whom many if not most would best be characterized as predominately poor on standard Western indices of consumerist clout, the sheer numbers still nonetheless shift the conventional target consumers of the global market significantly. In addition, as a broad generalization, Sen's stated goal of serving these strategic markets would not necessarily be the invention of perceived needs beyond subsistence but instead the improvement of standards of living and the development of capabilities to function freely toward uncompromising ideals of the justice, equality, and material conditions requisite for assuring individual responsibility. Sen argues that the enhanced presence of China and India, and particularly the successes of China illustrate the pressing need to invert the distorted focus on mere income growth over the normatively richer and more humane focus on capability sets (Sen 2005, p. 189):

> The governments of both China and India have been making efforts for some time now (China from 1979 and India from 1991) to move toward a more open, internationally active, market-oriented economy. When Indian efforts have slowly met with some success, the kind of massive results that China has seen has failed to occur in India. An important factor in this contrast lies in the fact that from the standpoint of social preparedness, China is a great deal ahead of India in being able to make use of the market economy. While pre-reform China was deeply skeptical of markets, it was not skeptical of basic education and widely shared health care. (Sen 1999, p. 42)

As three brief instances that highlight the civilizational matrixes behind that proposed transitions in mentality—two from the Asian (Confucian, Taoist, Buddhist) context, and one Indian (Hindu–Buddhist)—I would like not only to reinforce Sen's attendant egalitarian and revisionist material assumptions but also provide a concise genealogical narrative that situates each of the three contemporary seeds of innovation in their wider respective non-Western civilizational contexts. While the choice of the examples was not merely arbitrary, I do not want to mislead the reader into thinking that these few examples are determinative for entire civilizations. Think of them as helpful illustrations for what the practical implementation of cosmoipolitan justice might look like as a political program. The need for sustained philosophical reflection in the construction of other such examples could not be greater, which for the sake of time and practical expedience I must leave as a program for others to continue to experiment in constructing. As a cautionary disclaimer, lamentably, the greater corpus of the relevant literature in Western business ethics on the cultural assumptions and practice of non-Western market participants read more as instrumental strategies for closing the deal with a (justifiably so) culturally resistant skeptic than honest moral reflection on how best to maximize mutual understanding within a shared commitment to optimization of the material dimensions of species-ethical well-being.

Shanzhai as Bandit Innovation

As for the first Asian case, the evocative term *shanzhai* (literally, as bandit or guerrilla innovation) can play the ambivalent role of either an adjective or verb (Wu and Li 2011, p. 214). In either of these descriptive or normative semantic frames, *shanzhai* roughly connotes the imitation of already achieved degree of product functionality with the minimal possible cost.

> One of the latest buzz words in China's popular culture of 2008 is "*shanzhai*" (literal translation: mountain village), which originally meant a fortress in a mountain occupied by outlaws. However, in its post-modern connotation, it refers to a wide-range of imitations of brand names. It is associated closely with the phenomenon of producing and consuming low-cost products, which imitate brand names. (Wu and Li 2011, p. 213)

The production process and ensuing consumption succeeds by changing the attendant large industry propriety over exclusive intellectual property rights to allow for smaller-scale indigenous Chinese companies to flourish, using similar resources, and copying design without losing the original function. The most prominent domain for such devices in Chinese culture would be in the realm of digital products, and specifically cell phone usage among Chinese youth:

> The "*shanzhai*" mobile phone, as the name indicates, carries a connotation of rebellion, resistance, periphery, and outlawing. Foremost, it is an antonym of the "brand-name" phone. The "brand-name" phone signifies the celebrated name, good quality, high price, recognized prestige and an enviable possession of social status. Whereas the "*shanzhai*" phone is associated with the no-name, shoddy quality, low price, dubious reputation and a distasteful piece of low class production. (Wu and Li 2011, pp. 213–214)

Insofar as such phones, in particular, occupy approximately 30% of the domestic market with a disproportionately large representation of the Chinese youth culture, studies have begun to investigate how these devises help shape self-expression via novelty of design, alternate experimental functioning, and individualized style. In addition, some have gone so far as to suggest the absence of a brand name shows an implicit rejection of large-scale consumer enterprises and can even be expressed as a symbol of national, non-Western, and/or patriotic expression. The deeper cultural roots lie in Confucianism. Akin to the Confucian proprietary expansion of elite virtues to be emulated by the commoner, the attendant democratization presupposes an inherently social, relational, and egalitarian conception of human nature.[3] Not only does the propriety rendered technological lead to the spread of elite communicative innovations to the masses, *shanzhai* also draws upon vestiges of Taoism. The humble status of remaining nameless in the non-identification with a popularized industrial brand name also carries the latent hope of minimizing social strife by cutting the association of conferred status through the procurement of a scarce consumer fetish. These sinological conceptions of human nature challenge the individualist Eurocentric assumptions of intellectual property ownership and, in turn, invert the conventional pyramid of elite innovators reaping the material benefits by proposing the alternative egalitarian dispersal that highlights the common good of the moral and material benefits to be accrued by society. In addition, civilizational roots can also be traced back to the Taoist concept of *wu wei* as a moral principle that seeks maximal results via minimal effort, thereby producing similar outcomes as name brands with minimal possible costs to the consumer with the approximated performance of a much more costly and foreign enterprise.

Guanzi as Neo-Confucian Social Capital

Also of a Chinese heritage would be the incredible scholarly attention given to the neo-Confucian dynamics of *guanzi* (literally, tacit proprieties and normative practices for social networking). The enormous attendant literature predominately geared toward business school and international professional has come about as Western corporations seek to make inroads with the lucrative array of emergent Chinese markets. While a social phenomenon that has warranted book-length treatments to explain just one angle on all the proprietary complexities, most simply stated, the conferral of status in *guanzi* draws from an eclectic mix of performance by merit, family and hereditary ties, common educational profiles, and shared regional cultures and/or birthplaces. The most telling neo-Confucian characteristic

[3] However, the advent of the cell phone has also stirred on strong expressions of individuality. Since prior Chinese experiences with phone calls typically emanated from a single phone as customary for an entire apartment complex, messages by courier could often get to the recipient more quickly than a phone call. This newfound expressive individually could initially befuddle a Western observer. For instance, it is commonplace for Chinese to leave important meetings to receive a cell phone call, to perhaps leave a public lecture or class multiple times, or even openly to take the call during the meeting, lecture, or class.

would be the tie to *jen/ren* as deeply informing the associated Chinese assumptions considering the ideal functioning of human nature (literally, compassion or universal benevolence in relationship):

> [A]ffectiveness, which has been referred to as *ren* in Confucian terminology, is the common component of *guanxi* in all domains. As for the instrumental component, it is implied in the reciprocal obligation in the family domain, it is not salient in the educational domain, but it becomes very salient in the daily-life domain. In fact, the major domain for *guanxi* practices in Chinese society is neither family nor school, but the so-called daily-life domain within or between organizations. (Hwang 2012, p. 302)

While this relational view of the person entails a commitment to reciprocity, typically construed as the Confucian Silver Rule of not doing to others what one would not have done to them, this presumption of the socialized capacity for empathy also allows for a current of instrumentally strategic rationality. Some attribute this unique balance of the competitive individual with the relational and institutional realities of always already being immersed in a wide array of social contexts as a major contributing factor to the economic success recently experienced in many East Asian societies:

> From this [relational view], Chinese culture created a deep psychological proclivity for individuals to actively cultivate and manipulate social relations for instrumental ends. The unanticipated rise of industrial East Asia generated a great deal of interest in explaining how collectively-oriented peoples could exhibit such dynamic entrepreneurial energy, something presumed [from a Western/Eurocentric perspective] to reside only in heroic individuals. (Gold et al. 2002, p. 11)

The ensuing account of human nature that follows in this neo-Confucian context would be the avoidance of the extremes of atomistic individualism, on the one hand, and corporate collectivism, on the other.[4] Given the strong preference for individualism in Western contexts, the attendant notions of *jen* and *guanxi* are most often mischaracterized by external observers as leading to an alarming collapse of the individual into the family, corporation, community, nation, state, and/or society. However, this would be a gross misconception as it would better be stated as expressive of human nature as inherently relationship-based: 'Each individual is at the center of an egocentric network with no explicit boundaries, always involved in social interactions (*guanxi*) of varying strength. This leads to a deep contextualization of behavioral expressions whereby people are continually evaluating and managing—through reciprocity—their relations to others' (Gold et al.2002, p. 10).

[4] Yadong Lao in *Guanxi and Business* (2007) describes the complex Confucian backdrop as follows: 'Although the cultivation of *guanzi* has become the focus of researcher attention only since the decentralization and privatization of the Chinese economy, its roots are deeply embedded in 2000 years of Chinese culture. Confucian social theory is concerned with the question of how to establish a harmonious secular order in a man-centered world. According to Confucian philosophy, the individual is never an isolated separate entity. All humans are social or interactive beings. Although *guanxi* was not found in the Confucian classics, the word *lun* was used. The concept of *lun* concerns the differentiation of individuals and the kinds of relationships to be established between individuals. Confucian social order is constructed upon the concept of *lun* (12–13).

In terms more germane to competitive market participation, perhaps the most crucial difference with Western norms concerning the fundamental objectives of business would be the aforementioned predominance of increasing one's social capital over an impersonal metric of amassing economic capital.[5] For instance, the outright misunderstanding of the preference of upholding and/or improving one's *guanzi* status as more primary to one's business dealing than sheer profit motivation has led some Western corporations desiring to create Chinese branches to reconsider their entire corporate culture for what constitutes the ultimate ends and goals of business. Luo articulates this contrast as follows:

> *Guanxi* is a form of social capital which creates economic value. Unlike economic capital, in which money and commodities are incorporated into circuits of production in order to produce more money, social capital is an aggregate of actual or potential resources linked to the possession of a durable network of more or less institutionalized relationships. Mutual acquaintance and recognition provide credentials which entitle people to various kinds of credit. Social capital includes obligations (not debts in the economic, legally enforceable sense), the advantages of connections or social position, and trust….Social capital is fundamentally tentative and insecure, unlike economic capital which is objective, certain, and enforceable. Social capital, designated by such things as obligation and trust, is by its very nature vague and unmeasurable. Obligation is always a potential rather than a concrete actuality. (Luo 2007, pp. 41–42)

Hwang likewise reinforces these distinctions between economic and social capital, claiming: 'the Chinese word for *guanxi* implies that connections with the right people are often more important business decision considerations than price, quality, or after service of the tendered product' (2012, p. 302). While social actors often overemphasize Western business prowess as a matter of individual autonomy or entitlement to resource accumulation as guaranteed by the state apparatus, the neo-Confucian dimensions of *guanzi* networks construe human individuals as inherently social beings, simultaneously playing multiple overlapping roles. *Guanzi* networks are inherently amorphous as they allow one to hold the status of manager of resources commensurate with one's shifting portfolio of capacities born on behalf of obligations and responsibilities to a larger, indispensable, and pluralized social entities.

In addition, in contrast to what Western business practices might associate with one's demographic profile, the *guanzi* nexus more likely ties less to ascribed characteristics and more to socially conferred statuses, leading some scholars to call *guanzi* both social capital and cultural capital. Luo argues that the two can be used interchangeably within the same context of fostering *guanxi*:

[5] My own initial interactions with Chinese philosophy professors in both Shanghai and Beijing were telling in this regard. My first introduction proceeded quickly to the following initial questions: 'I looked at your institutional profile on your website and could not tell who your boss was.' This was followed by: 'I also looked at the website and was still left wondering what things precisely that you are in charge of at your college.' My second interaction was even more awkward. I was met immediately with the proclamation that 'You cannot be an assistant professor.' I learned later that 35 years old in China constitutes the threshold for conferral of all of the filial proprieties associated with coming of age. Since I was under 35 years old, my counterpart could not confer me the social capital that the status of degree recipient had conferred in the US.

> Knowledge or skill concerning the cultivation and maintenance of *guanxi* can be termed cultural capital….In general, cultural capital consists of what the agent knows and is capable of doing; it can be used to generate privilege, products, income, or wealth. Cultural capital can be gained individually through the processed of education, learning, and cultivation. It can also be institutionalized, as when certain forms of cultivation are accorded recognition by authorities. (Luo 2007, p. 42)

Therefore, one's role in the corporate scheme would thus be commensurate to the amount of pull their social contacts carry in the overlapping networks of social life inside and outside the business office. In other words, the conferral of face and status that merits *guanxihaw*—one who has close personal relationships with those whom hold social and political power or influence—belies the Western goal of maximized individual autonomy. Instead, by immersing the superior person in a complex network of reciprocal obligations, entitlements, and responsibilities, their status also entails a demanding host of social obligations (Hwang 2012, p. 197). Lastly, while Western businesses often reassert this emphasis upon individual autonomy over to the level of inter-corporate dealings through brief relationships modeled on mutual presumptions of non-interference, the Chinese array of leveled proprieties to *guanzi* networks can lead to inter-institutional obligations, responsibilities, and social ties that cut across each and every social sphere. Such networks could traverse supply and demand chains the Westerner might otherwise deem as external to one's corporate responsibilities, leading to exotic corporate species. These include a wide array of diversified conglomerates, including but not limited to fully or partially state-owned enterprises, innovative social bonds that bear no current legal precedent, and a shifting environment of norms to guide behaviors that may vary widely by context at either the domestic, international, or global levels.

Jugaad as Frugal Engineering

As for the Indian case, the notion of *jugaad* (literally: frugal engineering) generally means to begin with only the resources at one's disposal in the unrelenting effort to thwart seemingly insurmountable obstacles. The goal is to produce a product or service otherwise deemed impossible to create in such an inhospitable and resource depraved environment. In order to understand this practice, we should contrast the corresponding attitude to innovation held by Western/developed nations versus non-Western/emerging markets:

> The developed world's consumer technology innovations are built for an ever-expanding bandwidth network and move toward fancier, costlier, and more network-hungry and status-conferring devices. In emerging markets, firms constantly seek new uses for cheap, basic innovations, such as those that allow people to use their mobile phones for banking, market reports, and employment prospects. (Kumar and Puranam 2012, p. 105)

In this respect, we must articulate the distinct contrast between (a) the abiding Western/Eurocentric presumption that the goal of a consumer society would be to fabricate the false perception of unlimited wants and needs, with (b) the Hindu-Buddhist backdrop of non-attachment to the fleeting and impermanent entities that comprise a perishing material world. Cast in this light, frugal engineering assumes a different conception of human nature than the Western civilizational assumptions. Recall that the goals of Hindu *moksha* (literally: liberation from the confines of the finite world) and of Buddhist *nirvana* (literally: burning away all temporal desires) carry this inherently minimalist attitude toward worldly consumption. The human achieves optimal fulfillment in a manner much different than the consumerist ideal of attaining security in identity through maximal possessions.

Jugaad, akin to the two illustrations from Chinese innovations, also bears the potential for radically reshaping distribution pyramids. Such pioneering innovations are already being produced in the non-Western context to be shipped to local consumers. This reversal of innovation patterns also belies the assumption of supply chain redistribution to focus on maximal profit margins through the highest price. Given the predominate focus on minimal production costs through maximizing local resources, the emphasis is upon the more local immediacy of providing capability enhancement for those possessing the greatest need. We thus find overlapping consensus on common material ideals from quite distinct background justification: echoing Marx's radically humanist, anti-capitalist adage from a Hindu context: from each according to ability, to each according to need.

Conventional examples of *jugaad* practices of frugal engineering include cars produced for less than $ 3000, eyeglasses at $ 10, and even models for assembly-line style health care via cost-reduced surgeries and ultra-specialized services. Other examples extend beyond just the manufacturing sectors to novel models of research and development that include university-styled ongoing education as part of corporate on-site learning facilities. In addition, one illustrative Indian example of technological innovation exemplifies Sen's ongoing emphasis on true development as eradication of endemic capability deprivations. The following illustration offers direct application to Sen's importance placed upon literacy for enhancing other key capability sets like search for employment, prudent health choices, women's equality, an active public media, critical input from a multi-lingual public sphere, and poverty eradication. In his relevant studies on knowledge production and human capital, Indian scholar R.A. Mashelkar points to the pioneering work of a leading innovator in Indian information technology, F.C. Kohli, who has recently addressed India's 200 million illiterate adults by developing a Computer-based Functional Literacy Program (CBFL) based on cognition, language, and communication (Mashelkar 2008, p. 74). Mashelkar estimates 'Kohli's innovative CBFL can help 854 million illiterates in the world. Such is the power of this new knowledge that has been created for those existing at the bottom of the pyramid' (74). In such a model of frugal innovation, by focusing on the untapped human capital at the lowest tier of the wealth pyramid, the method has effectively streamlined 200 h of intense teacher to pupil interaction required for literacy to the new computer-assisted model of villagers reading newspapers within 8–10 weeks (73–74).

> Kohli is an engineer who believes in pragmatic and affordable solutions. His team ran these lessons on Intel 486s and the earlier versions of Pentium PCs modified to display multimedia. There are around 200 million of such PCs in the world that are obsolete and have been

> discarded. They can be made available free of cost. By using these PCs, the cost of making one person literate would be less than Rs 100, slightly over two U.S. dollars. With CBFL, Kohli says he can increase literacy in India to 90–95 percent within three to five years, rather than [the current pace of] 20 years. (Mashelkar 2008, p. 74)

In addition, the CBFL model carries much promise in its international implications for radically transforming the capability deprivations suffered by the bottom tier of the global pyramid as it has already been tested on five states and five languages in India and has begun a piloting trial in South Africa (74).

Sacralized Redistribution: Towards an Indigenous Model for Bridging Axial Divides

As one potential critique of my casting of cosmoipolitan justice in the context of what Jaspers even conceded in the first chapter as a global rite of initiation, now that we have comprehensively surveyed the non-Western Axial traditions, how ought we account for societies that have passed into modernity but nonetheless still retain elements of pre-Axial traditions? While it constitutes a separate debate altogether whether to confer Axial status on additional groups not mentioned in this text, I should concede that my classification scheme for Axial remains open-ended, and there are plausible reasons for including the Ancient Greek philosophers (as does Jaspers and Bellah, and Habermas plans a whole chapter in his forthcoming book on the Axial Age just devoted to the Greek and Hebrew-Christian inter-Axial borrowing and competition), possibly Zorastrianism, and even African indigenous religions as having sufficiently achieved the Axial breakthrough (this was a position defended by Prof. Thaddeus Metz of Johannesburg at the Summer 2013 Frankfurt School conference on Critical Theory, Globalization, and the Postsecular).

However, let us assume for the moment that there are societies that had never undergone an Axial breakthrough but nonetheless are full participants in a globalized modernity (Eisenstadt was fascinated by this prospect, and concluded after decades of research that Japan seemed best to exemplify this phenomena). In her "Where do Axial Commitments Reside?—Problems in Thinking about the African Case," Ann Swidler takes up this issue as it applies to tribal kinship networks in Malawi, where she had conducted many years of field research on this dilemma (Swidler 2012, p. 222).

In an array of cases as diverse as aid and relief efforts, funeral and marriage ceremonies, material redistribution, and participation in global activism, Swidler encountered a unique blend of pre-Axial and Axial traditions that I will take license to term: sacralized redistribution. On the one hand, she noted that social access to participants in tribally based kinship networks still prevalent in Africa were typically mediated strictly through the local chieftain for the conferral of access, denial, or recognition of distinct specialized authority upon an outsider (229–230). She cites instances of spiritual significance, such as proprieties associated with burial rites that required conferral of access for their perceived ritual legitimacy. She noted that even when these were officiated by imams, priests, or pastors that represented the more universalistic scope of the Axial traditions, they nonetheless still required local authorization of the chieftain. In addition, the attendance of the chieftain carried significant conferral of enhanced status upon the sacral officiate. Likewise, the denial of access or absence of the local chieftain could be construed as a form of social rebuke or public means to ostracize someone of ill moral repute.

She also highlights cases of health awareness concerning AIDS that often required a delicate mix of the conferral of authority upon purportedly universal Western medical practices from local chieftains that still exercised authority over more tribally oriented traditions association with health. She notes an array of social imaginaries associated with health that might strike a Western observer as misplaced. These run as diverse in concern as proper communication with deceased ancestors (that nonetheless might influence the health and well-being of a living ancestor), replacement or redaction of local medicinal practices, and matters as pragmatic as how best to mediate communication between chieftain and family networks one would like either to help, consult, or request help. She notes that the local proprieties could differ as determined by relational proximity: chief to eldest male, chief to eldest female, and so on, typically descending by degrees of age, family bond, and geographic proximity.

Her findings associated with the charitable distribution of material resources from international aid networks also had a direct bearing on local understandings of the proper role and status of the chieftain (236). For instance, a chieftain that publically exhibited selfish motives and behaviors with respect to personal and collective access to resources was often depicted as covertly tied to witchcraft (232–233). They were also likely to be perceived as of explicit or implicit immoral standing, and likely to transfer negative spiritual energies to the detriment of the social group. Relatedly, any perception of stealing from others' resource allotment within or even outside one's tribal and kinship network could serve as grounds for immediate dismissal from one's chieftain functions to be followed by living the remainder on one's life as a wandering social outcaste (231).

These findings proved vitally significant to Swidler in disclosing these latent assumptions to aid workers offering resource, material, or monetary help to a particular impoverished area. Since even the overall success or failure of the aid effort was perceived as having a direct causal relation to one's chieftain, the ongoing sustainability of a prolonged aid effort required due recognition of the complex proprieties. These could be associated with status, communication, conferral of scientific or political standing, and the complex understandings of the supra-mundane qualities often presumed by a locality. The shared social imaginaries could vary by locality with respect to their land, their ancestral heritage, and historical precedent of peaceful or conflict-ridden relations with neighboring kinship networks, other non-tribal local political authority, region-wide, and national governance.

What Swidler observed was direct confirmation of Voegelin's famous 'mortgage' observation that: 'nothing is ever lost' (239). Voegelin found that even in his millennia of data reconstructing already completed transitions from the pre-Axial to Axial stages, that the transition from ritual and/or mythic stages always carried a layer of symbolic meaning that aided in the translation of new significance to a particular set of symbols endowed with transcendent symbolic meaning. In confirming

Voegelin's insight, Swidler found that the chieftains still played a crucial role and even carried over the symbolic significance of one's African self-identification as deeply embedded in one's tribal and kinship affinities. However, what she clearly articulated as *not* observing was a backwards culture striving to maintain an archaic past. Quite the contrary, she observed a fascination and, at times, even a deep-longing for the universal, the global, and the open-engagement with the achievements whether technological, scientific, moral, material, or conceptual that one could classify as distinctively modern (235–236).

As pertains to her engagement with Axial traditions recently introduced into the African context, she witnessed the rapid spread of Islamic and Christian Pentecostal traditions (223). While she observed that indubitable fervor for the global and universal was immediately associated with the introduction of these Axial traditions, she also found that the self-ascription of inclusion among active adherents to an Axial tradition did not mean necessarily giving up every single pre-Axial self-understanding or commitment that one held. Even outside the domain of a particular Axial tradition, what she found was the reflexive adaptation across the board that to be Malawian also meant to be a participant in the wider scope of world history as comprising the entirety of the human species. In other words, even in cases whereby the Axial breakthrough was recognized, accepted, and taken up in its manifold historical narratives, the active introduction to that onset of universality cannot be described from the perspective of the third-person observer but only from the participant view of an enhanced species-ethical and universal self-understanding that presumes radical dependence upon second personal relationships (227).

6.1.5 Concluding Lessons for Realizing Cosmoipolitan Justice as a Political Program: Towards a More Egalitarian Economic, Social, and Moral Interdependence

In agreement with Sen's remarks on globalization, we should concur that for cosmoipolitan justice to serve as more than a mere academic ideal, the mere aggregate utilitarian calculation of improved living standards never legitimates continued moral, social, and/or political domination. And insofar as traditions are never ossified in time, we can agree with both Jaspers and Onuma that we should endorse the transcivilizational perspective for revising, redacting, and reinventing international law on a more democratic global model. Until then, Western and non-Western Axial traditions must exercise healthy skepticism towards the norms and prevailing background assumptions of international law. This should hold as particularly salient in the domain of property rights, intellectual property, international commerce and finance, and the general dismissal of socio-economic rights in current academic discourses. In the meantime, we might at best expect rapid and ongoing adaptations, particularly those in the domain of the digital technologies that have reshaped Western and non-Western social networking, bandit innovation, and frugal engineering—perhaps more so as digitalized participatory common law than the customary international law that Onuma and Sen have given us good reason to challenge. We might also even concede an insight to Landers that while scientific and technological conditions for innovation may be present, a domestic, international, and global social-political context open to change is also needed.

At the institutional level, we ought also to concede from our four non-Western examples that the dual modification of both means (production, research and development, etc.) and ends (product, target market, etc.) create mutually reflexive loops of product *and* production innovative design change. The ongoing education needed for hyper-vigilance on the part of consumers simultaneously exposed to more pervasive social networking capacities and opportunities—including participation in global movements, new abilities for reproducing and comparing competing product lines, and new streamlined forms of frugal engineering—offer added value to the human capital needed to make an epistemic virtue of incessant competition. As for the moral-ethical domain, not only may the assumption of the *de facto* superiority of Western models be epistemically inaccurate (as Onuma and Sen argue)—but, perhaps worse—justifiably perceived as the continual hubris of prolonged neo-colonial global narrative as also forewarned too by a vast array of authoritative Western voices (Bellah 2012; Bohman 2013; Casanova 2013; Habermas et al. 2011; McCarthy 2013; Nussbaum 2012; Rawls 1999, pp. 121–22).

As a further institutional insight from Sen's recently published critical observations and philosophical interpretation of anti-globalization protestors, those he characterizes as anti-globalist are caught in a performative contradiction: isolationist attempts to resist globalization further entrench the systemic scope of the forces they resist (Sen 2002, p. A2–A6). For instance, Sen notes the odd and counter-productive result that anti-globalization protests serve as some of the most popularized events the world has seen to date via transmission and exposure from a transnational digital media that presumes global communication networks as its necessary precondition for success. We might here invoke Onuma's and Habermas's concern that, while desirable, a transcivilization media has yet to be established whereby competing civilizational voices are given equal access to a shared forum of open and honest debate concerning competing perspectives and interpretations of the same events. In agreement with Sen, given the asymmetrical scope of globalization in a multipolar world, benchmark comparisons against best practices emerging out of disparate civilizations should expect wide institutional variance, ever-more intense competition, and dispersed market segmentation rather than global convergence on endorsing one civilizational context to reign supreme.

However, we are ultimately left with a final problem we must address. Have we fallen prey to the same dilemma faced by first generation critical theorists? In rendering such skepticism against political cosmopolitanism, are we back to Marx's problem of having provided a philosophical critique devoid of practical political proposals? How ought we best institutionalize cosmoipolitan justice as a practical political program?

In reply, for starters, it would be easiest to clarify what my goal is not. Consider the following proposal for radical UN reform from Samuel Huntington's classical and provocative *Clash of Civilizations*:

> In a multicivilizational world ideally each major civilization should have at least one permanent seat on the Security Council. At present only three do. The United States has endorsed Japanese and German membership but it is clear they will become permanent members only if other countries do also. Brazil has suggested five new permanent members, albeit without veto power, Germany, Japan, India, Nigeria, and itself. That, however, would leave the world's 1 billion Muslims unrepresented, except insofar as Nigeria might undertake that responsibility. From a civilizational viewpoint, clearly Japan and India should be permanent members, and Africa, Latin America, and the Muslim would should have permanent seats, which could be occupied on a rotating basis by the leading states of those civilizations, selections being made by the Organization of the Islamic Conference, the Organization of African Unity, and the Organization of American States (the United States abstaining). It would also be appropriate to consolidate the British and French seats into a single European Union seat, the rotating occupant of which would be selected by the Union. Seven civilizations would thus each have one permanent seat and the West would have two, an allocation broadly representative of the distribution of people, power, and wealth in the world. (Huntington 1997, pp. 317–318)

While Huntington's model certainly has its appeal over the prevailing system, these sorts of concrete proposals for the global political design for cosmopolitan justice are certainly not what I have in mind for political implementation. As for some positive orientation to shape the future of cosmoipolitan justice as an alternative project, it would be best to return to its origins in the work of Jaspers, endorsing his distinction between what he terms world dominion verse world order.

> Schematically seen, the alternative is world dominion or world order. World dominion would be peace imposed on everyone by a single power working from one point on earth. World order would be unity without any compulsion to unity beyond what arises from negotiation and common agreement. On the one hand, all are suppressed by one power, on the other hand all live in an order achieved by the general renunciation of sovereignty. (Jaspers 1948, p. 53)

As far as world dominion is concerned, it would not be a reach to presume that the current world dominion would include the hegemony of neo-liberal capitalism as the single power. Distinct, but super-imposed upon this locus of dominion would be the uneven global distribution of military force mentioned earlier by Sen. However, I would again agree with Jaspers, that in the interest of liberty, we ought to refrain from too concrete of practical proposals:

> Rather is it of crucial importance to liberty that, in thinking out the possibility or impossibility of a world order, we should not lay down any picture of the future, any devised reality, as the goal toward which history is of necessity steering, which we ourselves assimilate as such into our fundamental wills, and with the attainment of which history would be consummated. Never shall we find a fulfillment of history, save in every present as this presentness itself. (Jaspers 1953, pp. 212–213)

So, we are left with the conundrum of what exactly Jaspers' view would entail if we were to promote a world order without lapsing into world dominion. In his *The European Spirit* (1948), he offers some insights that in the immediate wake of WWII are still 5 years prior to his *On the Origin and Goal of History* (1953). Jaspers recommends two spiritual transformations that must occur if a world order were ever to come to fruition:

> On the way to world order two spiritual transformations would take place: first, the purification of politics….The limitation of politics to its essential nature itself derives from a belief, the only belief that does not turn into a conflict of belief, namely, the belief in the communication of self-living beings (*selbstseiender Wesen*), that is to say, the belief that genuine discussion between men leads to truth and harmony. Politics, therefore, tries in unlimited patience to speak, even though it does not seem possible, even with the man who fights for his belief. For it presupposes that no man is only a fighter for his belief, but it also a man among his fellow men….The second transformation is the dispelling of the magic charm of the history of states. The picture of history whose compelling power lies in the greatness of the States, in mighty events, even though they are catastrophes, in sensational unheard-of deeds, in the myth of warlords and statesmen, in fame lasting hundreds and thousands of years, will fade away. The brightness falls now on the soaring flight of human existence. (Jaspers 1948, pp. 55–57)

Firstly, his purification of politics much resembles the optimism he has for the boundless communication that comes with the onset of the Axial Age. Here he even adds the additional provision of seeking mutual understanding even with those whom show strong tendencies toward the use of force or coercion. According to Arendt's reflections in Jaspers' work, she finds this provision, like Kant, to call for the all out end to warfare in all of its forms (Arendt 1981, p. 548–549). While to attempt to achieve this through coercion falls itself into a performative contradiction, it nonetheless remains a normative ideal and is connected to the second spiritual transformation.

Secondly, in the void left by states, we could project the species-ethic of each major Axial tradition as the universalizing impetus for discourse. However, Allen (2013), Jose Casanova (2014), Charles Taylor (2007) and others are correct to point out that states are the major secularizing forces institutionalizing procedures oriented toward legitimate democratic outcomes. Allen uses this observation as grounds for charging Habermas of wanting to have his cake and eat it too (2013). The cake that he would purportedly enjoy would be the universalizable legitimacy that the institutional procedure brings in providing a context-transcendent moment of truth. The simultaneous eating of the cake he wants to retain, according to Allen, would be the species-ethical universality of the particular Axial tradition under purview, as Habermas resets modernity and the learning potential its brings about at the onset of the Axial Age (Habermas 2013, pp. 364–365). With respect to the intercultural discourse between distinct Axial traditions, she finds Habermas's commitment difficult to reconcile:

> [S]ince at that [intercultural] level it is not individuals but states that are either secular or religious, hence it is difficult to see how Habermas's institutionalized version of the translation requirement, according to which individuals acting in the public political sphere must translate their religious claims into publically accessible hence secular terms, will be useful here. Religious states would most likely balk at the idea that they must translate their religious motivations into secular language at the level of international institutions such as the United Nations, even if not at the level of the global public sphere. They would likely view this requirement as an instance of a secular Eurocentric cultural imperialism or of a thinly veiled crusading American Christianity. (Allen 2013, p. 152)

As for the veiled crusade, Habermas concedes that only by the practical demonstration of its capacities for decentering can European sources of modernity retain their ability to be trusted as legitimate sources of second personal orientations toward mutual understanding (Habermas 2013, p. 366). And with respect to the charge of cultural imperialism apparently brought about by either a dubiously objective secularism or an instrumental approach to reason, in reply, he makes the recursive appeal back to a fallibilist self-understanding (363).

While she does concede to the intellectual prowess of Habermas that he has both ends of her critique covered in the corpus of his writings (2013, p. 362–366), she still leaves unsatisfied.

> There's a certain irony involved in saying that the way to avoid Eurocentricism is for the West to celebrate its own cultural achievements, to be even more like itself: even more reflexive and self-critical than it already is…Presumably, Habermas would agree that whether this cognitive resource should be viewed as a cultural achievement that has resulted from a learning process is a question that must be politically left open and viewed as essentially contestable in the ongoing and intensifying debates about multiple and alternate modernities. (Allen 2013, p. 152)

As a point of reconciliation, Habermas is right about the attendant risk of lapsing back into neo-paganism if we simply grant each Axial tradition its distinct contextualism with no ground for objective transcendence (2013, p. 364). In support of his position, perhaps we can look for hints of such 'European' achievements of practical decentering as an immanent source of pragmatic universality in other civilizational settings.

Fortunately, in our search for such non-Western instances from other Axial traditions, and in preserving the general flow of this concluding chapter, we find an ally once again in the work of Amartya Sen. He highlights Buddhism as a helpful illustration that can get around not just the charge of a Christocentic bias. Buddhism's unique agnostic roots lay to rest questions concerning the ultimate necessity to posit a genealogy that at some point had dropped the notion of a personal God to be redacted by species-ethical universality. According to Sen,

> Though Buddhism is a religion like any other, it began with at least two specific characteristics that were quite unusual, to wit, its foundational agnosticism and its commitment to public communication and discussion. The latter was responsible for the fact that some of the earliest open public meetings in the world, aimed specifically at settling disputes between different views, took place in India in elaborately organized Buddhist councils', where adherents of different points of view tried to argue out their differences, particularly on public practices as well as religious beliefs…The host of the largest of these councils (the third), Ashoka, even tried to establish, in the third century BCE, good rules for productive debating to be followed by all, with 'restraint in regard to speech' and with the points of view of all being 'duly honored in every way on all occasions'. In so far as public reasoning is central to democracy (as political philosophers like John Stuart Mill, John Rawls, and Jurgen Habermas have argued), parts of the global roots of democracy can indeed be traced to the tradition of public discussion that received much encouragement in both India and China (and also in Japan, Korea and elsewhere), from the dialogical commitment to Buddhist organization. (Sen 2005, p. 182; Sen and Dreze 2013, p. 248)

This example offers substantive legitimacy to Habermas's postulation that, albeit learned, second-personal reciprocal role taking shows strong hints of something akin to a universal species-ethical capacity that has emerged in multiple historical iterations. The example also poses an intriguing alternative to the prevailing academic views of Ancient Greece as the sole pre-modern forbearer of democratic culture and offers a substantive response to the East Asian values debate that surreptitiously bears claims to a tradition inimical to democratic discourse.

Sen lends further support to Habermas's position (and my own, and Jaspers') that the de-centering of one's civilizational perspective has been undertaken outside the bounds of Europe, also in the historical experience of China:

> One of the positive contributions Buddhist connections produced in China is the general sense that even the Chinese must, to some extent, look outwards. Indeed, not only did Buddhism suggest their were sources of wisdom outside of China, but it also led to the tendency of many Chinese intellectuals to go abroad, in particular to India, in search of enlightenment and understanding. Furthermore, since these visitors to India came back with tales of wonderful things they had seen in India, it was difficult to take an entirely Sino-centric view of world civilization. (Sen 2005, p. 172)

Although Buddhism has its origins in India, as it migrated into China and beyond, it not only challenged the limits of the Sino-centric 'Middle Kingdom' but also called India to reassess its own self-ascriptions as 'Middle Kingdom' of the earth/cosmos:

> In fact, some Chinese commentators felt threatened not only by the dilution of China's centrality, but—worse—by the tendency of some Buddhists to take India to be actually more central than China. Even though India was commonly referred to, at that time, as 'the Western kingdom' (giving China a more central position), the Buddhist perspective tended to favor putting India at the centre of things. For example, Faxian's fifth-century book on his travels described India as 'the Middle Kingdom', with China as frontier country. While all this was intensely irritating for believers in China's centrality, such heterodoxy did bring in a challenge to what would otherwise have been China's monolithic self-centeredness. This was certainly a moderating influence on China's insularity, and might even had made an indirect contribution to the interest and enthusiasm with which Chinese mathematicians and astronomers greeted Indian works in these fields...On the other side, Buddhist connections also helped to moderate Indian self-centeredness and sense of civilizational exclusiveness. (Sen 2005, p. 172)

The supplanting of these kingdom claims to cosmic centrality with Axial species-ethical universality shows no territorial center or geographic confine. These cases give us pragmatic instances out of both India and China of what Europe would later experience with Latin Christendom and its geographic decentering initially southward, across the Atlantic, and then with its own waves of global diaspora. While Jaspers has originally left the empirical work to substantiate his axial thesis open-ended, he would surely not object to such historical instances now finding their scholarly justification. We can also be assured that even in cases of overlapping historiogenesis, such radical shifts in species self-understanding truly were multi-polar in a simultaneous emergence that cannot merely be given a reductivist narrative of cultural dissemination from a single source.

As for my own casting of cosmoipolitan justice as a political project, I hope that the extensive empirical work done especially in Chap. 2 and 3 only further substantiate these claims that certainly do not merely stand or fall on the aforementioned brief references to Sen's work. While I agree with Jaspers that a truly global philosophy, especially in its political and social scientific orientations ought to take the Axial Age as the onset of boundless communication, I ultimately do not see any pressing need to posit an Encompassing as the ultimate ground of truth upon which the whole edifice rests. Taking each of the Axial traditions as internally constituted by ciphers of transcendence deflates the epistemic quality of each of their claims to universality, rather than improve them. Moreover, in maintaining Habermas's adherence to a post-metaphysical political philosophy, the appeal to the Encompassing as an impersonal absolute offers little pragmatic efficacy for the grounding of a communicative ethic that places paramount importance on achieving mutual understanding with a second person.

References

Allen, Amy. 2013. Having one's cake and eating it too: Habermas's genealogy of postsecular reason. In *Habermas and religion,* eds. Craig Calhoun, Eduardo Mendieta, and Jonathan VanAntwerpen, 132–153. Cambridge: Polity Press.

Arendt, Hannah. 1981. Karl Jaspers: Citizen of the world. In *The philosophy of Karl Jaspers: The library of living philosophers*, 2nd augmented, ed. Paul A. Schilpp, 539–549. La Salle: Open Court Publishing Company.

Bellah, Robert. 2012. The heritage of the axial age: Resource or burden? In *The axial age and its consequences,* eds. Robert H. Bellah and Hans Joas, 447–466. Cambridge: Belknap Press of Harvard University.

Bohman, James. 1996. *Public deliberation*. Cambridge: MIT Press.

Bohman, James. 2013. A postsecular global order? The pluralism of forms of life and communicative freedom. In *Habermas and religion,* eds. Craig Calhoun, Eduardo Mendieta, and Jonathan VanAntwerpen, 179–202. Cambridge: Polity Press.

Casanova, Jose. 2013. Exploring the postsecular: Three meanings of "the secular" and their possible transcendence. In *Habermas and religion,* eds. Craig Calhoun, Eduardo Mendieta, and Jonathan VanAntwerpen, 27–48. Cambridge: Polity Press.

Casanova, Jose. 2014. The two dimensions, temporal and spatial, of the secular: Comparative reflections on the Nordic Protestant and Southern Catholic patterns from a global perspective. In *Secular and sacred? The Scandinavian case of religion in human rights, law and public space,* eds. Van den Breemer, Jose Casanova, and Trygve Wyller, 21–33. Bristol: Vandenhoeck and Ruprecht.

Gold, Thomas, Doug, Guthrie, and David Wank. 2002. An introduction to the study of *Guanxi*. In *Social connections in China: Institutions, culture, and the changing nature of Guanxi,* eds. Thomas Gold, Doug Guthrie, and David Wank, 3–20. New York: Cambridge University Press.

Habermas, Jurgen. 2013. Reply to my critics. In *Habermas and religion,* ed. Craig Calhoun, Eduardo Mendieta, and Jonathan VanAntwerpen, 347–390. Cambridge: Polity Press.

Habermas, J., Butler J., Taylor C., and West C. 2011. In *The power of religion in the public sphere,* eds. Eduardo Mendieta and Jonathan VanAntwerpen. New York: Columbia University Press. (Translated by Ciarin Cronin).

Huntington, Samuel. 1997. *The clash of civilizations and the remaking of world order*. New York: Simon and Schuster.

Hwang, Kwang-Kuo. 2012. *Foundations of Chinese psychology: Confucian social relations*. New York: Springer.

Jaspers, Karl. 1948. *The European spirit*. Trans: R. G. Smith. London: SCM Press Ltd.

Jaspers, Karl. 1953. *The origin and goal of history*. Trans: M. Bullock. New Haven: Yale University Press.

Kumar, Nirmalya and Phanish Puranam. 2012. *India inside: The emerging innovation challenge to the west*. Boston: Harvard Business Review Press.

Landes, Mark. 1998. *On the wealth and poverty of nations: Why some are so rich and some so poor*. New York: W.W. Norton and Company.

Luo, Yadong. 2007. *Guanxi and business*. 2nd ed. New Jersey: World Scientific Publishing Company.

Mashelkar, R. A. 2008. Knowledge production and human capital: An Indian perspective. In *Education for Innovation: Implications for India, China, and America,* eds. R. L. DeHann and K. M. Venkat Narayan, 63–82. Rotterdam: Sense Publishers.

McCarthy, Thomas. 2013. The burdens of modernized faith and postmetaphysical reason in Habermas's "unfinished project of Enlightenment". In *Habermas and religion,* eds. Craig Calhoun, Eduardo Mendieta, and Jonathan VanAntwerpen, 115–131. Cambridge: Polity Press.

Nussbaum, Martha. 2011. *Creating capabilities: The human development approach*. Cambridge: Harvard University Press.

Nussbaum, Martha. 2012. *The new religious intolerance: Overcoming the politics of fear in an anxious age*. Cambridge: Belknap Press of Harvard University Press.

Onuma, Yasuaki. 2010. *A transcivilizational approach to international law*. (Pocketbooks of the Hague Academy of International Law). Leiden: Martinus Nijhoff Publishers.

Rawls, John. 1999. *The law of peoples*. Cambridge: Harvard University Press.

Sen, Amartya. 1992. *Inequality reexamined*. New York: Harvard University Press.

Sen, Amartya. 1999. *Development as freedom*. New York: Anchor Books.

Sen, Amartya. 2002. How to judge globalism. In *The American Prospect*. Special Issue: Globalism and poverty. Winter, A2–A6. http://prospect.org/article/how-judge-globalism. Accessed 15 Aug 2014

Sen, Amartya. 2005. *The argumentative Indian: Writings on Indian history, culture, and identity*. New York: Farrar, Straus, and Giroux.

Sen, Amartya. 2010. *The idea of justice*. New York: Penguin Books.

Sen, Amartya, and Jean Dreze. 2013. *An uncertain glory: India and its contradictions*. Princeton: Princeton University Press.

Swidler, Ann. 2012. Where do axial commitments reside?—Problems in thinking about the African case. In *The axial age and its consequences,* eds. Robert N. Bellah and Hans Joas, 222–246. Cambridge: Belknap Press of Harvard University Press.

Taylor, Charles. 2007. *A secular age*. Cambridge: Belknap Press.

Wooldridge, Adrian. 17 April 2010. The world turned upside down: A special report on innovation in emerging markets. *The Economist* 6–18. http://www.scribd.com/doc/29980704/The-Economist-Special-Report-Innovation-in-Emerging-Markets-April-17th-2010. Accessed 31 July 2014

Wu, Mei, and Hongye Li. 2011. The triumph of *shanzhai*: No name brand mobile phones and youth identity culture in China. In *Global media convergence and cultural transformation: Emerging patterns and characteristics,* ed. Dal Yong Jin, 213–232. New York: Information Science Reference.

Zakaria, Fareed. 2008. *The post-American world*. New York: W.W. Norton and Company.

Index

A

Adorno, T., 3, 121, 144, 145, 147, 148, 149, 155, 160, 164
Allen, Amy, 308
An-Naim, Abdullah, 17, 122, 178
Aquinas, T., 169, 246
Arnason, Johann, 12
Asad, Talal, 17, 22, 53, 122, 178, 186, 193, 195
Authenticity, 10, 22, 29, 125, 172, 212, 214, 218
Axial Age, 5, 6, 7, 8, 9, 10, 13, 14, 20, 23, 24, 25, 26, 31, 34, 37, 39, 40, 51, 52, 54, 62, 66, 67, 68, 72, 88, 110, 123, 126, 132, 139, 149, 150, 152, 153, 154, 156, 157, 163, 164, 179, 212, 213, 247, 285, 303, 308, 311
  concept of, 11, 12

B

Bellah, Robert, 11, 34, 72, 215
Biblical religion, 15, 16, 41, 120, 121, 122, 123, 124, 125, 127, 130, 137, 139, 142, 152, 153, 154, 155, 156, 157, 158, 159, 161, 164, 166, 177, 178, 179, 180, 181, 182, 184, 185, 187, 189, 190, 193, 199, 200, 202, 205, 213, 220, 221, 245
Bohman, James, 225
Buddhism, 12, 30, 40, 54, 62, 73, 79, 85, 86, 110, 114, 115, 309

C

Capabilities, 2, 21, 37, 73, 86, 286, 292, 294, 295, 296
  based material, 22
Casanova, Jose, 8, 21, 34, 42, 213, 215, 228, 229, 268, 308
Catholicism, 205, 220, 238, 244, 246
China, 10, 30, 31, 43, 86, 94, 95, 99, 120, 156, 157, 179, 182, 185, 205, 272, 284, 286, 288, 291, 295, 296, 310
Christendom, Latin, 34, 53, 120, 122, 132, 160, 179, 184, 195, 213, 220, 228, 230, 236, 237, 238, 242, 244, 245, 272, 310
Christianity, 12, 30, 31, 72, 116, 120, 150, 152, 153, 154, 155, 156, 157, 159, 178, 179, 181, 183, 185, 205, 206, 221, 224
Ciphers, 52, 131, 164, 165, 181, 311
Communicative action, 16, 18, 21, 27, 34, 50, 51, 53, 54, 55, 56, 57, 61, 111, 125, 166, 167, 172, 174, 176, 187
Confucianism, 54, 86, 88, 91, 97, 100, 114, 115, 182, 296, 298
Cooke, Maeve, 161, 172
Cosmion, 14, 64, 131
Cosmoipolitan, 32, 33, 34, 35, 36, 37, 38, 39, 41, 43, 50, 51, 52, 54, 61, 123, 125, 149, 155, 199, 212, 213, 214, 226, 227, 229, 232, 273, 297, 303, 306, 310
  justice, 3, 4, 7, 9, 14, 21, 34
Cosmopolitanism, 2, 4, 6, 59, 116, 176, 178, 202, 203, 212, 213, 214, 219, 223, 242, 273, 306
Critical theory, 3, 6, 10, 18, 24, 36, 50, 61, 115, 121, 125, 143, 144, 148, 149, 161, 164, 166, 168, 170, 303

D

Deconfessionalized state, 40
Democracy, 59, 206, 225, 228, 248, 254, 284, 293
Democratic deficit, 227, 232, 238, 254, 267
Development, 2, 27, 43, 53, 57, 62, 86, 108, 168, 247, 306

J. Bowman, *Cosmoipolitan Justice*, Studies in Global Justice 15,
DOI 10.1007/978-3-319-12709-5

E
Eastern Orthodoxy, 205, 243, 244
Ecumene, 13, 83
Eisenstadt, S.N., 4, 5
Encompassing, 51, 59, 79, 131, 144, 155, 156, 163, 164, 165, 179, 180, 182, 183, 184, 213, 218, 270, 311
Epistemic authoritarianism, 15, 161, 180, 187
European Union, 203, 233, 236, 237, 238, 248, 249, 253, 307
Existential historiography, 120, 132
Exodus event, 121, 127, 129, 137, 143

F
Follesdal, Andreas, 252, 256

G
Galactic polity, 85
Global denominationalism, 43, 213, 229, 231, 266
Globalization, 2, 9, 21, 50, 53, 286, 294, 295, 305, 306
Gnosticism, 23, 36, 161, 309
Gospel of John, 173
Guanxi, 287, 299, 300, 301

H
Habermas, Jurgen, 2, 34, 49, 202
Hegel, G.W., 8, 53, 146, 153, 156, 166, 243
Heideggar, Martin, 108
Hinduism, 30, 54, 61, 66, 67, 68, 73, 76, 79, 83, 115, 182, 229
Historical critical method, 37
Historiogenesis, 14, 35, 127, 128, 129, 169, 182
Horkheimer, Max, 3, 114, 121, 126, 144, 145, 146, 147, 148, 149, 154, 155, 159, 160, 164
Human capital, 284, 295, 296, 302, 306

I
I am, 163, 165, 169, 170, 174
India, 8, 10, 24, 30, 31, 40, 62, 67, 69, 70, 71, 73, 115, 120, 156, 157, 179, 182, 184, 272, 284, 285, 286, 287, 289, 291, 295, 296, 302, 303, 307, 309, 310
Innovation, 2, 3, 60, 61, 77, 80, 88, 204, 241, 284, 286, 287, 288, 289, 291, 292, 293, 295, 297, 301, 302, 305
Inverse pyramid, 295, 296
Islam, 12, 15, 30, 31, 115, 116, 122, 156, 177, 178, 179, 180, 181, 182, 183, 184, 185, 190, 193, 194, 195, 198, 199, 200, 201, 202, 204, 205, 213, 221, 224, 227, 228, 229

J
Jaspers, Karl, 6, 34, 176, 212, 220
Jesus Christ, 16, 122, 156, 157, 158, 170
Judaism, 12, 30, 38, 116, 122, 138, 150, 152, 154, 156, 169, 178, 179, 181, 183, 185, 204, 224, 229
Jugaad, 287, 301, 302

K
Kant, Immanuel, 2, 157, 159, 160, 202

L
Lander, Marc, 286
Lisbon Treaty, 222, 257
Logos, 16, 109, 121, 150, 151, 157, 158, 169
Lutheran state, 40, 166, 179

M
Mandate of heaven, 41, 94, 96, 97, 98, 103, 182
Marx, Karl, 255, 285
McCarthy, Thomas, 4, 5, 247
Mead, G.H., 20, 33, 52, 111, 266
Mendieta, Eduardo, 4, 172
Middle Kingdom, 89, 291, 310
Moses, 16, 122, 127, 132, 133, 134, 135, 137, 138, 139, 140, 151, 169, 174
Multiperspectival principle, 240, 270, 271

N
Neocolonialism, 2, 290, 293
Nova effect, 30, 36, 132, 213, 215, 221, 223, 227, 228, 229, 265

O
Onuma, Yusuaki, 4, 6, 17, 22, 33, 53, 199, 286, 289, 291, 306
Original position, 31, 32, 33, 34, 35, 36, 37, 38, 39, 247
Overlapping consensus, 3, 35, 84, 91, 122, 162, 177, 178, 187, 202, 204, 205, 216, 218, 220, 223, 226, 227, 231, 239, 244, 247, 249, 253, 254, 266, 273, 302

P
Patocka, Jan, 12
Postsecular, 21, 22, 30, 39, 42, 162, 169, 171, 172, 194, 206, 213, 216, 230, 232, 241, 245, 249, 253, 272, 303
  society, 17
Pragmatic presuppositions, 37, 50, 51, 55, 106, 111, 124, 135, 178, 188
Promissory narrative, 151, 157, 158, 163, 173
Protestant, 29, 42, 53, 156, 179, 205, 237, 238, 244, 245, 248, 262, 288

R
Radical Orthodoxy, 244, 246, 247
Rasmussen, D., 3
Rawls, John, 31, 122, 178, 202, 309
Reciprocal role-taking, 32, 266
Reflexivity, 23, 24, 25, 27, 52, 56, 74, 93, 114, 171, 179, 240, 241, 267
Right speech, 54, 74, 75, 76, 78, 79, 81, 85, 114, 115
Rokkan, Stein, 240, 255

S
Sacralized redistribution, 287, 303
Samuel Huntington, 306
Scandinavian region, 256
Second person, 17, 38, 51, 53, 54, 55, 56, 64, 77, 89, 120, 121, 124, 131, 142, 158, 162, 164, 171, 174, 178
Secular, 8, 21, 22, 40, 41, 53, 54, 81, 84, 86, 115, 116, 119, 120, 127, 130, 131, 145, 149, 150, 157, 158, 160, 162, 166, 171, 172, 173, 176, 178, 186, 195, 196, 199, 200, 201, 205, 206, 212, 213, 217, 237, 266
  narratives, 9
Sen, Amartya, 17, 273, 284, 292, 309
Sermon on the Mount, 121, 150, 151, 153, 157, 158, 173
Shanzhai, 287, 297, 298
Smith, Adam, 284, 285, 286, 287
Social welfare, 240, 250, 252, 261, 286, 294, 295
Species ethic, 21, 23, 100, 174, 212, 214, 217, 218, 244
Stadial consciousness, 8, 9, 35, 59, 141, 242
Stump, Eleonore, 17, 18, 20
Subsidiarity, 42, 233, 236, 237, 238, 239, 240, 242, 249, 250, 251, 252, 254, 255, 256, 257, 258, 259, 260, 261, 262, 263, 264, 265, 266, 267, 268, 269, 270, 271, 273
  deterritorialized principle of, 5

T
Taoism, 12, 30, 40, 54, 99, 100, 101, 103, 104, 105, 107, 108, 109, 110, 113, 114, 115, 298
Taylor, Charles, 7, 11, 17, 34, 35, 36, 112, 157, 231, 238, 245, 265
Theocracy, 133, 138, 139, 141
Theopolity, 133, 136, 138, 139, 141, 150, 153, 186, 193, 195, 198, 199
Third person, 57, 110, 131, 134, 142, 165
Transcensus, 12, 14, 15, 23, 26, 27, 29, 39, 69, 71, 73, 87, 103, 157, 191, 195, 199
  characteristics of, 12
  concept of, 13
Truth disclosure, 54

V
Voegelin, Eric, 8, 33, 34, 36, 38, 126, 191

W
Weber, Max, 8, 29, 242, 245, 255
Wellhausen school, 133, 134, 136, 186

Y
Yahweh, 124, 126, 128, 130, 132, 134, 135, 136, 137, 138, 139, 140, 141, 144, 146, 153, 191

Printed by Printforce, the Netherlands